THE ABBOTT TOUCH

Pal Joey, Damn Yankees, and the Theatre of George Abbott

Thomas Hischak

methuen | drama
LONDON • NEW YORK • OXFORD • NEW DELHI • SYDNEY

METHUEN DRAMA
Bloomsbury Publishing Plc
50 Bedford Square, London, WC1B 3DP, UK
1385 Broadway, New York, NY 10018, USA
29 Earlsfort Terrace, Dublin 2, Ireland

BLOOMSBURY, METHUEN DRAMA and the Methuen Drama logo are trademarks of Bloomsbury Publishing Plc

First published in Great Britain 2023

Copyright © Thomas Hischak, 2023

Thomas Hischak has asserted his right under the Copyright, Designs and Patents Act, 1988, to be identified as author of this work.

For legal purposes the Acknowledgments on p. xi constitute an extension of this copyright page.

Cover design: Jess Stevens
Cover image: George Abbott sitting in a theatre during rehearsals for
A Soft Touch © Ray Fisher / Getty Images

All rights reserved. No part of this publication may be reproduced or transmitted in any form or by any means, electronic or mechanical, including photocopying, recording, or any information storage or retrieval system, without prior permission in writing from the publishers.

Bloomsbury Publishing Plc does not have any control over, or responsibility for, any third-party websites referred to or in this book. All internet addresses given in this book were correct at the time of going to press. The author and publisher regret any inconvenience caused if addresses have changed or sites have ceased to exist, but can accept no responsibility for any such changes.

A catalogue record for this book is available from the British Library.

A catalog record for this book is available from the Library of Congress.

ISBN: HB: 978-1-3503-4059-6
       PB: 978-1-3503-4058-9
       ePDF: 978-1-3503-4061-9
       eBook: 978-1-3503-4060-2

Typeset by RefineCatch Limited, Bungay, Suffolk
Printed and bound in Great Britain

To find out more about our authors and books visit www.bloomsbury.com and sign up for our newsletters.

CONTENTS

Preface viii
Acknowledgments xi

    Prologue: The Paradox of Mister George Abbott 1

1 Pounding and Progressing on 42nd Street (1913–1925) 9

The Misleading Lady • Lightnin' • Daddies • The Broken Wing • Dulcy • Zander the Great • White Desert • Hell Bent for Heaven • Lazybones • Processional

2 If You Want It Done Right, Write It and Direct It Yourself (1925–1934) 21

The Fall Guy • A Holy Terror • Love 'Em and Leave 'Em • Broadway • Chicago • Spread Eagle • Four Walls • Coquette • Bless You, Sister • Gentlemen of the Press • Ringside • Jarnegan • Poppa • Those We Love • Louder, Please • The Great Magoo • Small Miracle • Ladies' Money • Page Miss Glory

3 If You Really Want It Done Better, Produce It Yourself (1932–1940) 35

Lilly Turner • Heat Lightning • The Drums Begin • John Brown • Kill that Story • Sweet River • Angel Island • Brown Sugar • The Primrose Path • Ring Two • The Unconquered • Goodbye in the Night

4 How Did I Get Typecast in Farce? (1932–1939) 43

Twentieth Century • Three Men on a Horse • Boy Meets Girl • Brother Rat • Room Service • All that Glitters • What a Life! • See My Lawyer

5 The Celluloid Sidestep (1918–1931) 59

The Imposter • The Carnival Man • The Bishop's Candlesticks • Why Bring that Up? • The Saturday Night Kid • Halfway to Heaven • All Quiet on the Western Front • Manslaughter • The Sea God • Stolen Heaven • Secrets of a Secretary • My Sin • The Cheat

6 Adding Songwriters to the Mix (1935–1945) 67

Jumbo • On Your Toes • The Boys from Syracuse • Too Many Girls • Best Foot Forward • Beat the Band

7 Entertaining the Homefront (1942–1945) 81

Jason • Sweet Charity • Kiss & Tell • Get Away, Old Man • A Highland Fling • Snafu

8 Working with New (and Usually Younger) Faces (1944–1949) 103

On the Town • Billion Dollar Baby • Barefoot Boy with Cheek • High Button Shoes • Look Ma, I'm Dancin'! • Where's Charley? • Touch and Go

9 Post-War Blues (1946–1961) 115

The Dancer • It Takes Two • Mrs. Gibbons' Boys • The Number • In Any Language • Drink to Me Only • A Call on Kuprin • The Skin of Our Teeth (revival)

10 That's Entertainment? (1940–1960) 121

Pal Joey • Beggar's Holiday • A Tree Grows in Brooklyn • New Girl in Town • Fiorello! • Tenderloin

11 All They Want Is Musicals (1950–1955) 139

Call Me Madam • Out of This World • Wonderful Town • Me and Juliet • The Pajama Game • On Your Toes (revival) *• Damn Yankees*

12 Ignoring the Sixties (1959–1962) 159

Take Her, She's Mine • Never Too Late • Once Upon a Mattress • A Funny Thing Happened on the Way to the Forum

13 Almost But Not Quite (1964–1989) 171

Fade Out—Fade In • Flora, the Red Menace • Anya • Help Stamp Out Marriage! • Agatha Sue, I Love You • How Now, Dow Jones • The Education of H*Y*M*A*N K*A*P*L*A*N • The Fig Leaves Are Falling • Norman, Is That You? • Not Now, Darling • Music Is • Tropicana • Frankie

14 Looking Back with Dubious Success (1969–1994) 193

Three Men on a Horse (revival) • *The Pajama Game* (revival) • *On Your Toes* (revival) • *Broadway* (revival) • *Damn Yankees* (revival)

Epilogue: No Exit Music, Please 201

Appendices 207
Notes 227
Selected Bibliography 237
Index 243
About the Author 259

PREFACE

In the summer of 1986, my wife and I spent a few days in Stratford, Ontario, Canada, cramming in as many evening and matinee performances in the repertory schedule of the Stratford Festival as we could. For some years prior, Stratford had been presenting Broadway musicals in their largest venue, the quasi-Elizabethan space called the Festival Theatre. Productions of *My Fair Lady* and *Cabaret* brought in enough income to allow the Festival to offer *Henry V* and *The Duchess of Malfi* in their smaller spaces. Sometimes the musicals had a Shakespeare connection, such as *Kiss Me, Kate* and *The Boys from Syracuse*. That summer, they were offering the latter and we thought it would be enjoyable to see the Rodgers and Hart musical performed on that practical Globe-like stage that lent itself to so much creativity. So we went.

You notice I identified *The Boys from Syracuse* as a Rodgers and Hart musical. Everyone does. Yet I feel guilty repeating it because George Abbott wrote the libretto for that musical and it would not still be performed if he hadn't written it. Those wonderful songs could have gone the way of such forgotten Rodgers and Hart shows as *Heads Up!* (1929) or *Higher and Higher* (1940) without Abbott's book. He also produced and directed the original *The Boys from Syracuse*. That certainly helped make it a hit in 1938. But we're sitting in a theatre in 1986 listening to the overture and waiting for the show to start because Abbott made it possible. Otherwise we'd be at a Rodgers and Hart musical revue or watching a PBS fundraiser program with other beloved songs from rarely produced shows.

But to get back to Stratford. The production is excellent. It is also uncut so we get to enjoy the "Big Brother" song and ballet. And of course that stage is perfect not only for all the farce but for the musical numbers as well. (The Festival's oft-used trap door comes in handy when one Dromio dives out of sight at the end of that ballet.) The show ends, the applause is loud and sincere, then disappointment comes. Susan Wright, who has stolen all her scenes as the saucy cook Luce, steps forward to make a curtain speech. Among the many things we love about Stratford is that there is *never ever* a curtain speech, before or after a performance. No collections for retired Canadian actors or chipper announcements about upcoming shows. Ms. Wright says something to the effect that "The Stratford Festival has a habit of producing dead playwrights but today is an exception. I am happy to announce that the playwright of *The Boys from Syracuse* is here with us today and I'd like to present him to you. Mr. George Abbott."

A ninety-nine-year-old Abbott rises from his seat in the front row and gives a slight wave to the audience. The applause is deafening, the audience rises (something not normally done on cue at Stratford), and Ms. Wright goes to Abbott, takes him by the arm, and walks him upstage and out the center exit to meet with the cast and staff backstage. My wife and I and several hundred other people are watching theatre history walk across that stage. Many (maybe us?) will brag that we saw George Abbott just before he died. But we would be wrong. He lived another nine years and worked on two more Broadway shows.

This book is not a biography. Abbott himself wrote his autobiography, *Mister Abbott*, in 1963 and, as Huck Finn says of Mark Twain, "He told the truth, mainly." It is a very personal and revealing memoir with plenty of anecdotes and even a few embarrassing true confessions. But he writes little about his theatre work. Abbott expresses opinions about actors in general, the trials of trying out a play or musical, and thoughts about people he liked or didn't like to work with. Yet when it comes to the actual productions, he mentions the title and says whether it was a hit or not. Early in his career, Abbott was known primarily as an actor. He hit it big when he got the plum role of the Southern mountain boy Sid Hunt in Hatcher Hughes' melodrama *Hell Bent for Heaven* in 1924. Abbott's account of this important stepping stone in his career: "*Hell Bent for Heaven* opened, was a hit, and later won the Pulitzer Prize. I enjoyed playing it, even having to eat an immense slab of cherry pie every night."[1] Or consider this, Abbott's entire account of *Damn Yankees*:

> Meanwhile back in New York an agent brought me a novel called *The Year the Yankees Lost the Pennant* by Douglass Wallop. Brisson, Griffith and Prince entered into the proposition with me, it was agreed that I write the book with Wallop and direct the musical. Again we secured the services of Adler and Ross. I named it *Damn Yankees*. It was a hit, comparable to *Pajama Game*.[2]

What you get from *Mister Abbott* is a book that tells you a great deal about the man but next to nothing about his work, his accomplishments, and why he is so important in twentieth-century American theatre.

This book is about the theatre of George Abbott. As an actor, playwright, director, librettist, play doctor, and/or producer, he was involved with over one hundred productions in New York over a period of sixty years. My hat is off to the great songwriters, co-authors, choreographers, performers, and designers who worked on those plays and musicals, but I want to view them as "Abbott shows." What did he contribute? How did he work? What innovations did he come up with? What were his strengths? How did he survive so long? And what exactly was the famous "Abbott touch"? I don't think there are simple answers to any of these questions. But I found the journey through Abbott's remarkable career enlightening, first as history, then as a study in craftsmanship and panache. Abbott's theatre world is gone but I think there is more to savor from it than revivals of *The Boys from Syracuse* and his other timeless shows. Looking at that long-gone world by focusing on George Abbot, I hope to bring those many famous and not-so-famous productions to life. Since I wasn't there, I must rely on the accounts by those who were there: performers and other theatre folk, friends and acquaintances, critics and scholars of the time, and even photographs and a few films and videos. And, of course, George Abbott himself. In a roundabout way, *Mister Abbott* sheds some light on the man's work because we get inside his head. Perhaps that's where the true "Abbott touch" resides.

ACKNOWLEDGMENTS

I would like to thank my editors at Bloomsbury Press: Dom O'Hanlon and Sam Nicholls. Special thanks to Rob Schneider, Robbie Rozelle, Joseph Turrin, Lara Teeter, and Robert Lindsay-Nassif.

For their thorough review of the manuscript and for their comments and encouragement, I wholeheartedly thank Mark A. Robinson and Cathy Hischak.

PROLOGUE

The Paradox of Mister George Abbott

Let's take a peek at a George Abbott rehearsal for a musical.

It could be anytime in the 1930s or 1940s or 1950s. It's late summer and the rehearsal room is hot. Abbott arrives wearing a perfectly pressed suit, white shirt, and subdued-colored tie. Everyone, including some staff members who are older than Abbott and have been with him for years, addresses him as "Mister Abbott." Rumors float among the cast that he is called "George" by his friends outside of rehearsal but it's difficult to imagine such a thing. Abbott, tall, athletic, and a bit forbidding, addresses the assembled actors and staff in a not-unfriendly but businesslike manner, clearly explaining what scenes will be worked on, the reason they need work, and what needs to be accomplished during the rehearsal.

The stage manager calls for places and, as two assistants set up the necessary pieces of rehearsal furniture, he approaches Abbott cautiously and informs him that the leading lady, the nominal "star," has not yet arrived. Abbott pauses only a moment then tells the stage manager that the rehearsal will commence with the understudy. This is standard Abbott practice. Should the star arrive ten minutes late or two hours late, she will see a much younger actress/singer doing her scenes. She will not be late again.

As the actors run a scene, Abbott remains standing, never more than ten feet from them. He moves about some, not in a nervous manner, but to get different perspectives of the scene. When he finds that he does not like a piece of blocking he gave the actors previously, he stops the rehearsal and methodically re-blocks the section with no hesitation or self-doubt. When the scene is repeated and Abbott says "Better," the actors don't know if he meant them or his re-staging. Abbott generally likes actors as long as they are talented and disciplined. When a show is not going well in rehearsals or in tryouts, he tends to blame the script (even his script) rather than the actors. He finds that their weak spot is believing their reviews. He has seen many a reasonable actor get a swollen head after being praised by the critics. Or if they get poor reviews, they lose all confidence in themselves. Actors are too fragile. Abbott is not at all fragile.

As the rehearsal continues, one of the actors delivers a line incorrectly. Before the stage manager can correct him, Abbott stops the scene. Without looking at the script (which he wrote), Abbott explains that the actor has taken a phrase from the end of the sentence and put it in the middle of the sentence. While the actor repeats the line correctly it is clear to Abbott that the actor doesn't realize the difference. "If you say it the other way," the playwright/director explains, "I guarantee you won't get a laugh in New Haven. Or anywhere else." The actor may fumble other lines in the future but he will never say that line wrong again.

An hour into the rehearsal there is noise out in the hallway. Voices, laughter, even some tap-tap-tapping on the floor are heard. The dancing chorus has arrived for a later rehearsal in a space down the hall. (Before the late 1960s, the dancing chorus was separate from the singing chorus which was separate from the "character" performers.) Abbott is not terribly fond of dancers. They are cliquish, smoke too much, and dress abominably for rehearsals. They also have a habit of sitting on the floor when there are plenty of chairs. The stage manager quickly goes to shut the door to the hall but before he can the choreographer has come into the rehearsal room and asks if Mister Abbott has a moment to spare. His concentration broken by the noise, Abbott tells the actors to relax for a minute and he goes to see the choreographer.

Abbott doesn't dislike choreographers. Some directors think choreographers are a necessary evil. But Abbott respects them and knows how important they are. He also notices that the dancing chorus tends to listen to and do anything a choreographer asks, just like needy children. Abbott does not like directing needy children. This choreographer is polite but clearly upset. The dance music arranger has informed him that Abbott has requested that eighteen measures near the end of the Act Two ballet (there always seems to be some sort of ballet in Act Two) be trimmed to a more effective six measures. Abbott knows that the choreographer has not yet staged the end of the ballet and wanted the music rearranged in time for today's rehearsal. The choreographer fumes . . . politely. There are plenty of "But you see, Mister Abbott" and "You must understand, Mister Abbott" but Abbott says he does see and he does understand and he knows what will make the ballet better. The more emotional the choreographer gets, the more unflappable Abbott appears. What Abbott doesn't mention is that he thinks that there hasn't been an Act Two ballet yet written that couldn't be improved upon by being shorter. Except maybe "Slaughter on Tenth Avenue" from *On Your Toes*.

While Abbott and the choreographer are in a not-very-private conference, the cast members (particularly those who have never worked with Abbott before) watch as their heads fill with tales and rumors they've heard. Word has it that Abbott went to military school. That is easy to see. They say he never drinks or smokes or gambles or fools around with women, not even actresses. As far as dining out, he prefers to have lunch with men, dinner with women. It is a fact that he was a successful actor for some years before he turned to writing, directing, and producing. They have trouble believing that. No one ever seemed more non-actorish to them. They say he's been married twice. The first wife died. The second union was a disaster. He doesn't talk about either woman. They also heard he doesn't enjoy talking over past shows. To him they were either hits, flops, or something in-between—all best forgotten.

The rehearsal resumes. Abbott has made the choreographer see reason without lifting his voice or offering anything close to an ultimatum. The choreographer has left, in a somewhat flustered state, and joined the noisy dancers down the hall. Abbott looks at his watch, silently regrets the time lost, and picks up the rehearsal where he left off. He has a schedule and, hysterical choreographer or no hysterical choreographer, he plans to stick to it. Within seconds he is back in what he will years later describe as his bubble of concentration. A rehearsal is a state of being in which the outside world (bad marriage, health issues, union difficulties, producer's money woes, etc.) is blocked out and one is, for a time, in total control. As far as Mister Abbott is concerned, life would be better if it were one long rehearsal.

The George Abbott we have just witnessed was an invention. He was invented by Francis Abbott, a scrappy teenager with a rotten upbringing, an unhappy home, and a continual habit of getting into trouble. He was a small-town hick who didn't know how to dress or talk well ... and he knew it. So at the age of twenty he invented George Abbott. He invented him so well that he played the part comfortably and successfully for eighty-seven years.

Abbott rarely told friends about his sordid beginnings because he thought such tales were boring and he was happy to forget all about them. When pressured by the celebrity editor Bennett Cerf to write his autobiography, Abbott demurred. Everyone famous writes an autobiography, Cerf argued. That was one reason Abbott didn't want to do it. Another was he believed writing about oneself was a form of conceit. Besides, who would be interested? Cerf and Random House assured him plenty of people would want to read about his life. Abbott had good instincts about whether an idea would make a hit show or not but when it came to books he figured Random House knew their business. Finally Abbott gave in and in 1963 he wrote a surprisingly personal history of his life revealing much about the man but little that wasn't already known about his career. Cerf insisted the book had to be titled *Mister Abbott*; Abbott balked at that but he figured Cerf must know titles. Then Abbott wrote in the introduction, "I plan to leave town on the day of publication and flee to some far-off state like Florida, where they don't read books."[1]

Mister Abbott was not an autobiography hit, like Moss Hart's *Act One* (1959) or Noel Coward's multi-volume memoirs. But it was read in its day. Today the book is out of print and resides mostly in academic libraries and in the possession of theatre buffs who paid inflated prices for used copies. My guess is Abbott was later sorry he wrote his autobiography. He gave too much away. After reading it, one was less in awe of Mister Abbott, although his stature in the American Theatre was not at all diminished. He just became more human. And the book made one realize that the invention of Mister Abbott was a remarkable achievement, as dazzling as any of his stage productions. So let us look at Francis Abbott before the age of twenty and consider the raw material with which he had to work. As previously stated, this book is not a biography, so I'll be brief.

All the reference books say George Francis Abbott was born on January 25, 1887, in Forestville, New York. It sounds like a bucolic suburb of New York City. In fact, it was an off-the-beaten-path berg located somewhere between Buffalo, New York, and Erie, Pennsylvania. The farm which his grandparents farmed went to seed so Abbott actually grew up in another backwater town, Salamanca, New York, on the Allegheny River between nowhere and noplace. It was about as far from New York City as you could get without leaving the state. Because his father was named George, the young Abbott was always called Francis. His father was an imposing man who was big stuff to the locals: twice mayor, named volunteer fire chief, a favorite in the tavern. In reality, he was a budding alcoholic who failed at just about every business venture he tried. Mrs. Abbott was a practical woman, consequently eternally frustrated in her marriage. She raised three children with a Christian Scientist philosophy. She disdained drinking and smoking, not for moral reasons but because she believed them to be unhealthy habits. It was not a happy home and young Francis, a nervous bedwetter who worshipped his mother and feared just about everyone else, was a loner. All the same, he had a daredevil streak in him. He'd swim the fast-flowing Allegheny in spring when it was the most dangerous. He found acceptance with the older boys through card playing. They were mostly dumb, he was mostly smart, and gambling income was the allowance he never got at home.

Probably using a lot of bluff and back slapping, Abbott's father got a job as a government land agent for the State of Wyoming so in 1898, eleven-year-old Francis went West with his family and lived in the city of Cheyenne for four years. Not exactly a scholar in the classroom, Francis thrived in the outdoors and embraced all the clichés of the Wild West. He learned to ride, shoot, hunt, rope, brand, and participate in cock fighting; he didn't feel like an outsider anymore. Francis made extra money putting up and patching fences but found it more lucrative delivering newspapers and buckets of beer to the city's Red Light District. He still floundered in school but he did develop a passion for reading books on his own. Not dime novels but Sir Walter Scott and *Tales from Shakespeare*. His head was full of stories and a vivid imagination. His exterior, though, grew more coarse and crude in Wyoming. He also grew tall, taller than his father, which came in handy when family arguments came to blows and his father (now a full-time alcoholic) had to back down because Francis was bigger and stronger than his old man. There was plenty of fighting outside the home as well. Francis got involved with local gangs who competed in stealing chickens and such and then trying to steal from each other. Such belligerent behavior spilled over into the classroom and Francis was expelled from school. His parents decided to send him to military school and found one they could afford in Nebraska. Kearney Military Academy was little more than a reform school and Francis knew it. He started off badly, tricked and beaten up by the older boys and punished by the authorities for not measuring up. But he soon learned to play their game and actually found he was happy in this no-nonsense environment. Francis was never a model "cadet" but he finally knew who and what he was.

George Abbott Sr. didn't succeed as a land agent and the family went back to New York State in 1902. Francis was allowed to return for the summer to Wyoming where he got a job on a large ranch in which he worked at farming, handling horses, and doing all the grunt work they could give him. He didn't complain and was sorry when the fall came and he had to return to military school. Francis continued to get in trouble but that didn't keep him from polishing his gambling skills; soon his card playing made him feel like a rich man. Also, he was put on the football team and learned to love the sport. Francis graduated from Kearney Military Academy without honors but with a better self image and a sense of being independent from his troubled family. Arriving back in New York State in 1904, he found that his mother had left his father and was living with her parents in Hamburg, New York. George Sr. took off to pursue a traveling salesman career; it did not last very long. Francis was not happy at Hamburg High School except for athletics in which he was impressive if not always completely disciplined. He worked each summer at the Lackawanna Steel Company where the jobs were dangerous and the management was uncaring. He was saving up money to go to college because the situation at home was worse than ever. His father had returned to Hamburg and was seen all over town drunk and getting into trouble. Francis swore he would never drink. The principal at the high school had gone to the University of Rochester and helped Francis apply and eventually get accepted there. Around the same time, Francis met Ednah Lewis, a recent graduate of the University of Rochester who was temporarily teaching English in town. As much as he found himself falling in love with her, Francis knew she was too refined and intelligent for the likes of him. They dated in Hamburg and promised that they would see each other in Rochester where he could meet her family and come to Sunday dinner. The thought thrilled him. And terrified him.

It was at this point that Francis decided to invent George Abbott. Not only would he use his true first name but he would become another person. No more gambling. No more fights. No coarse ranch talk or factory slang. He would take school seriously. He would become a more disciplined athlete. He would dress better, talk better, be a better person. Was it all to win the heart of Ednah Lewis? Probably not. Was it to become everything his father was not? Possibly. But the new George Abbott was filled with such resolve that all his energies and brains and brawn, which had been mostly wasted up to this point, now were focused and his determination was something powerful.

Of course it didn't come easy. No new invention does. He arrived in Rochester in 1908 a kid from a series of hick towns facing a (relatively) big city. Years later he wrote that he began life at the University of Rochester feeling like Sir Galahad searching for the Holy Grail. But he couldn't afford the proper armor or helmet or lance and it was clear as he walked across the campus of the university that he looked like a country bumpkin and the other students all looked like city slickers. He was daunted but not defeated. George Abbott (as we can rightfully call him now) lived in a modest rooming house, took on part-time jobs, slowly brought his wardrobe up to standard, and learned a lot by keeping his eyes and ears open. He struggled in the classroom at first but immediately found success in football and in an extra-curricular activity he had previously been unaware of: dramatics. By his sophomore year, Abbott was so involved in the University Dramatic Club that he couldn't decide whether he wanted to become Broadway's greatest actor or America's greatest playwright. Of course, he didn't quite know what Broadway was but he certainly knew what a good play was so he wrote several even as he performed in every production that he could. He and Ednah saw a lot of each other and unofficially got engaged, promising that marriage would come when he found success in the theater. It turned out to be a seven-year engagement.

At the end of four years of undergraduate college, Abbott set his eyes on Harvard University because he had heard that you could actually get a degree in drama there and that his favorite playwright, Edward Sheldon, had studied there under Professor George Pierce Baker. He submitted a play to a Harvard competition that offered free tuition. The play didn't win but Abbott was determined to go there anyway. A series of varied summer jobs (door-to-door salesman, basketball coach, summer camp counselor, etc.) had got him through his undergraduate years and he would work his way through Harvard come what may. At first Abbott found Cambridge too high-tone and snooty for his tastes. He was now rubbing shoulders with Ivy League students. But Professor Baker's class was everything he has hoped and dreamed of. For the rest of his long career, Abbott would return to Baker's simple but profound tenets for good playwriting. One of Abbott's first scripts for the class was a one-act tragedy about a farm boy who tries to protect his mother from his abusive father and is horsewhipped for his efforts. (One of Baker's axioms was to write about what you know.) Titled, *The Head of the Family*, it was produced by the Harvard Dramatic Club. Abbott took advantage of being in Cambridge and went to see as much theatre in Boston as possible. Today the year 1912 is not considered the heyday of American playwriting but Abbott got to see all the great actors and actresses of the day. They made those pre-Eugene O'Neill plays seem like gold and Abbott was further inspired in his acting and writing ambitions. More of his plays were presented on campus and Abbott took further classes with Baker, one on Elizabethan drama he particularly liked.

A little theatre in Boston, the Bijou, was run by a Josephine Clement. The theater offered a prize of one hundred dollars for the best one-act comedy so Abbott wrote *The Man in the Manhole*. It was about a Danish cable slicer and his assistant in a steel plant, something Abbott knew about first hand. The comedy not only won and was produced at the Bijou but Mrs. Clement was impressed enough with Abbott that she offered him a one-year job as her assistant at thirty dollars a week. Struggling to pay tuition and worried about his future, Abbott happily accepted her offer. He left Harvard at the end of the semester. The year at the Bijou taught Abbott a great deal about all facets of running a theater but he knew it was a small-time operation. Also, he was not getting much opportunity to pursue his two great ambitions: playwriting and acting. For that he knew he had to go to New York, a place he had never even seen. So after a summer working at a camp and saving every cent, George Abbott set off for New York in the fall of 1913. He would remain there for a very long time.

1 POUNDING AND PROGRESSING ON 42ND STREET

(1913–1925)

The Misleading Lady • *Lightnin'* • *Daddies* • *The Broken Wing* • *Dulcy* • *Zander the Great* • *White Desert* • *Hell Bent for Heaven* • *Lazybones* • *Processional*

George Abbott arrived in New York about seven years before what is generally considered the beginning of the Golden Age for American plays and musicals. Yet the activity on Broadway that fall was bustling with nineteen musicals and about sixty plays opening before the end of 1913. But the number of big hits was down from the previous season and there were some ominous signs of trouble ahead. The storm clouds of war in Europe were gathering and most Americans were aware of it. The idea of the US getting involved in any European war was not even thinkable. All the same, presenting German operettas on Broadway was looking less appealing to producers. A closer-to-home worry for the theatre business was watching some of New York's larger playhouses being renovated to show movies. But for many playmakers and playgoers, the idea of the flickers posing a threat to live theatre was also unthinkable.

Back in his hometown of Hamburg, Abbott had befriended the struggling actor Arthur Allen who had not only been to New York City but had studied at the American Academy of Dramatic Arts. Allen told Abbott that the best time to find work in the big city was at the end of August. So after Abbott's summer jobs ended, the two took the Lackawanna Railway into New York and found lodgings at the YMCA on Twenty-third Street. The cost was a reasonable three dollars a week, an amount that worried Abbott as his savings dwindled. Allen and Abbott were forced to be frugal, eating in cheap cafeterias or from push cart vendors. Abbott owned one decent suit and, to keep it from getting shabby, laid the trousers flat under his mattress each night to keep it pressed. By day the two hounded the producers' offices looking for acting jobs; by night, they saw theatre from the second balcony of the Manhattan playhouses. Abbott rarely got to see any producers in person. Office underlings were assigned to dismiss the many wanna-be actors. Getting past such barriers was frustrating and demoralizing. After a few weeks, Abbott was lonely and depressed. He took some comfort in leaving some of his scripts at producers' outer offices. Yet the thought that his plays were probably disposed of unread also discouraged him.

So what did Abbott see on Broadway upon on his arrival in Manhattan? The fall's four play hits were more audience favorites than critical triumphs. George M. Cohan's comedy-mystery *Seven Keys to Baldpate* would end up having the most enduring stage life with revivals and regional productions for decades. The tongue-in-cheek claptrap probably amused Abbott but what must have impressed him more was Cohan's rapid, very physical direction on a single set with a half a dozen doors, a staircase with plenty of landings, and the effects of the wind and snow banging on the windows. The twenty-six-year-old melodrama *Henrietta* was given a facelift and opened that fall as *The New Henrietta* with original star William H. Crane as the ruthless stockbroker Van Alstyne. So many changes were made in the script that the play was not considered a revival. Audiences didn't care one way or the other and came to see Crane (and newcomer Douglas Fairbanks) for a profitable run. A silly comedy titled *Grumpy* also failed to win over the press but playgoers loved character actor Cyril Maude as "Grumpy" Bullivant. After a very lucrative run in New York, Maude toured with the play for years, chalking up over 2,000 performances as the old curmudgeon. *Potash and Perlmutter* was the fourth fall hit. It was an extended vaudeville skit about two immigrants in the dressmaking business who slaughter the English language and get into a financial tangle until the contrived happy end. The critics scoffed, the audiences laughed, and *Potash and Perlmutter* was a smash hit. Of the nineteen fall musicals, the only one to have endured in any way was Victor Herbert's operetta *Sweethearts*. Also enjoying long and profitable runs were Rudolf Friml's *High Jinks* and Ivan Caryll's *The Little Café*. (Abbott had missed the two big summer musical attractions: *Ziegfeld Follies of 1913* and *The Passing Show of 1913*.)

If Abbott was not encountering superior plays and musicals that fall, he had an opportunity to see some outstanding acting. In revivals, flop plays, and touring repertories, Broadway presented such luminaries as Alice Brady, David Warfield, Grace George, Ethel and John Barrymore (though not together), Mary Boland, Laura Hope Crews, Elsie Ferguson, and the aging but still potent John Drew and J. Forbes-Robertson. Abbott had seen some of them on tour in Boston but such a treasure trove in one place over a period of four months must have been enthralling. It is little wonder his desire to get involved in the New York stage was enflamed. He was determined to succeed as a playwright or an actor. But his money was running out and he had to wire his mother for a loan. It was the first and last loan Abbott ever had.

One can say Abbott paid his dues pounding Forty-second Street and the many producers' offices in the Broadway District. Yet this period of struggle was short lived. Within a month of his arrival, Abbott was cast in a first-class production by the promising producer William Harris, Jr. He had had a major hit with *The Yellow Jacket* (1912) and was embarking on a notable career out from under the shadow of his father, the renowned producer William Harris, Sr., one of the co-founders of the Theatrical Syndicate. (Harris' elder brother, Henry B. Harris, was also a very successful producer; his career was cut short when Harris died in the sinking of the *Titanic* in 1912.) The junior Harris' latest theatrical venture, **The Misleading Lady** (1913) by Charles W. Goddard and Paul Dickey, was already in rehearsal when Abbott was spotted in the outer office by Harris himself. Here was a tall, muscular young fellow who looked right for the small role of a drunken college boy. The part was already cast but the actor playing it was deemed too wooden by Harris so he sent Abbott to the rehearsal taking place at the Fulton Theatre. As Abbott remembered it, co-author Dickey was in charge of the rehearsal and, a former athlete himself, he thought Abbott looked right. Without any audition or preparation, Abbott was given a script and told to do the scene. Dickey hardly paid any attention to the young Abbott, having more pressing things on his agenda. But Abbott sounded right and was hired. It was a small part, even less defined than another college drunk, Habe Merrill, who had more lines. When the actor assigned to that better role stopped coming to rehearsals, Abbott was promoted to the juicier part of Habe. *The Misleading Lady* was a raucous comedy that would never sit well with modern audiences. A temperamental actress (Inez Buck) is fond of toying with men but goes too far with one cast-off admirer (Lewis Stone) who abducts her, chains her foot to the bed in his Adirondacks cabin, and proceeds to teach her manners. This bizarre kidnapping-etiquette lesson is interrupted several times by eccentric characters stumbling onto the mountain retreat. By the final curtain, the actress is in love with her abductor and all's right with the world. The most amusing of the intruders is an escapee from the lunatic asylum (Frank Sylvester) who thinks he is Napoleon. (It is believed that this was the first time the "Napoleon Delusion" complex appeared in the mass media; it certainly wasn't the last.) Abbott's inebriated college lad was indeed a minor role but it paid forty-five dollars a week and *The Misleading Lady* ran out the season—twenty-three weeks. The critics, for the most part, found the offbeat comedy enjoyable. The unsigned *New York Times* notice declared the play a "theatrical crazy quilt [that] had the audience gaping with surprise or wondering what would happen next." Abbott may not have been mentioned in the reviews but he was on Broadway and he felt the world was his for the taking.

But it was not to be. Not yet. Two years of disappointment, hard times, and bad decisions followed. The first miscalculation was when Abbott declined to stay with

The Misleading Lady for its one-year cross-country tour. The pay was even higher than on Broadway but Abbott foolishly thought he was now an established actor and the new season would bring him many offers. Because of *The Misleading Lady*, he was now getting interviews with actual producers but no job offers came of it. Abbott married Ednah in the summer of 1914 and the responsibility of supporting a wife weighed heavily on him. He took work in vaudeville, played a small role in the tour of a farce titled *Some Baby*, and was an extra in silent films being shot in the New York-New Jersey area. Abbott got a small role in the comedy *The Ohio Lady* but it closed out of town. Perhaps a low point was when he played a Nubian slave in the Off-Broadway play *The Queen's Enemies*. Abbott estimated his income for the two years—the summer of 1915 to the fall of 1917—was two thousand dollars. And this during a time of prosperity in America. Ednah took a job as a secretary in her brother's law office and was, in essence, supporting her out-of-work actor-husband. Abbott still made the rounds to producers' offices and continued to write plays, telling himself that having a wife as the breadwinner was only a temporary situation. Steady work eventually came from the playwright-producer John Golden. He thought Abbott's scripts promising but not yet stageworthy. He offered Abbott a job in his office as an "assistant" and soon Abbott was serving as office boy, a play reader, a casting director's assistant, and even a script editor. When Austin Strong's *Three Wise Fools* was in trouble in rehearsals, Abbott was asked to rewrite some lines and even a scene or two. Very little of the young playwright's work made it to opening night but Abbott was thrilled to hear some of his words spoken on a Broadway stage for the first time.

It was as a play doctor of sorts on **Lightnin'** in 1918 that finally reversed Abbott's string of ill luck. The comedy by Winchell Smith and Frank Bacon came to Golden's attention and he thought it had the makings of a hit. All the same, he asked Abbott to do some revisions on the script and assigned him as assistant stage manager for the production. Golden felt that working on what looked like a hit would be a valuable experience for the thirty-year-old office assistant. The comedy is about Lightnin' Bill Jones (played by co-author Frank Bacon), a crusty, talkative boozer who owns a hotel that straddles the California-Utah state line. The part of the lobby that is in Utah is in much demand by fugitives from California state laws or wives wanting to get to Reno. There is a complicated plot about a shyster lawyer (Paul Stanton) who has cheated a widow out of valuable land that the railroad wants, a young couple (Ralph Morgan and Beatrice Nichols) in love but entangled in legal matters, and Mrs. Jones (Jessie Pringle) trying to sue Lightnin' for divorce. But the comedy came down to the colorful character of Lightnin' and Bacon's acclaimed performance. *Lightnin'* opened in the late summer of 1918 and ran until 1925, a total of 1,291 performances, which made it the longest run of the decade and the record-holder for ten years. We will never know just how much Abbott contributed to *Lightnin'*; in his autobiography, Abbott only writes about what an effective director Winchell Smith was. He was precise, clear, and definite—qualities which Abbott emulated throughout his career. But even if Abbott's hand in *Lightnin'* was minimal, the experience of working on a hit play was significant. He was learning the ropes from veteran playmakers and he was in the thick of Broadway theatre.

A month after *Lightnin'* opened, Abbott was back on stage again and this time he was acting under the direction and supervision of arguably the most important producer in town, David Belasco. With his Roman Catholic priest's garb, shock of white hair, and lisping voice, Belasco came across as something of a clown. Yet his dedication to detail in both acting and stagecraft was legendary and he had created and nurtured a series of famous female stage stars. Abbott was cast against type in the sentimental comedy **Daddies** (1918) by John L. Hobble. He played Henry Allen, a middle-aged confirmed bachelor who, upon graduating from college in 1901, had signed an agreement with four other graduates to forsake marriage and remain single. If any of the five men failed to stick to this arrangement, he was to pay the others $5,000. Years later, in the midst of a World War, the quintet agrees that it is only right that each adopts a war orphan from Europe. Henry/Abbott ends up with orphaned triplets who prove to be so terrifying that he weds just to get a woman's knowhow. But the other four bachelors have similar experiences and all five are married by the final curtain. While the role of Henry was substantial, the play centered on bachelor Robert Audrey (Bruce McRae) who ends up not with a sweet infant orphan but with seventeen-year-old Ruth Atkins. This character was played by Belasco's latest protege Jeanne Eagels, a blonde, vivacious, and even sultry actress who had found some recognition playing opposite George Arliss in a series of costume dramas. Eagels was miscast as the innocent youth Ruth but Belasco was smitten with her, as he was with many of his leading ladies, and was determined to make her a bigger star who would return his affections offstage. It didn't happen. Eagels was uncomfortable playing such a naive character and was unaffected by Belasco's wooing. Years later, Abbott recounted how careful Belasco was to not criticize Eagels in rehearsals. Instead he took his anger and lecturing out on newcomer Edith King, saying to her what he wanted to say to his star. Yet Abbott found the experience acting in *Daddies* to be everything he hoped for. Belasco's working with actors was charged with energy and always had a theatrical touch. He got to witness one of Belasco's favorite gimmicks. During a passionate moment in rehearsals, Belasco pulled out his gold watch, smashed it to pieces, then broke into tears as he explained it was the watch his father had given to him on his deathbed. Later Abbott learned that Belasco had a drawerful of imitation gold watches which he used in a like manner with every production. *Daddies* was criticized as sugary claptrap by the press but the critics adored Eagels. The *Times* found her "Quite masterly in [her] direct sincerity and unaffected power ... Her whole performance was on a very high level and probably marks the advent of an actress of distinguished quality." *The New York Clipper* was more enthusiastic about the whole production, reporting, "David Belasco's first offering of the new season proved to be one of the most charming comedies the local stage has seen." Dorothy Parker in *Vanity Fair* sounded a sour note. "*Daddies* is just one of those things that are just simply too sweet for words," she wrote. "It starts out being sweet the moment the curtain rises, and it gets steadily sweeter and sweeter as the evening advances. In fact when you go to see it, it's just as well to bring the bicarbonate of soda with you." Parker concluded her opinion with the quip, "As propaganda for birth control, [*Daddies*] was extraordinarily effective." Regardless, *Daddies* ran out the season and Abbott had work for eleven months. Eagels thought her performance was lacking and got out of her Broadway run contract early by claiming illness often enough that Belasco, unable to seduce the actress, let her go. This time when Abbott was offered the tour, he readily accepted and was able to build up his bankroll while Belasco paid for most of his living expenses. (As might be expected, Eagels did not tour with *Daddies*.)

Abbott was back in New York and on stage in November of 1920. The comedy-drama was **The Broken Wing** (1920) by the team of Paul Dickey and Charles W. Goddard, authors of *The Misleading Lady*. The Mexican beauty Inez Villera (Inez Plummer) lives with her American foster father (Henry Duggan) in a well-appointed home in Mexico dreaming of the day a true love will enter her life. Suddenly a plane crashes into the side of the house and the dazed American flyer Philip Marvin (Charles Trowbridge) enters. He's lost his memory but he knows he loves Inez at first sight. She is then wooed by the dashing Mexican bandit Innocencio Dos Santos (Alphonz Ethier) who risks his life to be with her. Inez chooses the American and flies away with Philip. Director and co-author Dickey had Abbott in mind when he wrote the character of Sylvester Cross, a crass oil man who turns out to be a secret service agent. The critics applauded *The Broken Wing* and praised the spectacular scene when the plane crashed on stage. Critic Heywood Bron thought he play a mixture of "ethnic phraseology, a naïve heroine, and mawkish sentiment achieved its burlesque purposes with an ample dose of melodrama." As for Abbott, his comic performances was pointed out by the press to be "breezy and uncouth." Critic Alexander Woollcott wrote in the *New York Times*, "Probably the most effective performance of the evening is given by George Abbott in a semi-comedy role—a thoroughly lifelike characterization." The play was a success and Abbott was employed for twenty-two weeks. A footnote regarding *The Broken Wing*: throughout the play, the Mexican peon Basilio (Joseph Spurin Calleia) went about his business as he hummed a tuneful ditty composed by the actor. Calleia asked Abbott to write a lyric for the tune and, under the title "Adelai," it was published. Nothing much came of it and Abbott himself declared his lyric to be "perfectly horrible."[1] Yet some years later "Adelai" enjoyed a brief spurt of popularity. It was the beginning and the end of Abbott's songwriting career.

A major hit which launched the careers of playwrights George S. Kaufman and Marc Connelly, as well as actress Lynn Fontanne, was the comedy **Dulcy** which played to full houses throughout the 1921–1922 season. Although she always means well, Dulcinea Smith (Fontanne) usually ends up making trouble for the people she wishes to help. When her husband Gordon (John Westley) is close to pulling off a merger with C. Rogers Forbes (Wallis Clark), Dulcy invites the Forbes family for the weekend and manages to say all the wrong things and inadvertently praises a rival company. When the Forbes daughter Angela (Norma Lee) shows an interest in the wealthy Schuyler Van Dyck (Gilbert Douglas), Dulcy suggests they elope. Once all the damage has been corrected, Dulcy promises Gordon she'll never interfere again, but no one quite believes her. The comedy made a stage star out of Fontanne and brought Kaufman and Connelly to the attention of the public. For the subsequent tour, Fontanne reprised her deliciously daffy Dulcy, James Gleason was cast as her husband Gordon, and Abbott was hired for a small role. It was a step backward after getting noticed on Broadway in *The Broken Wing* but Abbott and Ednah now had a daughter, Judith Ann, and a steady income was needed. During the tour, Abbott collaborated with two cast members on writing two different plays. With the leading man Gleason, he wrote an early version of *The Fall Guy* and with performer Ann Preston Bridgers he worked on a comedy which later became the melodrama *Coquette*. Although he was getting cast on a regular basis, Abbott still dreamt of becoming a successful playwright. These two plays that he worked on during the tour would eventually help establish his writing career but their success was a few years away.

By April of 1923, Abbott was on Broadway again and this time he had another attention-getting role. The sentimental comedy-drama was **Zander the Great** (1923) by Salisbury Field, a vehicle for Alice Brady who was now a film star as well as a stage favorite. She played the hard-working, motherly maid Mamie who has charge of the five-year-old orphan Alexander (Edwin Mills), called Zander by the New Jersey household. Having heard that Zander's father is alive and living in Arizona, Mamie packs up Zander and his belongings (including a passel of rabbits) in an old Ford Flivver and they head West where they have adventures with cowboy bootleggers and possible fathers. Finally, Mamie settles down with the reformed cowboy Dan Murchinson (Jerome Patrick) and they adopt Zander. Abbott played one of the bootleggers, the homespun, tobacco-chewing Tex, a role he could bring a level of authenticity because of his time working on a ranch. He was mentioned in some of the notices but most of the attention was on Brady's performance. As for the play itself, it was met with mixed reviews. John Corbin in the *Times* thought, "structurally the play is ragged," but could not deny its sentimental appeal. "It may or may not be true that all the world loves a lover," he wrote. "But ever since Bret Harte wrote *The Luck of Roaring Camp*, there has been no doubt in the mind of the melodramatist that men, especially bad men out West, love a baby." Percy Hammond in in the *Herald Tribune* was more concise with, "Nice, rough, nursery stuff, calculated to charm the sophisticated drama lover who wishes to be made a child again just for tonight." The highest praise was for Brady's lively, heartwarming performance (one newspaper declared her "vivacious, tender, defiant, saucy").

Speaking of saucy, Dorothy Parker in *Ainslee's* pronounced "*Zander the Great* is the best play that Miss Brady has had for many seasons. It must also be admitted that the preceding is just about the faintest praise ever lavished on a playwright and his effort." The play ran over ten weeks. In his autobiography, Abbott states that *Zander the Great* was a turning point in his acting career. From that play onward, he never had difficulty getting jobs as a performer.

In the fall of 1923, producer-director Brock Pemberton cast Abbott in a major role in a tragic piece titled **White Desert** (1923) by the struggling playwright Maxwell Anderson. Being a dark drama written in blank verse, Abbott knew its chances for success were limited but he was excited by the powerful writing and the opportunity to play such a demanding role. Set in the brutal winter of the North Dakota prairie, the tale centered on the sexually repressed Puritan Michael Kane (Frank Shannon) and his wife Mary (Beth Merrill) who is not afraid of sex and tells her husband so, much to his embarrassment. The tall, strapping neighbor Sverre Peterson (Abbott) is married to Annie (Ethel Wright) but is drawn to the sensual Mary. When Michael leaves for two days to get supplies, Mary has little difficulty in seducing Sverre, the two of them taking refuge in the cabin during a blizzard. When Michael returns, Mary brazenly tells him what she did. Michael tries to forgive her but finds he cannot so he shoots and kills her. Most critics dismissed *White Desert*, only a few finding any promise in the playwright. Corbin in the *Times* wrote, "*White Desert* has real admirable qualities that bespeak far better luck next time for its author." The cast was saluted for its ensemble work. Corbin again: "The actors, one and all, creep snugly into the skins of their parts and live there." *Time Magazine* thought, "Though [the author] has created an artistic cross-section of stark bitterness, he is too pessimistic, too penetrating, to be widely popular. Possibly thereby he proves his tragedy is true." Audiences were not interested and the drama could only manage twelve performances in the small Princess Theatre. Abbott befriended Anderson during the preparations for *White Desert* and the two promised each other to collaborate on a script sometime.

More successful was Hatcher Hughes' rural melodrama **Hell-Bent fer Heaven** (1924); this time the critics were much more approving and the piece even won the Pulitzer Prize. In the Appalachian Mountains, the Hunt family and the Lowry clan have always feuded but it looks like peace will come with the marriage of the likable war hero Sid Hunt (Abbott) and the pretty Jude Lowry (Margaret Borough). The religious fanatic Rufe Prior (John F. Hamilton) lusts after Jude himself so he tries to reignite the feud by convincing Jude's brother Andy (Glenn Anders) to kill Sid. Rufe's machinations almost succeed, with Andy trying but failing to shoot Sid. Rufe even blows up a dam so that the rushing waters will drown Sid. But Rufe's devious ways are revealed to both families. Andy wants to kill Rufe but the aged family patriarch, Grandpa Hunt (Augustin Duncan), allows the culprit to escape, thereby ending the feud for good. Producer Alonso Klaw insisted on Sid having an authentic Appalachian dialect and paid for Abbott to spend some time in Boone,

North Carolina, where he could listen to the real thing. (Abbott brought Maxwell Anderson with him and the two worked on their own drama about a backwoods feud.) Writing years later, Abbott noted, "What a difference it was to come into first rehearsal feeling confident, and how pleasant to take my place among the others with assurance—to know that as an actor I was somebody."[2] Sid was a life-affirming, good-hearted mountain boy who relished eating pie and chewing the fat with Grandpa about the difference between the Civil War and the recent Great War in Europe. Abbott was physically and vocally right for the role and he filled his scenes with bluster and humor. Writing in the *New York Mail*, James Craig pointed out that "George Abbott, whom we have seen heretofore in comedy cowboy roles, has more than justified the selection of him for the leading 'straight' part, the hero of the tale." Corbin in the *Times* noted,

> Quite the equal of [Duncan and Hamilton] was George Abbott's Sid Hunt, the hearty, amiable and sensitive young hero returned from the war. How much of all this is attributable to the acting, and how much to the writing ... it is impossible to say. It is enough that the two occur in the happiest possible conjunction.

Critical opinion for the drama itself varied, some commentators finding it crude and in poor taste with others praising its honesty and raw power. *Hellbent fer Heaven* took a while to settle in for a Broadway run of 122 performances. Producer Alonso Klaw wanted to bring the drama to his own playhouse but the Klaw Theatre was housing a comedy that turned out to run longer than expected. So Klaw offered *Hellbent fer Heaven* for a series of matinees when the theatre was free and word started circulating, slowly gaining an audience who was not offended by the seemingly irreligious tone of the piece. The day after it closed, the play won the Pulitzer Prize for Drama but not without controversy. A majority of the Pulitzer committee selected George Kelly's comedy *The Show-Off* but the higher-ups at Columbia University, which gives out the awards, overrode the earlier decision. The fact that playwright Hughes was on the faculty of Columbia did not go unnoticed. All the same, Burns Mantle chose *Hellbent fer Heaven* as one of the ten scripts featured in *The Best Plays of 1923–1924* and, though rarely produced today, it was a significant drama. Also, appearing in a major role in a prize-winning play certainly helped Abbott's career.

By the mid-1920s, Abbott was in the envious position of choosing which roles he wanted to play. Sometimes he was so impressed with a character that his judgement about the play was clouded. Such was the case with the comedy **Lazybones** (1924), a "chronicle of a country town" by the prolific Owen Davis. The character of the shiftless Maine fisherman Steve Tuttle was onstage practically all evening, allowed Abbott to age from his twenties to his forties, was filled with rural hokum, and gave him room for plenty of sentiment in the last act. Ednah read the script and pronounced it "trash." But the acclaimed director Guthrie McClintic was directing and the veteran producer Sam H. Harris was presenting it so how bad could it be? The "lazybones" of the title refers to Steve, a worthless local who returns from a fishing trip with a baby girl in a shopping basket which he found floating in White Creek. Steve's fiancée is suspicious and, when he decides to raise the baby with the help of his mother, she breaks off the engagement. Years pass and the child grows up into the attractive young woman Kit (Martha Bryan-Allen) who falls in love with her guardian. In the end it is learned that Kit's mother was the sister of Steve's ex-fiancée. Abbott could tell that even Guthrie lost interest in the claptrap piece during rehearsals. Yet the quirky play was a pleasing mixture of comedy and pathos and the press approved of it. But *Time* found Abbott's acting to be wanting: "George Abbott, recalled agreeably for his comic cowboy in *Zander the Great*, stepped beyond his depth in the lead. He seemed to manufacture the part instead of living in it." Gerald Bordman, in his chronicle of the period, writes, "Many critics compared the play favorably to *Lightnin'*, and praised the players. But the public only supported the play for ten weeks."³

Abbott was more proud of his acting in **Processional** (1925), a self-described "jazz symphony of American life" by John Howard Lawson that used music, vaudeville techniques, dramatic scenes, and even burlesque to create a theatrical collage. The Theatre Guild production, directed by Philip Moeller, foreshadowed the Leftist dramas that the Group Theatre would present during the Depression. (In the cast were future Group members Philip Loeb, Lee Strasberg, and Sanford Meisner.) The episodic drama was set during a strike in a West Virginia mining town and had several storylines. The main one concerned the radical Dynamite Jim (Abbott) who is blinded by the capitalist's goons and then is hunted by the Ku Klux Klan. After a touching scene with his mother (Blanche Friderici), Jim is allowed to wed the Jewish shop-keeper's daughter Sadie Cohen (June Walker) in a jazz wedding. It was all presented expressionistically which some critics found bold and innovative, other disparaged as nothing but "noise and confusion" and very "uneven and not very well produced." *Time* reported, "Two reactions are discernible in the audience. Most of it is irritated and resentful. The minority is excited, savagely amused and deeply grateful that from this formless experiment the Guild has translated some of the stubborn emotional symbols with which the hidden history of American life tells of truth." Alexander Woollcott in the *Times* perhaps summed up the situation with, "A play that the Guild should be respected for producing and the playgoer pardoned for avoiding." Developing a character in a non-realistic drama had its difficulties but Abbott was pleased with his performance, later stating that Dynamite Jim was "the best acting part I ever had."⁴ Stark Young in the *Times* noted,

> George Abbott as Dynamite Jim started off only so so; he improved for the scenes where the man returns after being strung to a tree and cut down and

rescued. In this scene the blind man finds his mother and the girl who is to bear his child. Here Mr. Abbott was excellent and June Walker equally good.

Because some playgoers were intrigued by what they heard about *Processional*, it managed to run ninety-six performances. (The drama was revived by the government-sponsored Federal Theatre Project in 1937 and found an audience for ten weeks.)

One dozen years after arriving in New York, Abbott was an established actor on Broadway and might have gone on to a long and substantial career as a performer. But writing and directing in the theatre remained his goal and he left acting behind rather suddenly. In fact, he got out of his contract in *Processional* when the first non-acting job beckoned. Had Abbott so quickly tired of performing? He never said so but I imagine he found it frustrating having no control in the theatrical process. He had worked with both excellent and ineffective directors and knew he could hold his own staging a play. And his burning desire to write for the theatre had never cooled. When the opportunity to direct and write came along, it seemed like the most exciting (if not the most practical) thing to do. So in the spring of 1925, Abbott embarked on the next phase of his Broadway career. He was soon more successful than ever and he rarely returned to acting again.

2 IF YOU WANT IT DONE RIGHT, WRITE IT AND DIRECT IT YOURSELF

(1925–1934)

The Fall Guy • *A Holy Terror* • *Love 'Em and Leave 'Em* • *Broadway* • *Chicago* • *Spread Eagle* • *Four Walls* • *Coquette* • *Bless You, Sister* • *Gentlemen of the Press* • *Ringside* • *Jarnegan* • *Poppa* • *Those We Love* • *Louder, Please* • *The Great Magoo* • *Small Miracle* • *Ladies' Money* • *Page Miss Glory*

Abbott made his Broadway writing and directing debut with one production, *The Fall Guy* in March of 1925. Actually, it was his co-writing and co-directing debut since he shared both jobs with James Gleason. The two had outlined and began working on the comedy back in 1922 when they were actors in the tour of *Dulcy*. Since that time, Gleason had become a popular leading man on Broadway and in 1925 he and Richard Taber wrote the hit comedy *Is Zat So?* which Gleason starred in. The Shubert Brothers had produced *Is Zat So?* and agreed to any future project Gleason brought them. Abbott and Gleason polished up *The Fall Guy* and Gleason insisted that Abbott serve as co-director. So in one swift negotiation, Abbott found himself co-directing his first script on Broadway. *The Fall Guy* was a gangster comedy. Out of work with a wife, a sister, and a loafer of a brother-in-law to support, New Yorker Johnnie Quinlan (Ernest Truex) is desperate for cash and agrees to transport a suitcase for mobster "Nifty" Herman (Hartley Power). A rival gang member, Charles Newton (Henry Mortimer), is also interested in the suitcase and Johnnie is caught in the middle of an underworld quarrel. Newton turns out to be a federal agent, Nifty is arrested, and Johnnie is offered a job with the government. The writing is filled with New Yorkese slang and has a breezy quality to it.

> **Bertha**   Don't you never wish you was free and could go running around like you used to—and not having a wife to bother you?
>
> **Johnnie**   Naw.
>
> **Bertha**   Do you still love me, Johnnie?
>
> **Johnnie**   What do *you* think?
>
> **Bertha**   I'm afraid I razz you too much.
>
> **Johnnie**   Oh, that's all right. If it wasn't for scrapping once in a while, we wouldn't have nuttin' to talk about.[1]

The fast-paced comedy and Truex's risible performance as Johnnie were cheered by the press. Stark Young in the *New York Times* called *The Fall Guy* a "sound, infectious little comedy... very welcome by its devoted and roaring audience." Percy Hammond in the *New York Herald Tribune* placed the play, "among the top notchers of American shows." *Best Plays* chronicler Burns Mantle even selected *The Fall Guy* as one of the ten best plays of the 1924–1925 season. Although the play was co-directed by Abbott and Gleason, the latter was tied up with several projects so Abbott did much of the staging. When *The Fall Guy* went to Atlantic City for tryouts, Gleason didn't go and left everything in Abbott's hands. During the out-of-town tryout, the Shuberts wanted Abbott to replace one of the key actors but Abbott (with Gleason's backing) refused, sensing the actor was going to turn in a fine comic performance. This was a rather bold move for a first-time director but Abbott stuck to his guns, the cast was not changed, and the production opened to laudatory reviews. (Writing about *The Fall Guy* forty years later, Abbott would not disclose which actor had nearly been fired.) *The Fall Guy* ran over five months, a profitable venture in 1925.

Abbott had worked with several top directors before he staged *The Fall Guy* but he felt the attention given to certain aspects of staging a play were lacking. In Abbott's opinion, David Belasco had a vivid sense of the stage picture but rarely concerned himself with character relationships. Guthrie McClintic was more into character study but was not strong on pacing. Brock Pemberton was too superficial, Augustin Duncan was too old-fashioned in his staging, and Philip Moeller was too vague. Abbott believed that every aspect of a production should be unified by one artistic vision and only a director could provide that. It was a rather pompous philosophy for a first-time director but Abbott attempted to follow through with his ideas. The key word in his thesis was *control*. Abbott felt that unity came from one power source. Although he was shy of forty years old, Abbott believed he was experienced enough to be this all-controlling person. Was the direction of *The Fall*

Guy noticeably different? Not obviously so but the successful production led to many other directing offers. Abbott was hungry for financial security and artistic freedom and took everything that came his way. In the next two years, he was involved with nine Broadway productions.

For ***A Holy Terror*** (1925), Abbott was co-author, co-director, and leading man—a feat rarely seen on Broadway since George M. Cohan's early years. The script was a melodrama that Abbott and Maxwell Anderson had worked on back in 1923. Since then, Anderson had found fame as the co-author of the acclaimed war drama *What Price Glory?* (1924). Producer John Golden liked the script for *A Holy Terror* but insisted the veteran playwright Winchell Smith be brought on board to rewrite it with Abbott. Anderson was paid $1,500 for his contribution and Abbott was signed on to co-direct with Smith and play the leading role. The writing and the rehearsals did not go well. Smith was easily distracted and then got so ill that Abbott ended up directing himself in the melodrama. The plot had possibilities but the writing was artificial. Dirk Yancey (Abbott) learned how to shoot, growing up in the midst of two West Virginia feuding families. When a mine strike turns violent in his community, Yancey is made chief of police. Mayor Goodlow (Bennet Musson) is shot and killed during the rioting. Yancey is the prime suspect because everyone knows that he's in love with the mayor's wife Ellen (Leona Hogarth). But Yancey defends himself in court and discovers the real culprit. Writing about *A Holy Terror* decades later, Abbott thought he and Smith were not right for the subject of the drama. The critics agreed and the reviews for the script and the large-cast, multi-set production were negative. An unsigned review in the *Times* noted that "the new melodrama provides several thrilling climaxes but it hardly contrives to be thrilling throughout the evening." Yet Abbott's acting was complimented with, "Mr. Abbott, knowing his own hero to the ground, is interesting and often exciting in the role." With no money notices and poor box office activity, Golden closed the play after thirty-two performances.

Such a failure was a blow to Abbott but he was already involved with a comedy that would be a success. ***Love 'Em and Leave 'Em*** (1926) was co-written with humorist John V. A. Weaver and was based on Weaver's best-selling comic novel of the same title. Weaver was known for his comic slang and the dialogue for the play was punctuated with such idioms as "the galloping bones" for a pair of dice. Mame Walsh (Florence Johns) and her sister Janie (Katherine Wilson) work in Ginberg's Department Store and room together at a boarding house run by Lem (Donald Meek) and Ma Woodruff (Camilla Crume). Janie steals Mame's beau, the clerk Billingsley (Donald MacDonald), as well as the money Mame has collected for the Welfare Service Association and its charity pageant. Mame wins the money back in a crap game with a scheming bookie then gets Billingsley back as well. *Love 'Em and Leave 'Em* was the first Broadway production in which Abbott was billed as sole director, although in essence he had staged his last two productions on his own. His direction was rapid and well focused. The *Times* noted, "Mr. Abbott as director, no less as co-author, has molded this disjointed material into a viable performance." *Time Magazine* described the comedy thusly: "Clerks and poor boardinghouse folk are their characters. Their touch is shrewd and their comedy genuinely entertaining." The cast was also well received, particularly Donald Meek who stole his scenes as the shiftless boarding house manager Lem Woodruff. *Love 'Em and Leave 'Em* also marked Abbott's first of several productions with young producer Jed Harris. Like everyone who would work with Harris over the years, Abbott would develop a love-hate relationship with the volatile, passionate producer (later director as well). Disagreements about the production while it was trying out in Atlantic City led to temper tantrums by Harris but when *Love 'Em and Leave 'Em* opened in New York to laudatory reviews, all was forgiven. The comedy ran five months and Harris' career as a Broadway producer was launched.

Harris produced Abbott's next venture, the melodrama **Broadway** (1926), which would be one of the biggest play hits of Abbott's career. It all started with an actor. Lee Tracy was a quirky kind of leading man, more character actor than romantic type. His rapid, slightly nasal speech made him distinctive and the first time Abbott saw him on stage, he wanted to write a character for him. Harris was also impressed with Tracy so when a script titled *Bright Lights* came his way he showed it to Abbott. The melodrama set in a Manhattan nightclub was by a stage manager named Philip Dunning and both Abbott and Harris thought it needed work. So Harris produced the rewritten version, retitled *The Roaring Forties* and then *Broadway*, which Abbott co-wrote and directed with Tracy in the leading role. David Sheward, in his book *It's a Hit!* about long-running plays in New York, noted, "The gangster film of the 1930s can trace their ancestry to a honky-tonk stage melodrama of the 1920s named after the street of its setting. . . *Broadway* contained all the elements movie fans would later cry for in the machine-gun shoot-em-ups starring Humphrey Bogart, Edward G. Robinson, and James Cagney."[2] After seeing so many gangster tales in the movies, modern audiences might consider *Broadway* rather tame and routine. But the play was exciting and new in 1926. At the Paradise Night Club, the hoofer Roy Lane (Tracy) is in love with the chorine Billie Moore (Sylvia Field) but lately she is seen on the arm of the big-time bootlegger Steve Crandall (Robert Glecker). When "Scar" Edwards (John Wray) tries to muscle in on Crandall's territory, Crandall shoots him in the back room of the nightclub. Roy and Billie see Crandall and his henchmen removing the body and are told it is a drunk they are taking to a cab. The police start to investigate the disappearance of Edwards and Roy and Billie are questioned, but Crandall is murdered by Edwards' mistress Pearl (Eloise Stream). The detective Dan McCorn (Thomas Jackson) realizes the truth but reports Crandall's death as suicide. Roy and Billie get a booking together in vaudeville and another kind of engagement is hinted at. *Broadway* was not a musical but the action all took place backstage and the nightclub's jazz band was sometimes heard. The melodrama, which had plenty of comedy as well, started off in the midst of a chorus line rehearsal and the dialogue came fast and sharp. The slangy talk moved as rapidly as the action and *Broadway* had a staccato rhythm to it.

Roy   It's not like Billie to fall down on the job. Why, that kid is one of the best lookers and neatest workers you got. You'll make one big mistake if you let her out—she's a might nifty little trick.

Nick   Why all the talk? You don't work for her—you work for me.

Roy   God knows I know that.

Nick   Whadda ya mean?

Roy   Well, not to pin any bouquets on myself, but where could you get a guy to do what I'm doing for the coffee-and-cake money you're paying me?.. You see, it ain't only I can dance, but I got personality—Personality plus . . .

Nick   Something else ya got is a terrible swell head.[3]

The mobster talk in *Broadway* is sharp and direct and would be made fun of in future plays and films. In 1926 it was not considered cliché-ridden but rather stimulating.

Scar   We stocked that territory and we got a right to it. My mob worked for four years to get things the way we got 'em—and nobody—get that—nobody is goin' to cut in from down here and spoil a nickel's worth of it. You hi-jacked another truckload last night, yes, and you been spillin' more jack around for protection than we can afford—we ain't never come down here to horn in on your Broadway trade, but you're ruinin' our game up there and I'm here to tell you that you can't get away with it . . . I come here for a show-down with you guys, see.[4]

On paper and on stage, the melodrama *moved*. Dunning figured out that there were more than 300 entrances and exits in *Broadway* and that no one scene lasted more than four minutes.

Although *Broadway* smelled like a success from the start, there were plenty of problems during tryouts, mostly due to Harris' bi-polar temperament. At one point he insisted the entire third act be rewritten. Later he wanted to remove Abbott as director and bring in the more experienced Hugh Ford. Dunning stood by Abbott both times and Harris had to back down. Another problem arose when Harris' producing partner Crosby Gaige insisted that his latest girlfriend be cast in one of the supporting roles. She was not talented and Abbott wanted to replace her but found out Gaige was financing the production so they were stuck with her. "It cost a good deal of time and energy to get a performance out of her," Abbott wrote years later. "But by the time we opened in New York she was acceptable."[5] Of course once

Broadway opened to rave notices and Harris was now a wealthy producer, all past grievances were overlooked. Few plays of the era got the kind of exemplary reviews that *Broadway* received. Hammond, writing in the *Herald-Tribune*, called *Broadway* the "most completely acted and perfectly directed show I have seen in thirty years of professional playgoing." *Variety* sent three commentators to the opening: a theatre critic, a nightclub reviewer, and an out-of-town press writer to give a non-Manhattan point of view; all three notices were propitious. Alexander Woollcott, writing the preface to the published version of *Broadway*, said it "most perfectly caught the accent of the city's voice . . . a taut and telling and tingling cartoon which [was] produced with uncommon imagination and resource."[6] The play ran a hefty 603 performances on Broadway and there were six touring companies in the States and four abroad. *Broadway* was a long-run hit in London where several "Gods" and "Gees" had to be cut in order to please the Lord Chamberlain's office on censorship. The melodrama was later filmed twice and was adapted for television three times.

The following season Abbott directed two hits written by others although in both cases he contributed some uncredited work on the scripts. Maurine Watkins was a reporter for the *Chicago Tribune* for a time and was more than slightly familiar with the more notorious murder cases in the Windy City. She wrote a scathing satire of celebrity in the Roaring Twenties and titled it simply **Chicago** (1926). Roxie Hart (Francine Larrimore) shoots her lover and gets her husband Amos (Charles Halton) to say he did it thinking it was a robbery. But the police see through the false confession and Roxie is arrested. Newspaper reporter Jake (Charles Bickford) smells a good story and takes Roxie under his wing, getting the hotshot lawyer Billy Flynn (Edward Ellis) to defend her and convincing columnist Mary Sunshine (Eda Heineman) to write sob stuff about Roxie in the paper. Coached by Flynn, Roxie performs the role of the innocent, convent-educated girl at the trial and is acquitted. When she is free, she dumps Amos and goes into vaudeville. Initially producer Sam H. Harris signed Jeanne Eagels to play Roxie. Eagels had had her greatest stage triumph as the *femme fatale* Sadie Thompson in *Rain* in 1922 and was more popular than ever. She remembered Abbott from *Daddies* and insisted he direct *Chicago*. Abbott agreed and worked with Watkins on the script. Serious trouble followed when Eagels started coming late to rehearsals, then missing them altogether. Citing health problems, she stopped coming to rehearsals and Harris and Abbott agreed that she be replaced by Francine Larrimore. (Eagels died four years later from a heroin overdose.) Watkins had written *Chicago* as a student in George Pierce Baker's playwriting class at Harvard University. It was her first playwriting effort and, while the characters were vivid and bigger than life, the plotting was awkward at times. Abbott did not have to do much rewriting on *Chicago* and was not credited as co-author. But his direction of the slam-bang comedy was vital to the success of the play, as was Larrimore's "intense yet brittle" performance as Roxie. *Chicago* was applauded by the press with few dissenting votes. Charles Brackett in *The New Yorker* thought

"*Chicago* is heavy handed satire of facts which satirize themselves so completely that such a treatment of them is far less interesting than would be a sympathetic and realistic study of the material. That would be quite funny enough and subtler." But Brooks Atkinson in the *Times* thought the play should have been tougher. "*Chicago* emerges in the performance not as a firm, compact satire, deadly in its import, but rather as a generally diverting entertainment." Yet he concluded, "*Chicago* might well be one of the most striking plays of the season." Audiences enjoyed the comedy for five months. There was a film version in 1942 titled *Roxie Hart* which starred Ginger Rogers. With the original title, a musical version of *Chicago* by John Kander and Fred Ebb opened on Broadway in 1975 and was a hit. A 1996 Broadway revival was even more successful, going on to become the longest-running musical revival on record.

Abbott temporarily buried the hatchet and agreed to work with Jed Harris again in the spring of 1927, directing the drama **Spread Eagle** by George S. Brooks and Walter B. Lister. Burns Mantle described *Spread Eagle* as "a cynical drama tracing the origins of America's wars to Wall Street"[7] and the play was indeed politically charged. Billionaire Martin Henderson (Fritz Williams) wants to protect the interests of his Spread Eagle Mining Company in Mexico so he manufactures a war. Paying General De Castro (Felix Kremb) to start a revolution, Henderson gets the American government and people riled up enough to declare war. He then arranges for the promising young American diplomat Charles Parkman (Allen Vincent) to be killed in the chaos, even though he is engaged to Henderson's daughter. His plan is successful, Parkman is wounded, but Henderson loses the respect of those who work for him, including his wry right-hand man Joe Cobb (Osgood Perkins) who sees what dirty tricks Henderson has done and how many will be killed just so he can make more money. In the gripping last scene, the recovered Parkman returns to Henderson and agrees to remain silent about his manufacturing the war because he still loves the billionaire's daughter. Parkman leaves to enlist and the deflated Henderson slumps down into a chair as "The Star-Spangled Banner" is heard from a band outside. "You son-of-a-bitch . . . Stand up!"[8] Cobb barks as the curtain falls. Although Abbott and Harris had no quarrels in putting together *Spread Eagle*, relations between the two were chilly. The press cheered the bold writing, the splendid cast, and the taut direction by Abbott, the *Times* stating that he "has quickly, but surely, come to mean convincing realism." As much as the reviews praised *Spread Eagle*, the public was not overly interested in such a political drama and the production struggled to run ten weeks.

Equally serious and only marginally more successful was **Four Walls** (1927), a drama Abbott co-wrote with novelist Dana Burnet. Benny Horowitz (Muni Wisenfrend) has served five years in Sing Sing and on his release he steers clear of his old cronies in crime and the type of women who mean trouble. But when a thug from his old gang is threatening a girl, Benny throws him off the roof of an apartment building. The grateful girl tells Benny she will say it was an accident when the police investigate, but Benny confesses to the murder, realizing that he could never escape the four walls of his conscience. Abbott had seen Wisenfrend playing an old man in a production by the Yiddish Art Theatre and was so impressed that he went backstage to meet him. Abbott was surprised to find an actor in his twenties and an ideal performer for the role of Benny. Producer John Golden trusted Abbott's hunch and Wisenfrend made his English-speaking stage debut in *Four Walls*. The critics unanimously extolled him, one review saying he was "the possessor of all the trade's tricks and a master of expression" but also "one of the best actors in town." (Wisenfrend would soon change his name to Paul Muni and enjoy a long stage and screen career.) The reviews for *Four Walls* were favorable enough to let the melodrama run a profitable four months. Abbott directed the fast-paced, multi-set production and, while it is difficult to determine Abbott's contribution to the script, his expert staging of the play was quite visible. As Atkinson in the *Times* wrote, "George Abbott has given the play some crafty, workmanlike touches both in staging and writing which make it, above all, effective footlight material."

Coquette (1927) was one of the most famous plays of its era but not always for the ideal reasons. Abbott would again find himself at odds with producer Jed Harris but the more exciting battle was between Harris and the play's star Helen Hayes. The script was one that Abbott and Ann Preston Bridgers began collaborating on back in 1922 when they were performing in the road tour of *Dulcy*. The play was then a comedy about a girl fighting with her father over a boy she likes. After many rewrites, it was clear the play was not working and the authors realized the piece made more sense as a drama. The conservative Southerner Dr. Besant (Charles Waldron) is not pleased that his daughter Norma (Helen Hayes) is seeing the uncouth Michael Jeffrey (Elliot Cabot), a youth who was shell shocked in the Great War. When the doctor finds out that Jeffrey has slept with his daughter, he shoots and kills him. The lawyers tell Norma the only way she can save her father from the death penalty is to give evidence in court that she is a virgin and that Jeffrey tried to rape her. Since Norma is now pregnant with Jeffrey's child, she refuses and, rather than face the awful future, she commits suicide. Abbott and Bridgers had tried unsuccessfully to interest Hayes, Broadway's newest star, in the piece. It was Harris who convinced Hayes to star in *Coquette* with the condition that he get to produce the play. Abbott refused to direct *Coquette* because he didn't want to deal with Harris again. But after a few weeks of rehearsals, Hayes went to Abbott and said things were not going well and pleaded with him to take over the direction. Abbott agreed on the condition that Harris not attend any rehearsals and have no contact with him. This was asking a lot from the egotistical Harris but he agreed because *Coquette*, as it currently was, was sure to fail. Abbott was able to save the production although it must be admitted that Hayes' performance is what allowed the drama to run eleven months on Broadway. Hayes was about to take *Coquette* on tour when she found out she was pregnant and quit the production.

Harris was furious and sued Hayes for breach of contract, demanding she pay him a small fortune in damages. The quarrel went to court and *Coquette* was suddenly on the front pages. It remained there all during the trial which finally decided in Hayes' favor, the court stating that having a baby was an "Act of God" which overrides a contract.

With all the free publicity, *Coquette* confirmed Hayes' star status and gave Harris another hit. Yet the play itself, while not likely to succeed with modern audiences, was a solidly-written tearjerker. (Abbott later described it as "the weeping wonder of the world—I don't think I ever saw so many people sob in a theatre."[9]) Again, Hayes' poignant, fiery performance can take much of the credit. Yet one cannot but admire some of the writing.

> **Norma**   Why don't you leave me alone? I wish I'd run away with Michael, that's what I wish.
>
> **Wentworth**   Our chance to save your father is based on the plea that he was defending your good name. You've got to say that you resented Michael's attentions; that your father protected you from insult, that you're proud of him.
>
> **Norma**   No, I won't! I hate him! I wish I'd never seen him! . . . He killed the one thing in the world that I loved! He did that to me, and I don't care what happens to him now. Let them put him in prison, I don't care!
>
> **Wentworth**   You don't realize what you're saying, dear.
>
> **Norma**   I could see him in prison for the rest of his life and not care! I can see him hung—I don't care what they do—I don't want to help—![10]

It may not be Henrik Ibsen but *Coquette* has the qualities of the well-made play and, more importantly, it worked on stage. At least in the 1920s. Brackett in *The New Yorker* was "rendered speechless with admiration . . . absolutely speechless" with the play and the *Times* review stated, "all those associated in the writing, directing and acting in *Coquette* have woven it into a hauntingly beautiful drama, brimming with loveliness and pathos."

Abbott doesn't even mention his next eight Broadway projects in his autobiography. Some are cases in which he doctored a play enough to be listed as co-author. Others were directing assignments. The popular, but controversial, evangelist Aimee Semple MacPherson had been in news since 1918 and in 1926 made headlines again when she was supposedly kidnapped. It was most likely a publicity stunt, quite in character for the crafty McPherson. So John Meehan and Robert Riskin's play **Bless You, Sister** (1927), about a thinly-disguised McPherson-like evangelist, sounded like a possible hit. The daughter of a failed preacher, Mary MacDonald (Alice Brady) takes up evangelizing and her dramatic way of preaching and her ability to stir up the worshippers soon make her a success. The shrewd

Bible salesman Timothy Bradley (Charles Bickford) becomes her manager and through his promotion Mary becomes famous. Her hometown sweetheart Freddie Gribble (Robert Ames) does not see through the showmanship and thinks Mary is some kind of miracle woman. When Bradley tries to bed her, Mary gives up the preaching business and settles down with Freddie. Co-author Riskin produced the play with his brother; his co-author Meehan was slated to direct it but early on Abbott was called in and did enough doctoring that he received co-directing credit. The press applauded Alice Brady's performance but little else. *Time* pointed out that "*Bless You, Sister* will offend many people. It scoffs sharply at religion, contending bitterly that in some phases the word of God is simply salesman's talk." But, at the same time, admitted, "*Bless You, Sister* has many faults, but dullness is not one of them." The drama folded in three weeks; it was Abbott's most significant failure yet.

When he directed Ward Morehouse's newspaper play **Gentlemen of the Press** (1928), Abbott found himself in a losing position. The play opened on Broadway eight days after *The Front Page* premiered, an instant classic in the genre, and *Gentlemen of the Press* paled in comparison. The gentlemanly news reporter Wick Snell (John Cromwell) is tired of the uncouth company he must keep in the world of journalism so he quits and becomes the head of publicity for a swank real estate company. He soon finds that people in business are just as vulgar and, after he has a fight with his boss, Wick returns to newspaper reporting. The comedy-drama received some favorable notices but it was upstaged by *The Front Page*. *Time* made the point that, "The comparison, though, was interesting for it proved that truth, stranger than fiction, is not as exciting when placed upon the stage. *Gentlemen of the Press* lacks the hectic, unreal, melodramatic turbulence of the Hecht-MacArthur piece and insomuch it is a more true and a less compelling drama." Writing in the *Times*, Atkinson acknowledged, "*Gentlemen of the Press* has been directed by George Abbott who has been sweeping the theatrical heavens like a comet since collaborated on *Broadway*. With all this talent behind it, how can the new play be indifferent entertainment? Well, what jinx has pursued every newspaper play—excepting one?" With the odds quite against it, the play could only manage to run sixteen weeks.

The boxing drama **Ringside** (1928) by Edward E. Paramore, Jr., and Hyatt Daab was doctored and directed by Abbott but there were several prizefight plays during the 1928–1929 season and this one was lost in the shuffle. *Time* thought, "The writing of *racket* plays has become a racket in itself. This play, the latest in the Fight Game series, improves on many of its predecessors by furnishing a complete set of characters of its own instead of 'ad-libbing' from the newspapers." The mobster John Zelli (Robert Glecker) bets a lot of money against the lightweight prizefighter Bobby Murray (Richard Taber) then uses booze and the sexy Paula Vornoff (Suzanne Caubaye) to convince Bobby to throw the fight. Bobby's father-trainer (John Meehan) gets word of the plot and kills Zelli. Reviewers praised Glecker, the

Tribune noting that he played "the part for every drop of poison it contains," but little else about the drama was recommended. The Gene Buck production closed after thirty-seven performances.

More successful was the drama ***Jarnegan*** (1928) by Charles Beahan and Garrett Fort, an unsentimental, dark look at Hollywood that was unique in its day. The alcoholic movie director Jack Jarnegan (Richard Bennett) gives up drink and loose woman when he falls in love with the sweet, innocent starlet Daisy Carol (Joan Bennett). But Daisy is seduced by the callous filmmaker Edward Bernard (Robert Cain) and she dies when she tries to have an abortion. Jarnegan goes on a drinking binge then returns to work, more bitter than ever. Based on Jim Tully's novel, the script needed work and the star Richard Bennett's direction was wanting; Abbott did uncredited work on the play and the production. The result was less than stellar. Brackett in *The New Yorker* thought the play "noisy enough surely, but most of the noise has a hollow sound." Some of the other notices found *Jarnegan* entertaining but the public wasn't interested enough to allow the production to run more than seventeen weeks.

Abbott worked on less ponderous material when he directed Bella and Samuel Spewack's warm Jewish comedy-drama ***Poppa*** (1928). The Jewish Pincus "Poppa" Schwitzky (Sam Jaffe) has been neglecting his insurance business ever since he started playing in politics in the East Side of New York. He gets elected as alderman and, when he doesn't play ball with the corrupt Jake Harris (William E. Morris), Poppa is brought up on charges of bribery by Harris. It takes Poppa's clever son Herbert (Harold Waldridge) to stage a fake jailbreak and trick Harris into confessing while the dictaphone machine is running and saves Poppa. Atkinson in the *Times* was among the critics who found the mixture of comedy and melodrama in Poppa unsettling. "For bombastic clowning, *Poppa* is too earnest. For domestic drama, it is too glib." But audiences found the play charming so it ran for three months.

Abbott returned to acting in ***Those We Love*** (1930), a play which he co-wrote with S. K. Lauren. Abbott was not supposed to play the major male role but, for reasons that are lost to time, a week before opening he found himself as co-author, director, and leading man for *Those We Love*. Directing himself in a play did not seem to concern Abbott much. He probably felt it was just one actor less that he had to deal with. Frederick Williston (Abbott) is a writer and needs quiet; his wife May (Armina Marshall) is a composer and needs to bang on a piano all day. The couple are often separated, working in different places, which leads May to suspect that Frederick is seeing another woman. He is innocent but her hounding him does push him into the arms of Valerie Parker (Helen Flint). Their teenage son, the bewildered but highly practical Rickie (Edwin Phillips), needs and loves both parents and keeps them from divorcing. Some critics welcomed Abbott back to acting but held more praise for other cast members, in particular Marshall, young Phillips, Josephine Hull, Charles Waldron, and Percy Kilbride. The press was not impressed with the sentimental play. In the *Times*, Atkinson wrote, "Although the authors have chosen a genuine subject, and striven to treat it in a genuine manner, the artful dodging of the theatre does permeate their play." Similarly, *Time* thought, "George Abbot presents an effortless, natural portrait of the casual Westchester man-of-letters. Edwin Phillips, as the son, is that great dramatic rarity—an accomplished, likable adolescent." Audiences liked *Those We Love* enough for the Philip Dunning production to run ten weeks.

The prolific playwright and screenwriter Norman Krasna made his Broadway debut with the satiric comedy **Louder, Please** (1931). Hollywood publicist Herbert White (Lee Tracy) wants to give fading movie star Polly Madison (Louise Brooks) a boost so he pretends she is lost at sea and enlists the Coast Guard and the navy to find her. The news hits the front pages but Detective Bailey (Robert Glecker) is suspicious of White and is about to expose the hoax when he is asked to lead the rescue and gets caught up in his own heroics. Krasna was commended by the press for his farcical, breezy comedy and Abbott, back on familiar territory with a rapid-paced comedy, was duly complimented for his direction. Robert Benchley in *The New Yorker* wrote, "George Abbott has taken what was possibly a moderately amusing play by Norman Krasna and turned it into a whirlwind, although there must be some of the highly comical conceits that were the author's originally." *Louder, Please* ran a respectable sixty-eight performances.

A huge Billy Rose production that was more intriguing than satisfying was **The Great Magoo** (1932) by Ben Hecht and Gene Fowler. The womanizer Nicky (Paul Kelly) is a barker with a sleazy carnival show and Julie Raquel (Claire Carlton) is a Salome dancer on the boardwalk. Their romance is a bumpy one, with Nicky getting caught with too many women and Julia heading to Broadway only to wind up on skid row. He rescues her there and the romance continues. The unflattering view of life, peopled with misfits and oddballs, did not appeal to the critics and the interesting play quickly closed after only eleven performances. Abbott's direction of the multi-scene, large-cast production was widely noted by the press. Atkinson in the *Times* wrote, "Having become the past master of the backstage whirligig, George Abbott has turned this one into the usual skillful lithograph. He can still perform as a showman although [this] script is not a play." Harsher words came from *Time*: "[A] vulgar, undistinguished, gratuitously profane presentation." *The Great Magoo* is only remembered today for the Harold Arlen–E. Y. Harburg song "It's Only a Paper Moon" which the songwriters wrote for a scene in the play.

Abbott fared better when he staged another Norman Krasna play three years later, the backstage melodrama **Small Miracle** (1934). In the downstairs lounge of a Broadway theatre, patrons and staff intermingle in a series of crises involving a pregnant usherette (Elspeth Eric), her unruly boyfriend (Owen Martin), a married lady (Ilka Chase) meeting her lover (Edward Crandall), the head usher (Myron McCormick), an escaped convict (Joseph Spurin-Celleia), and the detective (Joseph King) who is after him. The many threads of the plot climax when the convict guns down the guy who squealed on him and, in turn, the convict is shot and killed. Like *The Great Magoo*, the play was more a series of fragmented episodes than a well-structured piece. But the collection of colorful characters and Abbott's masterful staging on Boris Aronson's elaborate setting appealed to both the press and the public. Atkinson, by this time one of Abbott's most vocal supporters, wrote in the *Times*, "Mr. Abbott's methodical sense of theatre as a procession of details in the vernacular gives *Small Miracle* vivid illusion. You believe every line of it." The play managed a lucrative run of six months. Although he was not credited as such, Abbott served as co-producer on *Small Miracle*. Courtney Burr enjoyed the prestige and social gatherings of being a Broadway producer but was uninterested in the artistic side of the job. Abbott not only directed *Small Miracle* but made all artistic decisions, from casting to scenery. Soon Abbott would be involved officially with Broadway producing.

Burr also produced Abbott's next production, the melodrama **Ladies' Money** (1934), in which Abbott was the sole author. Actually it was another rewrite job but was so different from the original that the play carried the oddball credit "by George Abbott, previously written by Lawrence Hazard and Richard Flournoy." The residents of a Manhattan boarding house include the unemployed vaudevillians Fruity (Hal K. Dawson) and Eddie (Eric Linden), the down-on-his-luck former clerk Jim Harris (Robert R. Sloan), and the crook Nelson Blummer (Jerome Cowan) who has gotten the landlady's daughter Ruth (Joyce Arling) pregnant. The police close in on Blummer but before they can get him Jim stabs Blummer to death because he believes the man is having an affair with his wife. The action took place on two floors of an old Brownstone on 46th Street and Abbott skillfully staged the drama moving the actors up and down the staircase and in and out of various rooms. The press was not impressed with *Ladies' Money*, including the *Times* which noted, "Abbott continues making skin-deep plays out of commonplace materials." *Ladies' Money* folded after a month.

Abbott's next project, Joseph Schrank and Philip Dunning's comedy **Page Miss Glory** (1934), ran only two months. When a health salts company offers a prize of $2,500 for a photo of the most beautiful and healthy-looking girl in America, the unemployed Dan Wiley (Charles D. Brown) and ex-photographer Ed Olsen (James Stewart) put together a photo using the legs, arms, and other body parts from movie magazine pictures. Their composite entry, whom they call Miss Page Glory, wins the contest but trouble comes when there are huge offers by other advertising companies to hire the girl. They find a poor substitute in the sexy chambermaid Loretta (Dorothy Hall) but she turns out to be less wholesome than what the companies want. Various contrived complications are added to the mix until a happy ending is achieved. The comedy was one of many Broadway failures for young actor Stewart who had better luck when Hollywood beaconed in 1935. *Page Miss Glory* met with lackluster approval by the press, such as "a reasonably funny knockabout screed" and "an animated cartoon of low comedy fooling." Audiences came for eight weeks but the expensive production, which required a large cast of characters in varied locales, could not show a profit.

Despite an inordinate number of failures of late, Abbott by this time had secured himself a new component to his career. "Back in those days . . . I was getting one credit which I didn't deserve," he wrote in his autobiography.

> I was now considered the 'play doctor' *par excellence*. I was a genius; I could fix anything. Unfortunately, I began to believe my own publicity and I tackled almost any assignment that was offered me. Thus, for awhile, I was connected with a great many indifferent plays that should have been allowed to die peacefully on the road. I have no doubt that I made them better, but it is one thing to take a script, rewrite it and recast it from the beginning, and it is quite another to go out on the road with a cast already selected by someone else, and in a limited time given you refashion it into a hit.[11]

In the next chapter we will look at some of these plays that ought not have ever opened on Broadway. The tricky thing is, Abbott produced them.

3 IF YOU REALLY WANT IT DONE BETTER, PRODUCE IT YOURSELF

(1932–1940)

Lilly Turner • Heat Lightning • The Drums Begin • John Brown • Kill that Story • Sweet River • Angel Island • Brown Sugar • The Primrose Path • Ring Two • The Unconquered • Goodbye in the Night

By the early 1930s, Abbott had worked with a variety of producers; some efficient (John Golden), some flamboyant (David Belasco), some ineffective (Courtney Burr), and some irritating (Jed Harris). Yet regardless of who was presenting the production, Abbott often felt artistic decisions were made that he did not agree with. Broadway producers stood to make much more money than the creative talents and even if a show flopped, the producer lost face but not much money. It was the backers (then often called "angels") who took on the financial loss. All the same, it is unlikely that Abbott turned to producing for the money. He was a very established and in-demand director and did not have an extravagant lifestyle. He saw how other suddenly successful men started living far beyond their means, unaware of the fickle nature of the business. He was more interested in the work and how to best control his interests. Many producers on Broadway were attracted to the power the job brought but it is more likely that Abbott was drawn to this sense of control. As a director, he had sought to bring a cohesive artistic look and feel to each production. But this was hard to do if someone else called the shots on the casting, the scenery, the publicity, and so on.

Abbott started his official producing career with **Lilly Turner** (1932), a play he co-wrote, co-produced and co-directed with Philip Dunning. The comely Lil Turner (Dorothy Hall), the main attraction of the traveling Dr. McGill's Health

Exhibit, is married to the troupe's barker Dave (James Bell) but she gets involved with two men: the insane German strong man Frederick (Robert Barrat) and the taxi driver Bob Cross (John Litel) who replaces Frederick when he is carted off to the asylum. When Frederick escapes, he comes looking for Lilly and beats up both Bob and Dave. Frederick is again sent to the asylum and Lilly returns to Dave. The press compared the drama unfavorably to Abbott and Dunning's *Broadway* six years earlier. Brooks Atkinson, writing in the *New York Times*, noted, "Since it is staged in the sleazy halls and hotel bedrooms of a traveling medicine show, it discloses some of the tinsel romance that made *Broadway* famous. But the comparison can hardly go further than that." *Time Magazine* simply dismissed the drama with, "Creaking and groaning, the play tells [a] barely credible story." In the supporting role of a hick truck driver, Percy Kilbride stole all his scenes and was the only aspect of *Lilly Turner* unanimously lauded in the reviews. With such weak notices and little advance, Abbott and Dunning were forced to close the play after three weeks.

Their next venture fared only slightly better. Abbott and Dunning again shared producing and directing credit with the drama **Heat Lightning** (1933) which Abbott co-wrote with Leon Abrams. Sisters Olga (Jean Dixon) and Myra (Emily Lowry) run a filling station-lunch room in the Arizona desert and most of their patrons are drifters, hitchhikers, and divorcées traveling to and from Reno. Two gunmen, George (Robert Glecker) and Jeff (Robert Sloane), are on the run after robbing a bank in Salt Lake City and come to the diner because Olga was once George's sweetheart. He tries to make love to her while Jeff tries to break into the sisters' safe, but Olga sees through both of them and shoots George dead. *Heat Lightning* had possibilities but co-producer, co-director Abbott later thought that he miscalculated when he cast the wry comic actress Jean Dixon as Olga. Yet Wolcott Gibbs in *The New Yorker* found the play, "Fairly thin and threadbare stuff, but it is redeemed by competent and literate dialogue ... and by the fine and very skillful performances of Jean Dixon and Robert Glecker." Most of the other reviews focused on Glecker's powerful performance. The production struggled to run over five weeks. (A much more successful drama with criminals taking refuge in a filling station-diner in the Arizona desert was Robert Sherwood's *The Petrified Forest* two years later.)

Abbott's losing streak continued with Howard Irving Young's drama **The Drums Begin** (1933). After World War One, the French film director Andre Roussel (Walter Abel) makes a film called *No More War* and films it in both German and French so that it can be shown in both countries. The star of the movie is the bilingual Valerie Latour (Judith Anderson) whom Andre is in love with until he learns that she was a German spy during the Great War. He denounces her then she denounces all men who begin wars in the name of patriotism. The struggling producers were fortunate in securing the renowned actress Judith Anderson for their production, and she got glowing reviews; but the play itself was roundly panned and closed after eleven performances. Yet Burns Mantle noted in his chronicle of the 1933–1935 season that *The Drums Begin* was "an elaborate mixture of motion picture technique and imaginative drama... Rather a pity [the play] was weakened by its elaborations and muddled plot. A good idea."[1] It was during rehearsals of *The Drums Begin* that Abbott came upon his method for handling talented but temperamental stars. After Anderson was late for rehearsals a few days running, Abbott knew he had to do something. He had seen how some producers or directors scolded stars before the rest of the cast, thereby causing tension in rehearsals. On the other hand, he could not let Anderson continue her undisciplined ways. Soon others in the cast would pick up on her behavior and the rehearsals would be out of control. Anderson had a much younger understudy in *The Drums Begin*. If the star was not present for the start of the rehearsal, Abbott began with the understudy taking her place. When Anderson finally arrived and saw her role played by a younger, prettier, but far less talented actress, she became possessive and even felt threatened. She was not late again.

Instead of pulling back and trying to determine why all of his producing projects had failed, Abbott made a major miscalculation and acted as producer, director, and star of his next production: Ronald Gow's historical drama **John Brown** (1934). Under the title *The Gallows Glorious*, the biographical piece had played in London with some success. Abolitionist John Brown (Abbott) organizes a raid on the government arsenal at Harper's Ferry and arms the slaves to help him wipe out slavery in the South. The rebellion is put down by Col. Robert E. Lee (William Corbett) and Brown is executed. Abbott's usual partner Philip Dunning did not think producing *John Brown* was a good idea and withdrew from the project. Abbott stubbornly proceeded with a large cast and an elaborate, multi-set production. He tried in vain to get Lionel Barrymore and then Walter Huston to play the fiery Brown; so, rather than abandon the production, Abbott decided to play Brown himself. As he admitted years later, he was too young and did not have the powerful vocal demands the role required. The press agreed. The *Times* thought, "In spite of his monumental beard and careless clothing, Mr. Abbott's voice is weak, his accent is urbane, and he lacks the power of the prophet." Aware early on that the whole project was doomed, Abbott posted the closing notice on opening night and *John Brown* chalked up only two performances, one of the biggest flops of his career. The large-scale failure sent Abbott into depression followed by an honest re-evaluation of his producing career. He felt confident about his directing but admitted his choice of projects was often in error. It was a failing that would haunt him throughout his career. Among all of the many Abbott hits over the decades were always a number of embarrassing misfires. Some of this can be blamed on Abbott's workaholic temperament. Working on any production was better than not working at all. This drive to keep moving ahead often clouded his vision. It was Abbott's Achilles' heel.

Working with a Dunning script and re-teaming with his partner in co-producing the newspaper comedy-melodrama **Kill that Story** (1934), Abbott finally had a modest success. The script was by Harry Madden and Dunning and was the kind of hard-hitting social drama that Abbott was expert in staging. At a convention of newspaper publishers, the double-dealing Spike Taylor (Matt Briggs) is trying to buy out the crusading *Herald* in order to silence the newspaper's stories about his corrupt practices. Newsman Duke Devlin (James Bell) manages to stop Taylor by getting him to confess to an affair that ruined Duke's marriage to Margaret (Emily Lowry). Taylor is toppled and Duke and Margaret are reunited. Abbott's taut direction was again applauded by the press but there were few compliments for the writing. Gibbs in *The New Yorker* thought, "There ought to be very funny material in a convention of newspaper advertising men but somehow George Abbott and Philip Dunning ... have let everybody down pretty badly." All the same, *Kill that Story* enjoyed a four-month run.

Over the next six years, Abbott produced seven Broadway productions, all but one of them box office failures. The most expensive flop was a dramatization of Harriet Beecher Stowe's inflammatory novel *Uncle Tom's Cabin* which Abbott adapted and retitled **Sweet River** (1936). Stage versions of Stowe's book had predominated the American stage in the nineteenth century; in fact, *Uncle Tom's Cabin* was the most frequently produced play across the nation for over fifty years. But the story seemed cliché-ridden to Depression-era audiences and Abbott was faced with finding ways to make the story and characters "modern" in temperament. His adaptation avoided some of the familiar melodramatic scenes, such as the death of Little Eva (Betty Philson) surrounded by singing slaves; but he retained Eliza (Margaret Mullen) and her famous escape and flight across the icy Ohio River. Donald Oenslager's many sets were elaborate but burdensome so a special forty-five-foot-wide turntable was constructed to keep the production flowing. Unfortunately it took the large turntable a full minute to make a complete revolve so each scene change was too long to maintain the pace Abbott wanted. Looking back decades later, Abbott noted, "The whole production was built on the premise of speed [but] it turned out to be a slow freight. There were ghastly waits, for one minute is an intolerable time to spend in the dark waiting for the next scene."[2] Nevertheless, it was a beautiful production and the gospel singing, under the direction of Juanita Hall, was glorious. The critics were impressed by the splendid scenery, lighting, music, and most of the performances but they could not recommend the slow-moving, dated melodrama. Atkinson in the *Times* was gentle in his criticism, ending his review with, "All this human, scenic and vocal material Mr. Abbott keeps moving softly across the stage with an admirable sense of theatre reverie. For he has the courage of his sentiment, as well as the labor for his pains." Faced with poor reviews and such an expensive production, Abbott was forced to close *Sweet River* after only five performances. More modern clichés were to be found in Abbott's production of the murder mystery **Angel Island** (1937) by Mrs. Bernie Angus. Leo (Carroll Ashburn) and Carma Grainger (Lea Penman) buy the remote Angel Island off the coast of the Carolinas because they have heard buried treasure is hidden there. Soon a handful of various characters, unemployed because of the Depression, arrive on the island for the weekend and look for the treasure. Two of the visitors are murdered by an ice pick and the rest cannot escape because the motor boat that brought them there is disabled and the phone lines are cut. The survivors set a trap for the murderer and he is shot, revealing the culprit to be Leo. Although the press deemed the thriller well acted and solidly directed by Abbott, the script was sometimes downright silly. *Time* thought, "A thriller with so pat a formula is usually expected to move posthaste off the Broadway boards, but with the guidance of respected Play-Picker George Francis Abbott, this one, blackouts, screams, rowdy humor and all, seems likely to remain for a time." Looking back, *Time* also noticed, "Play Wizard Abbott has had uncommon success in the last few years pulling rabbits out of shabby theatrical hats and then turning them into ermine." But ermine or not, *Angel Island* closed inside of three weeks.

When Abbott produced another drama by Mrs. Angus a month later, it was an even bigger failure. **Brown Sugar** (1937) was about the African American truck driver Sam Jackson (Juan Hernandez) who is attracted to the light-skinned beauty Rosalinda (Christola Williams). When the police want Rosalinda for doping a white man's drink at a nightclub and killing him, Sam offers to hide her in his apartment, much to the displeasure of his wife Louella (Beulah E. Edmonds). Eventually the police close in, Sam takes a freighter to South America, Rosalinda is caught, and Louella bids a satisfied farewell to both. *Brown Sugar* boasted some superior African American actors, including Hernandez, Canada Lee, Richard Huey, Ruby Elzy, and Georgette Harvey, several who would go on to much better vehicles. But the performer noticed most by the critics was, according to Atkinson in the *Times*, "a high-stepping little dusky creature with a piping voice who describes herself as Butterfly McQueen." McQueen and the rest of the cast found themselves "at liberty" after four performances.

A rare profitable Abbott production in the 1930s was the off-color comedy **The Primrose Path** (1939) by Robert Buckner and Walter Hart. Although it received some of the harshest reviews of the season, the play found an audience. Three generations of Wallace women (Florida Friebus, Helen Westley, Betty Garde, and Betty Field) live in a shack outside of Buffalo, New York, and make ends meet with a little prostitution and robbery. One of the women (Field) nearly weds a Harvard grad (Philip Wood) and goes straight but he kills himself so things return back to normal. In the off-putting last scene, it looks like the twelve-year-old Eva Wallace (Marilyn Erskine) is going to happily follow in her family's immoral footsteps. Buckner and Hart based *The Primrose Path* on Victoria Lincoln's novel *February Hill*, turning the British tale of slum living into a Yankee variation reminiscent of *Tobacco Road*. The play made no effort to disguise the crude nature of the story and characters. In the first scene, little Eva tells her cat, "Lay still, you son-of-a-bitch!"[3]. Robert Benchley took a tongue-in-cheek approach to the play in *The New Yorker*. "There were moments on the opening night when I had a feeling that perhaps here was a rather grim and decidedly bitter tragedy and that the audience might be offending the authors ... by laughing so hard at it all. I knew that they couldn't offend George Abbott by laughing, but it did seem that there were some phases of this study in American degeneracy that an author might like to have taken seriously. With less of the 'George Abbott touch,' it could have been a depressing but rather fine excursion into the depths." The other critics were more direct and generally dismissed *The Primrose Path* as crude and even obscene. *Time* thought "*The Primrose Path* at its rosiest is all downhill and no brakes." Also, noting the discrepancy in style, the magazine observed, "For, though humor and pathos make the best of friends, realism and farce are immemorial foes." The play was scandalous enough to run twenty-one weeks for the curious. Decades later, Abbott wrote that he was not embarrassed by *The Primrose Path* and its success. He was drawn to the shocking script and thought it was beautifully acted. This is curious because Abbott usually showed good taste in his selection of plays, preferring the conservative point of view. Often he would insist that a line, a dance, or piece of business be cut if he found it in objectionable taste. *The Primrose Path* was certainly an exception to the rule.

Three more Abbott play productions that failed must be considered in this chapter before we move on to more successful ventures. **Ring Two** (1939), a comedy by Gladys Hurlbut, was called by the *Times* "the working draft of a comedy still to be written." After divorcing her husband Michael (Paul McGrath) and giving up her stage career, Mary Carr (June Walker) buys a Connecticut farmhouse and hopes to escape from the world. Instead she is bombarded by guests, from her former leading man Durward Nesbitt (Tom Powers) and his new mistress Rosa Romero (Betty Field) to her outspoken agent Maggie Brown (Edith Van Cleve) and Mary's opinionated daughter Peggy (Gene Tierney). When Michael gets stuck in a snowstorm and has to join the throng, Mary is forced to re-evaluate her feelings for her ex and, after three acts, realizes she still loves him. Despite a superior cast giving fine performances, *Ring Two* was too impotent to last more than five performances.

Distinctive Russian-born author Ayn Rand adapted her first novel, *We the Living*, for the stage in 1936. As in the novel, the sullen Russian aristocrat Leo Argounova (John Emery), whose father was killed by the Bolsheviks, and his life-affirming wife Kira (Helen Craig) struggle to survive in the Soviet Union in 1924. Kira arranges for the ailing Leo to have a rest in the Crimea by sleeping with the Soviet agent Andrei Taganov (Dean Jagger). When Leo finds out, he leaves Kira and the guilt-ridden Andrei kills himself. Kira is determined to survive and makes plans to escape from the Soviet nation, thereby finding her individual freedom. Soon after Rand's novel was published, she approached the Broadway producer Jerome Mayer about doing a stage version. He was interested but thought it needed a star and the strong anti-Communist tone of the play frightened off any name actresses he approached. Mayer dropped his option and Rand circulated *We the*

Living among friends. The Russian actress Eugenie Leontovich read the manuscript and wanted to play Kira even though she was far older than the character. Leontovich sent the play to Abbott who decided to produce and direct the drama even though it was often more philosophic than dramatic. Rand had seen many changes made to her play *Night of January 16th* (1934) and this time insisted on total control. Abbott tactfully reasoned with Rand and she agreed to have the celebrated playwright S. N. Behrman serve as script doctor. During rehearsals it was clear that Leontovich was miscast as Kira but Abbott persevered and the play, now retitled **The Unconquered**, opened in Baltimore to terrible reviews and audience dissatisfaction. Abbott postponed the Broadway opening, fired Leontovich, and replaced her with Helen Craig, a twenty-eight-year-old actress from Orson Welles' Mercury Theatre. *The Unconquered* opened in February of 1940 to scathing reviews: "slow-moving, uninspired soup," "a confusing mix of sentimental melodrama and political discussion," and "as interminable as the five-year plan." The play was also attacked by the Communist Party USA ("deadly dull ... Rand is a fourth-rate hack"[4]) and right wing politicos who thought it understated the dangers of communism. The only aspect of the drama that was generally favored by the press was Boris Aronson's bold and expressive scenery. Abbott was forced to close the play after only six performances. (*The Unconquered* was not published until 2014 and the play is now studied and re-evaluated by Rand scholars.)

Abbott was again producer and director for Jerome Mayer's lurid melodrama **Goodbye in the Night** (1940). The homicidal mental patient Ollie (James Bell) escapes from an asylum and returns to his family farm where he murders his brother-in-law Joe (Owen Martin) whom he blames for all his problems. While he is trying to dispose of Joe's body, tourists Cece Sawyer (Mary Mason) and her fiancé Kurt (Paul Ballantyne) come looking for lodging and Ollie forces them to bury the body. Ollie then tries to blame the murder on Cece and Kurt but the guards from the asylum arrive just in time. The most severe criticism was aimed at the script. The *Times* thought "the play is mystifying, not because there is anything very puzzling in the story, but because Mr. Mayer remains vague about ordinary information. This makes the characters seem a little more stupid than most members of the human race." *Goodbye in the Night* lasted only a week.

As we will see in later chapters, Abbott had plenty of play and musical hits in the 1930s. But those shows that failed could not be ignored. How did Abbott handle so many defeats among his track record? "I don't remember being too depressed," he wrote in his memoir.

> I felt that it was obvious that life was made up of both success and failure, of the smooth and the rough, and I didn't think I had lost my ability ... I believed that the mistakes I had made were in choice of subject matter and perhaps in writing, but not in direction. It seemed to me that my direction of these failures was just

as conscientious and just as good as it had been with the big successes. I have always been sure of myself as a director—perhaps even conceited. I have felt that I directed my shows better than anyone else could have done; what's more, and this is a very silly thing to admit, I have usually felt, when seeing other people's direction, I could improve on it.[5]

4 HOW DID I GET TYPECAST IN FARCE?

(1932–1939)

Twentieth Century • Three Men on a Horse • Boy Meets Girl • Brother Rat • Room Service • All that Glitters • What a Life! • See My Lawyer

Ever since Eugene O'Neill had come on the scene in a big way with *Beyond the Horizon* in 1920, Abbott the playwright wanted more than ever to write great (meaning serious) plays. He felt he came close with *Broadway* and *Coquette* in the 1920s. But by the 1930s he was most in demand as a director and he hoped an *Anna Christie* or a *Desire Under the Elms* would fall into his lap. Instead he was sought out for musicals, action melodramas and, that most difficult of all genres, farce. Being type-cast for certain genres was a life-long problem for Abbott. Looking back to the 1930s in his autobiography, Abbott wrote:

> There is a tendency on the part of newspapers and the public to type-cast people, to put a label on them ... There had been plenty of comedy in the things that I had written and directed up to that time, but my successes had been mostly of a serious or melodramatic nature. Without knowing it, I was now about to be typed in another direction: I was to become a producer of farces. Following that, although I little suspected it at the time, I was to be a producer of teen-age plays—the most loathsome label of all. Still later, people were to say to me, 'You never do anything but musical comedy, do you?' So art is long and fame is fleeting.[1]

Abbott was no stranger to farce. *The Fall Guy* (1925), his playwriting debut on Broadway, was a farce. So were three of his early directing assignments: *Love 'Em and Leave 'Em* (1926), *Poppa* (1928), and *Louder, Please* (1931). In each case the critics applauded Abbott's swift direction. But moving a play along quickly was sometimes just a way of covering over a weak script and keeping the audience from noticing the lack of logic in the plot. When he started directing (and sometimes also writing) better farces in the 1930s, Abbott had to rethink his approach to the genre. He had no training in staging farce and went by what was being done. Broadway veteran George M. Cohan was probably the best director to watch. Whether it was a musical or a comedy, he directed his actors to talk and move as rapidly as he himself did on stage. Even the rhythm of some of his songs (particularly the verses) were written to be talk-sung in double time. Was that all there was to farce? Speed?

The first farce of real quality that Abbott got to stage was **Twentieth Century** (1932). He realized that tempo on the stage was a deceptive thing. Two actors talking quickly does indeed move the show along. But if there is a moment's pause between their speeches, the scene *feels* slow. Abbott insisted that it was not a matter of how fast the lines were delivered but the linking of the lines that gave the illusion of a swift pace. He directed his actors to begin each line the second the cue line was concluding. Even better, begin it on the last syllable of the cue line (unless it is a punch line). An actor need not speak quickly but must be quick on the pick-up. This non-stop rhythm in the dialogue not only helped the pace but it also created verbal energy. Did Abbott invent this technique? Not by a long shot. It was used in vaudeville a lot, particularly by the "Dutch" comic duos. And some stand-up comics even used it when doing a solo act. Jack Benny and Will Rogers, for example, spoke slowly and carefully. The audience would laugh at a line and they would not continue to talk until the level of laughter started to subside. Actors are still taught this, cautioned not to step on a laugh or wait too long for a laugh to fade away. The innovation Abbott brought to his writing and direction of farce was to calculate ways to maintain a farce rhythm. As we shall see, this rhythm is not one consistent pace. Farce is not set to a single metronome speed. It is the way the director (as sometimes provided by the playwright's script) varies this tempo that makes for effective farce rhythm. Of course, physical action is involved in a major way. Few farces are all dialogue. Abbott's insistence on precise moves where and when he instructed became legendary. Over the years actors would talk (complain? marvel at?) about how detailed his blocking direction was. It was true for all his plays and musicals but most essential for farce. I do not think it is going too far to say that Abbott helped define American stage farce. Like all the other genres, American farce is made up of European models. We get the pratfalls and slapstick from Italy, the room with many slamming doors from France, the eccentric English aristocrats and fops hiding behind screens, the rough and tumble braggarts from Ireland, and so on. But American farce became more distinct in the 1920s and 1930s. On Broadway the characters are often gamblers, non-threatening crooks, con men, innocent dupes, egomaniacs, youthful misadventurers, tough dames, and, yes, theatre people. The plots often revolve around schemes to make money illegally or at least easily, to get out of paying money owed, to find fame on a massive enough scale to feed one's ego, or to get the girl against the most ridiculous odds. All of these will be found in the eight Abbott farces discussed in this chapter. Whether he co-wrote them or not, Abbott helped shape these eight scripts and directed them using "the Abbott touch." At this point we are still learning what that touch involved, but farce is an effective way to explore it.

During the Depression, farce was in demand and many such plays were offered on Broadway in the 1930s. Only a handful were successful and most of them were directed by Abbott. *Twentieth Century* was a surprise hit and the kind of show that put Abbott on the top of the go-to list for directors of farces. The comedy can claim four authors as it moved from producer to producer. Charles Bruce Millholland, an agent for the producer Morris Gest, wrote a comedy about his eccentric boss which he titled *The Napoleon of Broadway*. As eccentric producers go, Gest was small potatoes so Millholland changed the leading character to a spoof of the more colorful showman David Belasco. It soon became clear to Millholland that he was a better agent than a playwright so he showed the script to Ben Hecht and Charles MacArthur, the team behind the runaway success *The Front Page* (1928). Many in the theatre community, including Abbott, considered the former journalists Hecht and MacArthur the "Katzenjammer Kids of Broadway," a reference to two popular comic strip mischief-makers. They loved pulling practical jokes, wasting time, partying, and then coming up with funny stuff. Jed Harris had produced *The Front Page* and, like Abbott and everyone else who had ever worked with Harris, Hecht and MacArthur grew to despise the man. The team took Millholland's script, renamed it *Twentieth Century*, and based the obnoxious producer character on Harris. It was sweet revenge but with one problem: they were stuck in the third act. Try as they might, they couldn't solve that curse that afflicts so many playwrights: third act mental block. So Hecht and MacArthur went to Abbott and told him if he could lick the third act problem, he could direct it. Abbott agreed on the condition that he and his writing-producing partner Philip Dunning produce the show. Hecht and MacArthur, willing to work with anyone besides Harris, said sure and went off to party and play more practical jokes believing that *Twentieth Century* was a lost cause and nothing would come of it. Since Abbott was to go immediately into rehearsal for another play, he turned the rewriting over to Dunning who went to his home in Westport and, after not too long, came up with a dynamite third act.

Just as *The Front Page* had lampooned the newspaper racket, *Twentieth Century* was a satire on the hollow ethics of show business. Down-on-his-heels Broadway producer Oscar Jaffe (Moffat Johnston) has just lost $75,000 on a production in Chicago and, in order to escape his many creditors, he and his cohorts have to stow away on the *Twentieth Century Ltd.* traveling to New York. It turns out that in the compartment next to Oscar's is the popular movie star Lily Garland (Eugenie Leontovich), the former Mildred Plotka who Oscar discovered years ago and made into a stage star. They were once lovers but things turned sour and she left him to go off to Hollywood. Oscar's only chance for a triumphant comeback is to convince Lily to star in his next Broadway venture. Running across two German actors from the famous passion play in Germany, Oscar gets an idea for a sure-fire hit: a passion play with Lily playing Mary Magdalene. As the train speeds toward Manhattan and time is running out, Oscar makes little headway with Lily, who is furious at him for his past infidelities. When a religious fanatic on board, Matthew Clark (Etienne Girardot), offers to put $200,000 into the passion play, Lily is tempted by the chance to play Mary Magdalene. She is just about to sign a contract with Oscar when it is discovered that Clark is a penniless nut case and is carried off to a lunatic asylum. Lily vehemently refuses to work with Oscar so he pretends to shoot himself in despair. His dying wish is that Lily sign the contract as a farewell gesture. She does, he immediately recovers, and it looks like the wily Oscar and the fuming Lily will be working together again. As much as Hecht and MacArthur were pleased with the rewrite, they refused to give Dunning author credit. But as co-producer of *Twentieth Century*, Dunning was more than compensated when the show opened on Broadway in 1932 and ran 152 performances during the worst days of the Depression. The farce was hailed by the critics, most comparing it favorably to *The Front Page*. Percy Hammond in the *New York Herald Tribune* wrote, "Show business gets a cruel razzing from [Hecht and MacArthur] ... in which those impish bad boys of the Drama kick it earnestly [in] its pants and inspire, thereby, much hilarity." And *Time Magazine* announced, "Even if it did take two years to write the third act, this muscular successor to Messrs. Hecht & MacArthur's *Front Page* was well worth the wait. It is the saga of one wild trip." The cast, which also included such delightful character actors as William Frawley, Matt Briggs, Roy Roberts, and Henry Sherwood, was roundly applauded by the press but there were just as many compliments for Abbott's ingenious direction.

So what exactly did Abbott do with *Twentieth Century* that got so much attention? The script itself forced Abbott to overcome a unique obstacle. Almost the entire farce takes place on a train. The scenery was designed by the team of Cirker and Robbins. We see an observation car early in the play but then much of the subsequent action is in the two adjoining private compartments of Oscar and Lily. Farce demands doors yet there are only three for Abbott to work with: one for each compartment and an adjoining door between the two staterooms. Yet Abbott made brilliant use of the small space, managing to keep the movement lively and clever by having bodies climbing over each other in the claustrophobic compartments. The adjoining door became a comic prop as characters eavesdropped, fell through, or were pushed though the door. Sometimes there was action going on independently in the two compartments, giving the audience two farces for the price of one. Abbott had turned a significant obstacle into a hilarious asset. Looking back years later, Abbott confessed that he did not like Hecht and MacArthur and did not enjoy working with them. Staging farce is serious business and the Katzenjammer Kids took nothing seriously. Abbott was happiest when the two playwrights were not to be found at rehearsals or anywhere else. He would later work with the duo on the musical *Jumbo* but that's another story in another chapter. Working with Eugenie Leontovich on *Twentieth Century* posed another difficulty, though a very different one. The Russian-born Leontovich was a member of the Moscow Art Theatre before the Russian Revolution broke out in 1917 and she escaped to Paris. Arriving in America in 1922 with a thick Russian accent, she was limited to playing foreigners on the stage, most memorably the ballerina Grushinskaia in *Grand Hotel* (1930). The casting of Leontovich as the temperamental film star was odd yet perfect and Abbott thought her performance was outstanding. But rehearsals were trying with her employing Konstantin Stanislavski techniques and looking for meaning in every move and line delivery. Abbott, of course, just wanted her to go where he told her and say the lines the way he instructed her. As frustrating as the situation was, Abbott maintained a cool and businesslike tone. When Leontovich suggested one of her entrances be changed, Abbott agreed, saying it would serve the leading man better that way. This did not please Leontovich and, later at lunch with Abbott, she insisted they return to the original blocking. Abbott lost his cool demeanor, called her a phony actress and a selfish ham who only cared about herself and not the play, then stormed out of the restaurant. He was followed by a smiling Leontovich who was so pleased to see a man with so much control loose his temper for once. From that point they got on fine and she was, according to Abbott, a pleasure to work with.

Twentieth Century has enjoyed a longer life than most 1930s farces. There was a deliciously daffy movie version made in 1934 with John Barrymore and Carole Lombard, and two Broadway revivals: a 1950 production starring José Ferrer and Gloria Swanson that ran longer than the original and a poorly received, significantly edited 2004 revival featuring Alec Baldwin and Anne Heche. Television adaptations of *Twentieth Century* were broadcast in 1949, 1953, and 1956. The play also was turned into the successful Broadway musical *On the Twentieth Century* in 1978. Abbott was not involved in any of the above.

One of Abbott's most successful doctoring jobs, the farce **Three Men on a Horse** (1935), turned out to be one of the longest-running comedies of the decade. The actor-director-playwright John Cecil Holm had an idea for a farce about a nerdy, mousy fellow who gets mixed up with gamblers. The idea was not a new one but then Holm came up with the right comic twist: the nebbish has a talent for picking thoroughbred winners even though he has never been to a race track. Titled *Hobby Horses*, the manuscript interested Warner Brothers enough to want to invest in the play with the idea of filming it later. But the script had problems and the studio insisted on bringing in director-writer Abbott. He strengthened the plot, put some zing in the dialogue, found ways to make the characters broader and funnier, and solved that persistent third act problem. Because Abbott would also direct what he retitled *Three Men on a Horse*, he made sure that the plot moved quickly, paring down the excess and tightening the speeches. How good or poor Holm's original script was will never be known but the final version of *Three Men on a Horse* is American farce at its best.

The milquetoast greeting card poet Erwin Trowbridge (William Lynn) looks at the newspaper daily and likes to pick the winning horses at the race track, though he never bets on them himself, and he invariably chooses the winners. After a tiff with his wife Audrey (Joyce Arling), Erwin takes refuge in a Manhattan bar where the down-and-out gamblers Patsy (Sam Levene), Frankie (Teddy Hart), and Charlie (Millard Mitchell) hang out with Patsy's girl Mabel (Shirley Booth). When they find out about Erwin's talent, they get him drunk, hole him up in a hotel room, and force him to pick winners for them. The crooks win big until they insist that Erwin bet his own money as well. As soon as he does, Erwin's gift deserts him. So Erwin makes peace with his worried wife and returns to writing greeting card poetry. *Three Men on a Horse* is a small-cast farce and doesn't rely on a great deal of physical action. Instead the Abbott-Holm script boasts a handful of well-drawn farce characters. Patsy is the central character even though the play starts and ends with Erwin. Insulting, frantic, bossy, and desperate, Patsy is a comic delight. He moves from utter despair to high-flying optimism at every turn of the plot. His cronies Charlie and Frankie are distinctively different, trying to keep up with Patsy but critical of him at every new scheme. Erwin is the opposite. Such a meek, innocent, and fearful man, he is amusingly irritating. He plays the horses on paper as a kind of secret hobby. That is about as exciting as his life can handle. Mabel is the tough girl with a soft spot for Erwin because he is the kind of guy she'll never get. Mabel tries to protect Erwin from Patsy's out-of-control enthusiasm for making a bundle. Erwin likes making so much money so quickly for others but he only feels at home writing sentimental verses for the greeting card company.

The action in *Three Men on a Horse* is limited to three rooms where there is not a lot of coming and going by extra characters. Erwin and Audrey's home in Ozone Heights, New Jersey, represents the safe and unimaginative world he inhabits. The bar in the basement of the Lavillere Hotel in Manhattan is dark and seedy, everything Ozone Heights is not. The room in the same hotel where Erwin is shanghaied is far from glamorous. Abbott worked with designer Boris Aronson for the first time with *Three Men on a Horse* and both made demands of the other. Aronson made the Erwin home as ugly as possible (walls painted "cockroach brown" with green trim!) and purchased all of the decor's bric-a-brac from Woolworths. The two hotel settings were stark and uncluttered. None of the sets were realistic. Aronson slightly stylized it all, using painted windows and exaggerated wallpaper. Abbott thought it quite unusual for a farce but agreed to the design if the set changes could be done quickly. Since all three box sets filled the stage and the action went back and forth from one place to another, Aronson had to use a system call "jack knifing" in which the walls separated and were stored behind other walls when not needed. When the scenery was complete and the set changes were executed quickly and (mostly) silently, Aronson asked Abbott if he was pleased. All the director said was "Make sure the doors don't shake!"[2]

The revised manuscript by Holm and Abbott satisfied Warner Brothers who invested in the play which Alex Yokel produced. Abbott was impressed by the character actor Sam Levene who had a small but memorable role in *Dinner at Eight* (1932). He cast Levene as Patsy then the rest of the cast fell into place. William Lyon was typecast as Erwin as were Teddy Hart and Millard Mitchell as Patsy's cronies Frankie and Charlie. Finally getting some recognition was Shirley Booth as Mabel. She had been appearing in forgettable Broadway shows for ten years but was not noticed until her funny, touching performance in *Three Men on a Horse*. In a small role was Garson Kanin who also acted as Abbott's assistant. Like Levene and Booth, he had a prodigious career ahead of him, though not as an actor. Kanin became one of show business' multi-hyphenates: writer, director, and producer on Broadway and in Hollywood.

Three Men on a Horse opened to favorable but not rave reviews. For example, Robert Benchley in *The New Yorker* called it "distinctly low in tone, broad in method, and ostensibly mad in design, but there is an underlying comic truth running through it." Brooks Atkinson in the *New York Times* was similarly cautious: "A topsy-turvy comedy that is not so funny as inspired fooling but it is funnier than most journeyman's jobs. What humors the notion contains Mr. Holm and Mr. Abbott have shot helter-skelter across the stage." It was the enthusiastic word of mouth that allowed the farce to run for two years: 835 performances. The play made Levene a star and he began a long and memorable career playing Patsy-like characters. He was the master at portraying lovable gamblers, small-time crooks, and similar low-lifes, perhaps most memorably Nathan Detroit in the original *Guys and Dolls* (1950). The critics also cited the newcomer Booth as Mabel and, once again, Abbott's sure-fire direction was applauded. While it was still running in New York, *Three Men on a Horse* had three road companies crisscrossing the nation and there was a London mounting. It was also a favorite later with all kinds of theatre groups. The play has returned to New York on four occasions. William Lynn reprised his Edwin and Teddy Hart was once again Frankie in a 1942 production that failed to catch fire. Co-author Holm directed and it was clear the Abbott touch was needed. Critics felt the farce lacked the sprightly tone of the original even though Holm tried to recreate Abbott's direction. But copying the 1935 blocking did not work, proving once again what a fragile thing farce can be. Levene and Abbott returned to the farce for a popular 1969 mounting which featured Jack Gilford (Erwin), Rosemary Prinz (Audrey), Dorothy Loudon (Mabel), Hal Linden (Charlie), and Al Nesor (Frankie). The well-reviewed revival directed by Abbott ran three months. Television favorites Tony Randall (Erwin) and Jack Klugman (Patsy) re-teamed for the National Actors Theatre revival in 1993 and audiences were pleased, even if critics pointed out the two performers were too old and sluggish for the farcical characters. Because the initial Broadway reviews and business for *Three Men on a Horse* were so lackluster, Warner Brothers was able to buy the screen rights for only $75,000. The 1936 film adaptation gave Sam Levene and Teddy Hart a chance to reprise their stage performances as Patsy and Frankie. Frank McHugh played Erwin and the supporting cast included Joan Blondell (Mabel), Allen Jenkins (Charlie), and Carol Hughes (Audrey). Mervyn LeRoy directed the movie which was fairly accurate to the play. The film drags at times but it is worth watching to see Levene and why the play made him a stage and screen favorite. *Three Men on a Horse* was musicalized for Broadway twice but without success. *Banjo Eyes* (1941) and *Let It Ride!* (1961) both failed to run despite some major talents involved; Abbott was not among them.

Rarely done today but very popular in its day was the Hollywood spoof **Boy Meets Girl** (1935) which Abbott produced and directed. Ironically, the two main characters in this Bella and Sam Spewack farce are based on Hecht and MacArthur. Abbott may have balked at working again with the Katzenjammer Kids as playwrights but not as characters. The Spewacks made no effort to disguise their characters' source but, for legal reasons, said all the characters were fictional. Robert Law (Allyn Joslyn) and J. Carlyle Benson (Jerome Cowan) are two wacko Hollywood screenwriters who thrive on practical jokes and driving the studio heads crazy. When the studio boss C. F. Friday (Royal Beal) assigns Law and Benson to devise a scenario to save the sagging career of cowboy star Larry Toms (Charles McClelland), the duo laugh off the assignment as an impossible task. Then they learn that the unmarried studio waitress Susie (Joyce Arling) is about to give birth and they have a brainstorm. Law and Benson obtain power of attorney and, as soon as the infant is born, set about making the baby, who is named Happy, into Larry's costar. The plan works and Happy not only becomes a child star but saves Larry's career, though the cowboy hates being upstaged by the cute tot. Trouble arises when a lawyer schemes and gets the power of attorney away from the writers and lets a rival studio cash in on Happy. Law and Carlyle try to tarnish the baby's image by hiring a studio extra, Rodney (James MacColl), to claim that he is the baby's real father. Susie and Rodney are in love but she still plans to run off with Larry and save Happy's career. When Larry catches the measles from the baby, he is furious and his true dislike for Happy becomes clear. So Susie ends up with Rodney, who turns out to be a titled Englishman.

The Spewacks brought their broad, wisecracking script to Abbott who decided to produce and direct the farce. He raised the capital from Warner Brothers by assuring them of the movie rights and then staged *Boy Meets Girl* as a high-speed parade of Hollywood clichés. A studio producer, starlet, yes-man, lawyer, songwriter, doctor, nurse, and a British major filled the stage as the action rarely slowed down. Scenic designer Arne Lundborg provided C. F.'s lavish office where most of the action occurred though there was one scene set in a hospital corridor. This time there was no shortage of doors for Abbott to work with and each one was used extensively. The script calls for a number of people to enter and exit and

Abbott made sure they did so without a second of dead space. He directed Royal Beal to play C. F. always on the brink of a nervous breakdown so that Allyn Joslyn and Jerome Cowan, as the two roguish writers, need not maintain a high level of clowning. In fact, their joking in C. F.'s presence became a wry commentary on everything going on around them. Although the scenery did not change much, there were many costume changes and Abbott abhorred the time needed between scenes. So he hired a dozen musicians and put them in the two theatre boxes closest to the stage and they broke into the music on the last spoken syllable of each scene. When questioned about the musicians, Abbott replied, "I always wondered what those theatre boxes were for. Now I know."[3]

Most of the critics agreed with the *Times*' Atkinson who called the show "An extraordinarily hilarious comedy." *Time* thought, "What gives the show the final gilt-edged touch, however, is the fact that Producer Abbott has cast it with the care and attention a professional diver gives his air hose." *Boy Meets Girl* ran 669 performances, by far the biggest comedy hit of the season. In the preface to the published version of *Boy Meets Girl*, Abbott wrote that he thought it the "best play that has yet appeared about Hollywood. It is the real thing ... because Bella and Samuel Spewack are reporters as well as dramatists and they report what they see and observe, not what convention would want them to see."[4] The Spewacks were also seasoned screenwriters, having already contributed to a dozen movies with many more to come. What Abbott doesn't mention is that he himself had considerable experience with moviemaking. By 1935 he had written and/or directed over a dozen films and thought the whole business of the movies to be disorganized, inefficient, and run by people with no sense of solid entertainment. The money Abbott earned was welcome but the moviemaking experience was usually very frustrating, as we shall see in Chapter 5. As for the husband–wife team of Bella and Samuel Spewack, they later had another comedy hit on Broadway with *My Three Angels* (1953) but the triumph of their career was their brilliant libretto for *Kiss Me, Kate* (1948). Ironically, Warner Brothers' 1938 screen version of *Boy Meets Girl* was neither a popular nor critical success. James Cagney and Pat O'Brien are in robust form as the conniving writers and director Lloyd Bacon keeps things fast-paced but the movie is more frantic than fun. The Spewack's screenplay, cleaned up for the screen (no unmarried pregnant Susie in a Hollywood movie), is still sharp but the movie is oddly unsatisfying. Once again, faster did not translate to better. *Boy Meets Girl* has not fared well in Broadway revivals either. Presented in 1943 and 1976 with no involvement with Abbott, the farce sparked no fireworks.

Abbott got to introduce a trio of little known actors (who would not be unknown for long) when he produced and directed **Brother Rat** (1936), a farce by two former cadets at the Virginia Military Institute. John Monks, Jr., and Fred F. Finklehoffe had had several run-ins with their teachers and officers while they were students at VMI. At one point they had gotten into a brawl and were put in jail where they began exchanging stories about cadet life and how they would make for a jocular novel or play. After graduation, Finklehoffe became a lawyer and Monks pursued a writing career. Some time had passed before the two young men got together and returned to their idea of writing about their days in military school. After various titles and numerous plot changes, the would-be playwrights had a comedy they titled *Brother Rat*. The title phrase is a term of gruff affection used by the cadets at VMI. The two authors claimed to have sent the script to thirty-one producers and been rejected the same number of times before they managed to get inside Abbott's office. Their timing could not have been worse. Abbott was recovering from the biggest flop yet of his career: his elaborate stage version of *Uncle Tom's Cabin* titled *Sweet River* had folded after five performances. Also, there had already been two plays that season about military schools: *Honor Bright* (1936) and *So Proudly We Hail* (1936). Both were about how cruelly the freshmen cadets were treated and the dramas portrayed such academies as breeding grounds for power-hungry leaders. Both plays failed to run. Abbott looked at the pair of twenty-six-year-old writers, who argued that they had fond memories of military school and that their play was a comedy, and could not help but think back on his own years at Kearney Military Academy in Nebraska. So he read their play and, after some script suggestions, decided to produce and direct *Brother Rat*.

The plot centers on senior cadet Bing Edwards (Eddie Albert), the school's star pitcher, and his two pals Billy (Jack Albertson) and Dan (José Ferrer). Against school rules, Bing has secretly married a local girl Kate Rice (Kathleen Fitz) and needs money to support a wife after graduation. He is counting on winning the VMI's $200 award as its best athlete. Bing gives Billy fifty dollars to put in Bing's bank account but Billy and Dan decide to do Bing a favor and they bet the money on VMI winning the big game. Right before the game, Bing learns that Kate is pregnant and the news so unnerves him that his pitching is lousy and VMI loses the baseball game. The distraught Bing faces graduation with dread (Billy and Dan find out about the pregnancy and suggest Bing name the baby Commencement) but a happy ending comes in the form of a check for $300. It seems Bing is the first father of his class.

Abbott decided from the start that the cast had to be young. "They're playing the part of Virginia Military Institute cadets," he said. "College men and prom trotters— and we'll not have a middle-ager in the crowd."[5] He cast newcomers Eddie Albert and José Ferrer as Bing and Dan; Jack Albertson had already found some recognition in the film *Alice Adams* (1935) but was still the right age for a cadet. The action of the play was mostly set in and around the school barracks, a milieu Abbott was more than casually familiar with. He directed the cadets to behave with authentic rough-housing and tussling with each other at every turn. Just as the Finklehoffe-Monks dialogue sounded like the real thing, so too did the young cast behave in a believably adolescent manner. As Gilbert Gabriel wrote in the *American*, the play was a "double quick-step march of jovial events by a company of immediately likable juveniles." When *Brother Rat* opened on Broadway in 1936, the notices echoed Gabriel's sentiments. *Time* said, "Able George Abbott's first production of the season is an ingenuous farce which is never as screamingly funny as his *Boy Meets Girl*, but which brims with nice young people and gentle laughter." The critics lauded the script, pointed out Abbott's tight direction, and there was plenty of praise for Albert, Albertson, and Ferrer whose facile performances were a highlight of the show. With such reviews and strong word of mouth, *Brother Rat* ran a very profitable 575 performances. Broadway never saw the comedy revived but the inferior 1938 movie, with Eddie Albert reprising his Bing Edwards, was popular enough to warrant a sequel, *Brother Rat and a Baby* (1940). Hollywood also made a musical of the property in 1952. Titled *About Face*, it starred Gordon MacRae, Eddie Bracken, and Dick Wesson as the three cadets.

Although he was not credited, Abbott did a lot of rewriting on the script for **Room Service** (1937), another hit farce which he produced and directed. John Murray and Allen Boretz's original version had interested producer Sam H. Harris and the show was cast, rehearsed, and trying out in Philadelphia when it was clear they had a flop on their hands. Harris closed the production but Murray and Boretz weren't giving up. They brought their script to Garson Kanin, Abbott's assistant, who told them he thought Abbott could fix it. Abbott saw definite farce possibilities in the script but, like many such plays in the genre, the story wasn't strong enough to sustain the premise. Working with Murray and Boretz, Abbott built the plot up so that the desperation of the main character, a failed Broadway producer, would force him to take drastic measures leading up to a somewhat logical resolution. Satisfied with the new script, Abbott cast the production mostly with actors he'd worked with in farces before, in particular Sam Levene and Teddy Hart from *Three Men on a Horse* and Eddie Albert from *Brother Rat*. Abbott later stated it was a most satisfying rehearsal process because the actors were in sync with him and with each other.

The action all takes place in a Manhattan hotel suite with a sufficient number of doors—a classic farce setting. Abbott made the most of it and there were plenty of entrances, exits, and concealing oneself under bedcovers. The penny-ante producer Gordon Miller (Levene) has a contract on a play titled *Godspeed* by the unknown playwright Leo Davis (Albert) from Oswego, New York. Miller also has an impatient director Harry Binion (Philip Loeb), a cast of twenty-two actors, and a possible lease on a theatre. What he doesn't have is the money to pay for any of it. The bill for housing the company in the White Way Hotel is mounting daily so Miller and his cohort Faker Englund (Hart) sell a ten-percent interest in the show to Joseph Gribble (Cliff Dunstan), Faker's brother-in-law who is also the manager of the hotel. The bills continue to mount up and Gribble panics when the supervisor of the hotel chain, Mr. Wagner (Donald McBride), notices the unpaid account and threatens to oust the company. Miller convinces the thick-headed Leo to pretend that he has the measles and is too ill and contagious to be moved. The ploy works for awhile but Wagner is adamant and, measles or no measles, he says out they go. So Miller goes one step further and tells the management that Leo has committed suicide and they stall for time by claiming they must attend to the funeral. In desperation, the hotel management puts money in Miller's production just to get rid of him. The play opens and is a smash hit. Happily paying off Wagner, Miller tells him, "This may be the first hotel to win the Pulitzer Prize!"[6]

With its one setting, three doors, a closet, and two beds, the farce was a blank palette on which Abbott created sportive chaos. Because of the high level of tension on the part of the theatrical producer Miller, everything that occurred in the hotel room was in panic mode. Yet Abbott did not fall into the trap of racing through the script. By this time he had learned how to control the speedometer of a farce and realized the importance of variety. With *Room Service*'s one setting and no scene or major costume changes, he had total control over the timing of the evening. Abbott was able to instruct the actors which sections of dialogue or action should be played fortissimo then suddenly when to slow down or even stop to accentuate a plot or character detail. Such a series of builds and descents gave the audience a chance to catch its breath. For example, Miller and his cohorts are cutting off the ends of each other's lines as they argue about money and deadlines in a scene in Act One. But the minute the would-be investor Simon Jenkins is brought in, the tempo immediately becomes a genteel pattern of politeness and sophistication. As soon as Jenkins exits, Gribble enters with news that room service has been discontinued, the actors are hungry, and we are off again in break-neck panic mode. Because *Room Service* is mostly one long extended joke, Abbott had to hide the script's shortcomings and put variety in the staging to make up for the variety that was missing on the page.

Shortcomings not withstanding, *Room Service* was an immediate hit with the press and the public. Atkinson in the *Times* called it a "very funny escapade in the helter-skelter vein of slapdash American fooling" and Richard Watts, Jr., in the *New York Post* went so far as to proclaim *Room Service* "the funniest play that New York has seen in years and years." *Time* echoed their sentiments with, "It pumps its subject full of fun in veterinary doses. [Other] than this pinchbeck legend of Longacre Square, there is no funnier show in town." The production ran a lucrative 500 performances and soon was a favorite on the road and in little theatres. RKO bought the film rights for the record price of $255,000, the most Hollywood had yet paid for a non-musical property. The unfortunate 1938 film adaptation was tailored for the Marx Brothers and it was an uncomfortable fit; it was neither a faithful version of the play nor a fully satisfying Marx vehicle. In 1944, Hollywood made a musical version of *Room Service* titled *Step Lively* with Frank Sinatra and George Murphy. Broadway saw a short-lived revival of *Room Service* in 1953, a version in 1983 that closed on the way to New York, and two laudable Off-Broadway productions in 1970 and 1985.

The only farce that Abbott presented in the 1930s that did not enjoy a long run was **All that Glitters** (1938) and even that ran a not-embarrassing sixty-nine performances. John Baragwanath and Kenneth Simpson wrote the "revenge comedy" which bordered on farce on occasion because of the risible main character, practical joker Muggy Williams (Allyn Joslyn). A Muggy sample, taken from Robert Benchley's review in *The New Yorker*: "A lecher is a man who collects lechings." When Muggy brings his fiancée Kitty Clark (Carmel White) to a gathering sponsored by the Park Avenue social maven Mrs. E. Mortimer Townsend (Helen Gardner), the snotty hostess snubs Kitty. Muggy vows to get even. He picks up the prostitute Elena (Arlene Francis), newly arrived from Latin America, and introduces her to Mrs. Townsend as a Spanish countess. Elena is soon part of the social circle and, just as Muggy is about to reveal who Elena really is, she ensnares his best friend George Ten Eyck (Judson Laire) who also thinks she's an aristocrat. Muggy breaks up the romance, Elena elopes with a rich playboy, and Mrs. Townsend pleads with Muggy not to let her mistake get into the papers. The Abbott production boasted a first-class cast and he directed it with precision but *All that Glitters* never rose above mildly enjoyable. The reviews were mixed. Benchley in *The New Yorker* called *All that Glitters* "an agreeable entertainment for pun-lovers and those who do not mind much where the ball is thrown as long as it keeps in the air." *Time* discussed Abbott at length: "News that George Abbott is directing a play interests Broadway more than who wrote it, or who acts in it. Abbott is noted for discovering merit in scripts rejected by other producers, is able by skillful play-doctoring, casting and directing to whip up a hit out of what looked like nothing. Nevertheless, Abbott's whip hand sometimes falters: his first two shows this season (*Angel Island, Brown Sugar*) were flops. But last week his third attempt looked as if it might last." Most critics praised newcomer Arlene Francis, an actress from Orson Welles' Mercury Theatre. Audiences got to enjoy her performance for nine weeks.

As the producer of a hit Broadway play or musical, Abbott benefited financially when the property was sold to Hollywood. In the case of the juvenile comedy **What a Life!** (1938), a windfall came when it was turned into a radio show, eleven movies, and a television series. Not bad for a script that no one would consider until Abbott saw possibilities in it. In 1936, Clifford Goldsmith wrote an amiable comedy titled *Enter to Learn* about a good-hearted high school student named Henry Aldrich who got into a series of scrapes at school. The script was little more than an aimless parade of misadventures with some mildly funny characters popping in and out. After several rejections by producers, Goldsmith rewrote the play, retitled it *What a Life!*, and managed to get it to Abbott. Perhaps Abbott saw something of his own adolescence in Henry or he just detected the premise for a strong farce. Regardless, Abbott made several suggestions to Goldsmith and, taking no writing credit, produced and directed *What a Life!* on Broadway where it ran a very happy 538 performances.

All the action takes place in Central High School, specifically Principal Bradley's office, a place to which the fun-loving but unlucky Henry Aldrich (Ezra Stone) is frequently summoned. On one occasion he was in English class where they were studying *Hamlet* but Henry was drawing a cartoon of a whale wearing eyeglasses and labeled it "Moby Bradley." Henry's mother (Lea Penman) has also been summoned to Bradley's office and, not for the first time, tries to defend her hapless son. She promises Henry that she will give him money to go to the Spring Dance if he passes his history test. Henry is smitten with the comely Barbara Pierson (Betty Field) and dreams of taking her to the dance despite the competition from his rival George Bigelow (James Cromer). The trouble is, Henry has lost his history textbook. Before you know it, Henry is back in Mr. Bradley's office for cheating on his history test. But such infractions are nothing compared to what happens a few days before the dance. All of the school's band instruments are stolen and hocked and all the evidence points to Henry. It looks like Henry's future is to be reform school until it is proven that George stole the instruments and Henry is free and able to take Barbara to the dance—though he has to borrow carfare from her to get them there.

Today we would consider such lighthearted goings-on more a sit-com entertainment than farce but Abbott, audiences, and the critics didn't see it that way. Respected columnist John Mason Brown called *What a Life!* a "veritable Utopia of farce" and *Variety* declared it "the funniest play of the season." In his report on the 1937–1938 season, Burns Mantle summed up the play's appeal. "It is a story of High School life that is basically human and sufficiently plausible to re-create for a majority in every audience a picture of their own school-time adventures."[7] The comedy was not situational but came from the characters, in particular the haphazard yet philosophical Henry Aldrich who takes life as it is handed to him. His father was a Phi Beta Kappa at Princeton and never lets his son forget it. Henry is expected to go to Princeton someday and his parents have been putting aside money for tuition. It is referred to as Henry's "sinking fund." When asked why he is always in trouble, Henry reasons, "I guess it's just the way I'm built or something. You know what I mean? You can ask any of my teachers and they'll all tell you the same thing . . . I guess some people are just built like that."[8] There was enough of Francis Abbott in Henry that Abbot made sure the character was never sentimentalized. It helped that young Ezra Stone was superb in the role, never forcing the character and endearing himself to everyone without seeming to try.

Abbot took a lighter touch in directing *What a Life!* Because he was not dealing with con men or scheming producers, there was a softer edge to the play's tone. The only villain in the plot was George Bigelow and he was an adolescent bully. The characters did not rush in and out of Principal Bradley's office as they did in bars and hotel rooms in other farces. All the same, timing was essential. Henry spoke in a haphazard rhythm, often trying to make things up or answer questions he didn't know the answer to. In his conversations with the principal, for example, Mr. Bradley is forced to pick up on Henry's scattered tempo and soon the two are doing something akin to a vaudeville act. At the same time, Abbott insisted on absolute sincerity from the cast. The characters in *What a Life!* are more than stereotypes and he knew the audience would like them if they found them believable. *Time* certainly thought they were believable, describing Henry as "always ingenious, never crafty, always there with an answer, never with the right one, brash, bouncing, rumpled, rattled, rueful by turns, Henry grows into that rare thing on the stage—a person." But the unsigned critic went on to say, "*What a Life* is so long on character portrayal that it is terribly short on plot, never quite masses its laughs through mounting situations, merely sprinkles them brightly at regular intervals. As slight of build as the kids it treats of, *What a Life!* is, like them, young, lively, fast on its feet, full of agonies a first kiss or even an ice-cream soda could drive away." Abbott liked working with Ezra Stone who was a natural for Henry. Unfortunately, the actor was typecast from then on and, Abbott felt, never developed into the actor he should have become.

While *What a Life!* was still filling the house on Broadway, Goldsmith wrote new sketches involving Henry Aldrich and they were heard on Rudy Vallee's radio program. The sketches went over so well, Goldsmith was soon writing Henry's own radio show, *Henry Aldrich*. The opening of the program was soon familiar and echoed across America. Mrs. Aldrich would screech, "Hen-reeeeeeeeeeeee! Hen-ree Al-drich!," and he responded with a breaking adolescent voice, "Com-ing, Mother!" Stone left the Broadway company and voiced Henry on the radio for the program's three seasons. It was followed by another radio show, *The Aldrich Family*, which was on the air from 1939 to 1953. There were also eleven Henry Aldrich films between 1939 to 1944, many of them featuring Jackie Cooper as Henry and Eddie Bracken as his pal Dizzy. There was even a television series, also titled *The Aldrich Family*, which ran on NBC from 1949 to 1953. Abbott did not participate in Henry Aldrich's long life but Goldsmith gave up the theatre and spent the rest of his life writing, producing, and supervising the many versions of his teenage hero. It was an entire career ignited by a handful of script suggestions made by Abbott.

The last farce of the 1930s produced by Abbott was **See My Lawyer** (1939), a rapid-fire comedy by Richard Mailbaum and Harry Clork. Abbott was too occupied with other projects so he left the directing to Ezra Hunt. He was missed. The script had its moments, the cast was first-rate, and the pacing was fast. Some critics felt it was too fast. But tempo in a farce is not a matter of speed, as Abbott had demonstrated on previous occasions. *See My Lawyer* needed a stronger hand at the helm. In true farce fashion, all the action is set in the Manhattan law offices of Lee, Russo and O'Rourke which had the sufficient number of doors and desks. Business is so slow in the new legal firm that Arthur Lee (Milton Berle), Peter Russo (Gary Merrill), and Joseph O'Rourke (Millard Mitchell) keep bread rolls in the office's petty cash box. They even allow the funny little ambulance chaser Morris Schneerner (Teddy Hart) to occupy rent-free the extra desk hoping he might bring them some business. Things liven up considerably when eccentric millionaire Robert Carlin (Eddie Nugent) drives his car through the office wall. They are on the twenty-second floor and Carlin was anxious to see them so he drove up via the freight elevator. It seems Carlin has practically run over their office boy down on the street and he has come to them for a settlement. Carlin takes a liking to the three young lawyers, gives them $25,000 in cash and asks them to handle all his legal affairs. The trio of young attorneys celebrate their good fortune but it doesn't last long. Carlin is a nut case, his legal complications are a nightmare, and the firm of Lee, Russo and O'Rourke is more than happy when Carlin decides to take his business elsewhere. There was unanimous praise in the press for the cast, in particular for Berle and Hart, but most reviewers thought the farce was more furious than funny. Atkinson in the *Times* thought some of *See My Lawyer* was "a hilarious scuffle when the crisis grows desperate" and deemed the farce "second-rate . . . but second-rate is nothing to be sneezed at just now." John Anderson in the *Journal-American* described the comedy as "more athletic than amusing" and wished "it were only funnier." *Time* was even less enthused: "The show has laughs, but never (as a farce must) piles up its laughter; everybody works a little too hard, tries to be a little too crazy. It's the old George Abbott formula minus the old George Abbott form." Audiences were less critical and enjoyed the play so producer Abbott made a wise decision: he moved *See My Lawyer* to a larger theatre, lowered the ticket price from $3.30 to $1.10, and the show ran a profitable 224 performances.

By the end of the 1930s, Abbott was a twenty-five-year veteran of Broadway with some two dozen plays and musicals to his credit. One might assume that the "Abbott touch" was well established and set in stone by this time. Yet new and different theatre experiences were still to come and what had worked for *Jumbo* in 1935 was not necessarily going to be right for *Pal Joey* in 1940. If I had to select a genre that forced Abbott to refine his touch, I would say it was his 1930s farces. As a producer, director, and sometimes co-author of these farces, he created a unique style not only for himself but for American farce. It was more subtle than George M. Cohan and perhaps more precise than George S. Kaufman, the writer-director who came closest to Abbott. Because he experimented less when selecting his farce productions than he did in his melodramas, Abbott was on sure ground when he presented a farce. The genre is difficult enough in its basic form that Abbott rarely looked for unconventional scripts. The challenge was already there; save the ground-breaking projects for other genres.

The eight farces in the 1930s that Abbott was involved with as co-author, director and/or producer ran a total of 3,562 performances. Add to that the successful musicals and melodramas he was involved with, it is little wonder that for much of the decade Abbott had three shows running simultaneously on Broadway. At one point, he had five different theatres presenting his productions. Abbott did a few more farces later in his career but the heyday of that genre was over by the war years and rarely came back. The comedies got gentler, starting with the long-run champ *Life with Father* (1939), and only in a handful of musicals did the inspired silliness of farce find a home. Abbott was responsible for some of them, as we'll see in later chapters.

5 THE CELLULOID SIDESTEP

(1918–1931)

The Imposter • The Carnival Man • The Bishop's Candlesticks • Why Bring that Up? • The Saturday Night Kid • Halfway to Heaven • All Quiet on the Western Front • Manslaughter • The Sea God • Stolen Heaven • Secrets of a Secretary • My Sin • The Cheat

While this book is about the theatre of George Abbott, it would be remiss not to include some discussion of his film career. It is a career that is too little known and includes acting, writing, and directing credits for the silent screen, the early talkies, and some big-budget musicals in the 1950s. Many of Abbott's stage works made it to screen without his involvement. We will concentrate on the movies in which he actively participated as an actor, screenwriter, and/or director. His first association with the movies came in 1914 when, unable to find work as an actor on Broadway, Abbott took jobs as an extra in silent films. This was long before the Screen Actors Guild (SAG) existed and the extras in movies were poorly paid and treated like expendable minions. Decades later, Abbott recalled, "Each of us felt ashamed of having such a lowly job, and many were the face-saving lies to be heard as we hung around waiting for the next shot."[1] (SAG was not founded until 1933 when screen extras were finally unionized.) While some extras' goal was to be noticed by the director and became a featured player, Abbott was not very interested in the movies and took film jobs out of necessity. Also, most movies in 1914 were made on the East coast, particularly on Long Island and in New Jersey, so he was able to do films without relocating to California. There is no record of how many shorts and features Abbott appeared in in those early days of cinema but he worked steadily for two years while his theatre career was floundering. Also, he noticed that movie producers and directors at the time were far from experienced. "Those in power were there by virtue of having been first in the field," he wrote, "rather than as a result of worth."[2] So later, when he was offered jobs writing and/or directing films, Abbott knew he was more than qualified.

The first such offer Abbott received was as co-director for *The Impostor*, a fifty-minute feature by the Empire All Star Corp. released in 1918. The tale of an innocent girl (Anna Murdock) from the church choir, who goes to the Big City to pursue a music career, bordered on the "mellerdrama" as she encountered wolf-like men and snide society cads before ending up in the arms of David Powell. Abbott had no hand in the screenplay but he was hired to co-direct the picture with Dell Henderson and played the minor role of Lem, one of the men in the heroine's adventures. When Abbott's play *Love 'Em and Leave 'Em* was filmed by Famous Players-Lasky Corp. in 1926 with the mesmerizing Louise Brooks in the lead, he was not involved in the project. Neither was he asked to participate when his play *A Holy Terror* was filmed by Fox as *Hills of Peril* in 1927. Both were silent features and held little interest for the now-successful Broadway writer-director-actor Abbott. It was when sound came in that Abbott took movies more seriously. "Talking pictures had just begun," he later recalled, "and I was one of those who felt that this medium was going to be important."[3] He wrote the screenplay for the 1928 MGM film of his play *Four Walls*, the first sound version of an Abbott work. The popular silent star John Gilbert played the ex-convict Benny opposite Joan Crawford; her star was rising, his was descending, and the movie was not popular. Another silent star, Mary Pickford, made her talkie debut in Abbott's *Coquette* released by United Artists in 1929. Pickford was cast against type as the "fallen woman" Norma and audiences were not interested. More successful was the first film version of Abbott's *Broadway* made by Universal in 1929. He was among the handful of those who contributed to the screenplay and the comedy-melodrama translated well to the screen.

By this time Abbott's reputation as a Broadway director got the attention of Paramount and the studio asked him to direct two shorts on the East coast before bringing him out to California. ***The Carnival Man*** and ***The Bishop's Candlesticks***, both released in 1929 and featuring the stage star Walter Huston, showed promise. The latter was based on an episode in Victor Hugo's novel *Les Misérables* and was the first screen adaptation of the French classic. Abbott arrived in Hollywood in 1929 where his first assignment was co-writing and directing ***Why Bring that Up?***, a comedy-drama about show business. The vaudeville team of Charles Mack and George Moran, known as the black-face comedians Two Black Crows, played themselves in the film. The duo makes it to Broadway but the partners fight over the pretty performer Betty (Evelyn Brent) so the act eventually breaks up. *Why Bring That Up?* is difficult for modern audiences to watch but Abbott's swift direction of the backstage film recalls some of his vivacious staging from *Broadway*. (He also played the cameo role of the Director in the movie.) Paramount re-made Abbott's *Love 'Em and Leave 'Em* as *The Saturday Night Kid* (1929) as a vehicle for silent screen favorite Clara Bow and newcomer Jean Arthur. (Edna May Oliver made her screen debut in a supporting role in the film.) Abbott was not involved with the movie but Paramount had him write and direct ***Half Way to Heaven*** (1929), a melodrama about trapeze artists in a circus. Two "swing men" (Charles "Buddy" Rogers and Paul Lukas) are rivals for the affections of the trapeze girl (Jean Arthur) so when one man fails to "catch" the other during a performance, death and complications ensue. *Half Way to Heaven* was well received and Abbott was noticed by other studios.

At Universal, a screen version of Erich Maria Remarque's acclaimed war novel ***All Quiet on the Western Front*** was being filmed with a screenplay by playwright Maxwell Anderson. The studio was not happy with the script and hired Abbott to rewrite it. The story of a German youth (Lew Ayres), who enters the army with high ideals but finds disillusionment and death in the Great War, was a powerful one and, as directed by Lewis Milestone, *All Quiet on the Western Front* (1930) became one of the first talkie classics in American cinema. It won Oscars for Best Picture and for Milestone and was nominated for Best Cinematography and Best Writing Achievement. The screenplay credit was confusing: "Screen Story by George Abbott. Adaptation by Maxwell Anderson. Dialogue by Maxwell Anderson and George Abbott." Abbott's script is indeed excellent but Anderson's contribution and Remarque's German-language novel *Im Westen Nichts Neues* (*Nothing New in the West*) must also be credited. As for the movie itself, *All Quiet on the Western Front* is one of Hollywood's greatest war films. Director Milestone hired German refugees living in California for many of the soldiers in the film and was not afraid to show the horrors of war. Made before the Production Code forbade graphic images on screen, *All Quiet on the Western Front* included some very disturbing scenes which kept some distributors in the States from showing it. (For its anti-Nazi stance, the film was banned in Germany and Italy for many years.) One of the most horrifying moments in the movie, when a soldier's severed hands are seen grasping the barbed wire, was not in the novel nor was it Abbott's work. One of the German extras told Milestone about having seen such a thing and the director added it to the film. Yet there are several aspects of *All Quiet on the Western Front* that are most likely Abbott's contribution, such as the movie's ending in which the hero is killed while reaching out for a butterfly. The reviews for the movie were exemplary. *Variety* called it, "A harrowing, gruesome, morbid tale of war, so compelling in its realism, bigness and repulsiveness... For this is a war and what Sherman said goes double here." In the *New York Daily News*, Irene Thirer wrote:

> It smack[s] of directional genius—nothing short of this; sensitive performances by a marvelous cast and the most remarkable camera work which has been performed on either silent or sound screen, round about the Hollywood studios ... We have praise for everyone concerned with this picture." The film afforded Abbott's only Oscar nomination during his long career yet he doesn't even

mention the honor in his autobiography. Abbott only notes that he "was paid a magnificent salary to rewrite the picture."[4]

He was more proud of **Manslaughter** (1930) which he wrote and directed for Paramount. "*Manslaughter* was the best picture I made because it had the most believable story," Abbott wrote years later.[5] A spoiled socialite (Claudette Colbert) accidentally kills a pedestrian while driving recklessly and the District Attorney (Fredric March) gets a manslaughter conviction for her. She loathes the D.A. for sending her to prison but while there the self-centered girl sees a whole new world of people without her privileges. She even falls in love with the D.A. and the two are united after she serves her time. The film was based on the novel by Alice Duer Miller which Cecil B. DeMille had filmed back in 1922. Clara Bow was originally cast in the remake but the unreliable actress was in her final years of acting and no longer the attractive star of the mid-1920s. Colbert, in one of the first good roles in her screen career, shone in the part and was well matched with March. Abbott recalled them both as "superb"[6] and admired how Colbert insisted on doing her own water skiing in one scene even though she had never skied before. *Manslaughter* was a success and Paramount studio head Adolph Zukor renewed Abbott's contract. His next assignment was as screenwriter and director for **The Sea God** (1930), an exotic romance-adventure set in the Solomon Islands. Cargo ship captain Pink Barker (Richard Arlen) bets with rival shipper Big Schultz (Robert Glecker) that he can make it back to port before him. But Barker sacrifices his chances of winning when he picks up an old castaway on a raft who tells him of a bed of sea pearls off a nearby island. The local natives are cannibals but are calmed when Barker comes out of the sea wearing the cumbersome diving outfit, causing the islanders to think he is a god. The plot gets more complicated when Schultz and his men arrive on the island and are killed by the natives and Barker has to rescue his sweetheart Daisy (Fay Wray) and his pal Square Deal (Eugene Pallette) from danger. The movie, based a short story by pulp writer John Russell, was filmed off Catalina Island and included several underwater scenes, some more convincing than others. Abbott expanded on the short story to make a feature film and it is perhaps overstuffed with action. Also, the subject matter was far from Abbott's usual sphere of experience. Yet *The Sea God* is still a passable adventure yarn and did well enough at the box office.

It should be pointed out how rare it was to get sole writing credit for a movie in the 1930s and even more rare for a sole artist to write and direct a feature film. Yet after only one year in Hollywood, Abbott was doing just that. He could have easily abandoned the theatre and had a very substantial, maybe even a celebrated, career in films. But he missed New York and Broadway. Also, his wife Ednah had elected to live with her family in Rochester, New York, when Abbott was working in California. She was the vital lifeline in Abbott's existence and he measured his success by her opinions. So it was quite an upset when Ednah's family requested he return to Rochester because she was seriously ill. In fact, she was dying of cancer and had only a short time to live. Ever the practical partner, Ednah made arrangements for their daughter Judith to be brought up in her sister's household in Rochester, thereby freeing Abbott for either a movie or theatre career. Abbott still had some films to make under Paramount's contract but the studio, according to him, "showed more heart than is generally attributed to large corporations by arranging immediately for me to continue the work I owed them in their Long Island studios."[7] Ednah died in September of 1931; they had been together for twenty-two years, married for sixteen years. At first Abbott was devastated. Then he returned to work and it dawned on him, somewhat guiltily, that he was a free and independent person for the first time in his life. Abbott realized he had never had the opportunity to live a bachelor's life and he found the prospect a "feeling of great exultation."[8] For the next fifteen years he lived, not like a playboy, but as a self-sufficient man of means. He indulged in things that he was too practical to consider before. Fine clothes, excellent food, comfortable living, playing golf, and foreign travel became important to him. Yet Abbott was always conscious of how fickle show business could be and he never lost sight of saving money, particularly as the Depression was nearing its lowest point in 1931. His solution was to keep working, be it in films or theatre, as a director or a writer.

This new perspective on life may have carried over to his next film project. The Paramount romantic drama ***Stolen Heaven*** (1931) was a vehicle for the adorable, very popular, star Nancy Carroll. The screenplay by Abbott and Dana Burnet concerned the streetwalker Mary (Carroll) and the petty thief Joe (Phillips Holmes) who make a pact: steal $20,000, spend it foolishly, then commit suicide together. They manage to get the money and begin a week of careless spending but Joe's conscience starts to bother him and he realizes he loves Mary. So Joe confesses to the robbery and goes to jail knowing Mary will be there when he gets out. The melodrama gets a bit thick at times but the performances by Carroll and Holmes are so convincing that *Stolen Heaven* ended up being very moving. The story was set in Palm Beach, Florida, but was filmed on Long Island. To help capture a romantic Latin atmosphere, Abbott hired a band from Cuba who played the rhumba, conga, bolero, and other native music still unfamiliar to most moviegoers in 1931. While the music was authentic, the dancing in the Palm Beach resort was "a sort of bastard foxtrot,"[9] as Abbott later complained. Perhaps the most notable aspect of Abbott's direction of *Stolen Heaven* is the way he handled the actors, getting superior performances from both the stars and the supporting players, most memorably Louis Calhern.

Abbott was back in Hollywood as the sole writer and director on Paramount's melodrama ***Secrets of a Secretary*** (1931), reuniting him again with Claudette Colbert. She played the frivolous heiress Helen Blake who, happily drunk one night, marries the gigolo and gold digger Frank D'Agnoll (Georges Metaxa). When her father dies and Helen finds out the family fortune has been wiped out by the stock market crash, Frank abandons her. Helen gets a job as the social secretary for her late father's friend Ogden Hunt Merrill (Burton Churchill) and helps plan the wedding of Sylvia Merrill (Betty Lawford) and the English Lord Paul Danforth (Herbert Marshall). The complications quickly pile up: Sylvia starts seeing Frank on the side, Paul and Helen fall in love, Frank tries a little blackmail and is shot by mobsters, and Helen's marriage to Frank is revealed and makes her a prime suspect in his murder. A happy ending is achieved by Frank's killer jumping to his death, Sylvia breaking off her engagement and going off on a cruise, and Paul and Helen getting together. Abbott's messy screenplay was based on a story by prolific screenwriter Charles Brackett who probably saw the many problems in his contrived plot and decided not to write the script himself. Abbott's direction is as clear and direct as the screenplay is convoluted. What makes the movie memorable is Colbert's expert performance, one of a handful in the early 1930s that made her a major star.

Acting as a film producer for the first time with **My Sin** (1931), Abbott also directed the tearjerker and played a minor role in the picture. The star was the sultry, temperamental Tallulah Bankhead but she and Abbott got along fine and later that year he worked with her on another movie. *My Sin* was based on a play and there were several hands (including Abbott's) working on the screenplay. The Panama nightclub hostess Carlotta (Bankhead) kills a man in self defense but, because of her bad reputation, no lawyer will represent her except the alcoholic Dick Grady (Fredric March). He surprises himself, Carlotta, and everyone else when he gets her off and suggests she start life anew. So Carlotta moves to New York City and becomes the successful interior decorator Ann Trevor. She also becomes engaged to the monied Larry Gordon (Scott Kolk) without telling him about her past. Dick, who fell in love with Carlotta in Panama, moves to New York and tells her of his feelings. She does not return them and, when revealing the truth about her past to the Gordon family, realizes the marriage would never have worked. A year later, Ann/Carlotta is hired to decorate the house intended for her and Larry and finds out Dick owns it. The two are reunited and Carlotta realizes she loves Dick. *My Sin* was a satisfying "women's picture" and a success for the new producer.

Abbott did not think much of the movie but enjoyed working with Bankhead so he ended his Paramount contract directing her in **The Cheat** (1931), the remake of a melodrama first filmed by Cecil B. DeMille in 1915. Abbott did not write the script and shared directing credit with Berthold Viertel. It is believed that Bankhead was not pleased with Viertel and asked for Abbott's help. The heroine was again a bad lady, Elsa Carlyle, who loses $10,000 in gambling. So that her husband Jeffrey (Harvey Stephens) won't find out, she embezzles money from a charity function and tries to gamble it up to $10,000. Instead she loses it all and goes deeper into debt. The slick businessman Hardy Livingstone (Irving Pichel) lusts after Elsa and offers to settle her gambling debts if she becomes his mistress. She takes

Livingstone's money but, before he can collect on her sexual favors, Elsa tries to repay the money. When Livingstone tries to rape her, Elsa shoots him dead. Jeffrey finds out the whole story and turns himself into the police, saying he killed Livingstone in a jealous rage. But at the trial, Elsa breaks down and tells the truth. Jeffrey is cleared, Elsa is acquitted, and the couple begins to make amends to each other. It was all hot-blooded derring-do in those pre-Code days and audiences loved it. Abbott's direction helped Bankhead give one of her best screen performances.

Abbott turned his back on Hollywood writing, directing, and producing in 1932. He was kept very busy on Broadway and didn't miss films, though the money was more lucrative in movies than on the stage. Several of his play scripts were filmed and re-filmed over the next few decades but Abbott was not involved in the projects. (See the Appendix for the complete statistics on all his films.) As for his Broadway musicals, most of them were filmed and sometimes he acted as director and/or producer. They will be covered in the discussion of those stage works. Abbott's actual Hollywood career as a writer/director/producer only lasted three years (from 1928 to 1931) yet it was significant. If Abbott truly wanted to be practical, he would have stayed in California and become very rich. Instead he chose the theatre and never regretted it.

6 ADDING SONGWRITERS TO THE MIX

(1935–1945)

Jumbo • On Your Toes • The Boys from Syracuse • Too Many Girls • Best Foot Forward • Beat the Band

Considering how popular musicals had always been on Broadway and the large number of them that were presented each season, it might surprise one that Abbott did not get involved with a musical until 1935. This was not totally accidental. Abbott was thought of as the author and director of dramas, melodramas, comedies, and farces. Broadway, then as now, had a habit of typecasting artists into certain categories. It is also unlikely Abbott pursued getting work in musicals. He was smart enough to know that a musical has many elements and these were usually done by several different people. With a non-musical play he had to deal with the producer, the director, and the author, jobs which he often did himself. He liked working with actors; singers and dancers were another breed. With a musical production, Abbott knew he would also have to work with a choreographer, musical director, dance arranger, vocal coaches, and who knows who else. For a man who valued total control, musicals were dangerous.

It was songwriters Richard Rodgers (music) and Lorenz Hart (lyrics) who first approached Abbott about doing a musical. They were impressed with Abbott's brisk, fast-talking, often satirical staging and thought he was ideal for a show they had in mind. It was about a Broadway hoofer who gets entangled with a Russian ballet company. They wanted Abbott to write the book and direct the musical. But before they could secure a producer for what would eventually become *On Your Toes*, the eager impresario Billy Rose approached the team about writing the songs for his "musical extravaganza" ***Jumbo*** (1935) at the Hippodrome Theatre. Built in 1905 as a venue for large-scale entertainment, the 45,000-seat Hippodrome had housed circuses, rodeos, operas, aquacades, and even baseball games. It had fallen on hard times during the Depression and was dark most of the time but Rose envisioned a spectacular program that would bring back the glory days of the huge dinosaur of a theatre.

Jumbo was a musical set in a circus and much of the evening would involve aerialists, animal acts, acrobats, clowns, and a real elephant to play the title character. Rose wanted only the best talent for *Jumbo*. He hired playwrights Ben Hecht and Charles MacArthur for the book (even though they had never written a musical before), Rodgers and Hart for the songs, Paul Whiteman and his orchestra for the onstage band, Jimmy Durante for the laughs, and, to put it all together, John Murray Anderson who was something of an egotistical impresario himself. The script that Hecht and MacArthur came up with was a tired *Romeo and Juliet* tale that was as thin as the Hippodrome was oversized. Rival circus owners Matthew Mulligan (W. J. McCarthy) and John A. Considine (Arthur Sinclair) have always been suspicious of each other so neither is especially happy when Considine's daughter Mickey (Gloria Grafton) and Mulligan's son Matt (Donald Novis) fall in love. Considine already has enough problems, like his drinking and the bankruptcy his circus is facing. His ambitious but inept press agent, Claudius B. Bowers (Jimmy Durante), tries to fix things by burning down Considine's house to collect the insurance. The two lovers solve everything by merging the two circuses into one and securing peace and prosperity. Rose and Murray didn't want too many songs because the book and score were, in their mind, secondary. In fact, Murray told the songwriters that he was not at all interested in either story or songs and planned to not waste much of his time on them. Naturally, this worried Rodgers and Hart who had been striving to make their musicals more cohesive. They told Abbott that *On Your Toes* was put on hold and asked him to direct the book scenes and musical numbers for *Jumbo*. Even though Abbott reminded them that he had no experience in such musical entertainment, they talked him into using *Jumbo* to gain that experience and then they would all go on to do a "real" musical.

Directing *Jumbo* was like trial by fire. Murray insisted on doing the sets, costumes, circus acts, and big dance numbers and left Abbott to stage the story and the Rodgers and Hart songs. The team wrote an excellent score which produced three standards—"My Romance," "Little Girl Blue," and "The Most Beautiful Girl in the World"—as well as "The Circus is on Parade," "Laugh," and "Over and Over Again." But frankly, such delights were lost in the tinsel and sawdust that was *Jumbo*. (The quaint duet "There's a Small Hotel" was cut from the production and surfaced later in *On Your Toes*.) Because Rose would not "give away" the songs for free by allowing radio play of any of the numbers, it took some time for such memorable musical moments to become famous. As for Abbott's contribution, it consisted more of traffic cop than director. But there was one rare tender moment in *Jumbo* that Abbott devised. With the stage washed in blue light, Mickey/Gloria Grafton recalled her childhood and sang "Little Girl Blue" as ghostly images of circus performers danced around her. The official billing for *Jumbo* stated "Entire Production Staged by John Murray Anderson," but in his autobiography *Musical Stages*, Rodgers says it was Abbott who made it all work. "George Abbott was a tall, sharp-featured ramrod of a man who, more than anyone else, was responsible for tying all the disparate elements of the production together."[1] Abbott's thoughts on his entry into musical theatre are not known. In his autobiography, he only discusses how uneasy he felt watching the aerialists, fearful that they would fall to the hard floor and die, so he saw very few performances of *Jumbo*.

Rose spent $350,000 on the production, easily twice what a large musical cost at the time. He convinced Actors' Equity that the show was categorized as a circus rather than a musical so he didn't have to pay the actors during the unheard of rehearsal period of nearly six months. When *Jumbo* opened in November of 1935, the reviews were very enthusiastic. Critics dismissed the book and concentrated on the enjoyable extravaganza, recommending it highly. *Time Magazine* described the experience thusly:

> Last week minuscule Billy Rose finally presented in Manhattan's Hippodrome the spectacle that was supposed to be BIGGER THAN A SHOW, BETTER THAN A CIRCUS. First-nighters were provided with a scale by which to judge the production as soon as they got their tickets, which were precisely nine times the normal size. When they took their seats in what is still the world's fourth largest theatre, they received further premonition of the grandeur that was to come. But when the cylindrical curtain around the protruding ring-stage at last rose, the result could only be described by a word from the lexicon of *Jumbo*'s chief comic Jimmy Durante: 'Colossial!'

The New York Times called it "mumbo-jumbo handsome—original and happily endearing." Audiences came for five months but the large venue was rarely filled and the expensive production made it difficult to meet the weekly operating costs. The whole enterprise closed in the red. It was the last hurrah for the Hippodrome. The venue remained dark for three years then was demolished in 1939. As for *Jumbo*, revivals have been out of the question. The musical wasn't turned into a film until twenty-seven years later. Titled *Billy Rose's Jumbo*, the 1962 MGM movie made some changes in the book and added a few songs, the best ones sung by Doris Day. Durante now played one of the circus owners, Pop Wonder, and he and Martha Raye provided the laughs. It is an enjoyable film and did well at the box office, probably due to the popularity of Day at the time. Abbott had no involvement in the movie.

Abbott, Rodgers, and Hart happily returned to a normal-sized show with **On Your Toes** (1936), Abbott's first fully-directed musical. The project had begun back when Rodgers and Hart were still in Hollywood and they wrote a scenario hoping to interest Fred Astaire in doing it. But the dancing hero they presented was not the top-hatted, "white tie and tails" figure that Astaire felt most comfortable with so he turned it down. Impressed with young Hollywood dancer Ray Bolger, the songwriters turned the proposal into a Broadway musical and the Shubert Brothers took an option on it. It was at this point that Abbott was approached to write and direct. He read Rodgers and Hart's sketchy script, thought it flawed but promising, then pretty much came up with a whole new libretto. Hoofer Phil Dolan Jr. (Bolger) grew up dancing in vaudeville. Years later he is teaching music at Knickerbocker University where his sweetheart Frankie Frayne (Doris Carson) writes songs like "It's Got to Be Love" and his student Sidney Cohn (David Morris) composes modern ballets, such as "Slaughter on Tenth Avenue." Junior convinces the wealthy patroness of the arts Peggy Porterfield (Luella Gear) to get Sergei Alexandrvitch (Monty Woolley) to have his Russian ballet company present the new jazz ballet. During rehearsals the prima ballerina Vera Barnova (Tamara Geva) gets a little too interested in Junior. This causes distress for Frankie and arouses enough anger in Vera's jealous boyfriend-dancing partner Konstantine Morrosine (Demetrios Vilan) that he hires two hit men to shoot Junior when the ballet ends. While Phil is dancing in "Slaughter on Tenth Avenue," he is slipped a note about the murder plot and is instructed to keep dancing no matter what. So Junior keeps dancing until the police arrive and both the ballet and musical can end happily. Both Broadway dancing and European ballet were spoofed, the characters were fun, and the score was outstanding. It was due to Abbott's libretto that the dance numbers were part of the plot and not just musical interruptions. Because there was so much dance in the show, there were fewer songs, yet all were first-rate and the ballads "There's a Small Hotel" and "Glad to Be Unhappy" became standards. More sardonic and playful were "It's Got to Be Love," "The Heart Is Quicker Than the Eye," "The Three B's," "Too Good for the Average Man," and the contagiously repetitive title song. Also, Rodgers' music for the dance sections revealed new facets of his composing talents. Most "ballets" in previous musicals were jazz pieces with modern dance. One only saw true ballet and ballet dancers as specialty acts in Broadway revues. The two extended ballet numbers in *On Your Toes*, the "Princess Zenobia" ballet and the justly-famous "Slaughter on Tenth Avenue," were not highbrow interpolations but witty and even satiric pieces that were, nonetheless, performed by classically trained dancers. The renowned choreographer George Balanchine, who had never worked on a Broadway musical before, was asked to provide all the dance in *On Your Toes* and he was drawn to the project because it allowed him to stage a variety of dance styles.

When the Shuberts' option on the musical ran out, the project was picked up by the successful producer Dwight Deere Wiman. But in the depths of the Depression, Wiman had trouble raising the money and the production was postponed a few times. Abbott got restless, opted out of directing the show, and went to Palm Beach to play golf. Wiman finally got the money and *On Your Toes* went into rehearsals with Worthington Miner directing. He immediately started making book changes and altered the nature of some of the characters. By the time *On Your Toes* started tryouts in Boston, the show was in big trouble. Both Wiman and Rodgers pleaded with Abbott to come to Boston and fix things, arguing that it was his duty to come and save *his* musical. Abbott went to Boston and watched a performance. He later recalled,

> Ray Bolger was sensational in the lead, and 'Slaughter on Tenth Avenue' remains in my memory as one of the best numbers I've ever seen in the theatre, both musically and choreographically. The book, however was a mess. The story had been destroyed by experimenting and the actors were out of hand.[2]

Abbott agreed to "fix" things. Rodgers wrote years later, "All George did was cut out the new material and go back to his original book. And it worked. In almost no time we were right back where we started, and from which we should never had left."[3] *On Your Toes* was the first of eight musicals in which Abbott worked with the prolific designer Jo Mielziner. Wiman hired Mielziner, who already had a reputation for his estimable scenic and lighting designs. The set for *On Your Toes* was in the traditional style of a series of drops that revealed alternately large and small scenes. The nightclub setting for "Slaughter on Tenth Avenue" was particularly impressive, the gaudy joint bathed in red light.

On Your Toes opened on Broadway in April of 1936 and met with even better reviews than *Jumbo*. Special attention this time was paid to the book which critics found "delightfully tongue-in-cheek." Woolcott Gibbs in *The New Yorker* declared, "I don't suppose *On Your Toes* really approaches brilliance anywhere, except perhaps in Ray Bolger's dancing, but I'm sure it's the pleasantest show that's been around in a long time, and that's saying a lot." *Time Magazine* thought it, "A definite milestone in musical theatre." The musical ran 315 performances, an impressive (and profitable) number during hard times. Three years later, Warner–First National made a screen version of *On Your Toes* without Ray Bolger, which was odd since he had already been featured in three movie musicals and had just completed *The Wizard of Oz* (1939). But even Bolger would not have been able to save the hatchet job that Warner Brothers did to *On Your Toes*. None of the songs were sung, some were heard as background music only, and only the (much abridged) ballet music was used. The screenplay was dreary, Eddie Albert was a tiresome Junior, and only Balanchine's choreography featuring Vera Zorina had a spark of life to it. What could have been one of the great movie musicals was botched beyond recognition. Abbott was more than pleased that he had nothing to do with the film.

On Your Toes is considered a landmark musical for its use of dance but it is equally important because it introduced the Abbott libretto. This kind of sassy, smart writing revealed a new facet of Abbott's talents.

Peggy   Sergei, I have a brilliant idea. At first you're not going to like it. A wonderful piece of music has come into my hands for a jazz ballet.

Sergei   I don't hear you so good. Jazz?

Peggy   It will take the public and the critics by surprise.

Sergei   Me too. Never.

Peggy   But you'll be broad-minded. You'll think about it.

Sergei   Certainly I'll think about it. (pause) I thought about it. No. That kind of talk—

Peggy   Your public is sick to death of *Scherezade*, *Le Spectre de la Rose*— They've seen all those Russian turkeys at the Capitol for forty cents. This is something different. It's a jazz ballet. It'll be sensational! They'll say it's art!

Sergei   We will never do this ballet. The Russian ballet has traditions.

Peggy   Who cares?

Sergei   I do! My ballets have been done for our Tsar and the Tsar's father.

Peggy   With the same troupe.

Sergei   I am loyal to my Tsar.

Peggy   Haven't you heard about the Revolution?

Sergei   Yes, but I do not recognize it.[4]

Abbott plotted out his libretto in the same manner in which he directed. He already knew that with multi-set shows, efficiency of time could be attained by writing scenes in such a way as to keep the action moving. Musicals usually had more scenic demands than plays and often involved several locales. He perfected the old practical devise of writing musical scenes "in one." Shorter scenes involving fewer characters are played in front of a curtain or backdrop, while a large, more populated scene is being set up behind. This not only keeps the show lively and facilitates scenery changes but also gives a musical an effective pattern. Full stage spectacle is relieved by simple, more intimate character scenes. It is a pattern that can be traced back to the Greek theatre with its alternating episodes and choral interludes. Under Abbott's writing and directing of musicals, the device reaches its most refined state. In *On Your Toes*, for example, Meilziner's backdrop comes down at the end of a "big" scene and a few of the Broadway dancers enter for some dialogue. They start singing and dancing to the title number then the Russian ballet dancers enter. A dance competition begins, the backdrop rises, and the full stage is available for one of the show's most memorable numbers, a combative ballet in which tap and ballet face off. This kind of writing/directing is present in most of Abbott's subsequent thirty-two musicals. (Two of those productions were revivals of *On Your Toes* which he again directed in 1954 and 1983. They will be discussed in later chapters with other Abbott revivals.) It was probably fortuitous that Abbott's first musicals were with Rodgers and Hart. Along with Cole Porter, the duo brought a sophistication to American musical comedy not seen since the Princess Musicals of the 1910s. Because there was wit and attitude in so many Rodgers and Hart songs, their shows tended to be more "modern" than the usual period musicals and operettas. Abbott's librettos for these Rodgers and Hart musicals are arguably his best, even though some have dated poorly. Of course, their 1930s slang and clichés is what is so charming about them. Let us look at two examples: the readily revivable *The Boys from Syracuse* (1938) and the problematic *Too Many Girls* (1939). Both were written, directed, and produced by Abbott and were hits in their day but they couldn't be more different.

With its tight, solid libretto based on Shakespeare's *The Comedy of Errors* and its scintillating score by Rodgers and Hart, **The Boys From Syracuse** (1938) is one of the most revived of all 1930s musicals. It is also one of the best musical farces in the American theatre. That said, it should be pointed out that there have been very few successful musical farces. And only a handful hold the stage today. Farce depends on a swift pace, broad characters, and lots of plot. Musical numbers tend to interfere with farce. Dancing usually interrupts the story, dream ballets notwithstanding. Abbott, working solo with Shakespeare's original, had plenty of experience writing and directing farce and knew its inherent difficulties. His script for *The Boys from Syracuse* does not depart radically from Shakespeare's plot line. In the ancient city of Ephesus, the master Antipholus (Eddie Albert) and his slave Dromio (Jimmy Savo) arrive from Syracuse and are immediately confused with their twins, the local Antipholus (Ronald Graham) and his slave Dromio (Teddy Hart) who are married to Adriana (Muriel Angelus) and Luce (Wynn Murray), respectively. Complications ensue, especially when the Syracusan Antipholus falls in love with Adriana's sister Luciana. Only after the two Antipholuses's aged father Aegeon (John O'Shaughnessy), who earlier explained how the two sets of twins were separated in a shipwreck, discovers them both in town does everything end happily. It all sounds so simple but, like any good farce, the complications pile up quickly and every cockeyed scene adds to the comedy. Abbott used only one line from *The Comedy of Errors*. When the Seeress quotes "The venom clamours of a jealous woman poisons more deadly than a mad dog's tooth," the clown Dromio sticks his head onto the scene and proclaims, "Shakespeare!"[5] Instead of trying to paraphrase the Elizabethan dialogue, Abbott wrote prose in a slangy, anachronistic manner.

> **Sorcerer**   Oh, the courtesans! There's my public. (**Courtesans** *enter*) Tricks, tricks! Ten cents a trick. Here you are. The Indian rope trick reduced in honor of Mother's Day.

Courtesan Not now, Sorcerer.

Sorcerer How about me dropping in this evening and doing a little entertaining?

Courtesan Well, maybe. I'll ask my secretary. Fatima, what appointments have I this evening?

Secretary Oh, there are some Rotarians in town.

Courtesan Oh, I know. Those dull Senators from Rome. On a cruise. Oh, yes. Well, all right. Sorcerer, drop around later, but don't bother me now.

Sorcerer It will cost you practically nothing. I work on the barter system.[6]

There was more than a touch of vaudeville in the script.

Luce (*to her husband* **Dromio**) Are you a man or a mouse? Well? Squeak up![7]

Hart echoed this silliness in his funny, as well as in his romantic, lyrics. The fact that the sets and costumes were in a cartoonish antiquity style supported the anachronisms in the dialogue. Jo Mielziner again designed the scenery and lighting and again efficiency was the key element. The ancient Roman comedies usually took place on a street with doorways to three houses. But the action in *The Boys from Syracuse* also took place inside the houses. Mielziner designed the large set pieces to slide in from the wings while a backdrop, with (as he described it) "a feeling of a fourteenth-century Tuscan painting, with complete disregard for perspective,"[8] remained behind. Irene Sharaff's costumes similarly conjured up the past but had modern touches. Even the title of the musical was a contemporary joke lost on audiences today. In the 1930s, everyone knew that the powerful Shubert Brothers came from Syracuse, New York.

The inspiration for the show came from Rodgers and Hart who wondered why there were no musicals based on Shakespeare's works. So many musicals taken from the Bard's plays have been presented since 1938 that one must remember that it was an original idea with *The Boys from Syracuse*. The songwriters considered several of Shakespeare's comedies and settled on *The Comedy of Errors* because of the importance of twins in the plot. Hart's brother Teddy, a funny character actor, was always being mistaken for the comic Jimmy Savo, both of them being short and rather dumpy. It was ideal casting for the two Dromios. Rodgers recalls in *Musical Stages*,

When we started talking about a director for this kind of musical farce, we could come up with only one name: George Abbott. Moreover, George was so enthusiastic that he decided to produce the show himself. At first Larry and I were supposed to collaborate on the script with him, but he had it all finished before we could get started ... neither Larry or I wanted to change a line.[9]

Neither did Abbott want to make many changes during the rehearsal process. "Everything in the show fell into place so easily," Abbott later wrote. "I don't recall changing the order of any numbers or adding any material once we began to perform the play."[10] The only problem that arose was Lorenz Hart, who was drinking heavily, missing rehearsals, and couldn't be found during the out-of-town tryouts. Luckily the score was in great shape and lyric rewrites were not needed. *The Boys from Syracuse* boasts one of Rodgers and Harts' brightest scores. "Falling in Love with Love" and "This Can't Be Love" were instant hits but the song that brought the house down each night was the swinging trio "Sing for Your Supper." Also outstanding is the mock revival number "Oh, Diogenes," the soft-shoe "Dear Old Syracuse," the comic duet "What Can You Do with a Man?," and the expository opening "I Had Twins." George Balanchine again served as choreographer but there were fewer dances than in *On Your Toes*, the second act ballet "Big Brother" being the notable exception.

The Boys from Syracuse opened on Broadway in November of 1938 to another round of rave notices. The *New York World Telegram* was so bold as to write, "I believe it will be regarded as the greatest musical comedy of its time. Richard Watts, Jr., in the *New York Herald Tribune* stated, "If you have been wondering all these years just what was wrong with *The Comedy of Errors*, it is now possible to tell you. It has been waiting for a score by Rodgers and Hart and direction by George Abbott." Robert Benchley in *Life Magazine* was in the minority, finding the musical entertaining but not any kind of a landmark. "George Abbott has given it one of those productions which make you sure you are witnessing a hit," he wrote, "even if you don't happen to be." *The Boys from Syracuse* ran a profitable ten months on Broadway. Yet the musical did not join the repertory of revived musicals until a charming 1963 production Off-Broadway. This faithful version (no outside Rodgers and Hart songs were added) ran nearly twice as long as the original and allowed *The Boys From Syracuse* to become a revival favorite. It also created enough interest for the first British mounting of the musical in 1963 at London's Drury Lane Theatre, leading to productions in Australia and Germany in the 1960s, followed by others wherever American musicals are enjoyed. *The Boys From Syracuse* was revived on Broadway in 2002. Despite a strong cast, the production received lukewarm notices and was not extended beyond its seventy-three-performance engagement. Like *On Your Toes*, the 1940 film version of *The Boys from Syracuse* was a misbegotten disaster. The screenplay reduced the tale to a 73-minute sketch. The garish production, complete with cigar-smoking citizens of antiquity and chariots checkered like modern taxicabs, was neither humorous nor popular. The Rodgers and Hart score was decimated; some songs were cut, some numbers reduced to background music, and others edited to the point of becoming teasers. The whole enterprise was so dreary that the film buried the original show in the minds of many for decades. Once again, Abbott was happily uninvolved in the Universal movie.

The process of putting together his first three musicals with Rodgers and Hart was relatively painless. Abbott later noted, "At this stage in my career, musical comedy seemed very easy to me. I was as yet unaware of its trials and tribulations."[11] These would come with **Too Many Girls** (1939). Screenwriter George Marion, Jr., wrote the college musical as a Hollywood project but the film was never made. Abbott read the script and brought it to Rodgers and Hart as a possibility for a Broadway musical. Why?, one might ask. It was a tired tale about college athletes, pretty coeds, and the Big Game. What clouded Abbott's vision was the fact that one of the characters was a Cuban musician and singer. By this time, Abbott had fallen in love with Cuba and often vacationed there between projects. He relished the idea of working with the Cuban nightclub performers Desi Arnaz and Diosa Costello and got Rodgers and Hart excited about the idea. Surprisingly, Abbott went with Marion's script when he obviously could have come up with a better libretto himself. The wealthy Harvey Casey (Clyde Fillmore) of Skohegan, Maine, has a wild daughter, Consuelo (Marcy Westcott), so when he sends her to Stop Gap, New Mexico, to attend school at Pottawatomie College, he secretly hires four All-American football players to enroll as well and keep an eye on her. Clint Kelley (Richard Kollmar) arrives in New Mexico with his pals Jojo Jordan (Eddie Bracken), Al Terwilliger (Hal LeRoy), and Manuelito (Arnaz), and when they are put on the football team the college starts winning. Clint and Consuelo fall in love, just as the other three men are getting romantically involved with coeds, but on the night before the big game Consuelo finds out why Clint is really there and plans to return home. Since Clint and the boys have orders to stick to Consuelo, they will all miss the crucial football game if they follow her. Consuelo is finally convinced that Clint really loves her, everyone stays in New Mexico, and Pottawatomie is victorious on the field. Broadway had seen more than its fair share of college musicals over the decades and *Too Many Girls* offered nothing new. (Even the title of the show sounded like a tired escapist frolic for the tired businessman.) Yet the show had three things in its favor: another sprightly score by Rodgers and Hart, a cast filled with young and exciting talent, and Abbott's astute direction which was noted by the critics for its swift pace and efficient staging. It is more than likely that such qualities were needed to keep audiences from dwelling on the lackluster plot. The characters were also trite but the press and the audience loved Bracken, Arnaz, Kollmar, and LeRoy and didn't get weary of their predictable college antics. As for the score, the runaway hit was the intoxicating ballad "I Didn't Know What Time It Was" but there was exceptional lyric work in the comic numbers as well and Rodgers' Latin-flavored music was fresh and contagious. "Give It Back to the Indians," "I Like to Recognize the Tune," "Love Never Went to College," "Spic and Spanish," and "She Could Shake the Maracas" were among the musical highlights.

Too Many Girls did not have an easy birth. Hart's drinking was worse than ever and this time he was needed during rehearsals and tryouts since many changes were being made. But often Hart was not to be found. Abbott recalls that Rodgers had to write the lyric for at least one song. Jo Mielziner again did sets and costumes and he had fun creating large adobe structures to suggest the campus in a desert setting. Robert Alton was the choreographer this time around and he was able to provide some spirited Latin dance numbers. But mostly they were unmotivated specialty acts and *Too Many Girls* ended up being pretty much a routine patch job. The creative staff was surprised when the reviews were so laudatory, particularly Abbott who as producer had much to gain from a musical hit. The reason for its appeal is explained in Burns Mantle's summing up of the season in the *Best Plays of 1939–1940*: "The first musical comedy hit of the year . . . here was a cast studded with talent, a better than average book . . . and an agreeably clean entertainment that missed being stuffy. The combination richly deserved the season's run it got."[12] The show had a healthy run of 249 performances on Broadway and toured with success but has rarely been revived over the years. This time Abbott was involved with the movie version, making his movie musical directing debut. The 1940 RKO picture featured Bracken, Arnaz, and LeRoy from the original company and Van Johnson from the tour, all making their film debuts. With half of the Broadway score carried over as well, it was a very faithful rendering of the stage hit. Lucille Ball (dubbed by Trudy Erwin) and Richard Carlson were Consuelo and Clint; Ball/Erwin got to sing the pleasing new Rodgers and Hart ballad "You're Nearer." Ann Miller and Frances Langford were among the coeds and both got to show off their dancing and singing talents with the Broadway cast members. The movie was choreographed by LeRoy Prinz and, with no major changes to the story, the film ended up being the most accurate transfer of a Rodgers and Hart musical to the screen. That said, it is not an exceptional musical by any means. Abbott directed with verve but the film is edited poorly and seems sluggish. Also, the performances are disappointing, with no chemistry between Carlson and Ball. (It seems any romantic sparks that were taking place backstage were between Ball and Arnaz who first met on the set and married a few months later.)

In 1941, Abbott again served as director and producer on a musical that he didn't write. **Best Foot Forward** also had an academic setting, this time a preppy high school, and it also was a hit. The score was by Hugh Martin and Ralph Blane (each wrote both music and lyrics) and John Cecil Holm penned the libretto inspired by an episode from his school days. Bud Hooper (Gil Stratton, Jr.), a student at Winsocki Prep School, invites movie star Gale Joy (Rosemary Lane) to his high school prom and, to his surprise, she accepts. It is all a publicity stunt set up by Gale's press agent Jack Haggerty (Marty May) to boost up her sagging career. Bud's excitement over his date with Joy angers his girlfriend Helen Schlessinger (Maureen Cannon) and the whole campus goes Hollywood crazy. The night of the prom, chaos erupts as the jealous girls tear Joy's gown to shreds on the dance floor. Haggerty gets Joy safely away and Bud and Helen make up. Abbott liked the script and cast the show mostly with unknowns, two of whom would not be unknown for long. June Allyson and Nancy Walker shone in supporting roles but the entire cast was young and exciting. Again one wonders why Abbott chose such a routine musical to present on Broadway. He did like working with new talent and Holm's script was not without merit. Also, Abbott wanted to hire Gene Kelly, the *Pal Joey* of the year before, to choreograph the musical before he headed to Hollywood. Richard Rodgers, weary of waiting for Lorenz Hart to get to work on something, ended up co-producing *Best Foot Forward* but he insisted on not being credited, knowing it would upset Hart.

For a campus musical, *Best Foot Forward* broke the mold by concentrating on a big dance rather than a football game. Ironically, the most famous song from the show is the rousing school fight song "Buckle Down, Winsocki." (Rodgers is credited with coming up with the fictitious name for the school.) The whole Martin-Blane score is excellent and undeservedly little known today. Other highlights include the fervent "That's How I Love the Blues," the slangy "Just a Little Joint with a Juke Box," the torch song "Ev'ry Time," the lament "The Guy Who Brought Me (Can't Send Me)," and the jumping "The Three B's" about barrelhouse, boogie-woogie, and the blues. The vivacious score shouted "youth" and Abbott directed the musical with an energy that matched the young cast. Because most of the characters were prep-school age, Abbott was able to hire a cast of inexpensive unknown actors who were too young to be drafted. Abbott and Kelly were the only familiar names on the bill so *Best Foot Forward* was considered a surprise hit. (Martin and Blane would not find fame until the film *Meet Me in St. Louis* three years later.) The critics declared the musical an escapist frolic, something audiences wanted even more than ever once America went to war two months after the opening. In *The New Yorker*, Wolcott Gibbs wrote, "George Abbott took us all right back to prep school and, forbidding as this excursion may sound, it was really quite a lot of fun." *Best Foot Forward* ran a profitable 326 performances and Abbott and Rodgers sold the movie right to MGM for a tidy sum. Neither was involved with the 1943 film but it must have pleased them to see much of the Broadway cast hired for the screen version. Because of the war, Winsocki was changed to a military academy but much else remained the same. Lucille Ball (this time her singing dubbed by Martha Mears) played herself as the visiting movie star and Tommy Dix, who had a supporting role on Broadway, graduated to the leading character of Bud. Arthur Freed produced the film, Edward Buzzell directed, and Charles Walters did the energetic choreography. *Best Foot Forward* has been infrequently revived on stage over the decades, though there was a notable Off-Broadway production in 1963 which ran 224 performances. It also featured a cast of unknowns with a promising future, including Liza Minnelli, Paula Wayne, and Christopher Walken (who was then going by the name Ronald Walken).

Abbott next explored the world of swing bands with **Beat the Band** (1942) but, according to him, the show was destroyed by a series of mistakes on his part. As the producer, director, and co-author, it was really difficult to blame anyone else. He did make a wise choice in hiring the acclaimed music arranger and composer Johnny Green who had just returned East from Hollywood. And it was a good idea to put Green's full orchestra on stage and for them to cut loose in the nightclub scenes. This was music more to be danced to or listened to with tapping feet rather than sung to. Two numbers stood out: the red hot "The Steam Is on the Beam" (set in a boiler room, no less) and the frenetic "America Loves a Band." But it was the book, which Abbott co-wrote with George Marion, Jr., from *Too Many Girls*, that was the problem. It was more than thin; it was nearly nonexistent. An heiress from the Caribbean, Querida (Susan Miller), comes to New York and looks up the address where her godfather lives, only to find that it is occupied by band leader Damon Dillingham (Jack Whiting). The two fall into a romance which is interrupted by some bumbling gangsters, annoying detectives, and a comic press agent (Jerry Lester). Even Green's band members were thrown into the mix, such as the notable trumpet player Leonard Sues and drummer Johnny Mack playing themselves and adding some schtick.

Leonard Sues Want to go bowling?

Johnny Mack I can't. I got a date with your wife.

Leonard Sues Why don't you try and get away later?[13]

It was quite clear by the time *Beat the Band* was trying out in New Haven that the show was in big trouble but Abbott stubbornly persevered and kept trying to fix it. When the press agent informed him that he could cancel the production photographer and save some money, Abbott fumed. Even after *Beat the Band* opened in New York, Abbott continued to tinker with the book and some of the stage business. After nine weeks, he pulled the plug on the production. "It was the poorest job of producing and directing that I ever did," Abbott wrote years later. "I was guilty of mistake after mistake. The first mistake was in thinking that it was any good; the second was in casting; and the third and biggest was in not abandoning it when it obviously was a failure."[14] Ironically, the reviews for *Beat the Band* were not that bad. Most critics accepted the musical as the kind of mindless, escapist entertainment that war-weary audiences wanted. Brooks Atkinson in the *Times* wrote, "Although *Beat the Band* was not one of Mr. Abbott's most triumphant festivals, it is fresh, interesting and overflowing with vitality." Lawrence Perry in the *Washington Star* was much more enthusiastic: "Here is a joyous, dynamic, tuneful, deftly constructed piece involving a host of lovely, talented girls, risible comedians, amazing dancers of both sexes—in brief, all you need to send you forth into the midtown dimout with an enlivening sense of having been well entertained." A sour note was expressed by critic George Jean Nathan, in his *The Theatre Book of The Year, 1942–1943*, when he wrote about *Beat the Band*. "The attitude of a portion of our theatrical producers seems to be that what people want in war time is not serious drama but entertainment, and then not providing it."[15] The house was rarely full but the show ran nine weeks.

Throughout the 1940s, Nathan headed a one-man crusade criticizing Abbott at every turn. Of course, the acerbic critic had many other targets as well. He was a tricky man to figure out. Nathan was clearly highbrow; he had attended Harvard and took George Pierce Baker's famous drama course. But sometimes the lowest form of entertainment pleased Nathan greatly. (In 1943, he preferred *Something for the Boys* to *Oklahoma!*) He never missed an opportunity to disparage not only Abbott's writing but his directing as well. Abbott, on the other hand, only saw reviews as "money" notices or "closing" notices. It was business, not personal. "I think critics are people like the rest of us," he wrote in his autobiography.

> [They have] the same anxieties, loyalties, prejudices, headaches and ambitions. Disappointed playwrights, some people call them. Is that bad? I don't think so. It only means that a love of the theatre has been turned into another channel. The critics have great power, it is true, and they can destroy a play. But in my opinion the plays they destroy usually deserve it; in fact, I believe that there is more justice in accusing them of being soft than in accusing them of being destructive. In certain respects they seem to me very vulnerable."[16]

Of course he is referring to a time when there were many New York City newspapers and many critics. The era of the all-powerful *New York Times* came after he wrote those words in 1963.

Just as bumpy as his career had been of late, so too was Abbott's personal life. For several years he was involved with a married woman, the successful model and fashion designer, Neysa McMein. It was a volatile relationship at times and, although the two boldly appeared together in high society and in travel junkets around the world, marriage seemed far from either of their minds. On the contrary, when Abbott met the actress Mary Sinclair in 1946, he was immediately smitten and they were soon married. The marriage lasted until 1951 when it ended with an amicable divorce.

7 ENTERTAINING THE HOMEFRONT

(1942–1945)

Jason • *Sweet Charity* • *Kiss & Tell* • *Get Away, Old Man* • *A Highland Fling* • *Snafu*

Just as some of Abbott's second-rate musicals found an audience during wartime, so too did some of his comedies have profitable runs even when the reviews were not always favorable. There was much less activity on Broadway during World War Two and playgoers looking for escapist entertainment often found they had few choices. At the same time, theatre attendance was down, many male actors and other artists were serving in the military and were not available, and money for live theatre was tight. So producing on Broadway for the first half of the 1940s was tricky. Abbott was involved with nine comedies during the war years but only once did he benefit from the scarcity of light comedies and have a major hit.

The comedy *Jason* (1942) opened six weeks after the attack on Pearl Harbor and playgoers wanted something light and escapist so it was a modest success. Abbott produced the Samson Raphaelson script but, atypically, did not direct it. He let the author himself stage *Jason* which was about a theatre critic and a playwright. Those expecting a savage satire on the theatre profession were disappointed; the play was a harmless trifle. Snide theatre critic Jason Otis (Alexander Knox) is challenged by the young, idealistic playwright Mike Ambler (Nicholas Conte) to get out of his comfortable home and see the real world so that his reviews are more valid. Jason takes up the challenge, meets some colorful characters on the streets of Manhattan, and then learns that Ambler is having an affair with his wife Lisa (Helen Walker). Jason's review of Mike's new play is more vicious than usual but, when Lisa returns to him and says she loves him, Jason writes a more balanced critique before press time. As smug and egotistical as Jason was, Raphaelson did not write him as a caricature. The idealistic Mike, on the other hand, was an overbearing, preachy playwright and many playgoers saw him as a spoof of the outspoken writer William Saroyan. What most amused the press about *Jason* was the depiction of a theatre critic living in a plush house where at his leisure he dictates his reviews to his secretary (Ellen Hall). Veteran critic John Mason Brown in the *World-Telegram* pointed out, "I have not dictated a review at midnight in the luxurious fashion of *Jason* for exactly forty-one years. Neither, I suspect, have any of my confreres. Nor do drama critics drink sherry when they foregather. Or live as snugly as the over-fastidious Jason does in a country house in the city without a typewriter in sight." The notices for *Jason* were not pans but neither did they strongly recommend the play. Audiences thought otherwise and kept it on the boards for four months. Abbott must have been relieved when he only directed the comedy **Sweet Charity** (1942) rather than serve as its producer because it closed in a week. The Irving Brecher and Manuel Seff play centered on a ladies group, the Friendly Hand Club in a small Connecticut town, who are raising money for a nursery for children whose mothers are working for the war effort. The ladies hire the bandleader King Cole to play for a charity dance but are unable to pay him his $2,500 fee when a lawyer takes the money for a lawsuit involving the nursery. So the ladies pull off a few minor swindles and illegal shenanigans to get out of their jam. The only memorable scene in the comedy occurred when one of the ladies shares with her friends some cigarettes she accidentally took from the band's drummer. Since the cigarettes are marijuana, the ladies become quite uninhibited before the night is over, serving tea in a watering can, pouring it into a man's fedora hat, dancing the jitterbug, and even attempting to go swimming in the water cooler. Abbott directed the farcical scene with abandon and the prim ladies cutting loose was indeed hilarious. But one prankish scene in a tedious play does not spell success. George Jean Nathan led the naysayers in his chronicle of the season, continuing his dislike of Abbott's work: "As usual, Mr. Abbott relied upon his established brand of grasshopper direction, jumping and scooting the actors all over the stage, to invest his lifeless exhibit with an aspect of inner vitality."[1] The title *Sweet Charity* had been used on Broadway for a 1930 drama that closed after three performances; this time the title served for eight performances. Both were long forgotten by 1966 when *Sweet Charity* again appeared on a Broadway marquee for a successful musical which had nothing to do with the Abbott play.

Abbott's biggest non-musical hit during this period, indeed one of the biggest of his entire career, was the wartime comedy **Kiss and Tell** (1943) by F. Hugh Herbert. Years later, Abbott recalled: "Some plays need work, but once in a while one comes along that is, as they say, a natural. *Kiss and Tell* was one of these; there was scarcely anything to do except polish it."[2] Teenager Mildred Pringle (Judith Parrish) secretly marries her neighbor Lenny Archer (Richard Widmark), a lieutenant in the Air Force, and tells no one but Lenny's sister Corliss (Joan Caulfield) whom she swears to secrecy. The Archers and Pringle parents have not been on speaking terms ever since the time Corliss talked Mildred into working the kissing booth at the fair. When Mildred learns she is pregnant, Corliss accompanies her to the obstetrician and a neighbor sees only Corliss leaving the office. Rumors quickly spread that Corliss is pregnant and that the young introvert Dexter Franklin (Robert White) is the father. Mildred's father Harry (Robert Keith) confronts Dexter, who thinks the father is referring to the time he and Mildred slapped each. Dexter assures Mr. Archer that it was all in fun and that it won't happen again. When Lenny gets leave from the Air Force, he returns to town to say he has received a medal. The marriage is made public, Mildred announces that she's pregnant, and everything is straightened out. The sit-com piece was mildly endorsed by the press as a harmless and satisfying comedy, *Time* magazine calling it "another comfortable suburban hit." Wolcott Gibbs, writing in *The New Yorker*, was more critical. "George Abbott clearly has a way with children, just as he has with fairly childish plots. *Kiss and Tell* is largely populated by adolescents and its basic design isn't much more mature than *The Three Bears*." George Jean Nathan, in his *The Theatre Book of The Year, 1942–1943*, summed up the situation with, "In short, a successful Broadway box-office show not without some humorous merit, but less an authentic comedy of youngsterhood than an artfully maneuvered comic strip."[3] *Kiss and Tell* was an instant success with the public. It ran over two years on Broadway and spawned three road companies. As both producer and director, Abbott found himself sitting on a gold mine. He sold the film rights to Columbia for a hefty sum (Shirley Temple starred as Corliss in the 1945 movie) and the play was a favorite with all kinds of theatre groups for years. Today *Kiss and Tell* is probably too tame for audiences but during the war it was considered refreshing and thoroughly entertaining.

Playwright William Saroyan must have forgiven Abbott for the way he was lampooned in the hit comedy *Jason* because Saroyan entrusted Abbott to direct his own comedy, **Get Away, Old Man** (1943). On the other hand, he turned to Abbott only after being rejected by four other producers. It was a spoof of Hollywood's ways and means and was filled with bigger-than-life characters. "It had very obvious faults," Abbott later wrote, "but my admiration for the author was so great that I decided to produce it, faults and all."[4] Hired by Hollywood producer Patrick Hammer (Ed Begley) to write a movie inspired from the hymn "Ave Maria," eccentric writer Harry Bird (Richard Widmark) wastes his time in Tinsel Town getting drunk with his cynical new pal Sam (Glenn Anders), dating the would-be movie actress Martha Harper (Beatrice Pearson), and complaining about any changes or suggestions that the studio autocrats make about his screenplay. Harry finally gives up on Hollywood and returns home to San Francisco where he waits for further inspiration. Saroyan first approached producer-director Eddie Dowling, who had had a hit with the playwright's *The Time of Your Life* (1939). Dowling insisted on several changes but Saroyan refused and offered the play to Billy Rose and then Michael Meyerberg, both of whom turned it down. Producer Mike Todd was interested but also asked for changes. A frustrated Saroyan agreed, made the changes requested, then Todd dropped the project. It was then that the playwright went to Abbott who agreed to produce and direct *Get Away, Old Man* if further changes were made. Saroyan conceded, eliminating characters and even changing the ending. "With all his great gifts for words, Saroyan is not very good at construction," Abbott noted. "*Get Away, Old Man* did not hold together as a story and failed."[5] The press agreed, though many enjoyed the colorful Saroyan characters. Even Abbott's sharp direction could not save the comedy. Lewis Nichols in the *New York Times* wrote, "Mr. Abbott, who is one of the best directors in the business, has done what he could to give the play life, but life is not inherently there." Critic George Jean Nathan, who had read Saroyan's original manuscript, felt that every change made in the script on the way to Broadway further destroyed the charm of the original. He blamed Abbott for that and for his direction. "Strangely enough for the customarily ebullient Mr. Abbott, [he] paced the comedy in terms of [Russian playwright Maxim] Gorki, [and] lost sight entirely of the delicately vagrant mood in which Saroyan writes."[6] Abbott had to close the play after only thirteen performances.

Running only two weeks longer was **A Highland Fling** (1944), a fantasy-comedy by Margaret Curtis set in a remote village near the foot of Cairn McGorum in Scotland. Although he has been dead for 150 years, Scotsman Charlie MacKenzie (Ralph Forbes) was such a womanizer in life that he cannot get into heaven unless he does one good deed. So Charlie returns to earth as a ghost only seen by children and "dafties," such as the town's lovable lunatic, the Lady of Shalott, known as Silly Shally (played by author Margaret Curtis). Charlie does his good deed when he reforms the nasty sinner Rabbie MacGregor (Karl Swenson). Although this gets Charlie into heaven, he finds he doesn't like it there. Bidding his angel-wife Jeannie (Frances Reid) farewell, Charlie returns to earth to be with Silly Shally but, it turns out, the crazy woman doesn't remember him. Abbott produced and directed the large-cast, multi-set play which had tryouts out-of-town but was delayed in coming to Broadway because a playhouse with enough backstage space was not available. Eventually the Plymouth Theatre was secured and *A Highland Fling* opened to mixed reviews. Some critics thought the premise was a good idea but was unfulfilled. Others thought the play wavered between a fantasy, as with the ghosts, and a whimsical comedy, as with the characters in the local watering hole. Nichols in the *Times* wrote,

> In directing, Mr. Abbott has put his best foot in the pub scenes, but has not given some of the others enough gaiety or speed... Perhaps it is only a child or a daftie who can talk properly to a ghost; from all events, from an alien corner, *A Highland Fling* did not seem to be expressing itself as well as it might.

On the other hand, Nathan in his chronicle of the season, thought it "an exceptional play from the hands of a novice... combining originality, imagination and humor, it amounts in the aggregate to a refreshingly witty and winsome fantastic conceit."[7] Not surprisingly, Nathan thought Abbott was at fault. "The less deliberate reviews were confused into attributing to the author the heaviness of treatment for which [Abbott] was largely responsible."[8] When the notices were not auspicious, Abbott had to close the play after twenty-eight performances.

The wartime farce *Snafu* (1944) was more to the public's liking. Like *Kiss and Tell*, this was a comedy set on the Home Front during the war and managed to avoid any of the anxiety about the latest news from the battle lines. Screenwriters Louis Solomon and Harold Buchman were the authors and Abbott again produced and directed. The patriotic youth Ronald Stevens (Billy Redfield) enlisted in the army by lying about his age. Although he has been serving in the Pacific and has reached the rank of Sergeant, Ronald's mother (Elspeth Eric) informs the army that he is underage and she does not give her permission for Ronald to serve. Told by his superiors that "your mama wants you," Ronald is sent back to his California hometown where he is miserable. He tries to run the Stevens household like a military operation and hopes to impress his former sweetheart Kate Hereford (Bethel Leslie) with the bloody Japanese flag and suicide sword he obtained as souvenirs. Both efforts fail and he is embarrassed to be seen around town. When his army friend Danny Baker (Dort Clark) is on furlough and comes to visit Ronald, the pal gets drunk and breaks into the girls' dormitory. Although Danny escapes without being recognized and leaves town, Ronald is blamed for the incident. The whole town is against him until word comes that Ronald has been decorated with the Purple Heart for valor. Realizing that their son will not be happy unless he gets back in the army, his mother and father (Russell Hardie) finally give him permission to enlist legally. The title of the play was an acronym for "Situation Normal—All Fouled Up" but to anyone in the military it was more bluntly translated as "Situation normal, all fucked up." *Snafu* boasted a strong cast and Abbott was applauded by the press for his light-handed but firm directing. Gibbs in *The New Yorker* wrote that *Snafu* "amused me only fitfully" and went on to say, "the trouble is that the play has no really continuous mood. Sometimes it is a straight comedy of adolescence and sometimes—thanks, no doubt to the guiding hand of George Abbott—it is plain, old-fashioned roughhouse farce, relying on the sort of characters and devices that have served Mr. Abbott so handsomely in the past." Similarly, Nathan offered faint praise writing that Abbott and the authors "managed a farce-comedy periodically not without amusement."[9] Audiences enjoyed the domestic farce for five months.

Completing the list of Abbott's wartime plays were three productions he directed—*Mr. Cooper's Left Hand*, *Twilight Bar*, and *One Shoe Off*—all of which closed in 1945 during their tryout engagements. It was indeed a precarious time for the theatre. Looking at the plays in this chapter, one finds a common element. None of them were challenging endeavors, not in the writing, acting, directing, or even the playgoing. It is certainly a challenge to turn a poor play into a hit, there is no question. But these were works in which no one, least of all Abbott, aimed very high. One could blame it on the times. Did audiences want to be challenged? Probably not. But does that mean Abbott's mediocre work during this period can be excused? Did he really care more about playing golf in Florida in the winter than the theatre? As we will see in the future, Abbott did a lot of mediocre and even poor work because the only thing handed to him was inferior material. But he was at the top of his game in the war years so why such malaise? Fortunately, Abbott was involved with several musicals throughout the 1940s that did pose a challenge. Some these were successful by any standard, but even those which were not offered opportunities to do something admirable.

1. GEORGE ABBOTT This photo portrait was taken in 1925, the year in which Abbott's career took off when he co-wrote and co-directed the comedy hit *The Fall Guy* with James Gleason. *Photofest*

2. *ALL QUIET ON THE WESTERN FRONT* (1930) The German youth Paul (Lew Ayres) finds himself in a shell crater with a dying French soldier (Raymond Griffith). Abbott did screenplay rewrites for this classic First World War film, the most famous movie he ever worked on. He received an Oscar nomination for his efforts. *Photofest*

3. *TWENTIETH CENTURY* (1932) The impresario Oscar Jaffe (Gregory Ratoff, standing) must convince the film star Lilly Garland (Eugenie Leonvotich) to forget her fiancé George (Roy Roberts) and sign with him. The Ben Hecht-Charles MacArthur farce took place mostly on a train, causing some intriguing staging limitations and possibilities for director Abbott. *Photofest*

4. *THREE MEN ON A HORSE* (1937) The high-strung gambler Patsy (Sam Levene, far left) tells the meek greeting card poet Erwin (William Lynn) that if he keeps picking winning race horses, they will all be rich. Mabel (Shirley Booth) and Charlie (Horace MacMahon) totally agree. *Photofest*

5. *JUMBO* (1935) Abbott's first musical was a colossal circus musical that filled the huge stage of the Hippodrome Theatre. He directed the book scenes and the songs which took a back seat to the circus acts. Albert Johnson designed the over-sized scenery. *Photofest*

6. *ON YOUR TOES* (1936) Ray Bolger (kneeling) gets caught up in the roughhouse ballet "Slaughter on Tenth Avenue," the climax of this legendary musical that mixed ballet and jazz dance. The two speakeasy denizens fighting to the music are Tamara Geva and George Church. George Balanchine's choreography has been kept alive by the American Ballet Theatre. *Photofest*

7. *THE BOYS FROM SYRACUSE* (1938) The first successful musical based on a Shakespeare play, this Rodger and Hart show was produced, written, and directed by Abbott. Jo Mielziner designed the sets and Irene Sharaff the costumes. *Photofest*

8. *PAL JOEY* (1940) Gene Kelly became a Broadway star playing the incorrigible Joey Evans in this landmark musical produced and directed by Abbott. Soon after, Kelly went to Hollywood and never again appeared in a Broadway musical. *Photofest*

9. *BEST FOOT FORWARD* (1941) In this posed rehearsal shot, Abbott (wearing a tie) watches a scene he's staged. Left to right are cast members Victoria Schools, June Allyson, Kenneth Bowers, and Rosemary Lane in a clinch with an unidentified actor. Abbott also produced the collegiate musical. *Photofest*

10. *KISS AND TELL* (1943) Lieutenant Lenny Archer (Richard Widmark) asks his teenage sister Corliss (Joan Caulfield) to keep his marriage to Mildred Pringle a secret but she looks hesitant. Abbott produced and directed the war-time escapist comedy which ran two years on Broadway. *Photofest*

11. *ON THE TOWN* (1944) Sailors on leave explore Times Square in the landmark dance musical directed by Abbott and choreographed by Jerome Robbins. The clever scenic design was by Oliver Smith and the costumes by Alvin Colt. *Photofest*

12. *HIGH BUTTON SHOES* (1947) One of the most memorable dance pieces of the 1940s was the Mack Sennett ballet choreographed by Jerome Robbins which was inspired by the silent-screen comedies. Abbott directed the musical which had scenery by Oliver Smith and costumes by Miles White. *Photofest*

13. *WHERE'S CHARLEY?* (1948) Ray Bolger donned a dress and became a Broadway star in this musical farce based on the British comedy *Charley's Aunt*. Abbott wrote the libretto and directed the show and David Ffolkes designed the sets and costumes. *Photofest*

14. *CALL ME MADAM* (1950) Ethel Merman and Russell Nype stopped the show each night singing the contrapuntal (or double) song "You're Just in Love," Irving Berlin's last great composition. Abbott directed the political satire which ran two years. *Photofest*

15. *A TREE GROWS IN BROOKLYN* (1951) Johnny Nolan (Johnny Johnston) comes home in the middle of the night and is confronted by his wife Katie (Marcia Van Dyke) and his sister-in-law Cissy (Shirley Booth). Abbott produced, directed, and co-wrote the libretto, one of the most serious musicals of his career. *Photofest*

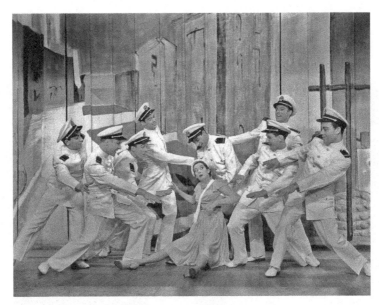

16. *WONDERFUL TOWN* (1952) When struggling journalist Ruth Sherwood (Rosalind Russell) tries to interview some visiting Brazilian sailors, all they want to do is to dance the conga. Abbott directed the musical which was choreographed by Donald Saddler with scenery and costumes by Raoul Pene du Bois. *Photofest*

17. *THE PAJAMA GAME* (1954) Manager Sid Sorokin (John Raitt) and union rep Babe Williams (Janis Paige) take time off from negotiating and enjoy the company picnic. The chorine poking her head into the shot is Shirley MacLaine. Abbott directed and co-wrote the musical, his first to run over one thousand performances. *Photofest*

18. *DAMN YANKEES* (1955) Gwen Verdon's first starring role on Broadway was the Devil's assistant Lola who tries to seduce the baseball slugger Joe Hardy (Stephen Douglass) in the locker room. Abbott co-wrote and directed the Faust musical and Bob Fosse provided the ingenious choreography. *Photofest*

19. *FIORELLO!* (1959) Fiorello La Guardia (Tom Bosley) campaigns for mayor of New York City in the Pulitzer Prize-winning musical based on the life of the beloved "little flower." Abbott co-wrote the libretto and directed the musical, the first outing by songwriters Sheldon Harnick and Jerry Bock. *Photofest*

20. *ONCE UPON A MATTRESS* (1959) Prince Dauntless (Joe Bova) finally finds a princess to his liking in the character of the hapless Winnifred (Carol Burnett). Abbott directed the fairy tale musical for adults and Joe Layton did the spirited choreography. Scenic design and costumes by William and Jean Eckart. *Photofest*

21. *A FUNNY THING HAPPENED ON THE WAY TO THE FORUM* (1962) The Roman slave Pseudolus (Zero Mostel, far right) believes "Everybody Ought to Have a Maid" and agreeing with him are (left to right) Lycus (John Carradine), Hysterium (Jack Gilford), and Senex (David Burns). Abbott directed the musical farce, the first Broadway show with both music and lyrics by Stephen Sondheim. *Photofest*

22. *NEVER TOO LATE* (1962) Harry Lambert (Paul Ford, seated) doesn't know what to make of things when his wife Edith (Maureen O'Sullivan) is expecting a late-in-life baby. The Lambert's son-in-law Charlie (Orson Bean) is amused by the situation. Abbott directed the domestic comedy which ran over one thousand performances on Broadway. *Photofest*

23. *FLORA, THE RED MENACE* (1965) Harry Toukarian (Bob Dishy) wants the art student Flora (Liza Minnelli) to join the Young Communist League with him. Minnelli made a sensational Broadway debut singing the John Kander-Fred Ebb score, their first for Broadway. Abbott co-wrote the libretto and directed the problematic musical. *Photofest*

24. *FRANKIE* (1989) Abbott's last new musical was a modern version of the Frankenstein story. Gathered together is the creative staff during a rehearsal at the York Theatre (left to right): Gloria Nissenson (lyricist), Donald Saddler (choreographer and co-director), Joseph Turrin (composer), and Abbott (co-director, librettist). *Used by permission by Joseph Turrin*

25. *DAMN YANKEES* (1994) Baseball manager Benny Van Buren (Dick Latessa, far right) encourages team players (left to right) Smokey (Jeff Blumenkrantz), Rocky (Scott Wise), and Sohovic (Gregory Jbara) with "(You Gotta Have) Heart." The popular revival was the last Broadway hit of Abbott's career, although his involvement in the production was minimal. *Photofest*

8 WORKING WITH NEW (AND USUALLY YOUNGER) FACES

(1944–1949)

On the Town • Billion Dollar Baby • Barefoot Boy with Cheek • High Button Shoes • Look Ma, I'm Dancin'! • Where's Charley? • Touch and Go

Because Abbott had such a long career in musical theatre, it is not surprising that he got to work with just about all of the songwriting giants, from Irving Berlin to Stephen Sondheim. Among the very few he did not collaborate with, Jerome Kern, George and Ira Gershwin, Alan Jay Lerner, and Frederick Loewe first come to mind. What *is* surprising is how many of the great songwriters he worked with early in their careers. Abbott was the Broadway veteran who helped launch the careers of such notable musical artists as Betty Comden, Adolph Green, Leonard Bernstein, Jerome Robbins, Nancy Walker, Gene Kelly, Richard Adler, Jerry Ross, Jule Styne, Bob Fosse, Ray Bolger, Sheldon Harnick, Jerry Bock, Harold Prince, Frank Loesser, John Kander, Fred Ebb, Liza Minnelli, Carol Burnett, Sondheim, and ... You get the idea. Most of these artists were decades younger than Abbott so one can safely say that he taught and influenced a couple of generations of new talent.

On the Town (1944) is a glowing example. Making their Broadway debuts were librettists-lyricists-performers Comden and Green, who were twenty-nine years old, composer Bernstein, and choreographer Robbins, who were both twenty-six years old; Abbott was fifty-seven. With so many unknowns on the bill, no wonder *On the Town* was a surprise hit. It started as a nineteen-minute ballet titled *Fancy Free*, which Bernstein composed and Robbins choreographed, that debuted at the Ballet Theatre (later called the American Ballet Theatre) in 1944. Three sailors on leave in New York City compete with each other for the women they encounter. The music was jazzy and the dancing was athletic and energetic. The young and gifted scenic designer Oliver Smith, who did the set for *Fancy Free*, thought the piece could be expanded into a full musical. He and his producing partner Paul Feigay wanted John Latouche to write the lyrics to songs to be composed by Bernstein but Bernstein wanted his college roommate Adolph Green and with Green came Comden. What the two writers came up with was very different from the short ballet. The three sailors were now buddies and each pursued (or was pursued by) a different girl with variable success. With a different plot line, Bernstein composed all new music and Robbins expanded on the original choreography. *Fancy Free* is still performed today and it sometimes surprises audiences with how different it is from *On the Town*. As Ethan Mordden wrote years later in his book about 1940s musicals *Beautiful Mornin'*, "*Fancy Free* is a burlesque. *On the Town* is a valentine."[1] This valentine concerns three couples but there is also a lot of affection for New York City. No other musical, before or since, celebrated the Big Apple like *On the Town*. And, also unique, that celebration is mostly in dance. The plot is thin but, because it is told in seamless song and dance, it feels complete. Sailors Ozzie (Adolph Green), Chip (Cris Alexander), and Gabey (John Battles), whose ship is docked at the Brooklyn Navy Yard, get a twenty-four leave and explore New York City looking for adventure and romance. They find it in the form of cab driver Hildy (Nancy Walker), anthropology student Claire de Loon (Betty Comden), and ballerina-cooch dancer Ivy (Sono Osato). At the end of the leave, the three couples part with bittersweet satisfaction. That's it. The oldest boy-meets-girl plot but, this time, boys do not get the girls. Yet they get so much more. They have experienced New York City and that serves as a satisfying happy ending.

Smith and Feigay had trouble raising the money for a show put together by promising beginners. They were also worried about the lack of story. As Abbott tells it,

> [The producers] knew that it had loose ends, and they wanted a more experienced hand to settle their battles and to give the enterprise some unity. I was approached, and I met with them and listened to the material ... I liked *On the Town* but I thought some things were wrong, and it seemed best to say so early in the game. For instance, there were many long and involved interruptions in the main plot by a judge and an old lady, two characters I thought unnecessary. They [Robbins, Comden and Green] argued until I finally said, 'You have to take your choice between me and the old lady.'[2]

Even with Abbott on board, Smith and Feigay had difficulty raising the money until they interested Arthur Freed at MGM. In a rare move at the time, the studio provided $250,000 for the production on the hunch that it would be a hit and make a popular movie. Ironically, most of the songs that Freed heard in the sales pitch were cut before the musical opened. Comden and Green took two of the major roles themselves and the rest of the cast was little known except for Walker who had shone in a supporting role in *Best Foot Forward*. Sono Osato, who played Ivy, came from the world of ballet. The Japanese-American dancer was a risky casting choice, though it proved to be a smart one; she was highly extolled by the critics. Anti-Japanese feelings were high in 1944. In fact, Osato's father was still in an internment camp and only after *On the Town* had been running for some time was he allowed to see his daughter dance on Broadway.

Bernstein composed over thirty minutes of dance music, more than had ever been heard in a Broadway musical before or since. And, with expert lyrics by Comden and Green, Bernstein provided a score that bursts with vitality and variety. Jazz, Latin rhythms, boogie-woogie, tender ballads, and raucous swing flowed out of the orchestra pit. The opening was particularly unique: an operetta air "I Feel Like I'm Not Out of Bed Yet" pierced by the jazzy anthem "New York, New York." Other memorable songs include the manic "I Get Carried Away," the torchy "Lonely Town," the quietly celebratory "Lucky to Be Me," the farcical "Come Up to My Place," the vivacious "You Got Me," the swinging "I Can Cook Too," and the poignant parting song "Some Other Time." Add to all that the scintillating "ballet" music and you have one of the great theatre scores. All the same, *On the Town* needed work out of town. Abbott complained about the short (ten days) Boston run, noting "this was much too brief by all normal standards," especially for a show with so many moving set pieces and so much dance. "We cut out a musical number and two songs, threw away one of our best-looking sets, added a new song, and changed stage managers."[3] This is where the veteran Abbott was needed; none of the novices on board had ever taken a musical out of town before. Yet there was little friction between the generations. Abbott later wrote, "We all worked together on this show in a way that I love to work: each putting forth his opinion, yet remaining objective, and subordinating everything to the main end; working with happy excitement, with passionate enthusiasm, with a wonderful feeling of warmth and togetherness."[4]

Although *On the Town* was a hit with 463 performances, it did not receive unanimously favorable reviews. What was different and exciting about the musical did not please everyone. John Chapman in the *New York Daily News* called it "a dullish musical comedy" and Burton Rascoe of the *World-Telegram* found the choreography "plastic rather than rhythmical and completely uninspired." But raves, such as Louis Kronenberger's "one of the freshest, gayest, liveliest musicals I have ever seen" in *PM* and *Newsweek*'s "The most original and engaging musical to hit New York since *Oklahoma!*," helped turn *On the Town* into a hit. Because the new talents were so impressive, Abbott was not given as much credit in the press as one might expect. In the billing, he was listed before everyone else but it was never considered an Abbott musical and he is still little mentioned when *On the Town* is written about. His contribution to the original production was later noticed in the 1971 and 1998 Broadway revivals which were directed by others. Despite some fine elements, both productions were short-lived. Only the 2014 revival, directed by John Rando and choreographed by Joshua Bergasse, captured the thrill of the original and found an audience for 368 performances in one of Broadway's biggest houses. Abbott's hand (or lack of it) is most obvious when one looks at the 1949 movie version of *On the Town*. Comden and Green wrote the screenplay that did not stray too far from the original stage story and the action moved briskly even if the plot seemed even less consequential on the big screen. The film, co-directed and co-choreographed by Stanley Donen and Gene Kelly, decimated the stage score but retained some of the lengthy ballets and the music Bernstein wrote for them. Producer Freed admitted he didn't like the stage songs so he hired Roger Edens to compose some new ones and Comden and Green wrote new lyrics, the best addition being "Prehistoric Man." Kelly was joined by Frank Sinatra and Jules Munshin to play the three sailors and Vera-Ellen, Betty Garrett, and Ann Miller were their love interests. In addition to the extended dance sequences, the movie was also unique in the way it used on-location filming in New York City, incorporating the celebrated tourist sights as the background for the action. The celluloid *On the Town* is some kind of movie musical classic but pales somewhat when viewed by those who love the stage version.

Abbott was reunited with lyricists-librettists Comden and Green and choreographer Robbins for **Billion Dollar Baby** (1945). Producers Smith and Feigay hoped for another *On the Town,* but Bernstein was busy with his rapid rise to fame as a concert maestro so Morton Gould was hired to write the music. Bernstein was sorely missed because Gould's music was dull and, for a Roaring Twenties spoof, sounded more swinging Forties than red-hot Twenties. Comden and Green wrote perhaps their least accomplished lyrics but came up with a merry, satiric tale of a gold digger who rises to the top. It was often funny but frequently nasty. The ambitious flapper Maribelle Jones (Joan McCracken) dances through the Jazz Age, dropping her Staten Island boyfriend Champ Watson (Danny Daniels) and taking up with small-time gangster Jerry Bonanza (Don DeLeo), then big-time mobster Dapper Welch (David Burns). She finally ends up with billionaire M. M. Montague (Robert Chisholm) but he loses his fortune in the stock market crash the day they are married. All the 1920s clichés were in place: speakeasy frolicking, underworld derring-do, stockbrokers riding the bull market, and *Ziegfeld Follies*-like revues with squealing chorines. There was even a Texas Guinan-like hostess named Georgie Motley (Mitzi Green) who entertained all the "suckers" at Chez Georgia. But two things were wrong. Maribelle and company were farcical but heartless and even off-putting. And second, Broadway audiences had no nostalgia or interest in the frivolous Twenties during the war years. McCracken as Maribelle was spot on with her wild dancing and shrill singing but one didn't really like her much. Similarly, Robbins' frenetic choreography was clever and even impressive but tiresome and sometimes empty. A second-act ballet, in which Maribelle imagines a life married to the bodyguard Rocky (William Tabbert), was intended as a spoof of the recent "Laurey Makes Up Her Mind" ballet in *Oklahoma!* (1943) but it was only mildly amusing. Abbott was quite at home staging this kind of 1920s silliness but his efforts were in vain. The reviews for *Billion Dollar Baby* were mixed, but even the naysayers found elements in the show that they liked. Chapman in the *Daily News* thought the musical "even better than *On the Town*" and declared that Robbins and Abbott were the "the real stars." But most commentators agreed with Rascoe in the *World-Telegram* that "there is a very satisfactory first act, fast moving, clever, rhythmical, broadly satiric, and diverting. But [in] the second act ... satiric inspiration lags, there is no surprise, and the comedy, anemic in the first place, gives up the ghost entirely." George Jean Nathan, who liked his dramas very heavy and his musicals very light, complained in his *The Theatre Book of The Year, 1944–1945* that "the show is another in the later day series of attempts to break away from the romantic musical and toughen it up in the interests of what is believed to be modernity."[5] Despite such notices, *Billion Dollar Baby* managed to run 220 performances.

That was twice as long as **Barefoot Boy with Cheek** (1947) lasted. Abbott so enjoyed working with Nancy Walker on the musicals *Best Foot Forward* and *On the Town* that he directed her in two more in the 1940s. This time Walker was the leading character in the musical satire *Barefoot Boy with Cheek* which had a very silly libretto by Max Shulman, based on his 1943 comic novel of the same name. At the University of Minnesota, the leftist coed Yetta Samovar (Walker) tries to make the campus more radical, in particular the boys of the Alpha Cholera Fraternity. She wins over the hick freshman Asa Hearthrug (Billy Redfield) and pushes his popularity until he is president of the Student Council. Yetta even manages to steal Asa's heart until he falls for the chirping coed Clothilde Pfefferkorn (Ellen Hanley). The sketchy plot was filled with comic types, all sporting ridiculous names: the frat boy Shyster Fiscal (Red Buttons), the dumb coed Noblesse Oblige (Betty Lou Watt), the young commie Boris Fiveyearplan (Martin Sameth), the dense football player Eino Ffliikkiimmenn (Benjamin Miller) from Finland, and so on. Walker was hilarious but couldn't overcome the weak score by Sidney Lippman (music) and Sylvia Dee (lyrics). One questions why Abbott would produce and direct another college musical, a genre that was pretty much worn out by the late 1940s. The opportunity to work again with Walker might have been enough or maybe the appeal was doing a show filled with young unknowns. Whatever the case, Abbott seemed to be in a repetitive pattern and the critics were not quiet about it. Writing in the *New York Post*, Richard Watts, Jr., noted, "There is something disconcerting in the thought that, while the rest of us are getting older, George Abbott keeps getting younger. At least his musical shows, which were never exactly middle-aged in their manner, appear to be rapidly becoming so callow that they are almost ostentatious about it." George Jean Nathan was even more critical in his *The Theatre*

Book of The Year, 1946–1947: "George Abbott, who both produced and staged the ephebolergy, is evidently suffering from arrested theatrical development, since such youthful collegiate affairs, long a favorite with him, have some time now been badly dated."[6] (I would be pleased to tell you what *ephebolergy* means, but Webster's and the Oxford dictionary and myself are unable to say. Possibly something to do with Athenian youth and the study of veins.) Most of the other reviews were more favorable but not the kind of money notices *Barefoot Boy with Cheek* needed to run more than fourteen weeks.

Abbott was not fortunate enough to produce the period musical **High Button Shoes** (1947) which turned out to be the biggest hit of the 1947–1948 season, running 727 performances. Show biz legend has it that lyricist Sammy Cahn saw an ad for a new book in the newspaper that had a 1910 photo of a family going for a drive in their Model-T Ford. Cahn was so taken with the image that he rushed to the home of composer-partner Jule Styne and said "This is our new musical." The ad was for Stephen Longstreet's semi-autobiographical novel *The Sisters Liked Them Handsome*. Styne asked Cahn if he'd like to meet the author to discuss it. Cahn enthusiastically replied in the positive. So Styne walked Cahn to the house across the street, knocked on the door, and when it was answered, said, "Sammy, this is Stephen Longstreet."[7] Monte Proser and Joseph Kipness were the lucky producers who optioned Longstreet's book and Styne and Cahn wrote their first Broadway score for the show that became *High Button Shoes*. Abbott was asked to direct and he loved the songs but thought the script "impossible."[8] But he was anxious to work so he accepted with the understanding that he would tinker with the script. Once Phil Silvers was cast in the starring role, the comic also contributed to the libretto. Evidently it was a major rewrite job and the producers kindly paid Abbott a royalty even though it wasn't in his contract. The carefree period musical comedy evoked Americana with a nostalgic smile. In 1913, con man Harrison Floy (Silvers) sells the people of New Brunswick, New Jersey, useless swamp land then, with his partner Pontdue (Joey Faye), takes the money and escapes to Atlantic City. Henry (Jack McCauley) and Sara Longstreet (Nanette Fabray), one of the families duped by Floy, follow him to the shore. A merry chase ensues, ending back in New Brunswick where Floy bets on the big football game between Princeton and Rutgers. He tries to bribe the Rutgers team into throwing the game but they double-cross him and Floy loses all the money he swindled from the New Jersey town folk. In the musical's subplot, Sara's sister Fran (Lois Lee) is in love with the Rutger's football star Hubert Ogglethorpe (Mark Dawson) but Floy tries, unsuccessfully, to woo her away from him. It wasn't the strongest of librettos but it worked, allowing song and dance to be added seamlessly. *High Button Shoes* was one of Abbott's better doctoring jobs. When Longstreet complained that Abbott was getting a royalty, the star Silvers told him, "Watch out. One of these nights we might play *your* script."[9]

Abbott was again working with new faces in *High Button Shoes*, including artists on the brink of fame. After supporting roles in several movies, Silvers became a

Broadway star with *High Button Shoes*. (He later became a bigger star as television's Sergeant Bilko.) Styne and Cahn had many film credits as well but this was their first show to reach Broadway. And, once again, most of the cast were young and unknown. The critics were not overly enthusiastic about the score though it is, by any standard, a superior one. The two standout numbers were the vivacious "Papa, Won't You Dance With Me?" and the quaint duet "I Still Get Jealous," both for the Longstreet couple. Floy sang three sparkling ditties: "There's Nothing Like a Model T," "On a Sunday By the Sea," and "Nobody Ever Died for Dear Old Rutgers." There were other noteworthy numbers but the entire score was eclipsed by a seven-minute dance-chase in the second act. Today known as the "Mack Sennett Ballet," the number was one of the funniest and most clever of the era. Any era, to be honest. It was Abbott's plot that set up the premise of Floy and Pontdue being chased by police and angry citizens in Atlantic City but it was Jerome Robbins who choreographed the sequence using various silent film elements, most memorably Keystone Kops and bathing beauties. The number, originally listed as the "Mack Sennett Ballet," was the dance highlight of the show. Sennett was still alive and sued the producers for using his name so the number was retitled the "Bathing Beauty Ballet." It was the one aspect of *High Button Shoes* that every critic extolled, even those who did not like the rest of the show. "The production has a lot of bounce," Howard Barnes wrote in the *Herald Tribune*, "The trouble is that the ball is extremely elusive." "There's so much good in the best of it," Robert Garland wrote in the *Journal-American*, "and so much bad in the worst of it." All the same, Robbins' handiwork was the talk of the town. "The hero of the evening is Jerome Robbins," Watts stated in the *Post*. "There is more humor and unconventional inventiveness and less stuffiness in Mr. Robbins than in most directors of the pirouette, and all of the dancing in *High Button Shoes* is agreeable." Even more so than his excellent work for *On the Town*, this production placed Robbins in the top ranks of Broadway choreographers. That ballet is so legendary that twenty-seven years later, when Gower Champion staged a Keystone Kops dance for *Mack & Mabel*, he made sure that none of his version echoed Robbins' original. *High Button Shoes* was never filmed but there were two television adaptations, in 1956 and 1966, but both were so abridged that the "Bathing Beauty Ballet" did not shine. Happily, Robbins recreated the famous number for *Jerome Robbins' Broadway* in 1988.

Despite mixed notices, *High Button Shoes* ran two years. When Abbott was reunited with Walker and Robbins for **Look, Ma, I'm Dancin'!** (1948), the result was less propitious. The idea for the production came from Robbins who wanted to do a musical comedy about the comic-sad workings of a ballet troupe. He presented his idea to playwrights Jerome Lawrence and Robert E. Lee; it was the team's first Broadway effort. Robbins also brought on songwriter Hugh Martin for the score. When Abbott was approached, he saw the show as a vehicle for Walker and signed on as producer and director. (So much of the finished product was Robbins' that he was eventually billed as co-director.) The plot had possibilities. The beer heiress Lily

Mallow (Walker) loves the ballet but has no dancing talent so she underwrites a touring dance company run by impresario Vladimir Luboff (Alexander March). She travels with the company, has a love-hate relationship with principal dancer-choreographer Eddie Winkler (Harold Lang), and eventually dances the prima ballerina role in some modern, cockeyed pieces that she introduces to modernize the art form. Because the musical would involve so much dance, Robbins asked for two weeks of rehearsal with the dancers before the rest of the cast was assembled. According to Abbott, Robbins needed the extra time to perfect "a rather spectacular ballet" for the show. Abbott agreed and kept out of the picture for the two weeks. "I kept getting word from my stage manager that progress seemed to be slow," Abbott recalled. Near the end of the two weeks, "a message came that Jerry wanted to see me immediately... He asked me to look at what he had done. It was not good; he knew it and wanted to have it verified. We immediately jettisoned the whole ballet and he started on a new one."[10] Such was a pattern that reappeared throughout Robbins' career. Yet Abbott also noted, "The best dance which Jerry did for the show was conceived and executed in two days while we were on the road."[11] Titled the "Sleepwalkers Ballet," the number required some dancers to stand on others' shoulders and move as if in a trance. There were other effective moments in *Look, Ma, I'm Dancin'!*, such as Walker's first entrance at a train station accompanied by a gigantic wolfhound as tall as she was. And the first act ended in a peculiar way. As the curtain fell on the disgruntled dance troupe, ushers brought a huge horseshoe of flowers down the aisle. Walker came on the stage and insisted they give the bouquet to her. "I paid for those flowers," she shouted. "And damnit, I'm going to get them!"[12] There were many things in the musical that were memorable. Walker's numbers "I'm the First Girl (In the Second Row in the Thirds Scene of the Fourth Number)" and "I'm Tired of Texas" were ideal for her comic talents. Lang got his big dance number with "Gotta Dance" and the duet "Shauny O'Shay" enjoyed some popularity in later years. Except for praises for Walker, the reviews were mixed. One of the few to fully advocate the musical was Robert Coleman in the *Daily Mirror*: "Rack up another hit for George Abbott. If you want to laugh, rush to the Adelphi [Theatre] immediately and buy your tickets. A fast, funny, zippy musical." Kronenberger in *PM* was disappointed. "The most I can say—to be schoolmarmish about [the musical]—is that it's one of the brightest children I ever flunked. It's a fine might-have-been; possibly even a fine should-have-been. It has good things in it, good people all about it, a good idea behind it. But it's not a good show." For once, Nathan did not blame Abbott. "George Abbott has done everything possible to get some life into the book, but the job he is up against is like trying to inject effervescence into a bottle of linseed oil."[13] And there were other problems. "Unfortunately Nancy kept losing her voice," Abbott wrote decades later. "And sometimes she was out for weeks at a time ... night after night we would have to disappoint our audience. Had it not been for this unfortunate illness, I think that the play would have been a hit."[14] Instead *Look, Ma, I'm Dancin'!* folded after an unprofitable 188 performances.

Songwriter Frank Loesser was another musical talent who debuted on Broadway under Abbott's sure hand. He had found success in Hollywood first as a lyricist then, since the wartime hit "Praise the Lord and Pass the Ammunition," as a composer as well. Also new to Broadway were producers Cy Feuer and Ernest H. Martin who bought the rights to Brandon Thomas' 1892 British farce *Charley's Aunt*. They had also secured the services of Ray Bolger, now a confirmed star because of *On Your Toes* and his Hollywood appearances. Feuer and Martin asked Abbott to write the script and direct the show and he didn't hesitate before saying yes. Just as he had condensed and tightened *The Comedy of Errors* for *The Boys from Syracuse*, Abbott did similar workmanship on *Charley's Aunt*. As hilarious as the classic farce is, it is a talky piece. Abbott simplified the plot and turned the Oxford student Charley Wyckeham (Ray Bolger) into the one who dresses up like his aunt from Brazil. (In the original play, it is fellow student Lord Fancourt Babberley who is convinced to go in drag.) In Abbott's version, Charley dons a dress and wig in order to provide a chaperone for himself as well as for his fellow student Jack Chesney (Byron Palmer) as they court Amy Spettigue (Allyn Ann McLerie) and Kitty Verdun (Doretta Morrow). Complications for Charley increase when Amy's guardian Mr. Spettigue (Horace Cooper) starts to woo the bewigged Charley and when the real aunt Donna Lucia (Jane Lawrence) arrives in Oxford. It seems she was once in love with Jack's father, Sir Francis Chesney (Paul England). Their rekindled romance meant the musical ended with three wedding engagements. I am among those who believe **Where's Charley?** (1948), as the musical was called, is more fun than the Thomas original. Abbott eliminated much of the verbal exposition and jumped right into the action.

Jack   Charley, where's your aunt?

Charley   Oh, she wasn't on the train.

Jack   Wasn't on it!

Charley   When she didn't arrive I read her letter more carefully and found she's coming on the twelve ...

Jack   Charley, you aunt will surely come, won't she?

Charley   How should I know? I've never seen the woman. All I know about her is what I read in those Sunday articles. She's frightfully rich and she wrote she'd visit me.

Jack   I've asked both girls to come here to lunch to meet your aunt.

Charley   They wouldn't accept. They couldn't!

Jack   They have! ... So all we have to worry about is your aunt for the chaperone.

Charley   Look, old boy! If my aunt is practical enough to marry one of the richest men in South America, she can certainly catch a train![15]

The songs are placed expertly so that they do not diminish the farce, a very tricky thing to do in a musical, as we have seen. Abbott's script and the musical numbers fell into place easily and early. "All the songs were kept in the production exactly as we planned them," Abbott wrote in his autobiography. "Usually there is a great shifting around of numbers, but in this case the only changes were at the end of Act One, which was, I regret to say, a dream ballet, a [kind of] number that was already beginning to be passé."[16] That first act finale, titled "Pernambuco," was actually not a dream but a farcical retelling of the aunt's supposedly hedonistic life in Brazil, complete with Latin music and clever choreography by George Balanchine. It was one of the few dances in the show, another necessity for musical farce. Because the whole Brazilian adventure is not seen in the original play, Abbott wrote a funny scene to set up the ballet.

Donna Lucia   You see, I know a great deal about you. You had quite a reputation, Donna Lucia.

Charley (*dressed as his aunt*)   I did? But I'm all right now . . .

Donna Lucia   [In] what part of Brazil did you live?

Charley   The residential part.

Donna Lucia   No, I meant the name.

Charley   Oh, oh that! Our town was named after a bottle of wine. What was it now? Pernambuco.

Donna Lucia   I see. Do tell us about the Brazileros.

Charley   Only the nicer girls wore them. Oh, lovely people, lovely people.

Donna Lucia   Do you speak the language?

Charley   What language? Oh—(a torrent of imitation Portuguese) Olay!

Donna Lucia   Interesting. Do tell us more . . .

Spettigue   You simply must! I want to know all about you.

Charley   Well, Brazil is situated—isn't it? Brazil is the land not only of nuts but of romance. And into this unbelievable place I came, an innocent English girl . . . picture if you will the life that greeted me. I stepped off the boat with high ideals and a small traveling bag. At first I was frightened, especially of that wonderful man with the big mustache. Whom I afterward married. He was brutal, but attractive. He was a good boy, a fine boy, a rich boy, so I married him. Ah, the romance of it all . . . Sometimes I can still hear those sounds—and smell those smells—and I wish I could live the whole thing over again.[17]

Things went so smoothly in rehearsals and tryouts that the creative staff must have been unnerved when *Where's Charley?* got such radically conflicting reviews. "An old-style book show ... Abbott's book is humorless," Ward Morehouse in the *New York Sun* declared, and Watts in the *Post* thought "all the humor [of *Charley's Aunt*] seemed to have been drained from it. For most of the time, everybody sat around and waited for Mr. Bolger to go into his dance." There were generally raves for Bolger but few of the positive reviews were complimentary to Loesser's score. Was it because he was the new kid on the block? How could one not appreciate, even on one hearing, the sprightly duet "Make a Miracle," the rousing "The New Ashmolean Marching Society and Students' Conservatory Band," the lilting ballad "My Darling, My Darling," the waltzing "At the Red Rose Cotillion," and the comic number "Serenade with Asides"? At least the press acknowledged the show's biggest hit song, "Once in Love With Amy," which Bolger turned into a sing-along number with the audience. Thanks to Bolger's box office clout and strong word of mouth, *Where's Charley?* survived its mixed notices and ran a very profitable 792 performances. It then went on tour with Bolger, returning to Broadway for six weeks in 1951 before he went to Hollywood to recreate his performance on screen. The 1952 Warner Brothers movie also retained Allyn Ann McLerie and Horace Cooper from the stage version but Abbott's script was changed slightly. David Butler directed, Michael Kidd did the playful choreography, and Bolger got to do more dancing than in the stage show. He also performed "Once in Love With Amy" as he had on Broadway, encouraging the movie audience to join in. The effect was not nearly as effective as with a live audience in a theatre but it gave the movie a silliness that was appropriate. Sadly, the film has been out of circulation for decades and can only be seen in bootleg copies.

There was, at the end of the decade, another Abbott production, **Touch and Go** (1949), his one and only musical revue. Again he worked with "newcomers," although Jean and Walter Kerr and Jay Gorney were not young beginners. Gorney was a veteran song composer who had contributed to Broadway revues since 1923, most memorably writing the Depression classic "Brother, Can You Spare a Dime" with lyricist E. Y. Harburg for *Americana* (1932). Jean Kerr had seen two of her plays already presented on Broadway and Walter Kerr was already the author of three Broadway plays. (His career as a notable New York City drama critic did not begin until 1951.) The Kerrs were on the drama faculty of Catholic University of America in Washington, DC, where they wrote a smart and funny revue titled *Thank You, Just Looking*. Walter Kerr directed the student cast and somehow Gorney was talked into providing the music. Abbott heard about the show from producer Joe Kipness and went to DC to check it out. With a professional cast and better choreography, Abbott thought it might do well on Broadway. Walter Kerr was retained as director and he brought with him two student performers. Abbott later thought the two amateurs hurt the quality of the New York production. He hired a cast of Equity members, got Helen Tamiris to redo the dances, and changed the title to *Touch and Go*. Nothing from the script was changed from the college production. The critics were surprisingly approving, enjoying the wit, some of the performers, and the music. Endorsements such as "good-humored, bright, original and intelligent" and "in the best professional taste, and mighty pleasant" were echoed in many of the reviews. This was still the age of the literate musical revue and *Touch and Go* held its own with the best of them. Highlights included *Hamlet* as done as the Rodgers and Hammerstein musical *Great Dane A-Comin'*, *Cinderella* as Tennessee Williams might have written it, a spoof of Hollywood heroines, and the songs "It'll Be All Right in a Hundred Years" and "Funny Little Old World." Out of the talented cast, Nancy Andrews was roundly applauded for her number "Miss Platt Selects a Mate." She and Dick Sykes shone in the desperate duet "This Had Better Be Love." Tamiris staged a mock-modern ballet titled "American Primitive" in front of Grandma Moses-like scenery. Also garnering praise from the critics were Helen Gallagher, Peggy Cass, Kyle MacDonald, George Hall, and Lewis (later Louie) Nye. The biggest laugh of the evening came in the *Cinderella* spoof when the Prince (Nye), searching for the girl with the glass slipper, asked the Stepmother (Muriel O'Malley) if there were no other maidens in the house. She assured him no one else was home, followed by the sound of a toilet flushing. Abbott thought the joke "vulgar" but the Kerrs fought to keep it in the show. Abbott later admitted, "It got one of the biggest laughs I have ever heard in the theatre."[18] *Touch and Go* had a modest run of 176 performances; it didn't make money but several accomplished actors got their first recognition with the revue.

9 POST-WAR BLUES

(1946–1961)

The Dancer • It Takes Two • Mrs. Gibbons' Boys • The Number • In Any Language • Drink to Me Only • A Call on Kuprin • The Skin of Our Teeth (revival)

The post-war years in America were a boom time for many industries but not for Broadway. Just as movie audiences were turning to television, theatregoers were moving to the suburbs and the tired business man did not feel like going back into the city after a long day at the office. Hollywood combated the small screen by making the movie screens wider and in glorious color. The theatre had no such recourses. Yet even as the number of plays and musicals plummeted, the era is now remembered as a golden age for great plays and classic musicals. Abbott would share in the latter but not in the former; all seven of his plays between 1946 and 1961 failed. It is worth noting that Abbott did not write any of the seven plays but was producer and/or director. In each case, the weakest aspect of the production was the script. So one questions Abbott's judgement in being involved with such inferior material. He hardly mentions these works in his autobiography but, in a few instances, one can guess what drew him to the project. Some outstanding performers can be found in several of the plays and Abbott enjoyed working with talented actors. In some cases, the project sounded intriguing on paper. But most of the time Abbott got involved because he wanted to work and had trouble saying no.

The Dancer (1946) was one of those embarrassing cases of a thriller that elicited snickers instead of chills from the audience. Abbott produced the melodrama by Milton Lewis and Julian Funt but let Everett Sloane direct it. It was not a good idea. The script was a turgid piece riddled with flaws and needed a sure hand in the staging. The world-famous ballet star Sergei Krainine (Anton Dolin) is mentally ill and for the past fifteen years has been kept secluded in a Paris apartment by the perverted impresario Aubrey Stewart (Colin Keith-Johnston). When Sergei gets drunk, he hears ballet music in his head and either breaks out into a dance or kills someone. When a local prostitute is murdered, the police suspects Sergei and converge on the apartment even as Sergei's wife Catherine (Helen Flint) and daughter Madeline (Bethel Leslie) come looking for him. The wife has the key to a safety box and is hoping for money. The daughter is engaged to be married but worries if her father's insanity is hereditary. Before the police can arrest him, Sergei kills both Catherine and Aubrey. The thinly disguised portrait of dancer Nijinsky and impresario Diaghilev was roundly panned by the press. Lewis Nichols in *The New York Times* wrote, "What Mr. Abbott seems to lack in his new enterprise ... is a play that is gripping or makes quite enough sense. *The Dancer* is one of those unhappy affairs that sets out to excite but through tortured writhings too often only amuses." George Jean Nathan, writing in *The Theatre Book of The Year, 1946–1947*, noted, "Hardly the best way to fashion any such thriller is to explain away everything at the start and then occupy the rest of the evening successively twisting the necks of the actors."[1] Abbott pulled the plug on the melodrama after five performances.

Laughs were expected with **It Takes Two** (1947), a comedy by Virginia Faulkner and Dana Suesse, but they were not forthcoming. When Todd Frazier (Hugh Marlowe) is mustered out of the army, he and his wife Connie (Martha Scott) find a small apartment in the Murray Hill section of Manhattan and settle down for a life of marital bliss. But it is not to be and soon the quarreling couple separate, though with the housing shortage they have to keep living together. While they take their time coming around to the fact that they still love each other, the plot was happily interrupted by some more interesting characters: Todd's old army buddy Monk Rathburn (Anthony Ross), the overbearing blonde Bea Clark (Vivian Vance), and their Mad Hatter neighbor Bill Renault (John Forsythe). Abbott directed and co-produced the unfunny comedy with Richard Aldrich. Nathan unsurprisingly criticized "the direction by George Abbott following his usual principle of making the actors appear to be running madly away from the script."[2] Aldrich and Abbott closed the play after eight performances. Will Glickman and Joseph Stein, who would later enjoy success writing musicals, provided the lean script for the comedy **Mrs. Gibbons' Boys** (1949) which Abbott produced and directed. The widowed Mrs. Peggy Gibbons (Lois Bolton) is about to accept the marriage proposal of timid Lester MacMichaels (Francis Compton) when she is visited by her three sons on whom she dotes with excess. Rudy (Tom Lewis) is on parole while Rodla (Ray Walston) and Francis X. (Richard Carlyle) have escaped from prison, bringing with them the boneheaded Horse Wagner (Royal Dano) who tends to throw people through windows. The four crooks hold mama and Lester hostage, but eventually she talks them into surrendering to the police. The unanimously negative notices were led by Wolcott Gibbs in *The New Yorker* who declared *Mrs. Gibbons' Boys* was "about as an annoying a little comedy we have had this season" and took Abbott to task with, "[the cast] was directed by George Abbott whose well-known theory that vehement activity is an acceptable substitute for funny lines and situations was pretty definitely exploded." Faced with such notices, Abbott closed *Mrs. Gibbon's Boys* after five performances.

Three plays Abbott worked on in the 1950s managed to run much longer but none of them showed a profit. The most successful of them was ***The Number*** (1951), a melodrama by Arthur Carter that lasted eleven weeks. Separated from her dull husband, Sylvia (Martha Scott) gets a job as a receptionist in the office of numbers-runner Maury (Mervyn Vye). She falls in love with the slick bettor Dominic Spizzilini (Dane Clark) who uses Sylvia to try and cheat Maury. The ruse is discovered by Maury who has Dominic rubbed out. The naive Sylvia quickly gets wise about the real world. Abbott did not produce *The Number* but he directed it with verve and the critics thought it a passable drama but complained about certain aspects of the plot. *Time Magazine* noted, "*The Number* has faults galore, but one very respectable virtue: it keeps its audience interested." In a rare move, Abbott made some significant changes in the production after opening night. A scene in the second act in which Sylvia fought with her husband over the custody of their child was cut. Abbott also made minor changes in the other two acts and invited the press to give *The Number* another look. Some did and the general consensus was that melodrama was tighter and more effective. In the past, Abbott had tinkered with his shows after opening. But this was a bolder move and got plenty of attention in press, helping the play to run as long as it did. An esteemed performance by Uta Hagen could not turn the comedy ***In Any Language*** (1952) into a hit but it did last nearly six weeks. Edmund Beloin and Henry Garson wrote the play about the past-her-prime movie star Hannah King (Hagen) who tries to resurrect her career by going to Italy and talking the celebrated director Aldo Carmenelli (Joe De Santis) into starring her in his next neo-realistic film. She succeeds, makes the art movie, but it is a flop. The experience is humbling but at least Hannah is reunited with her estranged husband Charlie (Walter Matthau) who she has not seen since the war. Rehearsals for *In Any Language* did not go smoothly and Abbott, who directed and co-produced with composer Jule Styne, did something he greatly disliked doing: replace actors in the final stages of rehearsals. In this case, two performers. Movie star Jeffrey Lynn was not working out as the husband Charlie so Matthau took over the role. Jean Casto was not satisfying as Hannah's brittle secretary Valerie McGuire so Anna Minot moved into the part, only to be replaced by Eileen Heckart by opening night. Such setbacks seemed not to perturb Abbott whose sure-fire staging of the broad comedy was noticed by the press. "George Abbott staged the performance at a pace that has not slackened perceptibly since *Three Men on a Horse, Room Service* and *Boy Meets Girl*," wrote Brooks Atkinson in *The New York Times*. "Although the seasons have been tottering by, Mr. Abbott's track time is still youthful. He plunges into these comic steeplechases with the eagerness of a yearling." These sentiments were echoed by *Time*: "With George Abbott to stage the show, no character very long remains stationary, no telephone silent, no door unentered; noises abound, gadgets accumulate, throngs assemble. But what is offered in the name of comedy is for the most part mere commotion." Critics were only impressed with Hagen who, having played Saint Joan the season before, was quite delightful as the temperamental Hannah.

Another widely-approved comic performance was the best thing about the Abbott-directed **Drink to Me Only** (1958) by Abram S. Ginnes and Ira Wallach. The young actor Tom Poston had the unenviable task of appearing drunk for most of three acts but the critics thought he pulled off well. The comedy was built on the premise that a man can imbibe alcohol heavily but still have the wherewithal to aim a gun accurately. The society playboy James Porterman (Paul Hartman) is on trial for trying to kill his wife Joyce (Undine Forrest). Although he had downed two quarts of whiskey within a twelve-hour period, Porterman claims he was still within his wits when he aimed the pistol at Joyce's buttocks, knowing it would not kill her. The prosecution says it was intent to kill and argues that any man with that much alcohol in him would pass out. Porterman's attorneys set out to prove their client truthful by having the youngest member of the firm, Miles Pringle (Poston), drink that much whiskey over the span of twelve hours. Miles survives the ordeal and is still able to stand up in court and prove the defense's point. As much as the reviews liked Jack Gilford, Paul Hartman, Sherry Britton, and John McGiver in colorful roles, they declared the evening belonged to Poston. There were also compliments for Abbott's ability to stage the one-joke show with panache. John Lardner in *The New Yorker* noted, "I doubt if Mr. Abbott (who, naturally, directed the play) has ever handled a more rewarding souse." *Time* thought "the nub of *Drink* lay in the staging, in what that master of accelerating insanity, George Abbott, could pipe into a yarn of careening drunkenness. Director Abbott and his downer of Scotch, Tom Poston, constitute the brighter side of the occasion. But *Drink to Me Only* is not an occasion, is not often very bright." The comedy struggled to run over nine weeks. Playwrights Jerome Lawrence and Robert E. Lee had struck gold twice, first with their 1955 drama *Inherit the Wind* and then with the comedy *Auntie Mame* the following year. So Abbott was willing to direct their complicated spy drama **A Call on Kuprin** (1961). He also did it as a favor for young producers Harold Prince and Robert E. Griffith whom he had worked with on *The Pajama Game* (1954) and *Damn Yankees* (1955). Because the play was based on an intricate novel by Maurice Edelman, it had a large cast and many different locations. When the Russian scientist V. V. Kuprin (George Voskovec) taught at an American university in Ohio, one of his students was Jonathan Smith (Jeffrey Lynn). The Soviets ordered Kuprin back to Russia to work on the space program by threatening to harm his aged mother (Eugenie Leontovich) if he didn't cooperate. Some years later, Smith is a noted scientist and when he visits Moscow he looks up his former professor. Kuprin wants to leave the USSR so Smith and the CIA arrange some subterfuges and spy tactics to get Kuprin and his family to America. What might have been interesting reading on the page became hackneyed on the stage. *Time* stated that "the authors have fitted their occasional thoughtfulness and sense of balance inside a framework of hackwork so that the play, in the end, has no more sustained topical value than theatrical impact." Kronenberger, writing in *The Best Plays of 1960–1961*, echoed the sentiments of the press when he wrote that *A Call on Kuprin* had "some brisk spy-and-counterspy hanky-panky, but was mostly routine comedy, routine satire, routine romance and routine sentiment."[3] The briskness came from Abbott's direction and the humor was provided by old Madame Kuprina (Leontovich) who wore turn-of-the-century clothes, spoke as if the Tsar was still alive, and thought Woodrow Wilson was still president. Because the production was so expensive and the reviews so disparaging, the producers closed the play after twelve performances. In his memoir *Sense of Occasion*, Prince blames an unfortunate historical coincidence. On the day *A Call on Krupin* started previews in Philadelphia, the USSR launched the space probe *Sputnik* and the newspapers were filled with stories about the successful mission. "We had lost a race with the headlines," he recalled. "All the mystery, the glamour of [our] story evaporated."[4]

One last play from the 1950s must be included here even though Abbott did not write, produce, or direct it. It was the celebrated 1955 revival of Thornton Wilder's 1942 play ***The Skin of Our Teeth*** in which Abbott played the leading male role. Producer Robert Whitehead and the American National Theatre and Academy (ANTA) put together a starry revival of the expressionistic play which was booked to go to Paris as part of an international exchange. Mary Martin and Helen Hayes were already signed up when Whitehead approached Abbott about playing Mr. Antrobus, the everyman who, with his family, survives the Ice Age, the Great Flood, and a World War. Not having acted on stage in twenty-one years, he was understandably reticent. At the same time Abbott was honored to be included in such fine company. He insisted that he audition for the part and Whitehead agreed but it was when Abbott was satisfied with his reading of Antrobus that he agreed to return to the stage. The director for the project was Alan Schneider, known at the time for his psychological approach to directing and later most remembered for staging the American premieres of such absurdist classics as *Waiting for Godot* and *Endgame*. Abbott was not impressed with Schneider as a director. "[His] method of direction was very personal," he wrote decades later. "He made notes then took each actor aside and talked to him privately. My method has always been to give all instruction in front of the entire cast or whoever happens to be on stage."[5] All the same, Abbott kept his opinions to himself and he admitted that rehearsals for *The Skin of Our Teeth* went well enough. "There was no pettiness... everybody took direction as well as he could."[6] The resulting production was considered first-rate by any standards. Helen Hayes was a fierce and funny Mrs. Antrobus, Mary Martin played the outspoken maid Sabina in a quixotic manner, Florence Reed (from the original 1942 production) shone as the Fortune Teller in Atlantic City, Don Murray was the restless son Henry, and Heller Halliday was a dense Gladys. Near the end of the Paris run, it was announced that the production would continue on: two weeks in Washington, another two in Chicago, and then a limited Broadway run of twenty-two performances. Abbott found acting hard work at his age (sixty-eight years old) and wanted to bow out of the cast after Paris but thought "I would ruin the project" so he stayed on.[7] The reviews when *The Skin of Our Teeth* arrived in New York were valentines. *The Times* called the production "perfect" and, while the most enthusiastic praise was for Martin and Hayes, Abbott was greeted warmly. "As Mr. Antrobus, George Abbott, the song-and-dance maestro, gives a pleasant and knowing performance," the *Times* noted. "A little small vocally but big in understanding." Abbott came away from the experience with a realization. "Sometimes I have been a little arrogant with actors and have told them acting wasn't work. Directing is work, writing is work . . . but not acting. Now I had to eat my words. After the age of thirty, acting *is* work."[8] *The Skin of Our Teeth* was Abbott the actor's swan song. He was never again tempted to return to performing.

10 THAT'S ENTERTAINMENT?

(1940–1960)

Pal Joey • *Beggar's Holiday* • *A Tree Grows in Brooklyn* • *New Girl in Town* • *Fiorello!* • *Tenderloin*

George Abbott is thought of as a conservative man of the arts. Throughout his career, some commentators considered him old fashioned and out of date in his writing and selection of projects. His career stretched out over so many eras that some critics had difficulty believing that a man who captured the Roaring Twenties on stage could also be relevant in the 1960s. Also, Abbott stubbornly refused to change his methods of working in the theatre. He believed that what worked effectively in the 1930s would still be useful in the 1970s and beyond. In this chapter, let us address the idea of Abbott being old fashioned and out of date throughout much of his career. As early as the 1940s, some critics already saw Abbott as a veteran and symbol of the past. Like the world in general, the theatre sees youth as the font of new ideas. We have looked at how Abbott often worked with young artists and was not afraid of those ideas. It is not a coincidence that he was involved with some very innovative and influential theatre productions, particularly in the musical genre. The already-discussed *On Your Toes* and *On the Town* are good examples. This chapter looks at six other Abbott musicals that were far from safe and conventional. As one might expect, few of them made much money.

When musical theatre aficionados consider shows that were ahead of their time, ***Pal Joey*** (1940) quickly comes to mind. It is often described as the first "adult" musical, not only for its sordid characters but for it total lack of sentimentality. It is also surprisingly well integrated for a musical three years before *Oklahoma!* It was author John O'Hara's idea to turn a series of his "Pal Joey" stories, currently running in *The New Yorker*, into a musical. Joey is a hoofer who finds work in sleazy clubs until he is fired for his womanizing, gambling, lies, and bad debts. The stories are all narrated by Joey whose uneducated, slangy way of telling a tale in run-on sentences makes him amusing but also somewhat despicable.

> One nite I am on my way out and some guy that had suspicions of me & his wife was waiting for me and I was doing some very fast talking when out of the corner of my eye I saw the Sailor and yelled to him and I must say what the Sailor can not do with his fist he does not have to do as he does it with the boot. I have seen some dirty fighting in my travels with the socialites and polo players I grew up with but nothing to compare with the Sailor who is a pleasure to watch work if you care for that sort of thing and I do especially when he is working on somebody that a minute ago was going to put their fist down my throat. Anyway the guy had the wrong party as it was not me but the drummer in the band. I had her sister and it was not even the right night he was referring to.[1]

O'Hara approached Richard Rodgers and Lorenz Hart in 1939 about the project. Rodgers, who tended to be conservative, was open-minded enough to think these tales would make a hard-hitting, truthful musical. Hart knew the characters and the seedy milieu only too well and jumped at the chance to write lyrics for such a show. O'Hara wanted to write the libretto even though he'd never written a play or a musical before. The songwriters asked Abbott to produce and direct *Pal Joey*, knowing that he could fix the book if O'Hara did not come through. Abbott was intrigued by the material but thought O'Hara's script too disjointed and meandering. He called it "a disorganized set of scenes without a good story line and required work before we would be ready for rehearsal."[2] Both Rodgers and Abbott, each writing about *Pal Joey* years later, complained about O'Hara's lack of involvement in the production. Abbott did the rewrites but O'Hara would disappear for days or even weeks. Rodgers was used to this kind of behavior from Hart but not from the librettist as well. So Abbott ended up writing *Pal Joey* (though he was not credited) and came up with a superior libretto.

Joey Evans (Gene Kelly) is a third-rate nightclub hoofer in Chicago who borrows money and beds chorus girls with no idea of taking responsibility for either action. He woos and wins the naive stenographer Linda English (Leila Ernst) then quickly dumps her when a bigger fish comes along in the form of the wealthy, bored society dame Vera Simpson (Vivienne Segal), a gal who barely keeps up a respectable front for her husband's sake. Vera and Joey are on the same wavelength and their torrid affair is without pretense on each of their parts. She rents a trysting place for them to meet and makes plans to build him a glitzy nightclub to star in. But when Vera tires of Joey, and some blackmailers make the situation sticky, she dismisses both problems with simple, professional ease. Vera, it turns out, is a smarter version of Joey. She offers the heel back to Linda who, having wised up to him, refuses, and Joey moves off into new territory and new, unsatisfying conquests. The tone throughout was tough and anti-romantic and the musical made no effort to charm or appease the audience. The dialogue was raw, funny, and smart.

> **Vera**   No, I've had no conversation with Mike. Give me some credit for intuition. After all, I am a woman.
>
> **Joey**   Yes, I'll say that for you.
>
> **Vera**   Intuition and mind changing. I decided last night that I'd never come here again. Tonight I change my mind. Oh, I can tell you the whole story. When we walked out of here last night, Mike was annoyed because he counted on our spending a lot of money. Right so far?
>
> **Joey**   Go ahead.
>
> **Vera**   So he fired you, but you said, "She'll be back, I know her kind." Right?
>
> **Joey**   I said, go ahead . . .
>
> **Vera**   Instead of appealing to my better nature, which you are sure I do not possess—Does it hurt? I hope?—you reveal yourself as a sensitive, understanding young man. And it worked. That's why I'm here . . . The reason it worked isn't because I was sucker enough to get angry. Oh, no. The reason it worked, dear Mr. Evans, was you were nice enough to treat me differently. Or is that a subtlety that escapes you? No matter. However, one thing you must never never never forget. I'm older than you, and I'm a very smart and ruthless woman, so don't try any fast ones. Come on.
>
> **Joey**   Where to?
>
> **Vera**   Oh, you know where to. You knew it last night. Get your hat and coat. I'll be waiting in the car.[3]

There is no such dialogue in the short stories, all of which are narrated by Joey. So either O'Hara or Abbott had to start from scratch to write dialogue for Vera and the other characters. Definitely Abbott provided the structure of the piece; as for this dialogue, it is not so easy to say who was responsible. One thing is clear: Hart wrote lyrics that matched the libretto's blunt style with a hard-as-nails attitude, even the love songs coming across as a con.

> Couldn't sleep
> And wouldn't sleep
> Until I could sleep where I shouldn't sleep.
> Bewitched, bothered and bewildered am I.[4]

For years Cole Porter had been suggesting sex in his lyrics with clever double entendres; Hart not only removed the double, he got rid of the entendres. The amoral Joey was not presented as a villain, but neither did he make any apologies to the world and he had no intention of changing. Joey was the American musical theatre's first anti-hero and he could fascinate even as he irritated. Likewise, Rodgers' music is cool, distant, and uncomfortably insincere. The score may not have produced as many hit songs as some of their previous shows but it was their most ambitious set of songs.

Rodgers had seen newcomer Gene Kelly shine in a small role in William Saroyan's play *The Time of Your Life* (1939) and thought of him first when it came to casting Joey. The wonderfully sly performer Vivienne Segal, who was so captivating in Rodgers and Hart's *I Married an Angel* (1938), was cast as Vera and the sparks between her and Kelly were thrilling. Yet the rehearsal process for *Pal Joey* was rocky. Not only were O'Hara and Hart often missing, Abbott caused difficulties of his own (according to Rodgers). He doesn't say so in his autobiography but Abbot most likely had second thoughts about producing and directing the controversial musical. Somewhere along the line he was convinced that *Pal Joey* was going to annoy and displease audiences and would be a quick flop. Abbott panicked and asked Rodgers and Hart to take a royalty cut, reduced the budget on Jo Mielziner's scenery, and refused to give choreographer Robert Alton the number of chorus girls he requested. Convinced that Abbott had lost faith in the project, Rodgers gave Abbott the opportunity to bow out as producer and director. The offer hurt Abbott's pride and from that point on he threw himself into presenting a daring, innovative musical, the audience's feelings be damned.

Pal Joey opened on Broadway in December of 1940 to mixed notices. Wolcott Gibbs in *The New Yorker* led the approving critics, applauding the "living, three-dimensional figures, talking and behaving like human beings." Brooks Atkinson was less enthusiastic in the *New York Times*, finding much to admire in the musical but wondering, "Can you draw sweet water from a foul well?" *Time Magazine* took the middle ground: "For those who can park their morals in the lobby, *Pal Joey* is a wow." Also failing to be generally appreciated by the press was the score. Even "Bewitched (Bothered, and Bewildered)," the musical's later popular hit song (though often with a cleaned-up lyric), was barely mentioned in the reviews. The flowing ballad "I Could Write a Book" also found some popularity after a time but in the context of the show it is just a lyrical con job. Virtually ignored were the caustic "Zip," the jazzy "You Mustn't Kick It Around," the amoral duet "Den of Iniquity," the sobering realization "Take Him," and the sarcastic "The Flower Garden of My Heart." Despite the mixed reaction by press and public, *Pal Joey* ran 374 performances on Broadway and did very well on the road. Cast recordings of a full score were not done in 1940 but in 1950 Vivienne Segal and Harold Lang made a studio recording of the score that was so popular they were cast in a 1952 Broadway revival that ran 540 performances.

This time around, more critics commended the musical, including Atkinson in the *Times* who now thought it "brimming over with good music and fast on its toes ... renews confidence in the professionalism of the theatre." Abbott did not direct the production and Jule Styne produced it with Leonard Key. There were less successful New York revivals in 1961, with Bob Fosse as Joey and Carol Bruce as Vera, in 1963 with Fosse and Viveca Lindfors, and in 1976 with Christopher Chadman and Joan Copeland. A revival by the Roundabout Theatre in 2008 had some book revisions by Richard Greenberg and was directed with uncompromising panache by Joe Mantello. The cast was headed by Stockard Channing as Vera and Matthew Risch as Joey and they, as well as the production, met with mixed press. Highly unsatisfying was the film version of *Pal Joey* released by Columbia in 1957. The movie was sanitized, watered down, and reconfigured piece that might have come out of the days of Hollywood's heaviest censorship. With Frank Sinatra as Joey, the character was changed from a Chicago dancer to a San Francisco crooner, Vera (Rita Hayworth, dubbed by Jo Ann Greer) was still high society but a former stripper (so that she could sing the risible song "Zip"), and Linda (Kim Novak, dubbed by Trudi Erwin) was now a dumb chorine. Nearly half of the stage score was dropped and famous, cheerier Rodgers and Hart numbers from other shows, such as "There's a Small Hotel," "My Funny Valentine," and "The Lady Is a Tramp," were inserted even though they did not fit the characters or the plot. There was even a happy ending with Joey reformed and going off into the sunset with Linda. How sad that Rodgers, who had been treated so shabbily by Hollywood in the 1930s and saw his scores with Hart mangled beyond recognition, should have to see the same thing happen to *Pal Joey* two decades later.

If *Pal Joey* is such an important musical, one must try to determine Abbott's contribution. His direction was roundly praised, from the staging of the nightclub numbers to the cunning dialogue scenes. Vivienne Segal was a seasoned actress, having starred on Broadway for the first time way back in 1925. But she had never been asked to play such a callous character before; actually, no one had. Kelly was a polished dancer but green as a singer-actor. His Broadway musical experience was limited to the chorus in *Leave It to Me!* (1938). Abbott must somehow be credited with getting superb performances out of Segal and Kelly. As for the script, we know something of the changes Abbott made in O'Hara's original. The character of Vera doesn't appear in the Joey stories and it was O'Hara who placed her as the leading lady in the musical. But there were scenes involving Vera—such as her attempt to fire a chorine she thinks Joey likes—that slowed down the action and muddied the focus. Abbott cut such scenes, as well as one in which Joey buys an expensive car with Vera's money. O'Hara had even written a happy ending in his script, Joey and Linda having a reconciliation and going to her sister's for dinner. Abbott's ending is more honest. Joey and Linda are seen outside the pet shop where they first met. Linda is cured; Joey is still lying.

Linda   Well goodbye. I guess I better be going.

Joey   I may shoot you wire and let you know how things are.

Linda   Oh, that would be wonderful. Goodbye. (*runs off left*)

Joey   And thanks, thanks a million. (*an attractive* **Girl** *enters, passes by, and exits right;* **Joey** *exits right.*)[5]

The age-old "Boy Meets Girl—Boy Loses Girl—Boy Gets Girl" plot is undone in *Pal Joey*. And it took an age-old pro like Abbott to do it.

Sometimes being called in to doctor a script and/or the direction of a production was a futile exercise for Abbott. Such was the case with the very intriguing musical ***Beggar's Holiday*** (1946), a jazz and blues reworking of John Gay's 1728 ballad opera *The Beggar's Opera*. The tale of the London outlaw Macheath and his enemies and lovers has held the European and American stages for three hundred years. Kurt Weill and Bertolt Brecht's adaptation 1928, *Die Dreigoschenoper* (*The Threepenny Opera*), had suffered a quick death on Broadway in 1933 but found wide acclaim Off-Broadway with Marc Blitzstein's version in 1954. In 1946, the property was little known by mainstream American audiences. *Beggar's Holiday*, with book and lyrics by John Latouche and music by Duke Ellington, was updated and given an American setting in the slums and political watering holes of the Big City. Alfred Drake played the dashing gangster Macheath, Jet MacDonald was his lover Polly Peacham, Zero Mostel her corrupt father, and Rollin Smith played the rival politician Lockit. Producers Perry Watkins and John R. Sheppard, Jr., tried to get Lena Horne for the multi-racial production but failed. John Houseman was hired to direct but it was soon clear he was not the right person for such a uniquely nuanced show. Abbott was asked to come in during late rehearsals to tinker with the book and take over the direction. In his version, "So much damage [had] already been done, so many wrong commitments made, that one [was] always in the position of trying to patch the sail with shoddy materials."[6] He asked for major changes in the cast, the dialogue, and even Oliver Smith's "breathtaking" scenery. "I think I could have made a hit show out of *Beggar's Holiday* had I been able to have the proper changes," Abbott wrote years later. "But having extravagantly squandered hundreds of thousands of dollars, the management now suddenly became penurious and was unwilling to squander a little more to salvage what they had already wasted. As a result, they lost it all."[7] Abbott moved on and Nicholas Ray was the final and credited director. The reviews for *Beggar's Holiday* praised the strong, integrated cast, Smith's settings, and Ellington's haunting music. Louis Kronenberger in *PM* probably best pinpointed the problem. "It is so far from a mere jazzed-up 'revival' that it can best be described as a very laudable attempt to do something really different in the musical field. Exactly what, however, you never find out—for the crushing reason that its fashioners seem not to have known themselves." George Jean Nathan, in his *The*

Theatre Book of The Year, 1945–1946, put it more simply: "*The Beggar's Holiday* vacillates nervously between satire and conventional musical comedy."[8] The huge, expensive production struggled to run an unprofitable fourteen weeks.

Could Abbott have saved *Beggar's Holiday*? It is difficult to say, this being a very offbeat musical and the slick Abbott Touch may not have been what was needed. I fear I make it sound like Abbott was only good at tinsel and tempo. He got to show a good deal of restraint and a more delicate touch with the gentle, nostalgic period musical *A Tree Grows in Brooklyn* (1951). The title means little to modern audiences but in its day *A Tree Grows in Brooklyn* was a best-selling novel by Betty Smith and a notable 1945 movie. The eager novice producer Robert Fryer had purchased the stage rights to the novel and Abbott heard about it. The inexperienced Fryer agreed to co-produce a musical version of *A Tree Grows in Brooklyn* with Abbott who would also direct and write the libretto with novelist Smith. As it turned out, Abbott did all the writing on his own while he took a cruise to various South American cities. Smith's novel is something of an epic, following a Brooklyn family for three generations. The film version had trimmed the book to focus on one troubled marriage and the daughter who is most affected by it. Abbott did likewise. In a turn-of-the-20th-century working-class neighborhood in Brooklyn, the hapless Johnny Nolan (Johnny Johnston) has trouble keeping a job or staying sober but he is loved all the same by his adoring wife Katie (Marcia Van Dyke) and their adolescent daughter Francie (Nomi Mitty). Katie's flamboyant oft-married sister Cissy (Shirley Booth) enters the picture with her own problems but ends up being some comfort to the family after Johnny dies. The writing is straightforward rather than poetic, though Johnny reaches some kind of poetry in his songs. He is a funny, tragic figure that audiences were getting used to in the "musical play" genre. At one point he tries to get his daughter Francie to face up to life.

Johnny   Look at me. See me for what I am . . . (*holds up a raffle ticket*) I hold in my hand the whole meaning of my life—a winning ticket on a second-hand piano that I can't even claim. I always meant to do better. I thought I had time. I thought I'd be young forever, and it ends like this . . . Don't ever throw away your bright young years, darlin'. Don't be a failure like me!

Francie   You're not, Papa! You're not![9]

This is not the usual Abbott territory. In fact, *A Tree Grows in Brooklyn* is probably the most delicate and affecting musical Abbott ever worked on. But there is a problem. Abbott doesn't quite trust the material he's working with. He doesn't trust his audience to accept a musical totally devoid of musical comedy. In some ways, he doesn't trust himself. In his libretto, the role of Aunt Cissy is enlarged and featured. She is the stuff of musical comedy. Did Cissy loom large over the musical because a star was cast in the role? Or did Shirley Booth, by her very presence, take over the show? Having won plaudits for her dramatic performance in *Come Back, Little Sheba* the previous season, Booth was established as one of the most versatile performers on Broadway. Her Cissy was alternately hilarious and pathetic. She never overdid it, never tried to steal focus. But she did. The reviews all centered on Booth's remarkable performance and musical comedy won out. More so than in the novel, Cissy comes alive in Abbott's writing.

Cissy   Stop thinking, Harry ...

Harry   Don't call me Harry.

Cissy   I call all my husbands Harry. It's an honor.

Harry   It ain't my name.

Cissy   But Harry's such a nice name in the dark.

Harry   Never mind that. Ain't you ashamed calling all them different men Harry?

Cissy   The first one's name really was Harry. And I was married to him too. On the level. He took me down to City Hall and we had a witness. Stuff like that gives a girl memories ... He sticks in my mind. He was so refined and had such a lovely build in the bargain.

Harry   You should-a stood with him.

Cissy   He had to go back to his wife.[10]

Another innovative aspect of *A Tree Grows in Brooklyn* was the evocative sets and lighting by Jo Mielziner. Taking the approach that this is a memory play though the eyes of young Francie, Mielziner did not portray Brooklyn realistically. The Brooklyn Bridge appeared in the background for every scene but it changed in character, from a bold, stiff structure in some street scenes to an impressionistic, free-floating figure during a ballet sequence. Mielziner's lighting was similarly surreal at times. In the designer's favorite moment, the stage was filled with clothes lines of laundry giving the grim neighborhood a bizarre carnival presence. Unfortunately, the design went when the laundry scene was cut.

Several critics pointed out the split personality of *A Tree Grows in Brooklyn*. "There are two shows within the stage version," Otis L. Guernsey, Jr. wrote in the *Herald Tribune*. "By far the better one is Shirley Booth singing and carrying on as a somewhat faded good-time girl." Guernsey was among the few who could not recommend the musical. John Chapman in the *Daily News* was more in line with the majority but even he had to acknowledge the dual nature of the piece. He thought the show "A splendid musical—or two musicals," he wrote. "The first act is marvelously funny ... the second act is very touching." Of the disparaging reviews, Frank Rizzo, in *Variety*, gave his opinion about the failure of the original production:

> The musical's failure was largely blamed on a script too tailored to accommodate the comic talents of Shirley Booth, in what was essentially a supporting role. But the show ... made other missteps. The arrival of the book's most appealing character—young Francie Nolan—was unnecessarily delayed, and an elaborate nightmare Halloween ballet in the second act, depicting the final descent of her goodhearted but alcoholic father Johnny Nolan, was a mistake.

There were enough money reviews to help *A Tree Grows in Brooklyn* chalk up a modest run of 270 performances; but finances as they were on Broadway, it was not enough to show a profit. Although revivals of *A Tree Grows in Brooklyn* are rare, the musical has developed a cult following over the years because of its sterling score. Arthur Schwartz (music) and Dorothy Fields (lyrics) wrote a resplendent set of songs that supported both sides of the musical's double personality. Among the highlights are the poignant "Make the Man Love Me," the lilting "It'll Buy You a Star," the catchy "Love Is the Reason," the vibrant "Look Who's Dancin'," and Cissy's farcical "He Had Refinement," one of the funniest and most revealing of all character songs. When Booth sang this delicious ditty about her former husband, *A Tree Grows in Brooklyn* firmly landed on the side of musical comedy.

Another Abbott musical with a hard-hitting subject that was softened by the presence of a Broadway star was **New Girl in Town** (1957). The source was Eugene O'Neill's 1921 drama *Anna Christie* and the star was Gwen Verdon. Since the play is not widely known today, let's look at O'Neill's plot. While not on his coal barge, the crusty Swede Chris Christopherson idles his time away at the Manhattan waterside dive run by Johnny-the-Priest with other sailors and the earthy Marthy Owen. Years ago Chris sent his daughter Anna to be raised by relatives in Minnesota but, unknown to him, she was sexually abused by her cousins and she ran off and became a prostitute. Chris gets a letter from Anna saying she is coming home and he thinks she is a refined, well-bred lady. When Anna arrives it is clear she is not so naive but to Chris she is the ideal of womanhood, a sentiment shared by the rough but good-hearted sailor Mat Burke who falls in love with her. When Anna eventually tells both Chris and Mat the truth about her history, the two get drunk and sign up on a ship going to Africa. Once they sober up they realize they both love Anna and accept her as she is. She promises to wait for their return and make a home for them both. The play is one of O'Neill's very few with a hopeful ending but, aside from that, this is not your typical musical theatre fodder. *Anna Christie* is a work of brutal realism overflowing with seedy atmosphere and dialogue that has a crude kind of poetry appropriate for its characters. It does not sound like something Abbott would readily agree to yet, oddly enough, it was Abbott who pursued the project. While in Hollywood filming *The Pajama Game*, the star Doris Day told him about a movie musical version of *Anna Christie* that Bob Merrill had scored and wanted her to make for MGM. Naturally the studio was fearful of a musical about a former prostitute, even if it starred Day. So Abbott listened to the songs, liked what he heard, and approached Harold Prince and Robert Griffith about doing it as a Broadway musical. Having just had a hit with *Damn Yankees*, Prince and Griffith wanted to be reunited with choreographer Bob Fosse and Verdon, again playing a floozie but this time for real. Frederick Brisson was brought on as another producer and a deal was made with MGM which owned the rights to the songs. Abbott agreed to write the adaptation and direct the show, but had his doubts about Verdon. Even though she had won over Broadway as Lola in *Damn Yankees*, Abbott insisted Verdon audition for Anna. She was insulted but complied, auditioning for Abbott who was not impressed. He gave her three weeks to rehearse and to then come back for a second look. Fosse worked with her and Abbott begrudgingly gave her the part. (In a very unusual move, Verdon had three standbys: one each for acting, singing and dancing.) As Abbott later explained, his hesitation was not a matter of talent. He just worried that the audience would expect Verdon to dance and everyone—Prince, Griffith, Abbott, Fosse, and even Verdon—agreed that Anna is not a dancing character and shouldn't dance. So Abbott charmed O'Neill's widow Carlotta Monterey into giving them the musical rights and *New Girl in Town*, as it was retitled, was a go.

For a musical that went relatively smoothly in rehearsals, *New Girl in Town* was quite obviously a big mistake when performed before an audience out of town. It was true to O'Neill, it was uncompromising in its execution, and the audience hated it. Clearly the public was not about to accept Gwen Verdon in a musical in which she doesn't dance. The artistic staff panicked and went about turning *New Girl in Town* into something totally different. Several dances were added, including an erotic ballet in the second act that attempted to visualize Anna's fantasy about working in a whorehouse. Prince, Griffith and Abbott wanted to cut the ballet because the audience reacted negatively to the somewhat-pornographic piece. Abbott later wrote that Fosse and Verdon "replied it was high art, that they didn't care what the audience liked."[11] Abbott even pointed out that "the ballet was false because it pictured the bordello in glamorous terms, whereas Anna Christie had nothing but loathing for her past."[12] Prince, looking back in his autobiography *Sense of Occasion*, confirms Abbott's version of the standoff. "We reached a poor compromise," he wrote, "The ballet was out in favor of another version ... The outcome was a pale imitation of the original. Still as out of place, but inoffensive. So much for compromise."[13] The further *New Girl in Town* moved away from *Anna Christie*, the more palatable it became. Audiences started to love it and, ironically, it got some very propitious reviews when it opened on Broadway in May of 1957. Most of them were valentines for Verdon, as with John Chapman's praise in the

Daily News: "Miss Verdon is remarkable. She acts with great honesty and effect, she sings bewitchingly, she dances with boundless skill, and is very beautiful." And there were high compliments for the show itself. "A thoroughly zestful and engaging period piece, a show with style, humor, and a rollicking score," wrote John McClain in the *Journal-American*. *Time*, on the other hand, thought "The result is no more a miraculous meeting—and mating—of extremes than a head-on catastrophe. It is, instead, an often pleasant but an always misguided show." Considering it was Merrill's first Broadway score, the press was generous in acknowledging the songs. Several numbers were well worth attention, including the expansive "It's Good to Be Alive," the sly duet "Flings," the rousing "There Ain't No Flies on Me," the kick-up-your-heels number "At the Check Apron Ball," and "On the Farm," a bitter solo for Anna in which she relates her sordid past and how she was sexually abused by her cousins. *New Girl in Town* also boasted a first-rate supporting cast. Cameron Prud'homme was her crusty father, George Wallace was a full-voiced Mat (spelled Matt in the musical), and Thelma Ritter stole all her scenes as the caustic Marthy. Riding on the good notices and the popularity of Verdon, the musical ran a profitable 431 performances. Prince later noted in his autobiography, "I have no regrets about *New Girl*. I think the lessons we learned were worth the trouble and we were paid for them. *New Girl* remains for us unique in that respect; a hit which I must consider a failure."[14]

Abbott also dismissed *New Girl in Town* as an artistic failure even though it made money. But there was much in the production that was admirable and Abbott was behind some of it. His script, for example, was very much in the style of O'Neill. He eliminated some of the thick, phonetically-written prose and replaced it with tight and blunt dialogue. In the original, Mat and Anna meet for the first time when he is dragged, more dead than alive, from a raft after days at sea. The two exchange long speeches about the sea. Abbott cuts to the chase.

Mat Ho, ho, I ain't dead. (**Anna** *enters with a whiskey*) Maybe I am dead.

Anna Here, drink this.

Mat It's a woman. A real live woman.

Anna Go on, drink. You'll need it, I guess.

Mat Or am I dreamin'?

Anna What a nut. Do you want it or don't you? Here.

Mat Whatever you say. (*drinks*) Wow! You're still here . . . How about a kiss for a dying sailor? You know what I thought at first? I thought you was a mermaid.

Anna Well, I'm not . . .

Mat   Have a heart, Baby. I've been at sea for four months. I've had a ship sunk under me. I thought I had seen my last woman and here I am standing safe—close enough to touch you.

Anna   Well, don't try it.[15]

The characters were sharply drawn and the seedy milieu was intact. Because all these were surrounded by nonintegrated dancing, the effect was softened but it was still there. Also, the staging of *New Girl in Town* had some masterful moments. For example, the opening scene, in which lusty sailors tumble off the ships and link up with the waterfront whores, was a more carnal version of the first scene in *On the Town*. The first act ended with the can-can number "There Ain't No Flies on Me," the curtain falling on the still-dancing ensemble. The second act curtain rose on the same scene, the cast all in movement as if the intermission had lasted only a few seconds. Of course Abbott kept the show moving; that was a given by this time. But he knew how to let everything stop to make an effect, such as Verdon/Anna's first entrance dripping with tacky accessories and wearing checkered spats; there was a breathless moment then the star-entrance applause broke the spell. Like *A Tree Grows in Brooklyn*, *New Girl in Town* was an ambitious musical play that slipped into musical comedy in its effort to please. Broadway audiences in the 1950s were not ready for musicals like *A Tree Grows in Brooklyn* or *New Girl in Town* as the creators originally intended. A decade later they would have been greeted very differently.

Abbott worked again with producers Prince and Griffith on two other unlikely musicals; one was triumphantly endorsed, the other viewed with disfavor. **Fiorello!** (1959) was a gamble that paid off even as it kept its integrity. *Tenderloin* was riskier and, consequently, an admirable failure. Both musicals were scored by newcomers Jerry Bock (music) and Sheldon Harnick (lyrics) and co-written with theatre novice Jerome Weidman, another case of Abbott supervising the first success of very talented youngsters. I say youngsters because, in 1959, Abbott was seventy-two years old. In America at that time, a good number of men were dead by that age. But Abbott found fresh blood in yet another new generation of talent. Still on the sidelines, Prince will eventually become the premiere director of Broadway musicals; the new George Abbott.

The idea of a musical about Fiorello LaGuardia came from Arthur Penn, a young and successful director of dramas (*The Miracle Worker*; *Two for the Seesaw*; *Toys in the Attic*) who wanted to break into musicals. He approached Prince and Griffith who liked the idea of doing a biographical political musical. That may not sound all that daring but consider how few examples existed before or since *Fiorello!* Musical bios were always about show biz, most conveniently about performers who easily break into song and dance. But politicians don't perform unless they are fictional cartoons as in *Of Thee I Sing* (1932) and *Louisiana Purchase*

(1940). It was Griffith who suggested Weidman for the libretto. He'd never worked on a musical before but Weidman had written some very astute novels about the New York political-commercial scene, as with *I Can Get it for You Wholesale* (which became a musical in 1962). Weidman started on the script, trying to contain LaGuardia's thirty-year political career within the confines of a musical. Prince and Griffith had been impressed with the short-lived boxing musical *The Body Beautiful* (1958) and approached Bock and Harnick. Without telling the songwriters what the musical was about, the producers asked if the duo would write three songs on spec. Given a long scene by Weidman set in a smoke-filled political caucus room, Bock and Harnick came up with the satirical "Politics and Poker." It perfectly captured the tone Prince and Griffith wanted: nostalgic for old-time political shenanigans but satiric as well. They didn't wait for the other two songs; Bock and Harnick were hired. Penn didn't like the song or what Weidman had written so far. He thought it was all too soft, not the hard-hitting exposé he imagined. So Penn bowed out of the project that he had instigated and the producers turned to Abbott to direct and contribute to the book. Abbott liked both the idea and Bock and Harnick's partially completed score. But, ever the play doctor, Abbott saw problems with Weidman's script. "Their attempt to do the story had, up to this time, been centered upon LaGuardia and Thea, Fiorello's first wife," Abbott later wrote. "Shortly after I began work, I became convinced that the second wife, Marie, was the principal woman character, and that the love story should center around her life-long devotion to the Little Flower."[16] In Weidman's original, Marie was only in the second act but Abbott introduced her early in the musical as Fiorello's secretary. But it was Weidman's idea to not include LaGuardia's years as mayor, events that 1959 audiences were all too familiar with from newsreels and radio broadcasts. Instead the musical would end with LaGuardia's second run for mayor with Marie at his side. (Marie LaGuardia was still alive and, not surprisingly, approved of this version.)

Prince later recalled in *Sense of Occasion* that Abbott and Weidman worked well together. "Abbott would outline a scene, Weidman would go home and write fifty pages overnight, and then Abbott would edit, rewrite, and structure the total."[17] The result was a splendid libretto that brought the man and his times to life. The musical begins in the 1910s with LaGuardia (Tom Bosley) as a small-time politician who is out to fight for the little people in New York City, particularly the newly-arrived immigrants. (Fiorello was half-Italian, half-Jewish.) When the Tammany Hall politicians, led by Ben Marino (Howard Da Silva), need a candidate for district office who is guaranteed to lose so that the status quo is not upset, they choose LaGuardia. To their surprise and disgust, the Italian ("Fiorello" means "little flower" in Italian) wins and begins to annoy members of the corrupt administration. With the outbreak of World War One, LaGuardia enlists. When he returns from Europe, Fiorello runs for mayor but loses to the swank (and well greased) "gentleman" Jimmy Walker. But the tables turn when the Walker administration is plagued with scandal and LaGuardia plans to run again. The romantic side of the story tells of Fiorello's courtship and marriage to Thea (Ellen Hanley), who dies in childbirth, and the realization that he loves the supportive Marie (Patricia Wilson). A subplot about the crooked cop Floyd (Mark Dawson) and the working girl Dora (Pat Stanley) provides some humor and is used to contrast Fiorello's high-minded ideals. The libretto has a slightly sarcastic approach to politics but is sincere enough that neither heroes or the villains turn into caricature. Throughout the script, Fiorello's sometimes-naive idealism is contrasted by Marino's cynicism. The two men have only a few dialogue exchanges in the musical but they often have parallel scenes, showing how each goes about his business in an opposite manner. Abbott provided the structure of the script but it is difficult to say who was responsible for the dialogue. In one scene, Fiorello and Marino argue about the Draft Act at the outbreak of war.

> **Marino** (*an angry outburst*)   If you really want to keep the boys at home, why do you go yelling your head off down there on the floor of the House? Why all this "let's pass this Draft Act" right away . . . ?
>
> **Fiorello** (*very quiet*)   Because when the people of the Fourteenth voted for me, and sent me down here, they changed me a little. They made me a little different from themselves. I can no longer think the way they think, as a single individual, a father or mother thinking about a son. I have to think about the whole country, all the people in it, what's best for all of them. I'm not a guy hanging around a political club any more, Ben. I'm a Congressman now.
>
> **Marino** (*sore*)   I wonder how your thinking would go if this Draft Act applied not only to people but also to Congressmen?
>
> **Fiorello** (*quiet*)   You can stop wondering about that. I enlisted this morning.[18]

Supporting the skillful script were Bock and Harnick's splendid songs. For the satiric side of the story, they wrote two dandy comic songs, "Politics and Poker" and "Little Tin Box," both of them showstoppers. There was also the plaintive ballad "When Did I Fall in Love?," the determined character song "The Very Next Man," the silly rhapsodic "I Love a Cop," and the waltzing "Til Tomorrow." Peter Gennaro provided the necessary dance and William and Jean Eckart's sets and costumes evoked the period beautifully. Casting an actor for the title role was problematic. Mature theatregoers remembered how LaGuardia looked and what he sounded like. After considering Eli Wallach for the role, Abbott and the producers came upon Tom Bosley, a plump 5'7" television actor who not only resembled Fiorello but had the easy-going charm of the popular mayor. In his Broadway debut, Bosley sparkled as Fiorello, and Howard Da Silva was a provocative and merry Ben Marino. As for Abbott's direction, the staging of *Fiorello!* departed from his most familiar look. Scenic designer Eckart used two turntables side by side to place the scenery on. The transition from scene to scene was circular rather than the flat drop scenery that Abbott usually worked on. This affected his writing as well as directing, for the short small-cast scenes in front of a drop were no longer necessary. With this cinematic approach and the newsreel footage used on occasion, *Fiorello!* did not look or move like an Abbott musical. The musical's opening was also unusual. Instead of a chorus number or dance, *Fiorello!* began with a spotlight on a chair where LaGuardia sat reading "Little Orphan Annie" and "Dick Tracy" into a microphone because there was a newspaper strike in the city. The familiar image so endeared audiences that they broke into applause each night. The critics took Abbott's nimble staging for granted. Walter Kerr in the *Herald Tribune* was one of the critics to acknowledge the veteran director. "George Abbott is younger than springtime," he wrote.

> He has been around long enough to have patented all the formulas. And the one thing Mr. Abbott isn't interested in is formula. Here he goes again. He forgets all those rules about how the dancing girls and boys had better hop out there every three or four minutes, how all the scenery had better be big and plush and picturesque, and how half of the ballads had better be tunes that are sufficiently unrelated to what is going on to make them sure-fire stuff with the disk jockeys.

Just about all the reviews for *Fiorello!* were raves. *Newsweek* called it, "One of the slickest, sassiest and most satisfying Broadway shows in years. *Fiorello!* is so much fun that it looks easy." The musical went on to win every award available, including the Pulitzer Prize. (It was only the third time a musical was so honored; *Of Thee I Sing* and *South Pacific* preceded it.) *Fiorello!* ran a very lucrative 795 performances and would have run longer, Prince notes, if an actors' strike hadn't interrupted the run and killed the momentum. Except for a two-week engagement by the New York City Light Opera in 1962, *Fiorello!* has not seen a full production in revival in New York. Few musicals with so many honors have fallen under the radar like this one. As the years passed and fewer and fewer New Yorkers remembered LaGuardia, *Fiorello!* lost its name recognition. Modern audiences wouldn't get it. You had to be there.

Pretty much the same team was reunited for **Tenderloin** (1960), another musical about New York politics. The time period was earlier than that of *Fiorello!* and the satire was nastier. Yet to the press and the public, it looked like Prince and Griffith were trying to replicate the formula that made *Fiorello!* such a hit. In truth, *Tenderloin* came about for personal reasons. "We had such a good time doing *Fiorello!*," Prince later wrote, "That we could not bear splitting up after it opened—so we did *Tenderloin*."[19] Such warm camaraderie is rare in the theatre but it is hardly the basis for doing a big-budget Broadway musical. So they had a team in place—Prince, Griffith, Abbott, Weidman, Bock, and Harnick—but no property. Prince read some galley proofs of a novel that Random House was to publish titled *Tenderloin* by Samuel Hopkins Adams. It was about Rev. Brockholst Farr (based on the true-life reformer Rev. Charles A. Parkhurst) who tried to clean up the district of sin in New York City in the 1880s. Prince and Griffith thought it would make a good musical. So did others, including producer Merrick, who does not easily take no for an answer. Somehow Random House went with Prince and there lay the problem. The team assembled, it turned out, was not the ideal one for such a property. Looking back sixty years later, Prince in his autobiography concluded, "We did not so much make a mistake in choosing to produce *Tenderloin* as we did in choosing *ourselves* to produce it. Merrick and Gower Champion would have knocked the ball out of the park, because of course it wouldn't have been about real hookers, but would have been a joyous musical comedy."[20] In other words, Prince and Co. here too highbrow to turn this tale into successful fluff. "The main problem with *Tenderloin* was that it was done too fast," Harnick was quoted in Philip Lambert's book about Bock and Harnick, *To Broadway, To Life!* "The experience on *Fiorello!* had been so good and there was such euphoria among Abbott, Griffith and Prince, Jerry [Bock] and myself, that I think even before *Fiorello!* opened we were talking about the next show. They had the rights to *Tenderloin* and we just plunged in."[21] Abbott makes no mention of *Tenderloin* in his autobiography but Prince reported that the veteran showman had his doubts. For example, the leading role of the reverend had to be funny, a bit mad, or at least interesting. Abbott wanted the British character actor Hugh Griffith for the role. Prince and Griffith instead cast the distinguished British Shakespearean actor Maurice Evans. He gave a polished performance but came across as annoying and, worse, dull. But one cannot totally blame the actor; it was a dull character. The script that Abbott and Weidman wrote departed from the novel in several ways, among then naming the Parkhurst-like character Rev. Andrew Brock. They also put their cards on the table with the musical's non-musical opening.

Tommy   You heard of Horatio Alger? That's gonna be me. Right to the top and I don't care how. Nuttin' can stop me—I mean nothing. See? I'm improvin' already ... What am I? Just a four-bit singer. But you watch where I go. Cause this is the land of opportunity.

* * *

Nita   When I was a kid, we didn't have hardly enough to eat. Then we come to this country and I find out I have something men will pay for. I'm the highest-paid girl in the Tenderloin. For America is indeed the land of opportunity.

* * *

Officer Schmidt   I have just been assigned to the Nineteenth Precinct—the Tenderloin. And there I get my percentage off of everybody and everything. In five years, I'll be rich. For this here is sure the land of opportunity.[22]

The plot was far from complicated. Brock (Evans) arrives in Manhattan and leads a righteous campaign to clean up the vice in the Tenderloin district. He enlists the help of journalist Tommy (Ron Husmann) in his muckraking activities. But Tommy is out to frame the minister and he succeeds, the reverend brought to court on a trumped up sex scandal. For a happy ending, Tommy sees the error of his methods by the loving choir singer Laura (Wynne Miller) and Brock is free to take his campaign to Detroit. Tommy and Laura part ways; he goes to Denver but he hints that he may someday return to New York. Much of the libretto is smart and pointed, showing the self-serving side of both the sinners and the crusaders. But the two primary characters failed to connect with the audience. Tommy is a smiling and shallow cad, and his redemption seems forced. Rev. Brock is full of rhetoric but we learn nothing about the man underneath. Only the prostitutes, led by Nita (Eileen Rodgers), are funny and human.

Richard Altman, who received a Ford Foundation grant to observe the rehearsals, previews, and opening of *Tenderloin*, kept a daily diary of everything that happened and included his findings in the book *The Making of a Musical* mostly about *Fiddler on the Roof* but starting with *Fiorello!* and *Tenderloin*. "My specific assignment was to report on the way George Abbott built and shaped a Broadway show," Altman explained. Although he was initially in awe of the "unyielding and glacial wizard of Broadway know-how," he "quickly became disenchanted with [Abbott's] directional methods, which to me seemed hopelessly mechanical." Altman admitted that he "was not fortunate enough to observe [Abbott's] work when he was at his peak."[23] Yet Abbott still had a handful of hits in his future. But *Tenderloin* was not to be one of them. Altman was also "surprised at [Abbott's] inability to come to grips with *Tenderloin*'s problem-ridden book early enough to make it work. He blindly followed his own rule of changing little or nothing until a show went out of town."[24]

Among *Tenderloin*'s many problems was a new member of the team. Prince and Griffith managed to get the esteemed British designer Cecil Beaton to do the sets and costumes. "Beaton did a beautiful job," Prince recalls. "But for the wrong show. It was tasteful and chic. It should have been vulgar." On the other hand, Beaton created grotesque makeup for the prostitutes. "We took some of the prettiest girls you ever saw in your life and made them ugly," Prince wrote.[25] A new team member who did work out was Joe Layton who came up with some effervescent choreography for *Tenderloin*. The musical also came to life with some of the Bock and Harnick songs. Altman observed that, "The pressure was never off the [songwriters] to keep coming up with new and better material. They worked around the clock and, as a result, five or six of the best songs in the show were inserted during the Boston run."[26] It is an exceptional score: sly, razor sharp, clever, and even tuneful. But too smart and knowing to catch on. (One number, the grossly insincere ballad "Artificial Flowers," was sung by Tommy to win over Laura and the reformers; taken out of context, it was a hit record for Bobby Darin.) The opening number, in which a hymn sung in church was overpowered by the denizens of the Tenderloin singing "Little Old New York Is Good Enough for Me," was as brilliant a start as you could wish. But then the Puritans took over and could only offer the naive "Good Clean Fun." Other significant numbers in this fine score included the sarcastic "The Picture of Happiness," the tongue-in-cheek "Reform," and the first-act closer "How the Money Changes Hands " which dramatizes the corrupt system flourishing in the Tenderloin district. The reviews for *Tenderloin* when it opened on Broadway in October of 1960 were mostly disparaging even as the critics had to point out the musical's enjoyable aspects. John McCarten in *The New Yorker* wrote "As soon as anyone in *Tenderloin* leaves off singing and dancing in order to keep the plot going with dialogue, the whole business becomes a bore." Prince and Griffith had had five hit musicals in a row so the press was unusually snide in celebrating their first failure. Because of a sizable advance, *Tenderloin* ran 216 performances; not enough to make a profit but not an embarrassment. Abbott still got kudos from some of the critics. Frank Aston in the *World-Telegram & Sun*, wrote, "George Abbott has whomped another whopper of a musical. I was completely Abbottized in song, dance, and merriment." Reviews like that kept Abbott in the ranks of the in-demand directors. But it would not last. By the later-1960s, when edgy and provocative musicals like *Cabaret* and *Hair* were finding an audience on Broadway, producers were no longer asking Abbott to stage them. There were disadvantages in being ahead of your time.

Although he never mentions it in his autobiography, Abbott worked in television for a while in the early 1950s. He foresaw how popular the medium would be and thought he should get involved. Prince first met Abbott not in theatre but through television. In his autobiography, Prince recalled in *Sense of Occasion*, "[A friend] had heard that George Abbott was organizing a small experimental TV unit and arranged an interview for me . . . I went straight over [to Abbott's office] and I never left."[27] Abbott produced a game show titled *Charades* for NBC and it was successful enough that the network hired Abbott to write and direct *The Hugh Martin Show*. Prince later wrote, "Television operation annoyed Abbott for many good reasons. There was *so* much activity: many shows on the air, much hysteria in the office . . . Abbott prefers *calm*."[28] When Abbott had Prince write and direct one episode of the show, the young assistant clashed with Hugh Martin and the episode was far from satisfactory. But Abbott must have seen something worthwhile in Prince. "Martin went to Abbott and insisted I be taken off the show," Prince remembered. Abbott refused. "Martin put it to Abbott: Prince or the show. Abbott chose Prince; the show went off the air."[29] So ended Abbott's foray into television.

11 ALL THEY WANT IS MUSICALS

(1950–1955)

Call Me Madam • Out of This World • Wonderful Town • Me and Juliet • The Pajama Game • On Your Toes (revival) *• Damn Yankees*

Although George Abbott would continue to stage plays on Broadway into the 1970s, he was pretty much pegged a director of musicals by the 1950s. It is not difficult to see why. In the Fifties, he had six musical hits. And while Abbott might have been categorized for musicals, he was not limited to one kind of musical. The variety in his 1950s credits is impressive. We have already looked at *New Girl in Town, Fiorello!*, and *Tenderloin*, atypical musicals for the time. Now we must consider his more conventional, and frequently more popular, musicals from that golden age of the 1950s.

Irving Berlin's first musical on Broadway was *Watch Your Step* way back in 1914. How interesting that Abbott did not do a Berlin musical until 1950 with **Call Me Madam**. Of course, many of Berlin's Broadway credits were revues, which Abbott seemed to avoid or was not considered for. But there were some 1940s Berlin musical comedies, such as *Louisiana Purchase* (1940) and *Annie Get Your Gun* (1946), that were definitely Abbott kind of shows. *Call Me Madam* certainly was one, though he was hired late in the process. Authors Howard Lindsay and Russel Crouse had to look no further than the current newspapers to get the idea for the musical. The celebrated Washington hostess Pearl Mesta had long been a mover and shaker in the social and political circles in DC. In 1948, President Harry Truman named Mesta the Ambassador to Luxembourg even though she had no official diplomatic experience. The idea of a society dame caught up in international diplomacy struck Lindsay and Crouse as funny and promising. Also, their comedy *State of the Union* (1945) had been a political comedy and had done very well. (It even won the Pulitzer Prize.) Leland Hayward had been the producer of that hit play so the authors had little difficulty convincing him to present their Pearl Mesta idea on Broadway, especially once Ethel Merman was interested in the property. The libretto for *Call Me Madam* is far from inspired but very workable and serviced the songs and Merman very well. The Texas oil widow Sally Adams (Merman) throws such grand parties in Washington that President Truman appoints her ambassador to the little European country of Lichtenburg. Willing to shower the needy nation with US dollars, she offends the dashing prime minister Cosmo Constantin (Paul Lukas) just as she is starting to fall in love with him. Sally's assistant Kenneth Gibson (Russell Nype) is also enamored of a Lichtenburg native, the Princess Maria (Galina Talva), and with Sally's help he wins her heart just as Cosmo and Sally are reconciled.

Merman wanted Irving Berlin for the songs and she usually got her way. It was fairly late in the game before Abbott joined the team as director. In his biography of Berlin titled *As Thousands Cheered*, Laurence Bergreen wrote that "George Abbott—Mr. Abbott to everyone—approached a new production as if he had been called in to quash a rebellion in a remote corner of the British Empire."[1] Abbott wanted George Balanchine to choreograph but Berlin wanted Jerome Robbins, who did the dances in his recent *Miss Liberty* (1949), and Berlin usually got his way. In fact, the only major concession made in creating of *Call Me Madam* was on the part of Robbins who saw one of his ballets cut. As Abbott recollected, Robbins "had conceived a big number about the wild men from the mountains coming down and dancing in the village."[2] Although Robbins had started dancing rehearsals early to have more time to put the ballet together, the creative team was in agreement that it "had to be jettisoned." There were also some tense moments when Lindsay arrived at a rehearsal and heard some lines of dialogue neither he nor Crouse had written. Abbott had tinkered with the script and had not yet had the opportunity to check the changes with the authors. Lindsay was furious and said in front of the cast, "Well, I hope we still have the same title."[3] It took some explaining before Abbott appeased Lindsay; but the changes were retained. During the tryouts in New Haven, Merman announced that, try as she could, she could not make her song "Mr. Monotony" work. The song, which had already been yanked out of two previous Berlin shows, created a Black Hole in the second act. It was cut and the hole got bigger. It is not clear where the idea came to replace it with a new duet for Merman and Russell Nype but Merman liked what Nype was doing with his secondary role of Kenneth in the first act. Berlin agreed to the idea but had trouble coming up with a song. It could not be a love duet (Kenneth is Sally's assistant/secretary) and Nype's singing voice was higher than Merman's. Again, there are various versions of what happened next but some sources say that Abbott was listening to a new recording of Berlin's 1914 hit "(Play a) Simple Melody" by Bing Crosby and his son Gary and he had an idea. The catchy "A Simple Melody" was a contrapuntal number; that is, two distinct melodies and lyrics that can be sung together. Abbott asked Berlin if he could write such a double song for Merman and Nype. It was just the kick-start Berlin needed and in a few days he completed "You're Just in Love," the best song in the *Call Me Madam* score and the last great song of Berlin's career.

Although Berlin's *Miss Liberty* had been a financial and critical failure the year before, the advance sale for *Call Me Madam* climbed close to $1 million by the time it opened on Broadway in October of 1950. The reviews were almost all raves with plaudits equally divided for Berlin and Merman. Robert Coleman in the *New York Daily Mirror* called Merman the Joe DiMaggio of Broadway. "It is the terrific Ethel who has to hit the homers after her associates have walked or singled. And she never lets the team down." Richard Watts, Jr., in the *New York Herald Tribune* declared, "The Irving Berlin songs and a superb production make *Call Me Madam* the gala it promised to me." While "You're Just in Love" got the most mention, Berlin's songs were roundly praised. The score remains one of Berlin's finest with such highlights as the chipper "The Hostess with The Mostes 'on the Ball," the gentle ballad "Marrying for Love," the jaunty "It's a Lovely Day Today," and the political ditty "They Like Ike." (The last number later became Eisenhower's campaign song when he successfully ran for President.) *Call Me Madam* ran a hefty 644 performances, toured, and in 1953 was turned into a commendable film by Twentieth-Century Fox. The movie provided Merman with one of the rare opportunities to recreate her stage role on screen and the result was a blockbuster for the star and the studio. Never considered thin and pretty enough for the camera, Merman saw her Annie Oakley and other Broadway roles made by others in Hollywood. But Sally is a middle-aged character and Fox took a chance and cast her; it is arguably her best film performance. Most of the Berlin score survived the transition and Donald O'Connor and Vera-Ellen were in fine form as Kenneth and the Princess Maria. Walter Lang directed the Sol C. Siegel production and Robert Alton did the choreography. The result is one of the more faithful stage-to-screen musicals and a thorough delight on every level.

Abbott's only musical with Berlin was a hit; Abbott's sole collaborations with Cole Porter and with Rodgers and Hammerstein were not nearly as successful. Porter (like Berlin) had seen the American musical change after *Oklahoma!* (1943) and thought his Broadway days were over. But just as Berlin had a huge hit in the new style with *Annie Get Your Gun* (1946), Porter found a second life on Broadway with *Kiss Me, Kate* (1948). Abbott doesn't even mention Porter's **Out of This World** (1950) in his autobiography even though he directed it (uncredited) and it was his only opportunity to work with the celebrated songwriter. Dwight Taylor wrote the libretto, a modern take on the ancient Greek tale of Amphitryon, the mortal whose wife Alcmene was seduced by Zeus. In this musical version, Zeus is now Jupiter (George Jongeyans) and is smitten with the newly-wed American Helen O'Malley (Priscilla Gillette). She is in modern Greece with her husband Art (William Eythe) trying to get an interview with the Chicago gangster Niki Skolianos (David Burns) on the run from the law. Jupiter sends the messenger god Mercury (William

Redfield) down to earth to arrange a tryst. Art is sent on a false lead and Jupiter, taking Art's human form, beds Helen. Jupiter's wife Juno (Charlotte Greenwood) finds out what is going on and goes down to earth to find her husband, only to pursue the wrong mortal. Knowing that his wife is after him, Jupiter returns to Mt. Olympus and Helen returns to her dull life with Art. Lemuel Ayers and Arnold Saint Subber, who had produced *Kiss Me, Kate*, liked Taylor's script and recruited Porter for the score, Agnes de Mille to direct, and Hanya Holm to choreograph. Before rehearsals began, Porter complained about how serious the script was so Reginald Lawrence was hired for rewrites. The producers tried unsuccessfully to interest Carol Channing and then Judy Holliday into playing Juno but ended up with the Hollywood character player Charlotte Greenwood who had not been on Broadway in two decades. Previews in Philadelphia did brisk business but *Out of This World* was fraught with problems as songs were deleted and then replaced. The libretto was still lacking and so Abbott was called in to fix things. Porter refused to make any more changes in the score but Abbott convinced him to remove a song from the second act because the singer (William Eythe) could not hit the notes. Porter agreed and "From This Moment On" was cut. Ironically, it would become a hit later when used in the screen version of *Kiss Me, Kate*.

Out of This World opened to mixed notices. The critics all loved the high-kicking Greenwood, John McClain in the *Journal-American* writing, "There is a gangling and engaging lady named Charlotte Greenwood, whose legs apparently emerge from her shoulder blades and whose arms hang to her ankles." The songs most cited by the press were Greenwood's comic numbers, "I Sleep Easier Now," "Nobody's Chasing Me," and I Got Beauty." Too few commentators appreciated the other songs, such as the dreamy "Use Your Imagination," the rhapsodic "I Am Loved," the merry list song "They Couldn't Compare to You," the witty "What Do You Think about Men?," and the lilting ballad "Where, Oh, Where?" Although few recognized it as such, Porter's score for *Out of This World* is now considered one of his finest. The other aspect of the musical that was universally applauded by the critics was co-producer Ayers' sets and costumes. John Chapman in the *New York Daily News* wrote, "You will not see again for some time so many lovely sets, costumes, curtains, and drops." But glittering visuals have rarely saved a musical from such critical comments as "second rate operetta" and, despite its healthy advance, *Out of This World* ran only five months in the huge (but only partially-filled) Century Theatre. As far as Abbott was concerned, it was another case of his coming in too late to save a musical riddled with problems.

Most of the team from *On the Town* was reunited with Abbott for **Wonderful Town** (1953): composer Leonard Bernstein, lyricists Betty Comden and Adolph Green, and choreographer Jerome Robbins. Ironically, only Abbott was in the original team for *Wonderful Town* put together by producer Robert Fryer. The property he optioned was far from fresh material. Ruth McKenny had written a series of semi-autobiographical stories in *The New Yorker* about the misadventures she and her sister Eileen had in Greenwich Village in the 1930s. The tales were collected and published together as *My Sister Eileen*. In 1940, Joseph Fields and Jerome Chodorov turned the stories into a long-running comedy, also titled *My Sister Eileen*. The play was successfully filmed in 1942 with Rosalind Russell as Ruth. Three attempts were made in trying to musicalize *My Sister Eileen* before it eventually became *Wonderful Town*. Producer Max Gordon optioned the property and hired Dorothy and Herbert Fields to write the libretto and lyrics for music by Burton Lane. The deal fell through because movie mogul Harry Cohn still had the rights from the movie made at Columbia Picture and was hesitant to release them. Nevertheless, producer Leland Hayward also put together a proposed production with Joseph Fields joining his brother and sister to write a script for an Irving Berlin score. When Berlin pulled out, Cole Porter was hired. Again the project fell apart. A third attempt was planned with Ella Logan playing Ruth but it did not get very far. In a fourth try, Fryer got Russell interested in reprising her Ruth in a musical, hired Fields and Chodorov to write the libretto, and Abbott was signed on as director. There were few surprises in the libretto but it was a workable script and retained what was so enjoyable about the stories and the play. The acerbic Ruth Sherwood (Russell) comes to New York City from Ohio with her pretty sister Eileen (Edith Adams) and they take lodgings in a Greenwich Village basement apartment. While Ruth pursues a writing career, Eileen hopes to become an actress. The city is not hospitable but eventually, through new-made friends and cockeyed luck, both end up with a sweetheart and a job. *Wonderful Town* was a simple tale with parallel (but very different) romantic relationships and a variety of fun characters. Leroy Anderson (music) and Arnold B. Horwitt (lyrics) were hired to write the score and Donald Saddler was brought on for the choreography. And so began a project about which Abbott later wrote, "There was more hysterical debate, more acrimony, more tension and more screaming connected with this play than with any other show I was ever involved with."[4]

It started with the songwriters stalling and giving excuses for why the score wasn't finished even as the date for beginning rehearsals loomed. When Anderson and Howitt finally presented some songs, Russell and the artistic staff thought they were so weak as to be unusable. Desperate for a score, Abbott approached Comden and Green to write new lyrics. They not only agreed but managed to get Bernstein to come back to Broadway and write the music. The trio had to work fast and they did not disappoint. The new songs came quickly and they were lively, funny, sarcastic, and fresh. Abbott, Fryer, and Russell were thrilled but Fields and Chodorov were not. They wanted to present a warm, nostalgic, romantic musical. They thought the new score was too modern, too facile, too slick. And so the battle began. Soon Robbins was brought in to redo some of Saddler's choreography. He restaged the opening number "Christopher Street" thereby giving the show a much stronger start. Then Bernstein added the dissonant number "Wrong Note Rag" which spoofed jazz, swing, and modern music; the librettists were furious. It all climaxed at the dress rehearsal the night before the first performance in New

Haven. Fields and Chodorov panicked, declared that everything about the production was wrong, and demanded several major changes be made right away. "We sat in that cold, empty theatre after that rehearsal," Abbott later wrote,

> Our quarrels out in the open, our voices penetrating to the deepest basement dressing room, shouting, arguing, name calling. Obscenities filled the air. As the director, I could not have made changes at this point even if I had approved of them. Any such decision would have thrown the cast into such confusion that our opening night would have inevitably become a shambles. I finally concluded the debate by walking out on it.[5]

Russell had not been on Broadway since *Garrick Gaieties* in 1930 and was very insecure in her singing. During the tryout tour, she lost her voice and then one night she was dropped during the "Conga" dance number and sprained her back. Russell was out of the show for a while but when she returned her singing improved thanks to co-star Adams, a trained singer who helped Russell get through the tricky harmonizing on "Ohio" by giving the star her starting note each performance. Everyone expected disaster so when the out-of-town audiences loved *Wonderful Town* it seemed tensions would decrease. "However, amity was never completely restored among all of us" wrote Abbott. "Sometimes a success will make all problems disappear, all differences evaporate, but in this case the antagonism between the writers of the book and all the rest of us continued."[6]

Wonderful Town opened on Broadway to the most glowing reviews of the season: "One of the gayest, smartest shows of recent times" . . . "[Russell] proves that she's as magnetic on stage as in the movies" . . . "Bernstein has achieved a score of remarkable quality" . . . "Comden and Green have written some extraordinarily inventive lyrics" . . . "The George Abbott touch is a grip of iron on [a] wonderful evening." Walter Kerr in the *Herald Tribune* made the point that, "If *Wonderful Town* belongs to the conventional rather than the adventurous school of musical comedy, its collaborators seem engagingly unaware of the fact; it is all new to them, and they make it all new to you." The musical ran a happy 559 performances with Carol Channing taking over for Russell later in the run. Oddly enough, no hit songs came from Bernstein's score. Was it that dissonant? Among the highlights were Ruth's riotous dance with some Brazilian sailors as they sang "Conga!" and a satirical nightclub act in a Greenwich Village watering hole with everyone singing and dancing to the "Wrong Note Rag." Other delectable songs from the show include the homesick ballad "Ohio," the revelatory "It's Love," the comic lament "One Hundred Easy Ways (To Lose a Man)," and the soothing ballads "A Quiet Girl" and "Never Felt This Way Before (A Little Bit in Love)." There was no movie version because Cohn planned his own movie musical with a different score. Reverting back to the title *My Sister Eileen*, the 1955 movie featured Betty Garrett, Janet Leigh, Jack Lemmon, and Bob Fosse who also staged a few of the dances. But

Russell did get to reprise her performance in a CBS television adaptation in 1958, the same year there was a limited-run revival by the New York City Opera starring Nancy Walker and Jo Sullivan as Ruth and Eileen. The same organization revived the musical in 1963 with Kaye Ballard (Ruth) and Jacquelyn McKeever (Eileen) and in 1967 with Elaine Stritch (Ruth) and Linda Bennett (Eileen), and the New York City Opera did a production at Lincoln Center in 1994 with Kay McClelland (Ruth) and Crista Moore (Eileen) leading the cast. Because she was known mostly for her dramatic roles in musicals, Donna Murphy surprised and delighted reviewers and audiences with her farcical performance as Ruth in the 2003 Broadway revival based on an earlier Encores! concert. Kathleen Marshall directed and choreographed the production and it ran 497 performances.

Three months after *Wonderful Town* opened, Abbott was again represented on Broadway as the director of Rodgers and Hammerstein's ***Me and Juliet*** (1953). This was a much anticipated event because the team had had five box office hits in a row. (Even the experimental *Allegro* in 1947 had run 315 performances.) Like *Allegro*, the new musical was an original idea and not based on a previous play or book. As Rodgers explains in his autobiography,

> *Me and Juliet* grew out of our fascination with the theatre ... One of our aims was to avoid all the clichés usually found in backstage stories ... The show within the show was a success. The backer didn't pull out, the star didn't quit and the chorus girl didn't take over. We simply used the production as a framework for a love story.[7]

Hammerstein's libretto sounds workable on paper. Backstage at the Broadway musical *Me and Juliet*, the Assistant Stage Manager Larry (Bill Hayes) falls in love with the chorine Jeanie (Isabel Bigley) and encourages her to audition for the understudy job to the leading lady. Jeanie's ex-lover, the bitter electrician Bob (Mark Dawson), tries to break up the lovers with threats and, while drunk, even drops a sandbag from the flies to kill Jeanie, but it misses. Larry and Jeanie decide to wed. In between scenes and songs from *Me and Juliet*, a romance also blossoms between the dancer Betty (Joan McCracken) and the Stage Manager Mac (Ray Walston). But Mac makes it a policy not to date girls in the show he is running so the affair is off until Mac gets a job with another show. When Rodgers approached Abbott about directing *Me and Juliet*, the veteran director "was eager to do so." He had worked with Rodgers several times but never with Hammerstein. They sent the script to Abbott who read it "with high hopes" but was greatly disappointed. "It was melodramatic and sentimental, and I didn't like it ... what I read was shoddy." But an invitation from Rodgers and Hammerstein was difficult to turn down. "Still, these were smart fellows," Abbott reasoned. "I could be wrong." So he met with the famous team to discuss the script and was somewhat relieved when Hammerstein said, "Take it home, cut it, makes notes, treat it as ruthlessly as though it were you own." But Abbott found that there was little he could do with the libretto. "In the main, my cuts were accepted," he later wrote, but the changes were far from "ruthless."[8] It was the whole idea that was wrong, not simply a character or a scene. *Me and Juliet* was dull and all one could hope is to disguise the fact with an impressive production.

Much has been written about every Rodgers and Hammerstein musical, even *Me and Juliet*. So the libretto for this problematic show has been studied with an eye for determining just where the thing fails. The uninteresting love stories with an equally routine love triangle, the show-within-the-show not arousing any curiosity, the lack of a strong climax, and even the absence of a star role have all been offered as excuses. But the real reason is perhaps less obvious. Ethan Mordden, in his book *Rodgers and Hammerstein*, suggests that the team's vow to avoid backstage clichés was flawed. "What backstage musicals? Broadway is already backstage. The backstager was developed in Hollywood, as were the clichés ... There were no clichés for R&H to subvert because, as far as backstage musicals went, there were no clichés."[9] In other words, showing a truthful depiction of professional theatre is not a very refreshing idea for a musical. Everything in *Me and Juliet* was highly polished and first-class but underlying all the work was the fact that the show had nothing to say. And for a Rodgers and Hammerstein musical to be mute and toothless meant disaster. None of this was obvious during the rehearsal process. The cast of unknowns was more than competent, several of the songs were immediately likable, and Abbott's staging and Robert Alton's choreography were more than satisfactory. Jo Mielziner's scenery and lighting magically moved the focus from backstage to onstage and back again, giving audiences one of the most complete depictions yet seen of the workings of a large theatre. This magic did not come easily or cheaply. Five tracks with motors were needed to move the large set pieces as the action moved from the bright musical being performed onstage to the backstage filled with shadows. It was all rather exciting to behold. Perhaps too exciting? The sets for *Me and Juliet* were so large and complex that the show didn't fit in the Shubert Theatre in New Haven so the out-of-town tryouts were in Cleveland and Boston. The audiences were mildly entertained in both cities but there was something wrong. Rodgers recalled, "Whatever flickering optimism any of us may have had about *Me and Juliet* was quickly doused when we heard people raving about the sets, without a word being said about the rest of the show."[10] So *Me and Juliet* opened on Broadway in May of 1953 to generally dismissive reviews. Brooks Atkinson in the *New York Times* wrote, "The book has no velocity ... [the musical] looks a little like a rehearsal—beautiful, talented, full of good things, but still disorganized." Coleman in the *Daily Mirror* noted, "Had it been penned and composed by a couple of [beginners, it would be] a fair start, showing promise of sorts. But coming from the atelier of the masters it was, to put it kindly, incredible." Because of its considerable advance, *Me and Juliet* ran 358 performances, enough to make a modest profit for Rodgers and Hammerstein who also produced the production.

Today *Me and Juliet* only exists as an original cast recording. (There were no film or television versions made.) Because Rodgers and Hammerstein were incapable of writing a worthless score, there are some sparkling songs in the musical. The only hit to come from the score was the tango-like ballad "No Other Love," but also highly enjoyable are the bubbly "It's Me," the cynical "We Deserve Each Other," the flowing ballad "Marriage Type Love," the sly "Intermission Talk," and the bizarre tribute to audiences called "The Big Black Giant." All are melodic and appealing but none go below the surface like a Rodgers and Hammerstein song can. Of course, *Me and Juliet* was not a musical play; the producers billed it as a "new musical comedy." The show was never all that funny but there were few things that were "new," mostly the visuals. Aside from the already mentioned scenery, there were aspects of *Me and Juliet* that were striking to look at. At one point, a fully costumed production number on stage shifted to a rehearsal of the same number with the cast in rehearsal clothes. This was Hammerstein's idea but it fell upon Abbott to devise a way of carrying them out. Mielziner worked out how to move his unwieldy set pieces but it was Abbott who figured out how to move people through the scenic labyrinth. The director for this kind of show is really more necessary as a traffic cop. Any creativity might have fallen to the choreographer. Robert Alton was near the end of his long career and best represented old Broadway hoofing. *Me and Juliet* needed the new breed to take Hammerstein's ideas and translate them into something visually radiant. Abbott thought so from the beginning, stating that the play-within-the-play was unclear from the libretto but could be saved by dance. "Remembering Rodgers' 'Slaughter on Tenth Avenue,' I had visions of magic moments," Abbott wrote. "[But] they had engaged a routine, old-fashioned choreographer, Bob Alton, to do this work, not George Balanchine."[11] When *Me and Juliet* was in Boston, the producers sensed that the dance aspect of the show was lacking and asked Jerome Robbins (who had staged the show-within-a-show "Small House of Uncle Thomas" in their *The King and I*) to redo some of Alton's choreography. Robbins refused, not wishing to upset the veteran dance master. If Alton was the wrong choreographer for *Me and Juliet*, it is likewise possible that Abbott was the wrong director. He was the expert at musical comedy; this troubled musical was something altogether different.

For good old-fashioned musical comedy, you couldn't do better than the Richard Adler-Jerry Ross musicals *The Pajama Game* and *Damn Yankees* which Abbott co-wrote and directed. Both were unpretentious, conventional, and safely accessible. This helped make them among the most successful musicals in a decade filled with hits. Not only are both shows set in the 1950s but they have such an Eisenhowish sensibility that when they are revived, which is often, they are usually set in that time period. While so many musicals between *The King and I* (1951) and *Gypsy* (1959) attempted to expand the parameters of the Broadway musical, both *The Pajama Game* and *Damn Yankees* were happily content to look back to 1930s musical comedy for their inspiration. Few playgoers were bothered by the old-fashioned aspect of these two shows because both were written, scored, directed, choreographed, and performed so expertly. There was a lot of escapism in the theatre, movies, and television of the 1950s. But too rarely were the products as polished and tuneful and entertaining as with this pair of winners. What does that say about Abbott who was a major force in shaping *The Pajama Game* and *Damn Yankees*? As a craftsman, he was at his peak; as a creative and influential artist, he was back-peddling.

Robert Griffith and Harold Prince, who had both worked in the Abbott office, wanted to go into producing and found a property that would launch their new career together. Richard Bissell's 1953 novel *7 1/2 Cents*, about a labor dispute at a pajama factory, looked like a strong possibility for a successful musical comedy. The book had hardly been a bestseller but had some lively characters and enough conflict to make for an engaging plot. Because Griffith and Prince had no clout on Broadway, they needed someone on the artistic team who did. Their ex-boss Abbott was the obvious choice. According to Prince, writing in his memoir *Sense of Occasion*, "Abbott was not attracted to [the novel]; it seems drab, and it was about a strike . . . Still, Abbott agreed to direct it if we got it properly adapted. This, I'm convinced, purely out of affection for Bobby Griffith."[12] Prince, Griffith, and Abbott all tried to interest some of Broadway's many librettists in adapting *7 1/2 Cents* for the stage but everyone turned them down. "Others seemed to be even more shy than I was," Abbott wrote. "They felt that a garment factory and a strike was too serious and controversial a subject for a jolly musical."[13] At some point, Abbott came up with the title **The Pajama Game** and started to see ways in which the property might work. He informed Prince and Griffith that he would be willing to collaborate with Bissell on the libretto. Abbott then tried to get Frank Loesser to do the score. He declined but strongly suggested two young protégés of his, Adler and Ross, who wrote both music and lyrics together. The pair auditioned some of their songs for a stone-faced Abbott. The songwriters were crestfallen, then Abbott said, "Good. I think you're ready."[14] Writing years later in his autobiography *You Gotta Have Heart*, Adler related how Abbott bluntly outlined the situation. "I'm going to direct and write the libretto. It's going to be based on a book called *7 1/2 Cents* by Richard Bissell. It's about a strike in a pajama factory." The two songwriters could not hide the bewildered look on their faces. "I know," Abbott sighed. "It doesn't sound like Rodgers and Hammerstein, which is why they're not writing the score."[15]

The libretto Abbott and Bissell came up with was straightforward and efficient. Labor-management relations at the Sleep-Tite Pajama Factory in Cedar Rapids, Iowa, are not improved when the new manager, Sid Sorokin (John Raitt), and the union spokesperson, Babe Williams (Janis Paige), fall in love. The relationship is further strained when the union insists on a 7 1/2-cent raise and Sid and Babe find themselves on opposite sides of the bargaining table. When Sid threatens to fire any employee who participates in a slow-down strike, a furious Babe kicks one of the machines and inadvertently shuts down the whole production line. Sid has to fire her but, learning from the wily secretary Gladys (Carol Haney) that the company has been overcharging consumers, he gets the workers their raise and gets Babe back. The comic subplot concerned efficiency expert Vernon Hines (Eddie Foy, Jr.) trying to overcome his jealousy concerning his flirtatious sweetheart Gladys. The libretto played it safe by not coming down on the side of labor or management. Instead the musical was light-headed and somewhat simple-minded. Abbott overcame the potentially dangerous aspect of the story by ignoring it. Prez, the head of the union, is an incompetent boob ("Hey, I lost my lunch bucket. Anybody seen my lunch bucket?"[16]) and Hasler, the head of the factory, is a penny-pinching crook ("Turn off those damn lights! Do you think J. P. Morgan got rich leaving lights burning all over Wall Street?"[17]). The plot was solid and the jokes were in place but there is no trace of wit or satire in the writing, only over-sexed characters and over-worked bits.

> **Prez** (*of the union*) We can't just sit around here and do nothing. We got to make plans. Hasler ain't going to give in easy.
>
> **Brenda** We got the slow-down.
>
> **Prez** I mean other things, more like for instance, like a suggestion here from Jake Fondermeyer. He says when he was working at the Ironclad Overalls Company and they was having trouble, why they spit tobacco juice in the back hip pockets of the overalls.
>
> **Mae** I draw the line at chewing tobacco.
>
> **Brenda** How about if the packers put the large size bottoms with the size small tops, and like that?
>
> **Joe** Sure.
>
> **Prez** Now that's what I mean. That's *constructive*![18]

Maybe it was Abbott's conservative political stand and the Red Scare that was going on in America at the time, but *The Pajama Game* was indeed escapist—in every sense of the word. Not that Bissell's novel was an incisive look at labor relations. The tale was told from Sid's point of view with mostly descriptions about working methods in a garment factory and details about the hero's sex life. The novel is surprisingly undramatic so it must have been Abbott who made the material stage worthy. (Bissell had never written a play before.) Hines is a very minor, very unfunny character in the original book, and the wily Gladys needed to be created to give the musical some oomph. Fortunately the Adler-Ross score had plenty of sparkle. The dreamy ballad "Hey, There" was the undisputed hit of the show with many recordings to follow. But just as memorable were the tango

"Hernando's Hideaway" and the jazzy "Steam Heat." Also laudable were the waltzing "I'm Not at All in Love," the comic duet "I'll Never Be Jealous Again," the rhythmic "Think of the Time I Save," and the country-western spoof "There Once Was a Man." Adler and Ross were very commercial songwriters (they had written the hit song "Rags to Riches" for Tony Bennett in 1953) with the Hit Parade in mind but their score for *The Pajama Game* was full of variety and served the plot well. Because this was their first full score, the producers put in a clause that an outside songwriter could be called in if needed. It was never necessary.

A similar clause was written into the contract for Bob Fosse, a dancer who had never choreographed a Broadway musical before. Abbott was most likely behind this, cautious about having so many newcomers on the staff. To protect himself and the production, Abbott also asked that Jerome Robbins be brought on to handle any musical numbers that were not working. Prince related in *Sense of Occasion*, "[Robbins] agreed in return for a co-directing credit; which I knew was unacceptable. I told [Abbott about] Jerry's demands, to which he replied, 'Oh Hal, give it to him—everyone will know who directed the show.'"[19] Of course Prince and Griffith were also novice producers but that did seem to worry Abbott much. Fortunately, Prince and Griffith were smart enough to enlist the help of Hollywood producer Frederick Brisson who invested in *The Pajama Game* and was named co-producer. All the same, it took 134 investors to come up with the $250,000, a modest budget for a musical even at the time. Abbott doesn't mention it in his autobiography, but the production was $28,000 short when it went into rehearsal. Abbott supplied the much-needed cash. (He was later paid back by Brisson.) Other problems came up once rehearsals began. Ralph Meeker was not working out as Sid so was replaced by John Raitt. (Abbott didn't care for Raitt, complaining that the actor was too stiff.) Robbins had to redo two of Fosse's numbers, "There Once Was a Man" and "7 1/2 Cents." The character played by comic actress Charlotte Rae was deemed superfluous and both character and actress were eliminated. Her song "There Once was a Man" was given to Sid and Babe. On the other hand, some fortuitous changes were made during the out-of-town tryouts. Abbott requested a song "about a kind of spooky nightclub, a sort of rundown nightclub, with a furtive look to it ... something very dark, a kind of speakeasy. Maybe Spanish."[20] The result was "Hernando's Hideaway." In previews, the ballet that opened up the second act was not working. Abbott wanted to replace it with a variety show put on the union members. Fosse asked the songwriters for something rhythmic for the amateurs to perform. "Something with a strong beat,"[21] Fosse suggested. Adler played "Steam Heat," a silly ditty he had begun writing years before in his bathroom listening to the beat of the steam in the pipes. Fosse loved the rhythm of the piece and, with some additional lyrics by Adler and Ross, it was put in the show, launching the second act with a bang.

Even though Prince and Griffith were not experienced producers, there was a sense of confidence felt during the rehearsals. Abbott was the reason. As Prince later wrote,

He was the most disciplined man in the theatre. Don't suffer fools, learn your lines, say your lines, and don't get hysterical. The theatre is a breeding ground for jealousy and insecurity, but Abbott never bothered with that. Presumably, he'd already been through it. By the time we did *The Pajama Game*, he was sixty-seven years old and had pretty much seen everything.[22]

Although the word from out of town was that *The Pajama Game* was going to be a hit, the production opened on Broadway in May of 1954 with an advance of only $15,000. "That means," Prince later wrote, "the show would have run a performance and a half."[23] The unqualified rave reviews quickly turned *The Pajama Game* into a giant hit, running 1,063 performances. Writing in the *Herald Tribune*, Kerr led the cheers. "The bright, brassy, and jubilantly sassy show is not just the best new musical of the season. That would be fairly easy. It's a show that takes a whole barrel full of gleaming new talents, and a handful of stimulating ideas as well, and sends them tumbling in happy profusion over the footlights." Coleman, mixing his metaphors in the *Daily Mirror*, called it, "A riot of fun . . . a deliriously daffy delight. A royal flush and a grand slam rolled into one," and McClain in *The New York Journal American* described it as "fast, raucous and rollicking … the story is told with incredible delight and ingenuity." The musical shone a spotlight on the new songwriters, the freshmen producers, and dancer-turned-choreographer Fosse. As for the veteran Abbott, he was not overshadowed. Kerr also wrote, "Of course, behind all the brand-new names and the brightly creative stage business stands a gentleman named George Abbott. As wizard of the enterprise, he has wrought a humdinger." Much of this wizardry in *The Pajama Game* was a matter of style over content. Abbott's cunning staging of the musical was as important as the script. If this was only a routine musical comedy, it was necessary to present it as something fresh and new. For example, it was Abbott's idea to have Sid sing "Hey, There" into his dictaphone, then play it back while making disparaging comments, then singing a duet with himself. What would have been a standard scene of the hero singing a ballad became something as affecting as it was masterful. Also very clever was how the number "Hernando's Hideaway" began in total darkness then, when the lyric referred to lighting a match, one was lit and one table was illuminated. The match burnt out, another was lit, and so on until enough matches were lit to see the whole stage. It was more than a slick gimmick; the nightclub was patronized by men who didn't want to be seen with their clandestine dates. Again, this was not choreography; like the dictaphone, it was an Abbott idea. In the opening scene in the factory, the men and the women sang in counterpart as sewing, waves of fabric, and boxes of pajamas moved as in a vaudeville act. No wonder no one worried about content. *The Pajama Game* was a dazzling circus of a show. Abbott won his first of seven Tony Awards for *The Pajama Game*. He would be nominated ten times in toto, rather good for someone who was working in the theatre three decades before the awards were established.

(See the Appendix for a list of all of Abbott's Tony Awards and nominations and other honors.)

One might argue that the hundreds of productions of *The Pajama Game* over the decades have played very well on stage without Abbott's direction. Thank the libretto and score for that. Yet even the New York revivals could not capture the excitement of the original, even when Abbott himself returned to direct them. The 1957 City Center production featuring Larry Douglas (Sid), Jane Kean (Babe), Pat Stanley (Gladys), and Paul Hartman (Hines), saw the original stage and choreography recreated by Jean Barrere. An interracial cast was the distinctive feature of the 1973 revival in which Cab Calloway's comic Hines and Hal Linden's full-voiced Sid were most appreciated by the press. Barbara McNair was Babe and Sharron Miller was Gladys. Abbott staged the production which ran 65 performances. The New York City Opera offered theatre performers Richard Munez (Sid), Judy Kaye (Babe), Lenora Nemetz (Gladys), and Avery Saltzman (Hines) in a 1989 production at Lincoln Center. In 2006, Kathleen Marshall directed and choreographed a Roundabout Theatre revival and she was applauded on both counts, as was the personable cast. Pop singer-songwriter Harry Connick, Jr., was a sexy, engaging Sid, Kelli O'Hara a smart and vibrant Babe, Megan Lawrence a dizzy, funny Gladys, and Michael McKean a jovial Hines. The limited run quickly sold out, then was extended for 129 performances before Connick had to move on to other commitments. *The Pajama Game* came to the screen in 1957 with just about the entire cast and creative staff of the original Broadway show and, though the film looked stage-bound on occasion, it was a delightful copy of the original. Doris Day played Babe and Abbott shared directing chores with Stanley Donen, but the rest was pretty much the same. Jean Eckert, who designed the costumes for the film, noted "Abbott was coaching the actors in an already established Broadway hit. Abbott's position on the set left Stanley Donen with little to do but stand behind the camera."[24] Only four of the fifteen Adler-Ross songs were dropped and there were no outside interpolations so musically the movie was very faithful to the Broadway show. Some of Fosse's choreography opened up nicely for the screen, particularly in the frolicking "Once a Year Day," and the final number "7 1/2 Cents" was turned into a pajama fashion show. All the performances were bright and funny and the movie musical remains unpretentious fun. (Bissell later wrote a novel, *Say, Darling*, about his experience working on a Broadway musical. Abbott and other members of the creative team were fictionalized and exaggerated in the book. It was turned into a musical with the same title in 1958.)

Before moving on to *Damn Yankees*, Abbott decided to produce and direct a revival of his 1936 hit **On Your Toes**. He was probably encouraged to do so after a production of his *Pal Joey* was brought back to Broadway in 1952 and ran 540 performances. The new *On Your Toes* featured Bobby Van (Junior), Vera Zorina (Vera), Kay Coulter (Frankie), Elaine Stritch (Peggy), and Ben Astar (Sergei), and

George Balanchine's original choreography was recreated, including the famous "Slaughter on Tenth Avenue" jazz ballet. But even with a strong cast and the Balanchine choreography, the show could not compete with all the new musicals on the boards. Also, the critics were not very helpful. In his summary of the 1954–1955 season, Louis Kronenberger dismissed the "uneven musical" and likened the revival to that season's unsuccessful return of the old chestnut *Abie's Irish Rose*. *On Your Toes* ran only two months. It would be thirty years before the musical would be a hit on Broadway again.

Abbott's other Adler-Ross success was **Damn Yankees**. The musical is so familiar to theatre lovers today that it is difficult to imagine what a long shot it was in 1955. Yes, it had the same producers, songwriters, director, and choreographer as *The Pajama Game* but recent success is no guarantee in the crazy world of musical comedy. *Damn Yankees* had two major hurdles to overcome. Musical fantasies were tricky and only on a few occasions did they succeed. And, secondly, there had never been a successful musical about baseball. (Hit musical fantasies are still rare and no musical about baseball has survived since *Damn Yankees*.) Prince, Griffith, Adler, Ross, and Fosse were young enough to miscalculate the challenge they had taken on; Abbott knew better. Yet he was determined to make *Damn Yankees* work and it ended up being one of the most challenging projects of his career. When a literary agent sent Abbott a copy of Douglas Wallop's novel *The Year the Yankees Lost the Pennant*, he read it, thought it promising, and sent it on to Adler and Ross. Everything quickly fell into place and the team from *The Pajama Game* was reassembled except this time Fosse was the sole choreographer. (Also, the clause in the contract about an outside songwriter or choreographer being called in was gone from their contracts.) Wallop was hired to co-write the libretto with Abbott even though he had never written a play. So Abbott was left pretty much alone in hammering out the sly, modern take on the Faust legend. Joe Boyd (Bob Shafer), a middle-aged fan of the Washington Senators baseball team, is so distressed at their losing record that he exclaims he would sell his soul for a winning season for the team. The devil, in the form of the slick and smiling Mr. Applegate (Ray Walston), immediately appears and makes a deal with the fan: he will be turned into the young slugger "Shoeless" Joe Hardy (Stephen Douglass) who will lead the team to victory over those damn New York Yankees. Joe agrees and is soon a celebrity as the Senators start winning and head to the pennant. To keep Joe from getting sentimental about leaving his loving wife Meg (Shannon Bolin), Applegate conjures up the funny, sexy temptress Lola (Gwen Verdon) to seduce the homesick Joe as she has seduced many others throughout history. But Joe's love for Meg is too strong and Lola ends up helping him outwit Applegate and help the Senators win the pennant. Applegate tries to win Joe back by promising that the team will win the World Series but Joe decides to return to his old self and his "good old girl."

There were a few holes in the plot and the second act had its problems but Abbott knew it could be fixed in rehearsals and during previews. His libretto echoed that alleged very first of all American musicals, *The Black Crook* (1866), in that it concerned a man selling his soul to the devil. Of course, that premise goes back hundreds of years to the Faust legend. One can better appreciate the libretto for *Damn Yankees* if it is compared to its source. Wallop's novel is only mildly funny and takes the form of science fiction rather than light fantasy. Wallop even set it in the future: 1958. Lola is a minor character and not a comic one at all. In fact, the novel's most serious moments are about her tragic love for Joe. Abbott took the main story and characters from the book and turned out a decent libretto. It is not as tight as *The Pajama Game* but at least this script had wit and some sass, even getting a bit subversive at points.

> **Applegate**   I've got too much on my mind. It slipped by me. I'm overworked.
>
> **Lola**   I know, poor dear, elections coming up.[25]

Abbott even returns to the punning kind of blackout-sketch of the past.

> **Teenager** (*looking for celebrities*)   Are you anybody?
>
> **Applegate**   Not a soul.[26]

The score for *Damn Yankees* parallels that of *The Pajama Game*. For the tango, there's the seductive "Whatever Lola Wants (Lola Gets)"; the hoe-down number this time is the raucous "Shoeless Joe From Hannibal, Mo"; the frantic dance piece was "Who's Got the Pain"; the jazzy Hit Parade duet was "Two Lost Souls"; the sing-along ditty was "(You've Gotta Have) Heart"; and "A Man Doesn't Know" and "Near to You" were the heartfelt ballads. Some of these songs did not come until late in the process; Adler and Ross saw several of their efforts discarded in rehearsals and New Haven.

Problems started early. Casting Lola, for example, was a bone of contention among the creative staff. After Mitzi Gaynor and Zizi Jeanmarie turned down the role, Fosse campaigned strongly for Gwen Verdon even though she had never carried a major Broadway musical before. But Fosse worked with her and convinced Abbott to cast her. But Verdon struggled throughout rehearsals and felt so overwhelmed that at one point she begged to be released from the show.

So many changes were made in the script and the score that it was not easy to notice that the story was sometimes confusing and unclear. The first preview out of town was an eye-opener. Audiences started the evening laughing and applauding but the more the musical dragged on the less they liked it. Something major was wrong and seeing *Damn Yankees* wither on stage told Abbott what it was. Actually, the audience reaction did as well. That night Abbott told his team,

> [The audience] is confused ... They don't know which storyline to follow, the baseball story, the love story, or the Faust story. The stories keep getting in the way of each other, and they hate us for it. Now the problem is to find the one they'll follow most easily, and still keep the other two in perspective.[27]

Ultimately it was the strong love Joe has for his wife that was turned into the principal story. The starring role of Lola could be as funny and sexy as she wanted but the audience's sympathy would remain with Joe and Meg. This realization saved the show but it meant more songs and dances thrown out and new scenes, songs, and dance added. At one point Applegate's only song, the wicked "Those Were the Good Old Days," was a duet with Lola. Despite the clever staging by Fosse, the number was not working. Abbott realized that Applegate could revel in all the terrible things he had done over the centuries but when Lola did likewise she lost the sympathy of the audience. The number was turned into a solo.

Damn Yankees was the first time Abbott worked with the married designers William and Jean Eckart. He did the sets and she did the costumes. Abbott immediately liked them both and trusted them to come through on several occasions here and thereafter. (The duo would design ten subsequent Abbott musicals and plays.) In his book about the Eckarts, Andrew B. Harris writes, "The Eckarts admired Abbott tremendously and were thrilled for the opportunity to work with him. They knew changes were the order of the day on an Abbott production but changes were also what created the excitement of working with him."[28] One change that happened out of town was the opening number. The show started off weakly and Abbott asked for a strong chorus number to set up the baseball theme. Adler and Ross wrote the spirited "Six Months Out of Every Year" in which the wives complained about the way baseball dominated their domestic lives each season. Abbott asked Jean Eckart to costume the housewives as if "they had gotten away from the stove just long enough to sing the song."[29] She put the women in aprons and the husbands in casual attire. When Abbott saw the men in the number, he told the Eckarts, "They look like a bunch of bums." But trusting them, he added, "But you'll fix it."[30] The most famous costume in *Damn Yankees* was Lola's sexy outfit in which she tries to seduce Young Joe in the locker room. Abbott expressed his ideas about what the costume should do then Jean Eckart and Gwen Verdon worked on it together. The furled skirt came off first, then a pair of lacy pants, until finally just a provocative black foundation garment. William Eckart's sets were also influenced by Abbott. Eckart had experimented with a collage affect in his scenery for *The Golden Apple* (1954) but now he had to conform to Abbott's traditional methods. The bigger scenes with detailed scenery and many performers alternated with brief scenes played "in one" in front of a drop or curtain. *Damn Yankees* was written this way so Eckart had to redo much of his preliminary scenic designs. Yet, as Harris points out, "George Abbott defined for [the Eckarts] what creating a musical was all about. During the creation of *Damn Yankees*, he became for them the ultimate collaborator."[31]

When *Damn Yankees* opened on Broadway in May of 1955, audiences and critics were enthralled. Verdon was declared Broadway's newest star, the libretto and score were roundly adulated, and Fosse firmly established his reputation as one of the top choreographers in the business. "That cagey old manager, George Abbot, and a team of actors, dancers, songwriters, and scene designers in championship form, played an all-hitter under the lights," wrote Chapman in the *Daily News*. Most of the notices also used baseball metaphors to praise *Damn Yankees*: "As shiny as a new baseball and almost as smooth ... There isn't a weak spot in the lineup ... A pennant winner if ever we saw one." Watts in the *Herald Tribune* pointed out that, "The funniest thing about the show is that it does the toughest things best." Despite such raves, Abbott, Prince, and Griffith were worried. Near the end of Act Two, Applegate punishes Lola by turning her into an ugly old hag. The out-of-town audiences didn't seem to mind it but the New Yorkers on opening night stopped laughing and even grumbled a bit. They obviously did not like Verdon treated so shabbily. A rehearsal was called the next day, a rewritten scene was rehearsed, and that night *Damn Yankees* never lost its audience. Prince even invited Walter Kerr back to see the improved second act; Kerr complied and reviewed the show again, liking it even more the second time around. A problem not so easy to fix was the box office. After being showered with critical approval, *Damn Yankees* was not selling as well as it should. Had the fantasy musical, and the subject of baseball, put a curse on the production? Why were people not buying tickets? Somebody (Prince? Abbott? Griffith?) suggested changing the publicity. The original poster and ads for *Damn Yankees* featured Verdon in a baseball uniform happily swinging a bat. It was very cute but very ... baseball. A new campaign pictured Verdon in the sexy underwear she wore in the "Whatever Lola Wants" number. Also, the baseball field green on the poster was changed to red. Tickets sales soared. Was it because baseball was eliminated from the sales pitch or was it the old adage "Sex sells"? Probably both reasons are valid.

Damn Yankees ran a very profitable 1,019 performances. There was a national tour starring the aging comic Bobby Clark as Applegate that was very popular even though Abbott thought him grossly miscast. There was also a London production which did not find success until celebrity ice-skater Belita was replaced by Elizabeth Seal as Lola. The 1958 film version of *Damn Yankees*, like that of *The Pajama Game*, was one of the most faithful stage-to-screen transitions of the decade. Again co-directed by Abbott and Stanley Donan and choreographed by Fosse, the Warner Brothers movie retained most of the Broadway cast. The only major change was casting current heart-throb Tab Hunter as Young Joe. (Neither Abbott or Donen wanted to use Hunter but Warner Brother mogul Jack Warner insisted.) Some scenes looked stagy but others opened up nicely for the big screen. Abbott's rapid theatre staging is lost and parts of the picture drag, but it's a wonderful record of a

Broadway favorite. There was also a television adaptation of *Damn Yankees* in 1967 with Phil Silvers in fine form as Applegate. The only Broadway revival of the musical came in 1994 and it was a solid hit, running 533 performances. (It will be discussed in Chapter 14 with some other Abbott revivals.) The team that put together the original *Damn Yankees* worked well together, weathering the stormy times on the way to success without losing their respect of each other's talents. The chance of them all reuniting for another show was erased in November of 1955 when Jerry Ross died from a life-long bronchial ailment. Adler tried to continue his career in the theatre without Ross but met with little success. He and Abbott would be reunited to work on a musical twenty-one years later.

12 IGNORING THE SIXTIES

(1959–1962)

Take Her, She's Mine • Never Too Late • Once Upon a Mattress • A Funny Thing Happened on the Way to the Forum

The 1960s were a turbulent time for America and this carried over to the theatre. The younger generation embraced film and abandoned the theatre. Broadway audiences got older and more conservative, sometimes as a reaction to the radical theatre that was dominating Off and Off-Off Broadway. Comedies and dramas on Broadway were infrequent and, for the most part, looking backwards. The musicals, on the other hand, could sometimes be very innovative but most shows were escapist entertainment. Abbott was involved with two hit plays and two successful musicals in the 1960s. They may have been old-fashioned but they appealed to the aging Broadway playgoer and ran. These were the last four new works in Abbott's career that would turn a profit.

Historians agree that the early 1960s were pretty much a continuation of the 1950s in tone and temperament. It was certainly true about Abbott's two comedies that opened early in the decade. In fact, *Take Her, She's Mine* and *Never Too Late* could have been written and enjoyed in the 1940s. They are both domestic comedies that take one away from your troubles because they are about nothing that much matters. Hal Prince's producing partner Robert Griffith died in 1961; he was only fifty-four years old. Prince had pictured a long future with the two of them producing together on Broadway. Instead he was forced to go solo and his first project was Phoebe and Henry Ephron's comedy **Take Her, She's Mine** (1961). Abbott agreed to direct because "most of the characters were college age" and he liked working with new talent.[1] Yet it was television star Art Carney as the father who dominated the play and was the reason it ran. Frank Michaelson (Carney) lives in Southern California with his wife Anne (Phyllis Thaxter) and two daughters whom he dotes on. When his elder daughter Mollie (Elizabeth Ashley) decides to go to a progressive women's college in New England, Frank panics. Not only will she be far away from home but she'll be within barking distance of the male wolves at Dartmouth, Yale, and Harvard. During Mollie's absence, Frank's wife and younger daughter Liz (June Harding) try to help Frank cope, going so far as to arrange for him to take rhumba lessons at an Arthur Murray studio. When Mollie comes home for Christmas, his worse fears are confirmed. Mollie sports a high-style Italian haircut, smokes cigarettes in a holder, and drinks "very dry" martinis. By sophomore year, Mollie is dating older men and playing guitar in a coffee house. Just about the time Frank gets resigned to the fact that Mollie is now an independent, self-assured woman, Liz announces she is going off to college and Frank starts to panic all over again.

For a thin little comedy, *Take Her, She's Mine* had a lot of characters and many different locations, making the show expensive to run. Designer William Eckart solved the scenic demands by using the style of "selective realism." Locales were suggested by pieces of realistic scenery and, as in a musical, scene changes were done in front of the audience. Since the script called for so many long-distance phone conversations between the California home and the East coast college, Eckart put a telephone pole on either side of the stage and, with dangling wires overhead, the phone metaphor was visual. Abbott staged *Take Her, She's Mine* like a musical as well. The action moved so swiftly from location to location that one hardly noticed this was essentially a staid domestic play that could have been told in a dull box set. For the most part, the press found the comedy insubstantial and did not recommend it. Walter Kerr's review in the *New York Herald Tribune* began with, "The problem with the new comedy . . . is that it hasn't got a problem." But audiences preferred to listen to Norman Nadel in the *World-Telegraph and Sun* who called the comedy "not only an honest and amusing play, but a wholesome one as well." Abbott kept the multi-set production moving and Carney's popularity and his droll performance made *Take Her, She's Mine* seem better than it was. Looking back, Prince wrote,

> It had some grace and charm, and it was what you call commercial, and I had a hit the first time out producing alone . . . But [it] could have been produced by anyone. A number of the shows that preceded it fit that category. Others, the best of them, the Abbott shows, had a texture that was his.[2]

Take Her, She's Mine ran a full year on Broadway, toured successfully and was sold to the movies for a tidy sum. Abbott related in his autobiography that the young stage cast was very talented and predicted "in fifteen years [one] will be astounded by the number of fine actors who played in the New York and national companies."[3] It was true for Elizabeth Ashley. Fame also came for Ashley's counterpart, the playwrights' daughter Nora Ephron who had a prominent career as a writer and director.

Abbott had an even bigger hit with an equally thin comedy by Sumner Arthur Long titled *Never Too Late* (1962). Long had gotten the idea for the comedy when he saw a middle-aged pregnant woman and wondered what her husband thought of the situation. Producers Eliot Martin and Daniel Hollywood sent Abbott the script, then titled *Cradle and All*. "It was underdeveloped," Abbott later wrote, "but it had good characters and a comic idea, and I thought I saw just what should be done to make it a hit."[4] Lumber yard owner Harry Lambert (Paul Ford) and his wife Edith (Maureen O'Sullivan) are a middle-aged couple who live in Calverton, Massachusetts, with their married daughter Kate (Fran Sharon) and their wisecracking son-in-law Charlie (Orson Bean) whom Harry cannot stand. When Harry learns that Edith is pregnant, he is the butt of so many jokes at the lumber company and around town that he is reduced to wearing dark glasses. As the day of delivery approaches, tensions in the Lambert house rise until one night Harry and Charlie get drunk together and come to some kind of understanding. The press felt the one-joke show was made palatable by the deft performances, particularly from Ford and Bean. Writing in *The Best Plays of 1962-1963*, editor Henry Hewes summed up the situation best:

> The season's new American comedies were fairly pale efforts. Most successful because of fine performances by Paul Ford and Orson Bean and shrewd George Abbott direction was *Never Too Late*, a creaky affair that started out as a comedy about what happens when the head of a household suddenly discovers that his middle-aged wife is pregnant again. But the fun of the play turned out to be the running battle between the parsimonious father and his dependent but frustratedly defiant son-in-law.[5]

All of *Never Too Late* took place in the Lambert living room and there was little physical action in the script. The closest to visual comedy in the play is a scene in which Harry and Charlie struggle to carry a new bathtub up to the second floor bathroom. Abbott and scenic designer William Eckart decided to give the staircase a landing and a turn to make the scene more farcical. The small-cast, one-set production was an economical moneymaker and played 1,007 performances. *Never Too Late* was one of the longest-running non-musicals in Abbott's career. At the end of the 1962-1963 season, Abbott was nominated for Best Directing Tony Awards for both *Never Too Late* and *A Funny Thing Happened on the Way to the Forum*, the first time anyone was ever nominated for a play and a musical in the same year.

In the case of Abbott's two 1960s hit musicals—*Once Upon a Mattress* and *A Funny Thing Happened on the Way to the Forum*—he was again working with beginning songwriters and, as with Carol Burnett, a future star. Musical scholar Ethan Mordden bluntly describes **Once Upon a Mattress** as "sheer unapologetic musical comedy ... the kind of thing George Abbott would do."[6] This suggests the show is stubbornly old-fashioned, which it is, but also in the style of Abbott's 1930s musicals, which it isn't. The score by Mary Rodgers (music) and Marshall Barer (lyrics) is tuneful and slangy like an old score but it is firmly integrated into the story *The Princess and the Pea*. Even some of the dance is part of the plot. As suggested by the title, *Once*

Upon a Mattress is adult; not in the way *Pal Joey* was but because it has a sly, grown-up tone. In the libretto by Barer, Jay Thompson, and Dean Fuller, no one in a fairy tale kingdom can marry until the hapless Prince Dauntless (Joe Bova) is wed, and his mother Queen Aggravaine (Jane White) has seen to it that no girl is good enough for her boy. But the unconventional, spunky Princess Winnifred (Burnett), from a distant and swampy kingdom, outwits the Queen, passes her test of sensitivity even as she sleeps on a pile of mattresses, and there is a happy ending for everyone, including the once-mute King (Jack Gilford) who silences his bossy wife. In a romantic subplot, the pregnant Lady Larken (Anne Jones) and her lover Sir Harry (Allen Case) help Winnifred and the Prince get together so that weddings are allowed in the kingdom again and Larkin and Harry can marry before she starts showing her approaching motherhood. The famous fairy tale is reimagined as an entertainment for grown-ups, even going so far as using an unplanned, out-of-wedlock pregnancy as a plot complication. *Once Upon a Mattress* began as a one-act entertainment at the Camp Tamiment resort in the mountains of Pennsylvania in the summer of 1958. Broadway designers Jean and William Eckart saw it and thought it belonged on Broadway so they became producers and would do the sets and costumes. The role of Winnifred was written as a star vehicle and Nancy Walker was in mind from the beginning. But the production team consisted of beginners and unknowns (even if the composer was Richard Rodgers' daughter). William Eckart later said,

> For Jean and me, getting George Abbott to direct was crucial. We set up an audition. George came, listened politely and said, 'Well, it's amusing, but it's only one act, and I don't think you can expand it.' We could tell that he thought it was too campy, but we said, 'If we expand it, and get it to you by such-and-such a date, would you look at it again?' . . . Honestly, he didn't have much faith in it as a project, but by that time, we did.[7]

According to Abbott, "The book seemed to be confused and naive—though often funny. I made suggestions for a rewrite; the authors and the Eckarts retired for a couple of weeks, and when they reappeared with a much improved version I said yes."[8]

With Abbott on board, raising the money for *The Princess and the Pea* (as it was still called) would not prove too difficult. The problem was in getting a theatre during a very busy season. So the Eckarts turned to Off-Broadway and the Phoenix Theatre Company. Starting a show Off-Broadway and then, if it was successful, moving it to Broadway was common practice by the end of 1960s. But in the spring of 1959 it was a rare occurrence. The celebrated George Abbott directing a musical Off-Broadway? It didn't seem to bother him. According to William Eckart,

> George agreed to direct the play for $100 per week for rehearsals. This was about enough to cover his cab fares and lunches. He also agreed to become one of our first investors although the investment was in the name of his

grandchildren. Another stipulation he made was that one of us would have to eat lunch with him every day ... [As this] was his first Off-Broadway show, he didn't like the idea of having to fend for himself on East 12th Street, which was not an upscale neighborhood.[9]

Nancy Walker had agreed to play Winnifred, even if it was Off-Broadway, so the Eckarts were shocked at the first production meeting to learn that Abbott did not want Walker. Mary Rodgers recalled, "Abbott said that Nancy was wonderful but he would rather not do the show with her because Nancy was already a star. He wanted someone who wasn't known." Abbott's logic was: "Remember you are putting the show on Off-Broadway. The lead should be someone the audience discovers."[10] Abbott's muscle was such that the producers and writers had to agree, Walker was out, and the hunt was on for a new face. Theatre manager Joe Harris had seen Carol Burnett on television's *The Garry Moore Show* in which she was a last minute replacement when Martha Raye was taken ill. After one audition for Abbott, Burnett was cast as Winnifred. So there was no star and the only truly seasoned actor in the cast was Jack Gilford who played the mute king. (Abbott doesn't mention it in his autobiography, but his casting of the African American actress Jane White as the Queen was probably the first case of color-blind casting on Broadway.)

As Burnett recalls in her memoir, "[Abbott] was everything I dreamed he would be. He had directed some of the biggest hits in Broadway history, but he treated us as if this was his very first one."[11] That did not mean rehearsal went smoothly. William Eckart, in Andrew Harris's book about the career of the designer husband and wife, related,

> Two people were replaced in rehearsal. One was a tenor named Robert Rounseville (the original Candide on Broadway). Abbott decided he was too stiff. The role of the Wizard had to be re-cast as well. Abbott had chosen Jack Good, an old vaudevillian, but everyone soon tired of his shtick. There were also problems with the Stage Manager chosen by the Phoenix [Theatre]. His name was George Quick. Unfortunately, he wasn't. A couple of days into rehearsal, Marshall [Barer] came up with, 'Good is bad, White is black, Quick is slow, and Rounseville is square.'[12]

A new and slightly suggestive title for the musical was provided by Jean Eckart who had to fight the rest of the team to accept *Once Upon a Mattress*. Yet this was an adult fairy tale with the focus on that pile of mattresses. A particularly difficult scene was a six-minute pantomime in the second act in which "Fred" struggles to get comfortable on the top mattress. There was no spoken words or music, just physical comedy. Burnett wrote years later,

I was supposed to flail about, roll myself up into a ball, jump up and down, sock the pillow, almost fall out the bed, and wind up exhausted, counting sheep ... It took all afternoon [to choreograph]. By the time we finished ... I *felt* like Winnifred. I was wiped out. But Mr. Abbott, who had been matching me move for move, looked as if he'd just had a good night's sleep. He was seventy-two and I was twenty-five.[13]

William and Jean Eckart did the sets and costumes, respectively, for *Once Upon a Mattress*, and they were as colorful as they were playful. The costumes were simple yet often accurate to the Medieval era. The baggy, disheveled dress Winnifred wore on her first entrance after swimming the moat was actually taken from a fifteenth-century tapestry. Far less experienced than the Eckarts were two other members of the team. *Once Upon a Mattress* was the first major musical for the prolific lighting designer Tharon Musser. And Joe Layton had only choreographed one Broadway show (the 1959 revival of *On the Town*) when he was brought on. He did himself proud, particularly in the frantic number "The Spanish Panic," a furious dance in which the Queen hoped to tire out "Fred" and cause her to sleep soundly. While none of the songs from *Once Upon a Mattress* became hits, they were a spirited bunch of numbers that sometimes echoed the past. The giddy "Happily Ever After," the playful "In a Little While," the robust "Shy," the old-time buck-and-wing "Very Soft Shoes," the pantomimed duet "Man to Man Talk," and the harmonizing "Normandy" were all splendid and tied into the plot surprisingly well. The reviews Off Broadway were auspicious enough that *Once Upon a Mattress* ran a happy 216 performances at the Phoenix. The theatre was booked for the next production so the show did indeed move to Broadway but had trouble finding available venues for very long. The musical played in no less than five different playhouses during its 244-performance Broadway run. Most of the Broadway reviews concentrated on Burnett, as with Brooks Atkinson in the *New York Times* proclaiming her "a lean, earthy young lady with a metallic voice, an ironic gleam, and an unfailing sense of the comic gesture." The notices for the musical itself were not all complimentary but enough critics championed the show that it caught on. *Variety* announced, "In a season of not-too-fresh musicals, this is a little gem," and *Newsweek* applauded the "new talent Broadway must reckon with."

Once Upon a Mattress was popular enough to warrant two road companies and was later produced in London and eventually just about everywhere. There has been one Broadway revival, a 1996 production featuring Sarah Jessica Parker. While she was considered a bright and personable performer, most critics felt her Princess Winifred was not raucous enough to hold together the musical. Yet Parker had her fans and the colorful, clever production, which included tap dancing knights in armor, was enjoyable enough that audiences came for 187 performances. There has been no film version of *Once Upon a Mattress* but there have been three television adaptations, each one starring Burnett. She reprised her "Fred" in a 1964 version on CBS-TV in which most of the Broadway cast appeared. Although musical numbers were cut to fit the show into the ninety-minute broadcast, the spirit of the stage musical was still there. A 1972 remake on CBS-TV reunited Burnett with other Broadway cast members in a ninety-minute new version with a slightly revised script. A 2005 television production on *The Wonderful World of Disney* starred Burnett again but this time she played the Queen and some scenes and songs were reassigned to build up the supporting role. Tracey Ullman was a farcical Winifred and the supporting cast was very talented. Kathleen Marshall directed and choreographed the broadcast which had colorful, fairy tale-like production values.

Abbott's last success with a new Broadway musical was ***A Funny Thing Happened on the Way to the Forum*** (1962). His contribution to this success has often been misunderstood. Erroneous legend has it that the aged Abbott lost his touch, failed to make the musical work, and that Jerome Robbins had to be called in to save it. This version is given some credibility by the fact that Abbott never again had a new hit musical on Broadway. His entry on the musical in the autobiography is not overly detailed.

> I entered this project late, and I found the authors almost swamped under half a dozen versions of this play. I took all the scripts up to the country and made such savage cuts that I feared my new associates would be horrified. Instead, I received heart-warming words of thanks. However, our problems were not over. The audience laughed at this show, but they didn't *like* it, and it was only after great travail—in fact, not until the last week of our tryouts in Washington—that we pulled it together and found a way to make the people out front laugh with us as well as at us. Of course my job was made immeasurably easier by the fact that Zero Mostel, Jack Gilford, David Burns, and John Carradine are all great comics.[14]

The above was written within a year of the events described so it was not the passage of time that simplified Abbott's memory. Perhaps "great travail" was as much as he wanted to say because the tryouts of *A Funny Thing Happened on the Way to the Forum* (hereafter abbreviated to *Forum*) were uniquely complicated. And, as Abbott wrote, he entered late into a project that was already filled with problems.

Burt Shevelove and Larry Gelbart, two friends and comedy writers from television, spent over two years working on the libretto for a musical based on a handful of short comedies by the Roman playwright Plautus. It was a promising idea for a play because Plautus had inspired Shakespeare to write *The Comedy of Errors* which had been musicalized successfully as *The Boys from Syracuse*. In the raucous libretto, the ancient Roman setting and characters were retained but the musical was also a vaudeville-like romp filled with merry anachronisms. The conniving slave Pseudolus (Zero Mostel) promises his young master Hero (Brian Davies) that he will get him the beautiful virgin Philia (Preshy Marker) for his wife in exchange for his freedom. But Philia is one of the girls-for-sale in the house of Marcus Lycus (John Carradine) and has been purchased by the puffed-up soldier Miles Gloriosus (Ronald Holgate). Also, Hero's hen-pecked father Senex (David Burns) lusts after the girl himself and tries to bed her while his shrewish wife Domina (Ruth Kobart) is out of town. To convince Miles that his intended has died of plague, Pseudolus stages a mock funeral with the fellow slave Hysterium (Jack Gilford) acting as the dead virgin. It all goes awry and, after a farcical chase involving all the characters, Hero gets Philia and Pseudolus wins his freedom. Today the libretto plays like gold. But there were two major difficulties in the idea: *The Comedy of Errors* was a full-length play with enough plot and characters to sustain an evening's entertainment while the short works Shevelove and Gelbart were working with were more akin to skits. The second difficulty we have encountered before: the musical was a farce. This fact would continue to plague *Forum* up until the New York previews.

Although Stephen Sondheim had written the lyrics for two hits—*West Side Story* and *Gypsy*—his music had not been heard anywhere. Yet Shevelove and Gelbart wanted Sondheim for the score from the beginning and Sondheim wanted Jerome Robbins to direct and choreograph it. They brought the script and score, both in rough form, to Robbins and producer David Merrick (who had presented *Gypsy*) and both were interested but agreed a lot of work was needed before rehearsals could begin. While rewrites were made, Merrick lost interest in the property but Hal Prince became excited about it. The authors wrote the central character of Pseudolus with comic Phil Silvers in mind so Prince sent the script to Silvers who quickly and firmly turned it down. Another blow came when Robbins got tired of waiting for a better script and asked to be released from the project. With no star, director, or choreographer signed up, rehearsals were postponed again. It was at this point that Abbott was approached and a reading of the script was arranged for him. *Forum* did not read well and Abbott excused himself and left before the reading was even finished. Prince was persistent and sent the script to Abbott's home in the Catskills. The next morning Abbott called Prince and said, "It is absolutely marvelous. I'll do it."[15] As Prince later wrote, "Abbott alone, in my experience, possesses the self confidence to alter his opinion totally without getting involved with *losing face*."[16]

Since Abbott had directed two of the American theatre's best musical farces—*The Boys from Syracuse* and *Where's Charley?*—the future of the project seemed secure. Prince and the staff tried to get Milton Berle to play Pseudolus but the star demanded too much money and approval of cast, designers, choreographer, and even which Broadway theatre he would perform in. When Prince suggested Zero Mostel for the star role, he was vehemently opposed by the authors and Sondheim who insisted a comic was needed, not an actor. They even brought the Dramatists

Guild into the argument, claiming cast approval in their contracts, and threatened to withdraw the play if Mostel were cast. As Prince bluntly put it in his memoir, "It got nasty."[17] Abbott sided with Prince and, with time running out, Shevelove, Gelbart, and Sondheim reluctantly agreed to Mostel. (The rotund actor also had his doubts and wanted to play Falstaff at the Stratford Festival in Connecticut until his wife talked Mostel into doing *Forum*.) Rehearsals began with Jack Cole as choreographer and Tony Walton doing the sets and costumes. Early on there was a problem with the opening number. Sondheim had written a witty number titled "Invocation" in which Pseudolus called upon the gods to bless the comic revels to follow. Abbott thought the lyric did a good job in preparing the audience for the farce to follow but he found Sondheim's music too atonal and far from hummable. Bowing to the master's experience and better judgement, Sondheim wrote a very hummable ditty titled "Love Is in the Air," an old-time soft-shoe number which was given to David Burns to sing. Abbott seemed satisfied and the show went to New Haven and Washington to tryout.

Being a musical farce, there was not a lot of dancing in *Forum*. But the second act called for a slapstick chase that had to be choreographed and Cole was slow in getting the number right. Also, the actors playing the juvenile Hero and the ingenue Philia were not working out and had to be replaced. (Prince had tried to get Joel Grey and Barbara Harris originally but it didn't happen.) Abbott's farcical staging seemed to be working in rehearsals but when Forum began performances in New Haven gloom settled on the musical. In *Finishing the Hat*, Sondheim recalls it most succinctly.

> The show was received with scathing reviews from the critics and indifference from the audiences. We couldn't understand why: every night Burt, Larry, George, Hal, and I would huddle in the back of the house, baffled at the long silences punctuated by mild and tiny spurts of laughter which greeted what we thought were screamingly funny scenes and lines. Even George Abbott, the theatre's most accomplished play doctor, murmured, 'I don't know—I guess we'll have to call in George Abbott.' . . . We didn't call in George Abbott, but in Washington, in our final week before coming to New York, at my suggestion and George's approval, we did call in Jerry (Robbins), or rather recalled him.[18]

Robbins immediately pointed out the problem; the opening number. "Love Is in the Air" was a sweet song but totally wrong for preparing the audience for what was to follow. Sondheim complained to Robbins that his original song "Invocation" had done precisely that but Abbott couldn't hum it and rejected it. Sondheim recalled, "Jerry replied . . . that I should stop complaining and get busy writing another song which accomplished the same thing, but one that George could hum."[19] The resulting number "Comedy Tonight" was written quickly and just as swiftly Robbins staged it, thereby changing a "catastrophe into a three-year hit." But how did Abbott react to Robbins coming in and saving the show? Prince later wrote, "They couldn't have been more compatible."[20] Robbins restaged the second act chase and even redid some bits in the book scenes. It was remarkable how quickly Robbins fixed things. Yet, he had originally planned on directing and choreographing the whole show so many of his ideas were already worked out in his head.

Forum opened on Broadway in May of 1962 to mostly raves. Some critics singled out the script, as with Robert Coleman in the *New York Daily Mirror*: "It's about as crazy as anything you've ever seen in old-time vaudeville or films." Several applauded Mostel, such as John McClain in the *Journal-American*: "Zero Mostel, a very animated blimp, will personally defy you not to like [*Forum*]." And Abbott was duly recognized, as in the case of Howard Taubman in the *Times*: "George Abbott, who has been around for a long time but surely staged nothing for the forum mob, has forgotten nothing and remembered everything." The only sour note was the critics mostly ignoring or disapproving of Sondheim's score, calling it "second rate" and the "lyrics far surpassed his music." Time has corrected such thoughts though the songs in *Forum* are often more serviceable than showstopping. After the opening number, "Everybody Ought to Have a Maid" is the catchiest song, something Abbott and everyone else can hum. Other highlights include the vapid love song "Lovely," the bouncy and wordy "Pretty Little Picture," the nervous character ditty "I'm Calm," and the sly duet "Impossible." Audiences may not flock to *Forum* to hear the score but the show needs the musical numbers in order to soar.

Coming in with bad word of mouth and a low box office advance, *Forum* was a surprise hit, running 964 performances. But was it still an Abbott show? Or was it now a Robbins musical? There is no question that Robbins' staging of "Comedy Tonight" was the turning point for *Forum*. Yet most everything else was already there. And it's still there. *Forum* has been revived professionally and by amateurs with success without Robbins' coming in to stage the opening. There have been two Broadway revivals. Shevelove directed a 1972 production that was highly praised but could only find an audience for five months. Phil Silvers, who had played Lycus in the film version, finally got to play Pseudolus and Larry Blyden was particularly applauded as Hysterium. Nathan Lane (and later Whoopie Goldberg) starred as Pseudolus in a sprightly 1996 revival directed by Jerry Zaks. Some critics quibbled about the young cast's ability to do the old-time schtick but admitted the musical was still a joyous romp. Audiences agreed for a very profitable 715 performances. United Artists released a movie version of *Forum* in 1966 with Zero Mostel and Jack Gilford from the Broadway cast but tossed out all but five of the songs, and three of them were heard in a very abridged form. The cast is strong throughout and the Richard Lester-directed movie certainly moves at a good clip. The result is a pleasing comedy but an unsatisfying musical.

It was after the success of these two plays and two musicals that Abbott wrote his autobiography, *Mister Abbott*. He was rather sanguine about his career filled with hits and misses. He was still working and planned to continue doing so for as long as he was still able. Had he retired in 1963, the story of Mister Abbott would have concluded with a strong second (third? fourth?) act. Instead he continued to take whatever was offered to him. The offerings were mostly inferior. But he never looked back, only forward. For another thirty years he only looked forward.

13 ALMOST BUT NOT QUITE

(1964–1989)

Fade Out—Fade In • Flora, the Red Menace • Anya • Help Stamp Out Marriage! • Agatha Sue, I Love You • How Now, Dow Jones • The Education of H*Y*M*A*N K*A*P*L*A*N • The Fig Leaves Are Falling • Norman, Is That You? • Not Now, Darling • Music Is • Tropicana • Frankie

In January of 1962, an entertainment-party-tribute was held to celebrate George Abbott's seventy-fifth birthday. The occasion also marked his fiftieth year in New York City theatre. It was well-attended, full of speeches, and featured skits and musical numbers from his many shows. Abbott found it "heart-warming to have so many friends there to wish me well, but it also contained a faint unspoken valedictorian tone which I didn't like—as if my past was being celebrated, I was a dean, an honorary member. I preferred to feel as though I were still on the team."[1] He was very much a player in 1962 with three shows running on Broadway. "I hadn't been put out to pasture just yet," he wrote near the end of his 1963 autobiography.[2]

For a time, Abbott continued to get the first-class offers, such as **Fade Out—Fade In** (1964). The producers—Lester Osterman, Jule Styne, and ABC-Paramount—were big-time operators with deep pockets, the star was Carol Burnett, and Betty Comden and Adolph Green wrote the libretto and also provided lyrics for Styne's music. On paper, this was a no-brainer. On stage as well, for the production was dazzling and the cast was sparkling. So the fate of *Fade Out—Fade In* was peculiarly sad—nasty even—which left a bad feeling between the star and the production's management that kept Burnett away from Broadway for thirty years. As United Press International writer Jack Gaver described it, the tale of Burnett and the musical was "a case unique among all of the odd things that have happened on Broadway."[3] Scheduled to open in the fall of 1963, *A Girl to Remember* (as the musical was then called) was pushed back to the late spring of 1964 when Burnett announced that she was pregnant. Burnett had established her Broadway clout with *Once Upon a Mattress* in 1959 but it was her television appearances since then that had made her even more popular. So everyone waited for Burnett. The producers had to return $1 million in group sales and pay off the cast and the theatre owners to the tune of about $40,000. Abbott was nonplussed. He went to Florida for the winter and played golf. The team was reassembled for rehearsals in April with an opening at the very end of the season. This was problematic because that season saw the musical hits *Hello, Dolly!* and *Funny Girl*, and musical star turns by the likes of Carol Channing, Barbra Streisand, Mary Martin, Florence Henderson, Josephine Baker, Angela Lansbury, and Beatrice Lillie. Comden and Green's libretto was a spoof of 1930s Hollywood. Hadn't the duo already done that with the film *Singin' in the Rain*? And didn't they do it superbly? The movie was not a success back in 1952 but old Hollywood was being rediscovered in the 1960s so *Singin' in the Rain* was finally being hailed as a classic. So Comden and Green were competing with themselves with *Fade Out—Fade In*, as the show was retitled. When the unknown chorus girl Hope Springfield (Burnett) comes to L.A. to become a film star, she ends up as an usher in a movie house. Only Rudolf Governor (Dick Patterson), the nephew of the movie mogul Lionel Z. Governor (Lou Jacobi), believes in Hope. Once inside the studio, Hope is put in the chorus but is accidentally given a major role in the Hollywood musical *The Fiddler and the Fighter*. The mistake is discovered and all prints of the movie are hidden away in the vault. It takes Rudolf to get *The Fiddler and the Fighter* to a preview audience who love it, encouraging the studio to release the film and making Hope a star. For a spoof of a Thirties movie musical, *Fade Out—Fade In* was less interesting than the films it was lampooning.

Happily, the script included some hilarious characters, such as the narcissistic leading man Byron Prong (Jack Cassidy), the bombastic boss Lionel Governor who requires a full-time psychiatrist at his side, the savvy African American Lou Williams (Tiger Haynes) who is clever enough to play dumb when the cameras are rolling, and the shallow starlet Gloria Currie (Tina Louise) who has a rivalry with the studio mascot, a seal named Smaxie. The ambitious Hope was not much of a comic character but Burnett turned it into a star role by doing various comic bits and impersonations, most memorably a facile Shirley Temple tap-dance number "You Mustn't Be Discouraged" with Haynes. There were some other noteworthy songs in the score: the yearning character song "The Usher from the Mezzanine" for Hope, the torchy "Notice Me" for Rudolf, and the brassy "Call Me Savage" for a production number in *The Fiddler and the Fighter*. The opening number, "(I've Never Been Here Before But) It's Good to Be Back Home," was staged by Abbott (and choreographed by Ernest Flatt) with all the panache of a hit musical. Hope arrives in Hollywood and outside the studio gates she encounters a bevy of movie stars ranging from Mae West to Dracula. Designer William Eckart's revolving stage was used cleverly throughout the musical, either for changing locales or allowing for Busby Berkeley-like production numbers in *The Fiddler and the Fighter*.

Although *Fade Out—Fade In* lacked a first-rate script or a top-notch score, it played like a sure thing. The reviews pointed out the show's weaknesses but enthusiastically endorsed Burnett and her glittering vehicle. "A World's Fair musical," John Chapman in the *New York Daily News* exclaimed. "[It has] something in it for everybody and everything in it for somebody." Norman Nadel in the *World-Telegraph & Sun* wrote, "Look no further than *Fade Out—Fade In*, which rode into town last night on a wave of laughter, to learn the ABCs of comedy. They are Abbott (George), Burnett (Carol) and Cassidy (Jack)." Nadel was also among those who credited the direction:

> George Abbott is endowed with that elusive and fragile talent known in academic circles as the old razz-ma-tazz ... he can so overwhelm an audience with showmanship that any weakness in dialogue, situations, or music go almost unnoticed. In his hands, *Fade Out - Fade In* maintains a wild pace. He has exploited every potential laugh, and probably invented a few of his own along the way.

With such notices, and the popularity of Burnett, *Fade Out - Fade In* was a box office bonanza, outgrossing *Hello, Dolly!* and *Funny Girl* each week. Then it all fell apart. Burnett was in a taxi cab accident, suffered whiplash, and was frequently out of the show. Audiences didn't want to see the musical without Burnett in it and the box office plummeted from $64,000 a week to $18,000. When Burnett was hospitalized, the show closed until she was available again. But Burnett did not wish to return to *Fade Out—Fade In* and was more anxious to return to her television show *The Entertainers*. She offered to buy out her Broadway contract for $500,000, enough money to allow the production to make a profit. But the producers insisted Burnett return to *Fade Out—Fade In* and held her to her contract. Things got ugly, with management arguing that if Burnett was well enough to do television, she was well enough to do Broadway. Burnett countered with accusations that the producers were trying to destroy her TV career. Actors' Equity got involved and, surprisingly, sided with management. Burnett was forced to return to *Fade Out—Fade In* for the remaining two months in her contract. Of course the momentum was gone and it took the glow off of everything knowing that the star was being forced to perform against her will. Some new songs and scenes were written during the hiatus but *Fade Out—Fade In* had not much improved. The show closed for good after a total 277 performances, not enough to make a profit in the ever-increasing economics of 1960s Broadway. *Fade Out—Fade In* has not been heard of since. The publicist for the musical, Harvey Sabinson, later wrote about the production in his memoir:

> A week after the closing, while engaging in informal athletic activities with her husband's children [from a previous marriage], Carol Burnett tripped and broke an ankle. I cannot say that the news provided much cheer for [producers] Osterman and Styne, but I doubt if they ever sent her a 'get well' card.[4]

As for Burnett, she would not appear on Broadway again until 1995 with the comedy *Moon Over Buffalo*.

For Abbott, the unfortunate fate of *Fade Out—Fade In* was out of his hands. He gave the musical a vibrant staging then watched it all dissolve. But Abbott never dwelled on the past when there were new projects waiting for him. **Flora, the Red Menace** (1965) did not have big names associated with it but it looked very promising. Once again, Abbott was supervising the Broadway debuts of very talented young people. In this case, songwriters John Kander and Fred Ebb and a nineteen-year old dynamo named Liza Minnelli. Also once again, Abbott was brought in late in the process. Producer Hal Prince thought Lester Atwill's 1963 novel *Love Is Just Around the Corner* would make a unique musical. The heroine was a struggling commercial artist in New York City during the Depression who comes under the influence of the Young Communist League. "It was the perfect time for it," Prince recalled. "McCarthy was dead."[5] Although the story was set in the 1930s, there were clearly parallels to Joe McCarthy's witch hunt for communists in the 1950s. One of the Hollywood writers who had been hassled by the Red hunters was Robert Russell. He also liked the novel and agreed to write the libretto with Barbra Streisand in mind for the heroine. It was soon clear to Prince that Russell did not know how to structure a musical. More disturbing to the producer, with each rewrite Russell's writing was getting softer and losing its bite. "I came to think he had an uneasy compact with failure," Prince recalled.[6] So he turned to Abbott who he knew could pull the script together. It was a disastrous decision. Abbott was apolitical, conservative even. His sympathies for the heroine were such that he wrote all the communist characters as either clowns or villains. Hardly anything of Russell's efforts remained; even the novel was left far behind. Kander, in his memoir written with Ebb, years later looked back and stated, "Abbott ... was probably the wrong person to direct that. As wonderful a man as he was, he really didn't have an affinity for the material. Hal [Prince] later said he wished he had directed it himself."[7]

Retitled *Flora, the Red Menace*, Abbott's libretto was built as a star vehicle for Eydie Gorme. It wasn't to be. The libretto focused on the recent art school graduate Flora Meszaros (Minnelli) who has trouble finding a job during the Depression. She meets and falls for the idealist Harry Toukarian (Bob Dishy), a stammering socialist who believes he can cure his speech impediment by putting pebbles in his mouth. Harry suggests Flora join him and get involved with the Young Communists. At a Party meeting, Flora is impressed by the ferocious resolve of Comrade Ada (Mary Louise Wilson) but is not convinced, especially after she finally gets a job as a fashion designer. When Harry is unfaithful to her with the oversexed Comrade Charlotte (Cathryn Damon), Flora realizes she doesn't need him or the Party to become a happy individual. Novice songwriters Kander and Ebb wrote a score filled with satiric numbers for the communists ("Sign Here" and "The Flame"), goofy love songs for Harry and Flora ("Not Every Day of the Week" and "Hello, Waves"), silly specialty numbers ("Knock, Knock" and "Palomino Pal"), and big-belt showstoppers for the female star ("All I Need Is One

Good Break," "A Quiet Thing," "Dear Love," and "Sing Happy"). When both Streisand and Gorme turned down the show, they were left without a leading lady. Ebb recalled,

> We had been having trouble finding a Flora. It seemed like the perfect thing for Liza to do. At the time she had another show that Richard Adler had written, based on the movie *Roman Holiday*, She was going to do that, but then she heard [the score for] *Flora* and obviously wanted to do it [instead].[8]

(Adler's *Roman Holiday* musical never happened.) Kander and Ebb worked with Minnelli to prepare her for a socko audition. She had gained some recognition in the Off-Broadway revival of *Best Foot Forward* in 1963 but, despite being the daughter of film director Vincente Minnelli and singer Judy Garland, she was unknown and unproven. Abbott was not impressed with Minnelli's audition but finally he begrudgingly conceded with, "All right take her. If you all like her, take her."[9] Such an attitude was detected in much of Abbott's work on *Flora, the Red Menace*. Scenic designer William Eckart recalled, "He didn't want to be in New York in the winter. He wanted to be in Miami."[10] Abbott was also losing some of his stubbornness and granite determination. One scene was set in Manhattan's Union Square and Eckart had designed a powerful setting in which a statue had "Down with Capital" graffiti painted on it. "George was thinking of cutting the Union Square set," Eckart recalled. "But after he saw the sketches, he said, 'Well, the set's good so we'll keep it.' In earlier years, he wouldn't have done that."[11] In fact, Abbott showed little enthusiasm for the show until it got encouraging reviews out of town and he was determined to make it better.

While everything seemed to be floundering in rehearsals and in previews, one thing was clear to all: Minnelli was able to carry a Broadway musical with remarkable energy and talent. And no one was more pleased that Abbott. "He fell completely in love with her," Kander recalled. "He loved young talent. That really excited him. On Liza's birthday, Mr. Abbott came waltzing into a rehearsal with a cake, which was something he would never ordinarily do."[12] "He loved the kind of singer she was," Ebb added. "I don't think she was ever less than aware of how important this show was for her, and Mr. Abbott was very protective of her. He insisted that Liza have an eleven o'clock number ... We wrote 'Sing Happy' out of town. She had to have a big song at the end."[13] By the time *Flora, the Red Menace* opened on Broadway in May of 1965, it was indeed a star vehicle and Minnelli was the undisputed star. "Individual, unduplicated and electrifying," Nadel raved in the *World Telegraph & Sun*. "She will be a star on her own terms for as many years as she can and will give so generously of her talent, spirit and love." But with such praise came a sour note. "Liza Minnelli brings her youth and eagerness to bear on the role," Howard Taubman wrote in the *New York Times*, "But her freshly burgeoning talent is not yet overpowering enough to save a faltering production." Neither was Minnelli able to keep *Flora, the Red Menace* on the boards for more than eighty-seven performances. By that time,

Prince had given up on the musical. "Of all the shows I have done which didn't work, I regret the failure of *Flora* most especially. What it could have been!"[14] It was clear to Prince that he had the wrong librettist and the wrong director. (From that point on, Prince directed all the musicals he produced.) It is questionable whether even an established star could have turned the show into a hit. Yet there was much to recommend in *Flora, the Red Menace* aside from Minnelli. The opening, for example, was very effective. The homeless and jobless on the street sang of waiting on breadlines then the scene shifted to Flora's graduation in which she and the students sang the anthem "Unafraid." It was a purely Abbott opening. At the Party meeting, the fervent but ridiculous song "The Flame" had the Communists chirping as if in some kind of cockeyed operetta. There was a mocking ballet for Comrade Charlotte and the Party members that was choreographed with style by Lee Theodore. And the ending, with the street-corner philosopher Mr. Weiss (Joe E. Marks) convincing Flora and the ensemble to be proud with "You Are You," was a spirited finale. But it wasn't enough; the show was done in by Abbott's libretto and his resolve to "pull its punches," as Walter Kerr noted in the *New York Herald Tribune*. While the idea and the structure of the script was solid, the characters were one-dimensional and the dialogue failed to sparkle.

Ada   It's easy, Comrade. First we give you a banner to carry.

Galka   With a slogan on it.

Jackson   "Down with Capitalism"!

Flora   Sure.

Charlotte   Suppose a cop comes at you with his club, what do you do?

Flora   I run?

Ada   No.

Flora   I scream?

Ada   No.

Charlotte   You hit him.

Flora   I do?

Ada   This is war. This isn't squat tag, Comrade.

Galka   You defend yourself against "police brutality."

Flora   Good. I got it. I hit him. (*hits an imaginary copy*) Pam! Pow!

Galka   Very good. You have the right spirit.[15]

Either because of Abbott's neglect or lack of interest in the subject., *Flora, the Red Menace* didn't completely come together. Kander later wrote, "Mr. Abbott later said he thought he was the person responsible for *Flora*'s not working."[16] Ebb agreed, noting that "His love for [Liza] killed the show. He wouldn't allow that spunky side of her to come out." Kander explained that, "Mr. Abbott didn't want to see Liza do anything ugly or unseemly at all. The one thing that became clear to us toward the end was that he couldn't bear the idea that Flora would be seriously in love with a Communist, because of his own political feelings."[17]

Flora, the Red Menace marked an unpleasant turning point in Abbott's career. When the production was trying out in Boston, Elinor Hughes in the *Boston Globe* noticed it. "Strangely enough for a George Abbott show," she wrote, "[It was] slow paced and not too organized." Pace and organization had been the hallmarks of an Abbott production. Perhaps, for the first time, the man who saved a musical was, instead, responsible for its failure. When *Flora, the Red Menace* was revived Off-Broadway in 1987 at the Vineyard Theatre, it had a totally new book by David Thompson which did not pull any punches. The musical was better reviewed but, despite an excellent production, was still wanting.

Minnelli won a Tony Award for her Broadway debut in *Flora, the Red Menace*. At this time it is worth pointing out how many performers won Tonys under Abbott's direction. Sixteen, to be exact. For the record: Ray Bolger in *Where's Charley?*; Ethel Merman and Russell Nype in *Call Me Madam*; Helen Gallagher and Natalia Makarova in two different revivals of *On Your Toes*; Rosalind Russell in *Wonderful Town*; Carol Haney in *The Pajama Game*; Gwen Verdon and Ray Walston in *Damn Yankees*; Gwen Verdon and Thelma Ritter in *New Girl in Town*; Tom Bosley in *Fiorello!*; Zero Mostel and David Burns in *A Funny Thing Happened on the Way to the Forum*; Liza Minnelli in *Flora, the Red Menace*; and Hiram Sherman in *How Now, Dow Jones*.

The day after *Flora, the Red Menace* opened, Prince met with Kander and Ebb in his office to discuss the next musical he had lined up, a work about the holocaust (and later known as *Cabaret*). Prince said he would direct it himself. There would be no compromising and no star turns. And no Abbott. After eleven Broadway shows together, they parted ways. Or, more accurately, Prince departed. Abbott never said "never" and rarely held a grudge. In fact, twenty-two years later, the two men *almost* collaborated again, as we shall see in Chapter 14. But in 1965, Abbott was moving on to a new project. Six months after *Flora, the Red Menace* opened, he was again represented on Broadway as the co-author and director of **Anya** (1965). Two musicals could not have been more different from each other. The legend of the Tsar's daughter Anastasia, who may or may not have survived the revolution, has often been dramatized. This musical version of the story was based on the French drama *Anastasia* by Marcelle Maurette which Guy Bolton adapted and it found success on Broadway in 1954. Producer Fred Fehlhaber hired Abbott to write the script and direct the new musical. Actually, it was not a musical but, in the old-fashioned sense of the word, an operetta. (Ethan Mordden, in his book about Sixties musicals *Open a New Window*, called *Anya* "the *last* operetta"[18] and

Ken Mandelbaum, in *Not Since Carrie*, labeled it "one of the last gasps of floperetta."[19]) A very serious tale about Russian hierarchy was a stretch for Abbott; an operetta was far out of his reach. Abbott had wisely avoided operettas in the 1920s, when they flourished, and in the 1930s, when they languished. So what was he doing working in operetta in the hip 1960s? Most likely Abbott was drawn to the project because *Song of Norway* (1944) and *Kismet* (1953) had been hits. Songwriters Robert Wright and George Forrest had taken music by Edvard Grieg for the former and themes by Alexandre Borodin for the later, added lyrics, and it all worked beautifully on stage. *Anya* could do the same thing, this time with music by Sergei Rachmaninoff; a real Russian composer providing the music for a very Russian tale. And given the lush and melodic sound of Rachmaninoff's music, it had to be an operetta. So *Anya* wasn't such a bad idea after all. But Abbott was obviously wrong for the job. He livened up the somber play with some animated new characters and he staged it efficiently, but to no avail. This was a show for another artist and for another time.

The story of Anastasia is seductive and would continue to resurface in the future. Abbott's libretto begins in a mental asylum in Berlin in 1925 in which the patient Anya (Constance Towers) tries to commit suicide by jumping into the river. When rescued, she claims to be the long-lost Anastasia, the Romanov child who escaped from the Bolshevik slaughter in 1917. A contingent of Russians in exile, led by the taxi-driver Bounine (Michael Kermoyan), hope to cash in on the wealthy Dowager Empress (Lillian Gish) by passing Anya off as the lost princess. Anya falls in love with Bounine and cooperates with him in the hoax. Yet when Anya does meet the Empress it appears she knows details that only the true princess would know. The Empress is convinced but the scam is revealed when Bounine is attracted to the Countess Genia (Karen Shepard) and Anya gets jealous, announcing to all that she is a fake. The exiled Prince Paul (John Michael King) is devastated because he has fallen in love with Anastasia. A happy ending of sorts was achieved by Bounine and Anya running off together. Abbott created the characters of the cafe owner Katrina (Irra Petina) and the raucous émigré Chernov (George S. Irving) to add a dash of spirit and have an excuse to use some of Rachmaninoff's more cheerful melodies. As with their previous efforts using classical music, Wright and Forrest composed a lot of "filler" but they knew when an old piece of music would translate to a highly accessible theatre song. The problem had more to do with the lyrics. The songwriters came up with some very accomplished lyrics for *Kismet* but the wordplay in *Anya* was flat and turgid. That left Rachmaninoff to carry the day and often he did. A recurring leitmotif, the haunting "A Song from Somewhere," was used as Anya remembered pieces of the past. There were the passion duets "This Is My Kind of Love" and "If This Is Goodbye" for Bounine and Anya, a minor-key ditty "That Prelude" for Katrina and the ensemble, the jaunty "Snowflakes and Sweethearts" for a flashback, and the stirring, nostalgic "Homeward" for Katrina and the émigrés. Most of the score required operetta-level singers but *Anya* ended up with a cast of theatre voices. The renowned opera baritone George England was originally cast as Bounine but he was gone early in rehearsals and was replaced by Michael Kermoyan who, like Constance Towers as Anya, was more in the Rodgers and Hammerstein range. Irra Petina trilled in the stratosphere without any problem but Lillian Gish, as the Empress, had to talk-sing her one song, "Little Hands." The bottom line in 1965 was that audiences didn't much care about operetta voices because they didn't much care about operetta.

Anya opened on Broadway in November of 1965 to either mildly dismissive notices or outright pans from the press. Comments such as "extremely dated" and "old-fashioned" and "an insensitive and tasteless treatment [of Rachmaninoff]" were repeated in all of the reviews. Some critics questioned Abbott's involvement in the whole venture. Nadel in the *World-Telegraph & Sun* noted, "George Abbott does some musicals notably well. However, both the writing and the direction of *Anya* indicate that he had the wrong concept from the very beginning," and Kerr in the *Herald Tribune* wrote, "No matter who the real Anastasia was, I am going to cling to my blind conviction that the George Abbott who is listed as co-librettist and director is not the real George Abbott." Without star power (Lillian Gish only appeared in the second act) or a big advance, *Anya* closed in two weeks. Could it have survived with someone else writing and directing the musical? Wright and Forrest thought so and over the next two-and-a-half decades they reworked the material. Productions of *Anya* with a revised book have surfaced in various theatres. A 1989 version, that was produced and recorded as *The Anastasia Game*, removed Katrina and Genia in order to simplify the story. Even the score was rethought. It still didn't work.

The year 1965 may have seen two Abbott musicals fail on Broadway but it also brought two honors that few theatre artists could boast. That year the playhouse at 152 West 54th Street was named the George Abbott Theatre. Built in 1928 as the Craig Theatre, the venue had housed three Abbott productions in the past: *On the Town* (1944), *Look Ma, I'm Dancin'* (1948), both when it was known as the Adelphi Theatre, and *Drink to Me* (1958), when the playhouse was called the 54th Street Theatre. Most theatres are named after actors or producers so it was unique that this one was named after a director, something only seen previously with the Belasco and John Golden Theatres. But the George Abbott Theatre was an unlucky playhouse, housing no hits during the next five years. Sadly, it was demolished in 1970 to make way for an addition to the Hilton Hotel. Several old playhouses were similarly torn down in the 1970s. More permanent (and even rarer) was the 1965 naming of the block on West 45th Street, between Seventh and Eighth Avenues, George Abbott Way. This was a prestigious piece of real estate, the location of six of Broadway's finest playhouses: the Booth, John Golden, Bernard B. Jacobs, Music Box, and Imperial Theatres. Abbott's theatre is gone but there is still an Abbott Way.

In the fall of 1966, Abbott directed two comedies that quickly closed, something they were more than likely to do no matter who directed them. Keith Waterhouse and Willis Hall's British farce **Help Stamp Out Marriage!** (1966) had managed to run in London under the title *Say Who You Are*. It was one of those silly contrivances that frequently amuse playgoers in Great Britain but leave American audiences baffled. Every Friday Sarah Lord (Valerie French) forces her husband David (Roddy Maude-Roxby) to take her to the movies so that her friend Valerie Pitman (Ann Bell) can use their London flat for a romantic tryst with Stuart Wheeler (Francis Matthews). To avoid marriage, Valerie tells Stuart she lives there with her husband David, so complications ensue when the foursome all end up in the same place one Friday night. Abbott was back in form staging an unequivocal farce but the critics quibbled. John McCarten in *The New Yorker* stated the case bluntly: "The oral acrobatics, I regret to say, were not amusing, and some of the exchanges between the characters are witless enough to be actively annoying." Audiences stayed away and *Help Stamp Out Marriage!* departed after twenty performances. It is difficult to believe, but this low-brow affair was produced by the Theatre Guild, once the bastion of high art, but in the Sixties the organization was struggling to survive. Also difficult to believe is that Abbott chose, or approved of, the new title. Less than three months later, Abbott was billed as director of **Agatha Sue, I Love You** (1966), a comedy by Abe Einhorn, a stagehand-turned-playwright. It again was a farce and it was co-produced by Edwin Wilson and Abbott's now-grown daughter Judith. Although it was set in the present, *Agatha Sue, I Love You* had the demeanor (if not the style and panache) of a 1930s comedy. The destitute Manhattan gamblers Jack (Corbett Monica) and Eddie (Ray Walston) are holed up in the Great White Way Hotel, a past-its-prime lodging in New York, where they live on minuscule portions of graham crackers and Cola-Cola and spend their time avoiding the shrewish proprietress Mrs. Gordon (Betty Garde). The desperate duo needs some cash to place on a horse, so they try to steal and pawn the guitar belonging to the pretty, young folk singer Agatha Sue (Lee Lawson) from next door. She misinterprets Jack's attentions as a proposal of marriage and moves in with the two men, happily giving them what money she has to bet on a horse called Flaming Arrow. The horse wins, Jack deserts Agatha Sue for the sexy blonde Sheila (Renee Taylor), so the optimistic singer heads to Chicago for a folk singing gig. The press noted the competent cast and Abbott's tight direction but felt that the script for *Agatha Sue, I Love You* was hopeless. Kerr in the *Times* wrote, "I will never understand how anyone succeeded in persuading George Abbott—who once directed *Three Men on a Horse* with a plot, and with real jokes besides—to stage so melancholy a collection of non-comic non sequiturs." After only five performances, the comedy was gone.

How Abbott worked in the New York theatre since the late 1950s without having to deal with David Merrick is no mystery. Abbott disliked the upstart, publicity-driven young producer and stayed clear of him. There are singing-dancing-acting stars and there are playwright stars and songwriting stars and even director stars but, in Abbott's thinking, there should never be a producer star. Producers are businessmen; audiences do not go to see businessmen in the theatre. Yet by 1967, Merrick was the star of his many plays and musicals, even when he optioned them in London and brought them to Broadway intact. Also, by the late Sixties, Merrick was in direct rivalry with Prince and Abbott knew where his loyalties lie. So when the Merrick musical *How Now, Dow Jones* (1967) opened on Broadway with Abbott billed as the director, one had to ask two questions: Was Abbott so desperate for work that he succumbed to Merrick? Or was a Merrick show in so much trouble that the producer had to beg the Master to fix things? One wants to hope that the latter was true. It certainly looked like it judging from the facts (such as we know them). Lyricist Carolyn Leigh came up with a terrible idea for a musical and somehow a lot of intelligent people thought it was a good idea. Merrick hired humorist Max Shulman to write the script, wooed the renowned Hollywood composer Elmer Bernstein to give Broadway a try, and had Leigh further develop her premise into lyrics. All these experienced artists went into rehearsals with a libretto that is celebrated as one of the worst of its era. Kate (Marlyn Mason) works on Wall Street as the "Voice of Dow Jones," announcing the Dow Jones Industrial Averages over the loudspeakers on the trading floor. She is engaged to the struggling trader Herbert (James Congdon) but has a fling with the suicidal Charley (Anthony Roberts) which leaves her pregnant. The more Kate pressures Herbert to marry her, the more insecure he becomes until, in a fit of desperation, he promises her that he will wed as soon as the Dow Jones average hits 1000. So Kate announces to all on the trading floor that the Dow has hit 1000, thereby causing a furor of buying followed by a crashing reaction. The reformed Charley saves the day by getting an aged multimillionaire to start a buying frenzy, the market returns to reasonable levels, and Kate dumps Herbert to marry Charley. The equally asinine subplot concerned the Wall Street mogul Wingate (Hiram Sherman) who connives to get his mistress Cynthia (Brenda Vaccaro) into a "love nest" then, once she's there, he forgets all about her.

If the libretto was fraught with difficulties, the production was just as problematic. The London choreographer Gillian Lynne was replaced by eager dancer Michael Bennett but Merrick gave him no program credit. The initially-cast George Coe was replaced by Congdon to play Herbert; the character of Miss Whipple, played by Madeleine Kahn, was cut and Kahn was out even though she understudied Vaccaro; and director Arthur Penn fled during the Philadelphia tryouts. So Abbott was brought in by Merrick, perhaps as an impossible challenge for the veteran director. One does not fix a libretto this bad. Instead Abbott used every trick in the book to draw attention away from . . . well, just about everything. Pace and organization were on full throttle and *How Now, Dow Jones* had the face of a big Broadway musical comedy. As Clive Barnes noted in the *Times*: "Abbott's direction—a positive powerhouse that has forgotten what it is doing with the power but keeps on pounding away." There were many compliments for the talented cast even though the characters made no sense. For the most part, the critics declared the show a mess, not knowing what it wanted to be or say. Kerr also reviewed the musical in the *Sunday Times* and thought, "*How Now, Dow Jones* is well put together by a man who has never had an identity crisis, George Abbott. Unfortunately, Mr. Abbott has only directed, and the show is shy a few things, such as an amusing book, melodic songs, lyrics with life to them, and dancing." Actually, what dancing there was was quite enjoyable, such as the merry march "[Will Everyone Here] Step to the Rear" in which Roberts cavorted with a group of widowed Jewish investors. It was a highlight in a score that was indeed disappointing. Still, Vaccaro got the fine comic number "He's Here" and Mason sang a memorable ballad titled "Walk Away." With reviews that ranged from mixed to pans, *How Now, Dow Jones* would have quickly closed. But Merrick was not Broadway's most brazen producer for nothing. His publicity machine started early and the show had an advance of $500,000 by the time it opened in December of 1967. Merrick & Co. kept the momentum going with television appearances and radio spots. *How Now, Dow Jones* ended up running six months and would have continued on had there not been an Actors' Union strike in June of 1968. To return to the question about why Abbott agreed to work with Merrick, there was an official answer from Abbott. When asked by a journalist why he took on a musical that was rumored to be in so much trouble, Abbott replied, "Listen, I had a couple of flops last year, and I was kinda glad to get something."[20]

As loud and tacky as *How Now, Dow Jones* came across, Abbott's next musical—***The Education of H*Y*M*A*N K*A*P*L*A*N*** (1968)—was gentle, quiet, and quaintly engaging; in essence, not what audiences and critics wanted in the restless 1960s. In 1937, Jewish humorist Leo Rosten wrote a series of short stories about the inquisitive immigrant Hyman Kaplan finding his way in Chicago during the Depression. With Rosten using the pseudonym Leonard Q. Ross, they were published in *The New Yorker* and were later collected into two award-winning volumes: *The Education of H*Y*M*A*N K*A*P*L*A*N* (1937) and *The Return of H*Y*M*A*N K*A*P*L*A*N* (1959). Rosten, sometimes referred to as the Jewish James Thurber, created a delightful character who was stereotypic but not a caricature. Songwriters Paul Nassau and Oscar Brand thought that Kaplan and the stories would make a fine subject for a musical. The libretto by Benjamin Bernard Zavin moved the tale to the Lower East Side of Manhattan in 1919, the period of the infamous Palmer Raids in which the district attorney rounded up alleged radicals among the immigrant neighborhoods and had them deported without a trial. While this historical reference tried to give *The Education of H*Y*M*A*N K*A*P*L*A*N* (hereafter called *K*A*P*L*A*N*) some dramatic weight, the musical was far from a heavy drama. The Jewish tailor Hyman Kaplan (Tom Bosley) wants to learn the language and customs of his new homeland so he enrolls in night classes with other immigrants. The teacher Mr. Parkhill (Gary Krawford) struggles to communicate with the multi-lingual students, often with humorous complications. Hyman is a willing but hopeless student. He asks too many questions and has too many opinions which accidentally gets him arrested as an anarchist. The misunderstanding is cleared up in time for Hyman to take the oath of citizenship with his fellow immigrants. There was a romantic triangle as well. Hyman falls for the young classmate Rose Mitnick (Barbara Minkus) but she faces an arranged marriage with the insufferable Yissel Fishbein (Hal Linden). It seems Fishbein paid the steamship passage for her and her mother (Mimi Sloan) and the family is indebted to him. But in the end, Rose finally refuses Fishbein and goes off with Hyman. Because the libretto was based on a series of stories, it was episodic and the highlights of K*A*P*L*A*N were the scenes at night school rather than the musical numbers. That said, there were two thrilling moments in the musical: the rousing "I Never Felt Better in My Life," choreographed with zest by Jamie Rogers, and Rose's defiant solo "When Will I Learn?" as she makes her bold move to take charge of her life. (Those annoying asterisks between the letters of Kaplan's name represented the stars that Hyman drew in his moniker to display his patriotism for his new country.)

K*A*P*L*A*N's three mostly-inexperienced producers—André Goulston, Jack Farren, and Stephen Mellow—were not too savvy about Broadway but even they knew Abbott was the man to rewrite and direct their musical, even though he had not had a hit since 1962. Abbott agreed and insisted designers William and Jean Eckart be brought on to do the sets and costumes. The producers wanted comic Red Buttons to play Hyman but Abbott refused, insisting on Tom Bosley from *Fiorello!* Abbott then rewrote some of the libretto, adding musical comedy laughs that did not always blend in with Rosten's less-sophisticated ethnic humor. Although Abbott was used to working with unknowns, he did not have a good rapport with the librettist, the songwriters, or the producers. As William Eckart later commented, "Abbott, who was directing his 110th Broadway show, wasn't working with people who knew how to respond to him."[21] So Abbott tended to spend much of his energy on working with the cast, a talented mixture of various types beyond the Jewish characters. Bosley was as likable and charming as Abbott had hoped though it was clear to many that Bosley was not ethnic enough—"too white bread," Eckart thought.[22] Still, Bosley had to carry the show and he did so with aplomb. A pleasing surprise was Hal Linden in his first notable role. Although Fishbein was not a likable character, Linden's performance was compelling and in his one song, "Old Fashioned Husband," he was splendid. (Just about every critic cheered Linden in the reviews.) One aspect of K*A*P*L*A*N that was true to the source material was the Eckarts' designs. The subdued color palette, the busy conglomeration of buildings, and the non-costume look of the clothes all helped evoke life on the Lower East Side of Manhattan.

Opening night of K*A*P*L*A*N—April 4, 1968—would turn out to be a terrible one, but not because of the quality of the show. There was a slight commotion at the back of the house near the end of the first act. Then some uniformed men made their way to where John Lindsay, the current mayor of New York City, was sitting with guests. The mayor was rushed out and then at intermission word quickly spread through the playgoers that Dr. Martin Luther King had been shot and there were potential riots in Harlem. It was with an uneasy, even terrified, audience that the second act of K*A*P*L*A*N was performed. Critics attended opening nights in those days so they also saw the musical under uncomfortable conditions. Some of the next day's reviews took in account the unusual circumstances while others did not mention Dr. King's death and the possible impact it had on the proceedings. The notices ranged widely from favorable nods to outright pans, most critics picking and choosing some elements of K*A*P*L*A*N to be commended. Abbott was not saved from some negativity. Some notices thought Abbott did the best he could under the circumstances but Martin Gottfried in *Women's Wear Daily* placed some of the blame on Abbott when he wrote, "The book is based on Leo Rosten stories, spiced—a better word would be smothered—by the unmistakable contributions of Mr. Abbott. There is no sense in carping on the inadequacies of the writing." The producers, perhaps unwisely, decided to take advantage of the situation surrounding their ill-timed production. They announced that for one particular upcoming performance of K*A*P*L*A*N, all of the box office receipts would be donated to Dr. King's Southern Christian Leadership Conference. The performance was a sellout and Sammy Davis, Jr., was on hand to make a speech at intermission. After that, the box office intake dwindled and the musical closed after twenty-eight performances, losing its entire investment of $550,000.

The Education of H*Y*M*A*N K*A*P*L*A*N (to use the full title one last time) was one of the musicals William Goldman thoroughly covered in his incisive book about the 1967–1968 Broadway season. He saw the show in rehearsals, out of town, and on Broadway and witnessed the way Abbott steadily improved the musical. But Goldman was not surprised by the outcome. He declared K*A*P*L*A*N was "Charming. Charm is the key word here. There are lots of charm shows, and when they become hits, as *My Fair Lady* did, they can run forever. But they have little power, and if the critics aren't in the mood for charm that night, they're dead."[23] Ken Mandelbaum, in his book about Broadway musical failures, perhaps summed up the situation best. "This was an evening of charm and light humor, rather than a blockbuster. And *Fiddler on the Roof*, then in its fourth year on Broadway, had set a standard for musicals about Russian Jews that was difficult for other musicals to live up to."[24]

Although he was not counting, K*A*P*L*A*N was Abbott's seventh consecutive Broadway flop in six years. Of course, in 1968 there had not been a musical hit on Broadway *by anyone* in two years. So the pickings were slim for everyone. That is probably why Abbott agreed to direct **The Fig Leaves Are Falling** (1969), a musical one cannot imagine him wanting to sit through no less direct. It was one of the handful of plays and musicals in the 1960s about the youth movement, written by and enjoyed by those who were far from young. Making fun of hippies, free love, protest songs, and the generation gap lost its sense of humor as events near the end of the decade turned ugly. But that didn't stop *The Fig Leaves Are Falling*, one of the most embarrassing failures of its day. Novelty song writer Allan Sherman wrote the libretto which was a thinly disguised version of his own mid-life crisis. Harry (Barry Nelson) and Lillian Stone (Dorothy Loudon) live in the suburb of Larchmont with their two teenage daughters. Harry is restless and feeling neglected so when his young secretary Pookie Chapman (Jenny O'Hara) tries to seduce him, Harry doesn't put up a fight. She is a founder of the Sexual Freedom League and represents the new Good Life to Harry. Soon he has moved out of the house and living the wild life of the younger generation. Of course, it doesn't last and Harry eventually returns to his wife and family. Allan was known for his silly lyrics set to existing music (often classical) but it was clear he could not write a play or a real song. Albert Hague wrote the music for Sherman's lyrics. He had written some admirable music for television but had had little luck on Broadway; *The Fig Leaves Are Falling* was no exception.

Producers Joseph Harris, Lawrence Carr, and John Bowab, for reasons that boggle the mind, hired actor Jack Klugman to direct their hip "now" musical. Before rehearsals began, Klugman wisely departed from the project. William and Jean Eckarts, who were doing the sets and costumes, suggested Abbott to replace Klugman. One assumes they did it out of friendship or loyalty because no one was more wrong for the subject matter than Abbott. The eighty-two-year-old disdained the new music, the mod look, and the whole counter-culture movement. But, wanting to work, Abbott agreed to direct *The Fig Leaves Are Falling* and went to work turning it into a colorful satire without any bite. Comic actor Jules Munshin, who was playing a supporting character, quit during rehearsals. Instead of trying to get another name, the understudy (Kenneth Kimmins) was given the role. Also during rehearsals, the underused Dorothy Loudon was proving to be the highlight of the show. Abbott took the song "All My Laughter" away from Pookie and gave it to the wife. Loudon's rendition of the number was so exciting it was used to close the first act of the musical. Perhaps Abbott went too far in his desperate attempts to make the musical lively. At one point in the evening, Harry and Pookie auction off a live chicken to the theatre audience.

The reviews when *The Fig Leaves Are Falling* opened in January of 1969 were devastating. Barnes in the *Times* felt all the show needed was "a new book, new music and lyrics, new settings, new direction, new choreography, and a partially new cast." Gottfried in *Women's Wear Daily* wrote, "*The Fig Leaves Are Falling* is so naive as musical theatre and as a point of view that I feel out of proportion attacking it as a menace." The other notices were not far behind. Yet on opening night, when Loudon sang "All My Laughter," the audience was so enthusiastic that they wouldn't let her get off stage until she had sung an encore. Unfortunately, she only got to wow the playgoers three more times; *The Fig Leaves Are Falling* closed after the fourth performance. Loudon did get a Tony nomination, which is remarkable considering how few opportunities the Tony voters had to see her in the show. By this time, the critics had stopped complimenting Abbott for doing his best with inferior material. The reviews for *The Fig Leaves Are Falling* either ignored him or criticized the staging.

How long was one able to give Abbott the benefit of a doubt? When it came to musicals, opportunities would only arise for a few more years. In the meantime, Abbott was offered two plays and, as dreadful as they were, he took them. It is unclear whether Abbott tinkered with the scripts or not. If he did, his efforts were in vain.

Plays on Broadway about homosexuals were still very rare in the early 1970s so when a deplorable work like **Norman, Is That You?** (1970) got produced, the damage was considerable. The problem of parents who have a gay son is turned into a joke and every laugh confirmed the public's stereotypic ideas on homosexuality. The play was the first theatre effort by television writers Ron Clark and Sam Bobrick and there was a definite sit-com feel to the proceedings. Ohio dry-cleaning mogul Ben Chambers (Lou Jacobi) finds out that his wife Beatrice (Maureen Stapleton) has run off to Mexico with his own brother. So Ben goes to New York City to commiserate with his son Norman (Martin Huston), only to find that the youth is living with his boyfriend Garson Hobart (Walter Willison) in a homosexual love nest. After the expected comic reaction and jokes about masculinity, Ben attempts to "straighten out" Norman by hiring the pretty prostitute Mary (Dorothy Emmerson). The tryst is a disaster and Ben starts to realize he cannot change his son. Beatrice, having tired of the brother, returns to Ben in New York and they are reconciled to each other. Norman is drafted into the army and Ben and Beatrice end up taking Garson back to Ohio with them. There was no hiding the offensive nature of the piece, especially in light of the slow acceptance in the theatre for realistic gay characters. Some critics expressed their disdain for the shabby way the authors treated their subject matter but most just decried the poor writing and lame jokes. Yet every notice applauded Jacobi and Stapleton's performances and some of Abbott's staging. Barnes in the *Times* wrote, "What might have given this pathetic little comedy of variants some passing interest are the enthusiastic and energetic direction of George Abbott, who flogs the play to within an inch of its death, and a couple of superbly conventional performances from Lou Jacobi and Maureen Stapleton." She only appeared in one scene at the end of the comedy. William Eckart, who designed the scenery for *Norman, Is That You?*, explained, "George got Maureen to do it ... she and George were having an affair at the time, so she couldn't say no."[25] The comedy could not survive the damning reviews and closed after twelve performances. So how much damage could the play do? Quite a bit, actually. *Norman, Is that You?* received many productions in less discriminating dinner and community theatres. One amateur theatre in Los Angeles, the Ebony Showcase Theatre, did the play in 1971, with an African American cast, and it ran seven years. The first international production was in Paris that same year, followed by versions in thirty-five countries. Hollywood latched onto the African American angle and made a film version in 1976 starring Redd Foxx and Pearly Bailey. So *Norman, Is that You?* was a flop play that went on to belittle homosexuality for thousands of playgoers and moviegoers, getting laughs all the way. Abbott's Broadway failures rarely hurt anyone; this one did.

It looked like Abbott was handed a sure thing when asked to direct the London hit comedy *Not Now, Darling* (1970) by Ray Cooney and John Chapman. The posh London furriers Arnold Crouch (Norman Wisdom) and Gilbert Bodley (Rex Garner), of the posh establishment of Bodley, Bodley, and Crouch, endure a day of furious misunderstandings in their salon when a husband is sold a fur for his wife that was intended for his mistress. Suspicious wives enter, scantily clad girls are hidden in closets, and everyone is doubled over with double entendres until the final curtain mercifully falls. As with Abbott's earlier *Help Stamp Out Marriage*, the peculiar kind of British farce failed to amuse Americans. The critics lowered their guns, calling the play "infantile," "singularly flat [and] lugubrious," and warning patrons to "check your mind at the door." The popular British stage star Norman Wisdom was cited as both the best and the worst of the frantic cast. Although *Not Now, Darling* went on to run two years in London, the Broadway version folded after twenty-one performances. It was the last non-musical that Abbott directed on Broadway, coming forty-five years after his first effort, *The Fall Guy* in 1925. His last new musical to reach Broadway came in 1976 with **Music Is**, a musical adaptation of Shakespeare's *Twelfth Night*. The comedy classic has been turned into a musical more often than any other play by the Bard, ranging from the rock-and-roll spoof *Your Own Thing* (1968) set in the psychedelic Sixties to the Duke Ellington juke box version *Play On!* (1997) set in the swinging Forties. This new version returned to Elizabethan times but was not strict in its adherence to the period. Some of the dialogue was modern, some right from Shakespeare. Similarly, the songs by Will Holt (lyrics) and Richard Adler (music), reunited with Abbott from *The Pajama Game* and *Damn Yankees,* had the flavor of the English Renaissance while others were standard Broadway and a few were actually quite modern. While this may sound like *Music Is* was inconsistent, the blending of different styles was one of its charms. The project originated with Abbott who wanted to return to the classics for a musical comedy as he had with *The Boys from Syracuse* and *A Funny Thing Happened on the Way to the Forum*. Abbott wrote his adaptation for the students at the Eastman School of Music in Rochester, New York, but when he showed the final script to Harold Prince, his past collaborator thought it "too good to waste on amateurs."[26] So Adler decided to co-produce a Broadway production with Roger Berlind and Edward R. Downe, Jr. In a very unusual move for the time (but common practice today), *Music Is* premiered first at a regional theatre—the Seattle Theatre Center—before doing the usual out-of-town tour heading to Broadway.

Abbott's condensing and altering of *Twelfth Night* into a musical comedy was done expertly. Barnes, in his review in the *Times*, did not endorse the show but he did admit, "In all fairness, George Abbott has done a very clever job of carpentry—indeed his skill at trimming, changing and bending the original narrative while being faithful to the main story is worth studying by any aspirant writers of musical books." As with Shakespeare, there is a clever love quadrangle. The Duke Orsino

(David Halliday) loves the Lady Olivia (Sherry Mathis) but she falls in love with Viola (Catherine Cox) who is disguised as a boy and is in love with the Duke. Olivia's steward Malvolio (Christopher Hewett) is tricked by the vulgar Sir Toby (David Sabin), the handmaiden Maria (Laura Waterbury), and the fop Sir Andrew Aguecheek (Joe Ponazecki) into thinking Olivia is in love with the somber Puritan, causing him to make a fool of himself. When Viola's twin brother Sebastian (Joel Higgins) arrives in town, mistaken identity results and the complications pile up nicely until they are resolved satisfactorily. While *The Comedy of Errors* was a farce, Shakespeare's *Twelfth Night* is romantic high comedy with farcical elements and *Music Is* was also in the more sophisticated mode. The quality of the score was uneven, often because of Holt's lyrics, but it had several memorable numbers: Viola's lovely ballad "Should I Speak of Loving You," Olivia's song of awakening "Suddenly Lilac," Malvolio's comic tour de force "I Am It," and the pleasing Sebastian-Olivia duet "Please Be Human." It is a score that deserves more recognition. Alas, there was no original cast album.

Music Is opened on Broadway in December of 1976 and was mostly trounced by the critics. Howard Kissel in *Women's Wear Daily* was kinder than most, writing, "There is no lack of inventiveness . . . in the show," but concluded, "*Music Is* is short on substance, and these days, alas, even in musicals, substance counts." The musical did suffer from a sense of identity and did not fall into place as it should have. Yet the reviews were dismissive and did not acknowledge the production's many joys. For example, the show's opening was dazzling. The entire cast marched across the stage in a colorful, Elizabethan parade, holding up banners that identified the artistic team. It was like the opening credits of some playful movie. The end of the first act was a furious dance choreographed by Patricia Birch. In a game of blindman's bluff, the cast bounced about the stage with the help of trampolines hidden behind the furniture. The said cast was filled with talented unknowns who did both Shakespeare and Abbott proud. Even the vibrant orchestrations by Hershy Kay were complimented by many of the critics. So why was *Music Is* treated so roughly by the press? The show was in competition with two previous musicals. Abbott's own *The Boys from Syracuse* was a well-known entity and the reviews compared it to *Music Is* and found the new show lacking, particularly regarding the score. Yet consider: in the 1970s no one, neither a Stephen Sondheim or a Jerry Herman, could turn out a Rodgers and Hart kind of score. *Music Is* was also compared to the earlier *Your Own Thing* which had a fresh approach to doing a musical version of the classic play. The satiric pop-rock show was indeed original; the press thought *Music Is* was old hat. With such negative reviews, the producers closed *Music Is* after only eight performances. In his autobiography, Adler wrote,

> Mr. Abbott was as gracious in defeat as he would have been with a hit. He told me he loved the music . . . [that] it hadn't been my fault, that there were two fatal flaws in the show: 'The book wasn't good enough,' he said, 'and I should have

made you write more Elizabethan music, like the opening number.' And that was it for him. He'd closed the ledger on this show and, characteristically, was ready to begin [the next].[27]

It was a sad end to Abbott's career as a creator of new work on Broadway.

But there was still Off and Off-Off Broadway and in the 1980s Abbott turned to these less-glamorous venues for his last two new works. The musicals had very limited runs and very small productions: bits of costume and scenery, solo piano, limited choreography, but boasted excellent performers which Abbott often picked from his previous productions. For example, Lara Teeter, who has been widely applauded in the 1983 Broadway revival of On Your Toes, played the central character in Abbott's new musical ***Tropicana*** (1985). It was an original script set on a fictitious South Seas island. where the American Bill Smith (Teeter) is shipwrecked and washed ashore. He is discovered more dead than alive by an island girl Ana Sanchez (Roxann Cabalero) and she nurses him to health and into an atmospheric island romance. The island is ruled by a cruel dictator, President Mendoza (Edmund Lyndeck), who keeps the people living in poverty while he thrives. Bill tries to help the people, is arrested and tortured by Mendoza, then escapes the island, unresolved love filling the air. The young songwriter Robert Lindsey-Nassif, who had composed music for Joseph Papp's Public Theatre, was hired to write both music and lyrics and worked with Abbott on the musical. Abbott was not pleased with some of the lyrics and, after Lindsey-Nassif provided new ones, he insisted that Peter Napolitano be brought in to write some new ones. (The final score was evenly divided with lyrics by Lindsey-Nassif and Napolitano.) As per the setting, the score for *Tropicana* was in the Latin style with calypso touches. Highlights from the score include the waltzing duet "Teach Me" for Ana and Bill with a distinctive rhumba beat; the haunting ballad "I Will Remember You" in which Ana recalls all departed ones; and the expansive contrapuntal duet "Now" with Ana and Bill celebrating the moment.

After a staged reading of *Tropicana*, the Off-Off Broadway group Musical Theatre Works planned a full production for the spring of 1985. This company was dedicated to presenting new works and had the sponsorship of important people. Hal Prince was on hand to promote the work of his old friend Abbott and encourage the young talent involved. A top-notch cast was secured for the sixteen-performance run and Broadway veteran Donald Saddler was brought in to choreograph. In my interview with Teeter, he recalled years later that Abbott directed the small-scale production "just as if it were a big Broadway show." Since Teeter had seen Abbott in action with On Your Toes, he noted "Nothing was different. He was the first to arrive at rehearsal and the last one to leave." The only concession the ninety-nine-year-old director allowed himself was "a cot to take a nap on and servings of lemon flavored soup."[28] During rehearsals it became clear *Tropicana* had an identity crisis. It brought up some very serious issues yet Abbott still directed it like a musical comedy while Lindsey-Nassif took the plight of the island characters very seriously. This conflict of ideas climaxed in the torture scene which Abbott insisted on playing for laughs. Although Musical Theatre Works was Off-Off Broadway, the production was a celebrity affair because the company's Artistic Director Anthony J. Stimac turned *Tropicana* into a celebration in honor of Abbott's 121st New York theatre production. Salutations, in the forms of ads in the program, came from the Who's Who of the theatre community. Those who actually attended met with a very uneven musical, some delightful songs, and a splendid cast of nineteen, most members of Equity. In addition to Teeter and those already mentioned, there were fine performances by Constance Carpenter as the wise grandmother and Natalie Costa, T. J. Harris, and Charles Goff as the three Mendoza offspring. The May–June 1985 run of *Tropicana* did not do what was intended: interest producers and/or investors in moving the musical on to the next level. No one was surprised. Even the show's composer-lyricist Lindsey-Nassif knew there was no future in *Tropicana*. "It was all very embarrassing," he said decades later in an interview for this book. "However, it led to my working with Hal Prince on many projects for the next twenty-five years."[29] Although there had been some friction between Lindsey-Nassif and Abbott, the director sought him out a year later to score another show, a musical version of his 1926 hit melodrama *Broadway*. That will be discussed in Chapter 14 with the infamous 1987 revival of *Broadway*.

Abbott's musical version of Mary Shelley's *Frankenstein*, with the unfortunate title of **Frankie** (1989), also suffered from lack of identity. Everyone knew the story but the musical didn't know if it was a horror tale, a romance, or a satiric comedy. The fact that Abbott's libretto was a little bit of each caused confusion instead of entertainment. The story was set in the present day with scientist Dr. Victor Stanford (Richard White) putting off his marriage to Elizabeth Blake (Elizabeth Walsh) until he gets to complete his ultimate experiment: to bring life to his creature Frankie (Gil Rogers). His brother Burton (Casper Roos) warns Victor of the dangers he is courting but, being somewhat mad, the scientist pursues his goal, brings Frankie to life, and even manages to civilize him somewhat. But Frankie turns wild, kidnaps Elizabeth and straps her to the operating table. It seems he wants to experiment just like his master. Elizabeth is rescued but Frankie goes on a rampage and, after a handful of murders, is put to sleep for good. The story ends with the African American maid Flora (Ellia English), who grew fond of Frankie in his gentle state, mourns his passing as the village joins her in singing a "Negro spiritual"-like number. Abbott took his libretto to Janet Hays Walker at The York Theatre, an Off-Off-Broadway organization that had received wide recognition of late, and convinced her to produce the show. For a composer, Abbott asked Donald Saddler (who would later co-direct and choreograph *Frankie*) if he could recommend someone. Saddler had worked with Joseph Turrin on the Emmy Award-winning TV movie *Verna: USO Girl* (1978) and suggested Abbott hear some of his music. Turrin was asked to meet Abbott in a hotel lobby where there was a piano. "There in the middle of folks coming and going," Turrin recalled in my interview with him,

> I sat at the piano and performed the pieces I had written. I'm not a singer and I sounded horrible but got through the set of songs regardless. God knows what the people in the lobby thought of this. George loved what I did and said he would be delighted to have me compose the score ... That's how it all started. Interestingly, in my first phone conversations with him I addressed him as Mr. Abbott and to my surprise he insisted I call him George.[30]

It was Abbott's intention from the start to modernize the Mary Shelley tale. "He thought a modern version might be interesting as told in a farcical way with the whole of the book set to music like an operetta," Turrin said.[31] Abbott, it seems, was impressed with the sung-through style of Andrew Lloyd-Webber's recent hit *The Phantom of the Opera* and wanted to use it for *Frankie*. "The music was continuous throughout the book," Turrin continued. "When we decided on spoken dialogue, the music would go into underscore like a movie track. In many of the singing sections, I used Abbott's dialogue as if they were lyrics."[32] But singing dialogue was not enough so Turrin suggested that his lyricist friend Gloria Nissenson be hired to turn parts of the dialogue into verse or recitative. Abbott agreed. The script for *Frankie* may have gone off in different directions but the score by Turrin and Gloria Nisssenson is in the romantic style. The duets between Victor and Elizabeth are rather formal and closer to opera recitative than melodic. Some numbers are mildly comic, such as a caustic duet by the two gravediggers. Victor sings of his future glory in "If I Succeed," both music and lyric having a disturbing undercurrent. Perhaps most satisfying is the simple hymn that Flora sings over the sleeping body of Frankie. Turrin remembered,

> George was constantly rewriting scenes as he often said to me it could always be better. Even at the age of 102 he was tireless and would often rewrite a scene five or ten times. Of course, I would then have to recalculate the amount of music under the scene and add or subtract bars. I once said to him: 'George, every time you rewrite a scene, I need to rewrite the music and that's a lot of work.' He said to me, 'That's your job, isn't it?' That shut me right up.[33]

As far as the director's job on *Frankie*, Abbott and Saddler staged the show together and Saddler handled the little choreography that was needed. Abbott did not use a walker or wheelchair so he was mostly stationary while staging scenes and Saddler was the movement director in more than dance. The two veterans (Saddler was a spry seventy years old at the time) worked well together, according to Turrin. "George and Don split the direction fifty-fifty, I would say. George was [very old] at this time so Don was very helpful."³⁴ Before *Frankie* played at the York, Arnold Middleman at the Cocoanut Grove Playhouse in Miami, Florida, presented a reading of the script and songs before a selected audience. Afterwards, Middleman wanted to make suggestions but was cautious about bringing them to Abbott so instead he approached Turrin about changes he recommended. Turrin said he agreed with the changes so Middleman found the courage to talk to Abbott. When Turrin asked Abbott about it later, he replied " I yes'ed him to death."³⁵

There was not as much hoopla over the premiere of *Frankie* at the York Theatre as had been for *Tropicana* at Musical Theatre Works. It was also more a bare-bones production with a smaller cast (total of ten players) and less money for scenery and costumes. But once again the reason for the production was to interest producers. If Abbott felt it was degrading that he had to "audition" his shows in an effort to get produced, he never said so. He approached *Frankie* the same way he did on an expensive Broadway venture, tinkering on it up until opening night. The York production ran twenty performances in May of 1989. Only a few critics covered the event and their reactions were far from favorable. Mel Gussow in the *Times* wrote, "Abbott & Co. misguidedly approached *Frankenstein* as a love story with a happy ending. The result is as simple-minded as if told from the monster's point of view." Much of the criticism was aimed at Abbott. Gussow thought,

> In his many years in the theater as director and author, Mr. Abbott has of course provided us with countless evenings of entertainment. But his book for *Frankie* lacks any sense of Gothic surprise, and the staging (by Mr. Abbott and Donald Saddler) is sedentary, except for those occasional moments when the monster lumbers from side to side.

Gussow attacked the musical again when he summarized the Off-Off Broadway season in *The Best Plays of 1989–1990*, "The York [Theatre], which in the past has offered fine revivals of Stephen Sondheim musicals, scraped musical (and OOB) bottom with *Frankie*, a woeful modernization of *Frankenstein*, conceived by the indomitable George Abbott."³⁶ As usual, Abbott was nonplussed. He was already thinking about a new project. Turrin, on the other hand, was discouraged by Gussow's review until Prince told him, "Don't pay any attention to the critics because what ever you're doing you're doing right. Just keep doing it."³⁷ It is interesting that even in a totally negative review, Gussow still had to admit that Abbott was "indomitable." That is the key word. Abbott had always been around and it was assumed he would come back for another drubbing. But it was not to be. *Frankie* was the end of the line, at least as far as new shows went. In the final chapter, we look at the Abbott-directed revivals between 1969 and 1994. Like his entire career, they range from the subordinate to the sublime.

14 LOOKING BACK WITH DUBIOUS SUCCESS

(1969–1994)

Three Men on a Horse (revival) • *The Pajama Game* (revival) • *On Your Toes* (revival) • *Broadway* (revival) • *Damn Yankees* (revival)

George Abbott may have been opposed to talking about his past productions, preferred to move ahead rather than look back, but he was not hesitant in directing revivals of his distant hits. This did not come from a sense of nostalgia but rather his insistence in getting things right. He was rarely satisfied with a show on opening night and sometimes called the cast in during the run to do some further tinkering. Abbott would have liked to direct revivals of some of his unsuccessful productions, proving that he could make it work a second time around. But Broadway was only interested in reviving hit musicals from the past, playing on the public's memory to build excitement over a new production (usually with a different star or two). While few revivals manage to equal the originals, there is something to be said for returning to theatre classics. Over the decades, Abbott directed several revivals of his successful plays and musicals. Let us consider five that he did in the later part of his career.

The 1937 comedy *Three Men on a Horse* by Abbott and John Cecil Holm had been given a revival in 1942 that was directed by Holm. It boasted the original leading player, William Lynn, as the mousey greeting card poet Erwin Trowbridge, but it was Sam Levene as the fast-talking gambler Patsy who gave the farce its sparkle back in 1937. Comic Sid Stone was only an adequate Patsy in the revival and, consequently, the production suffered, closing within a month. When Abbott was asked to direct the 1969 Broadway revival of *Three Men on a Horse*, he solved the Patsy problem by getting Levene to reprise his performance from thirty-two years earlier. Since the character could be most any age and Levene was as vibrant as ever, it worked beautifully. Levene was supported by an outstanding cast which included

Jack Gilford as Erwin, Rosemary Prinz as his wife Audrey, Hal Linden and Al Nesor as the gamblers Charlie and Frankie, Paul Ford as the crusty Mr. Carver, and Dorothy Loudon as Patsy's brassy gal Mabel. Abbott kept the play in its original 1930s setting and, as in 1937, the scenery moved swiftly from one location to another, keeping the farce tempo throughout. For the most part, the reviews were highly appreciative for the old play, the cast, and for Abbott. Barnes in the *Times* objected to the old comedy being billed as a "classic," but he praised "the admirable all-star cast who play together with the skill of accomplished farceurs," the performances that "range happily from wild idiosyncrasy to gentle camp," and for Abbott who "keeps everything superbly trim and shipshape." The revival ran 100 performances.

Abbott worked again with Hal Linden four years later with his 1973 Broadway revival of ***The Pajama Game*** (1954). Co-composer/lyricist Richard Adler co-produced the revival with Bert Wood for only $300,000, a frugal budget at the time. (That season's *A Little Night Music* cost $650,000.) Consequently more than one critic pointed out the bargain-basement look of the scenery and costumes. But what really mattered—the cast, direction, and choreography—was right in place and the revival was first-class entertainment. It is not clear whose idea it was to have an interracial cast and thereby add a new layer to the story. Most likely it was Abbott who was always looking for ways to "improve" even a classic. Linden played the new factory manager Sid and the popular African American singer Barbara McNair was his lover/nemesis. The legendary Cab Calloway was the comic Hines, adding a star quality to the event even though he was not an actor. With the characters now representing different races, Abbott and Adler rewrote some of the book to take advantage of the new sensibility, still keeping within the musical comedy mode.

Babe   It wouldn't work ... there's a little thing called social prejudice.

Sid   You mean you won't go out with us Polacks?[1]

Also, Adler added a new song, the ballad "Watch Your Heart," which was a revised version of a song he wrote for *Kwamina* (1961). Bob Fosse's original choreography was recreated by Zoya Leporska and "Steam Heat" again brought down the house. The new *The Pajama Game* met with mostly exemplary reviews. Some critics thought the black–white casting was a gimmick, others felt it added to the musical's depth. Linden, who had found fame in *The Rothschilds* (1970), was praised as an affable Sid. Most reviewers wrote that McNair was a beautiful and stylish singer but lacked the acting ability to make Babe the spunky heroine who opposes management. Sharron Miller's Gladys, on the other hand, was roundly applauded for her vivaciousness. Calloway was a natural as Hines but he sometimes broke what character he had to sing a few lines of his signature song "Minnie the Moocher." Clive Barnes in the *New York Times* thought, "The book, once so modern ... has passed, perhaps not happily, into history and its social conscience now seem *jejune.*" Yet he commended much of the production, adding, "Mr. Abbott has staged the show as bright as an old preserved penny." But Richard Watts, Jr., in the *New York Post* thought *The Pajama Game* "seems better; in fact brilliant" and Martin Gottfried in *Women's Wear Daily* agreed, writing "Though twenty years older, it is fresher and less old-fashioned." These were money reviews. But the economics of Broadway in the 1970s were challenging and, with a run of only sixty-five performances, *The Pajama Game* lost a bundle.

An even riskier venture was the 1983 revival of the even older musical, **On Your Toes** (1936), but this time fortune smiled and it was a surprise hit. ANTA and the Kennedy Center were among the slew of producers who wanted to present a classic American musical at the Kennedy Center then, hopefully, on Broadway. They asked Abbott to direct a revival of his 1940 success *Pal Joey* but he thought that uncompromisingly problematic show was not likely to please modern audiences. He recommended the older and lightweight *On Your Toes* and the producers agreed. Abbott asked Broadway veteran Donald Saddler to recreate George Balanchine's original choreography for the new production. Peter Martins from the New York City Ballet was hired to do the Balanchine ballets "Princess Zenobia" and "Slaughter on Tenth Avenue." (The later ballet was still in the repertory of the ABT.) Also, eighty-eight-year-old Hans Spialek was brought on board to recreate his original 1936 orchestrations and vocal arrangements. Abbott had directed the unsuccessful 1954 revival of *On Your Toes* in which he made some changes in the libretto. For example, he felt the opening scene, showing the young Junior Dolan tap dancing in the family vaudeville act, dated the script and was not accessible to 1950s audiences. For the 1983 revival, he rethought his decision and realized that opening number "Two a Day for Keith" did much to establish the character of Junior. So the number was put back in and it ended up starting the musical off with a boffo beginning. Other minor changes were made but the new production emphasized the old-fashioned charm of the 1936 original. In addition to the wonderful Balanchine/Saddler dances and ballets, Abbott insisted on old-time scenery and accurate period costumes from designer Zack Brown. The use of painted drops and "in-one" scenes in front of them was rarely used on Broadway by the 1980s so the look of *On Your Toes* was both quaint and refreshing. The original production had made a star out of Ray Bolger but Abbott did not want a "name" to play Junior. Yet finding a performer who could do both tap and ballet and have a comic-romantic charm was a challenge. Abbott had seemingly endless auditions and call-backs before deciding on Lara Teeter, a musical comedy hoofer whose only Broadway credits were in two major flops: *Happy New Year* (1982) and *Seven Brides for Seven Brothers* (1982). To play the prima ballerina Vera Baranova, Abbott cast the world-acclaimed ballet dancer Natalia Makarova who had never been in a Broadway show. These were daring casting choices, to say the least. Rounding out the cast were the veterans George S. Irving as the Russian impresario Sergei Alexandrovitch and Dina Merrill as the society patron Peggy Porterfield; and for

Junior's love interest Frankie, the young but established Christine Andreas, who had just finished playing Eliza Doolittle in the Broadway revival of *My Fair Lady*.

Because of the great amount of dancing, *On Your Toes* had a rigorous rehearsal schedule. Teeter, who did not have much of a background in ballet, was petrified to be dancing opposite a famous prima ballerina. But he soon found out that Makarova was just as frightened appearing in a Broadway musical comedy and the two relaxed and worked well together. Abbott, who was ninety-six at the time, showed boundless energy as he staged the large and complicated production. Seventy-nine-year-old Balanchine attended some of the rehearsals and the company felt connected to the great ballet master; when he died a month after the opening, a great loss was felt by Abbott and the cast. Teeter recalled that Abbott "was all business" during rehearsal. There was "no small talk" and his directions were precise and to the point. During a dress rehearsal at the Kennedy Center, a lone voice was heard in the dark that said "Take that wig off"; there was no question of who it was.[2] Abbott continued to tinker with the production through the engagement in Washington and during the pre-Broadway run in Seattle. Some six months after *On Your Toes* opened on Broadway, Abbott returned to check on the show and give notes to the cast. Teeter had improvised a few minor changes during the past weeks. Abbott's note to him was, "You were awful."[3]

The revival of *On Your Toes* finally opened on Broadway in March of 1983 and was greeted with mostly rave reviews. "Mostly" is the operative word here. While critics were calling the revival "a stunning new production . . . a heavenly gift" (*New York Daily News*), "a cause for rejoicing!" (*Women's Wear Daily*), "a sparkling new revival" (*New York Post*), and "thrilling and invigorating and terrific" (WCBS Radio), there was one dismissive note. It came from Frank Rich in the *Times* who not only disparaged *On Your Toes* but went out of his way to be vicious, attacking "the dreary book . . . with dull subplots and hoary gags," as well as the production ("its few assets as entertainment are scattered like sweet and frail petals on a stagnant pool"), and most of the cast ("Lara Teeter, a standard Broadway chorus dancer with little discernible personality"). Rich was less severe regarding Abbott, stating the staging "is the patented article—straightforward, uncampy, all-American in its four square ingeniousness." It seemed like the very existence of an old-fashioned musical like *On Your Toes* was anathema to Rich. One such rejection in a newspaper would not have mattered in the days of the original *On Your, Toes* but since the 1960s the *New York Times* had a monopoly on critical clout and Rich was in the position to close a show with a simple thumbs down. The future of the production was definitely in jeopardy. There was considerable backlash in the theatre community, once again protesting the power of the *Times* and the often-cruel nature of Rich's reviews. Support for the revival appeared in print and on radio and the cast members joined the fight by sporting "Get Rich Quick" buttons. Such efforts, and very strong word of mouth, helped *On Your Toes* find an audience and run 505 performances. At season's end, the show won the Tony Award for Best

Musical Revival and Makarova took home a statuette for Best Actress in a Musical. Teeter, Andreas, and Saddler received Tony nominations, rather good in a season in which *Cats* swept most of the awards. Although the Broadway run did not show a profit, the revival was very popular in London and paid off its investment.

Some biographical interruptions: In December of 1982, Abbott was given the Lifetime Achievement Award by the Kennedy Center. Although he received many honors during his lifetime, including seven Tony Awards, this one was significant in that it was not a theatre award. The Kennedy Center honors covered all of the arts so Abbott was being recognized by mainstream America. A single man since 1951, Abbott married for the third time in November of 1983. Joy Moana Valderrama had been his secretary for several years but after the success of *On Your Toes* he proposed marriage. Legend has it that Abbott asked Joy to meet him for dinner at a particular restaurant at a particular time. When she arrived exactly at the appointed time, he decided to propose. She remained his wife, secretary, caregiver, and eventually his nurse until Abbott's death in 1995. In 1985, the Stage Directors and Choreographers Foundation established the Mr. Abbott Award. The annual honor named for Abbott is given by a committee of peers to a Broadway director or choreographer for lifetime achievement. The first recipient was Hal Prince, an appropriate choice given his working relationship with Abbott over the years. Subsequent directors and choreographers to receive the Mr. Abbott Award include established artists, such as Agnes de Mille, Mike Nichols, Bob Fosse, and Lloyd Richards, as well as later generations of talents, as with Susan Stroman, George C. Wolfe, Joe Mantello, and Julie Taymor.

Abbott made many tactical mistakes in his long career but usually he was the only one harmed. Not so with a project which he pretty much sabotaged. It involves the 1987 revival of his early hit *Broadway*, the 1926 melodrama he co-wrote with Philip Dunning. But before looking at that revival it is necessary to go back a year or two. For many years, Abbott had toyed with the idea of a musical version of *Broadway*. He had even approached Leonard Bernstein with the idea. It was an excellent idea. The backstager was practically a musical already and the slangy Twenties talk and iconic characters were ripe for musicalization. Abbott got Hal Prince interested in the project which was not to be another Off-Off Broadway workshop. In fact, the plan was for Prince and Abbott to co-direct the show on Broadway. Abbott had liked the songs Robert Lindsey-Nassif had written for *Tropicana* and asked if he would write the score for the musical of *Broadway*. Lindsey-Nassif readily agreed, contracts were signed, and Lindsey-Nassif worked on the score for two years while Abbott tackled the libretto. It was the first time in Abbott's long career that he adapted one of his own plays for the musical stage. Yet the transition from play to musical came easily. Prince got producer Roger Peters interested in *Broadway* and a reading was planned once the first act was finished.

The year 1987 marked Abbott's 100th birthday and some theatres planned productions of Abbott plays and musicals as part of their season. When the Great

Lakes Theatre Festival was planning a celebration, Prince suggested they have Abbott go there and direct his play *Broadway*. The plan was for Prince and Lindsey-Nassif to see the non-musical work in Ohio in order to help create the musical version. The Great Lakes people agreed and that is what happened: *Broadway* was produced in Cleveland, Abbott directed, and Prince and Lindsey-Nassif attended the revival. Back in New York, just as rehearsals were to begin for the reading, *The New York Times* announced that the Great Lakes production of *Broadway* was heading to Broadway where it would play at the Royale Theatre in celebration of Abbott's birthday. "I was shellshocked," Lindsey-Nassif recalled in an interview for this book. "Abbott had not informed me, knowing full well it was a clear breach of our contract." Whenever a play is optioned for an adaption into a musical, a "freeze clause" is put in the contract stating that no production of the play can be presented in the vicinity of New York City. "I called Abbott in shock. I was furious, heartsick, and hardly able to speak," Lindsey-Nassif continued. "He said, essentially, he was an old man and that his attorney told him no one should stop him from taking this opportunity. Abbott knew full well I couldn't afford to sue him."[4] So while rehearsals began in the Minskoff rehearsal studio, the Great Lakes production was being loaded into the Royale Theatre across the street. The reading of the first act script and songs for *Broadway* the musical went very well. "Hal raved, saying there were two hit songs in the first act alone," Lindsey-Nassif said. "We would definitely go forward with the project and he urged me to finish the musical."[5]

Whether the revival of *Broadway* was a success or not, it would affect the prospects for the musical. If the play was a hit, there might be interest in a musical version down the road but not immediately. If the revival flopped, it would be difficult to get producers/investors interested in a musical version. As it happened, *Broadway* opened in June of 1987 to unanimous pans. Mimi Kramer in *The New Yorker* was one of the critics who tried to analyze the misbegotten production. "The mistake that this production made was of not trusting the audience. Like so many New York revivals, it assumed a public too stupid to understand or appreciate the material. *Broadway* is a period piece; it ought to have been played as a period piece, not as a sort of pastiche of dramatic clichés. But everything in this production of the play ... conspired to make *Broadway* look like a great big joke on itself." A few critics managed to compliment Lonny Price who played the leading role of hoofer Roy; Price was the only cast member not in the Great Lakes production. As for Abbott, the critics were careful and even polite. But it was clear they could find nothing good to say about his direction. What had been planned as a joyous birthday celebration quickly turned sour and the *Broadway* revival folded after four performances.

Prince assured Lindsey-Nassif that the musical project was still on and the songwriter spent another year finishing the score. But by then any interest in a musical version had evaporated. Both Prince and Abbott pulled out and when time ran out on the underlying rights, Abbott refused to renew them. After two years, the songwriter was left high and dry. "You cannot imagine what this did to me,"

Lindsey-Nassif stated. "Abbott destroyed me ... My family wasn't rich. I couldn't afford staying in New York very long. Abbott was a millionaire. A young artist has only so much time and money to spend pursuing [his] dreams. He robbed me of those years."[6] Abbott also robbed himself of one last chance for a new musical hit. Prince was right about the *Broadway* score; it was exceptional. The title song was a catchy, breezy Charleston number with sly lyrics. "Partners" was a slangy love duet that didn't take itself too seriously. The hero got the wordy "I am" song "Personal TNT" and the villain sang about "Everyone's Addicted to More." More serious was the heroine's song of yearning, "Castles in the Air," with a lyric that was much smarter than the clichéd title. Perhaps capturing the spirit of the show best was a risible number "What If I Told You" in which the character "Lil" in drag tries to tell his dense sweetheart Porky that he's a guy. This was all very promising material. There is no such thing as a sure thing in show business but Abbott destroyed what might be considered by some to be a sure thing.

Abbott's last Broadway revival, *Damn Yankees* in 1994, allowed him to go out on a high note, though his involvement in the production was minimal. The Old Globe Theatre in San Diego decided to do a revival of the 39-year-old musical with an eye on moving it to Broadway. Interested producers provided funds to the Old Globe, allowing the non-profit theatre to spend $1.2 million on the production. Jack O'Brien, who was artistic director at the Old Globe, agreed to direct the revival, though he thought the script might need to be revamped in spots. Over the period of a few months, he met with Abbott and discussed possible changes. Years later, O'Brien wrote in his memoir, "He was 105 years old when we met, and 107 when he finally died, vibrant, insistent, wise, and irascible to the bitter end."[7] The 1955 libretto was carefully pruned and clarified, although how much was Abbott's doing is hard to say. But he definitely approved of all the alterations. Using a "reverent backward glance," O'Brien kept the story in the 1950s but softened some things that wouldn't sit well with a contemporary audience. Joe Boyd refers to his wife Meg in dialogue and song as an "old girl" although she is probably in her forties. So O'Brien had Meg several times refer to Joe as "old boy," making it sound like the couple's pet names. Meg's reaction to Joe's disappearance has always struck some as too casual; the new script added lines in which she expresses her concerns, and even her anger, to young Joe. Some of the short crossover scenes, written to cover scenery changes, were cut because the sets by Douglas W. Schmidt moved more swiftly. The second act, always problematic in logic, was redone with emphasis on Applegate using his powers to jinx Joe's batting and trying to let the Yankees win. Lola, instead of turning into an old hag, distracts Applegate from carrying out his plan by getting him to sing the duet "Two Lost Souls." Just as important as what was cut was what was added. The show started out with a stadium organ playing "The Star-Spangled Banner" and the overture was punctuated with the sounds of a bat hitting a baseball. (The new orchestrations were by Douglas Besterman.) To show how incompetent the Washington Senators were, a quick series of blackout sketches used visual gags that landed nicely. The song "Shoeless Joe" was reprised for a series of TV commercials showing the rising popularity of Joe Hardy with product tie-ins. The new script was also filled with 1950s reference to set the period, including jokes about J. Edgar Hoover, Arthur Murray, Joe McCarthy, Eleanor Roosevelt, and Milton Berle ("some guy on television in a dress"). All these were significant additions and one questions if any were written by Abbott. The program credit read: "Book revisions by Jack O'Brien."

The Old Globe production ran in the fall of 1993 then headed to Broadway for a March 1994 opening. The cast was mostly the same, although Jere Shea as young Joe was replaced by newcomer Jarrod Emick who made a sensational debut, eventually winning a Tony Award for his performance. Victor Garber was a droll, dapper Applegate, and Bebe Neuwirth played Lola with wisecracking glee as she got to show off her singing and dancing talents. Vicki Lewis was a firecracker as the reporter Gloria. In addition to the changes made to the script, some songs were reassigned. To beef up Garber's role, "Two Lost Souls" was taken from Young Joe and given to Applegate to sing with Lola, which made no sense. Instead of the number being about Joe and Lola under the thumb of Applegate, it was just a charming duet about nothing. A music change that did work beautifully was bringing Old Joe (Dennis Kelly) on stage when Young Joe sings "Near to You" to Meg (Linda Stephens), turning the ballad from a duet to a trio, the two Joes assuring her that her husband is not gone for good. Since Old Joe was originally only seen in the first and last scenes of the musical, his appearance in the middle of the second act strengthened his character and allowed the audience to understand why Meg missed him so much.

The New York reviews were mostly raves, the critics approving of the alterations even as they cheered the old musical. Rob Marshall's choreography was so admired that comparisons with Bob Fosse's original (some of which was preserved in the 1958 film version) was not an issue. Just about all the reviews mentioned Abbott, though it was difficult to pinpoint just what aspects of the revival he was responsible for besides the script. Don Braunagel in *Variety* wrote, "This is one terrific production, a theatrical grand slam. Among the audience members it delighted were 106-year-old George Abbott, the original director and co-librettist, and Richard Adler, co-composer/lyricist of the marvelous score." Even the difficult-to-please John Simon in *New York Magazine* lauded the revival as "a remarkable case of modernization without anachronism." On January 1, 1995, the production went on hiatus to prepare to reopen in February with Jerry Lewis, in his Broadway debut, playing Applegate. *Damn Yankees* reopened on February 28 and played another 169 performances, for a total of 533 performances. Lewis took the musical on tour then to London.

George Abbott died of a stroke on January 31 in Miami. As was often the case over the previous eight decades, on that day, Abbott's name was on a bill outside a Broadway theatre.

EPILOGUE

No Exit Music, Please

It is either 1991 or 1992 and George Abbott, aged 104 or 105, is on a golf course in Florida. Two other players and his wife, Joy, who keeps careful watch over her husband, are with him. After a few holes, Abbott passes out. One of the golfers runs to call an ambulance and Joy tries to cradle Abbott's head in her lap. He is semiconscious.

> **Joy** Lay your head on my lap, George! Lay your head here!
>
> **George** (*guttural noises*)   Grrrrrrrr.
>
> **Joy** George! Lay your head here!
>
> **George** Grrrrrrr.
>
> **Joy** Can you hear me, George? Lay your head on my lap here!
>
> **George** (*opens his eyes*)   It's lie. Not lay.[1]

There are a lot of apocryphal stories about Abbott. This one happens to be true. But it doesn't matter. Like a Sam Goldwyn or a Groucho Marx, Abbott is credited with saying things he never said. I suppose this is what makes a person a legend. He had a reputation for being a certain way or doing certain things. For example, he was so well known as a play doctor that it was assumed he could fix anything and that he actually did. But even Abbott knew the truth and could joke about it. When *West Side Story* was trying out in Washington, DC, Hal Prince and Jerome Robbins asked Abbott to take the train down from New York and see a performance and give his opinion. Abbott took a train early enough to be treated to a fine dinner at a restaurant, watched the show in silence, then left the theatre without saying a word. Prince and Robbins followed him to the taxi cab waiting for him in front of the theatre. Once inside, Abbott rolled down the window and said to them, "Another show fixed!" and then the taxi drove off.[2]

Is this what happens to legends? They become so famous for doing something that they no longer need to do it anymore? Not in Abbott's case. He needed to work. He couldn't turn down offers no matter how unpromising. When I spoke with some of the people who worked with Abbott in his last decades, they immediately recognized the director I described in rehearsal in the Prologue of this book. Nothing had changed over the decades. Perhaps the Abbott Touch was something that was set in stone. We have seen how Abbott often found himself collaborating and/or directing younger generations of artists. They saw Abbott as the grand old man of the theatre, a shining example of the past. By the 1960s he was a legend, a figure perhaps more respected than actually revered. Writing his autobiography in 1963, Abbott was riding on some recent hits (*A Funny Thing Happened on the Way to the Forum* and *Never Too Late*) and looked back over the decades with satisfaction. The years of continual disappointment and back-to-back flops lay before him. He would keep working in the theatre just to keep working. He may have suspected that his best years were far behind him but he didn't let that stop him. He still wanted to fix things, make them better. What does a perfectionist do when everything he does fails? In the case of Abbott, you move on to the next thing.

William Goldman, writing about Abbott in 1969 in *The Season*, stated: "Whatever it is that he is, he is the last of it. In his own way, he is the ultimate superlative. He has probably brought in more blockbusters than anyone else in the century."[3] Which raises questions about the numbers. It is not possible, for example, to say exactly how many New York theatre productions Abbott worked on. For some of his play-doctor assignments, he contributed very little, others a lot. So it is debatable if some of his uncredited jobs should be counted. There were also some regional theatre directing jobs and, in the early days, some tours that have been mistakenly added to his Broadway credits. The best total number of New York productions I can come up with is 117. Not that Abbott kept track. When once asked if it was true that he was working on his 103rd Broadway show, Abbott said it didn't make any difference; all that counted was if it was a hit or not. So that is the more interesting number to determine. How many hits did Abbott have and how does that number compare to the number of his shows that did not make money? This is also tricky to determine because a play that ran 75 performances in the 1920s paid back its investors. The same number of performances in the 1970s indicated a major financial failure. But some effort must be made to figure out what Abbott's balance sheet is. Looking closely at those 117 productions, and examining what jobs he held for those same shows, it appears that it's a draw. Of the ninety-four productions he directed, forty-nine made money and forty-five didn't pay. Of the thirty-seven shows he produced or co-produced, eighteen paid back the investors while nineteen didn't. As an actor, Abbott fared better. He appeared in eleven plays and eight of them made money. What Goldman says about "blockbusters" is worth examining. Before World War Two, a play that ran 100 performances was called a hit and anything running over 300 was a blockbuster.

During that period Abbott had a dozen blockbusters. After the war, shows that reached 300 were considered hits and to be a blockbuster you had to run over 1,000 performances. During the post-war years, Abbott had fourteen hits and three blockbusters. A show that ran a week (eight performances) or less was considered a major flop no matter when it opened. Abbott had thirteen such flops during his career. No one went up to bat more often than Abbott and his batting average was .504 or fifty-nine hits out of 117 productions. It puts him in some kind of Hall of Fame.

But too often an evaluation of Abbott focuses on numbers: the longest, the oldest, the most successful, the number of performances, and so on. One must get away from the statistics so we can finally return to the man himself. Looking back years after the musical failure *Music Is*, Richard Adler expressed something in his autobiography that hasn't been thoroughly examined in these pages yet: the affection many (certainly not all) had for Abbott. While everyone who worked with him agreed that Abbott had a chilly and stoic personality, he often aroused great emotion in others. This is difficult to explain but it is definitely there. To some, such as Hal Prince and Robert Griffith, Abbott was a father figure. With that comes a whole set of conflicting feeling. To others, such as Carol Burnett and Liza Minnelli, he was a grandfather figure, helping scared kids get through an ordeal by his sense of calm and protection. He was indeed an authority figure to just about everyone he worked with. In a business filled with insecure, egotistical, nervous, desperate, fragile, and downright crazy individuals, Abbott was a rock. It is interesting to consider the ways that a rock can evoke affection but Abbott did. Returning to Adler, he wrote,

> The only compensation I received out of the experience of *Music Is* was working again with the great George Abbott, watching this tireless man perform his theatre magic ... the aura of George Abbott will always remain special and beautiful to me, and the time I spent on this and other productions with him will be times I will forever cherish. They form a bouquet that I've saved, pressing it carefully between the pages of my life.[4]

John Kander did only one musical with Abbott, *Flora, the Red Menace*. But, in his memoir written with Fred Ebb, Kander recalled, "Mr. Abbott was a terrific man, and I learned more about working in the theatre from him than any other single source." Kander explained that

> Mr. Abbott had a ritual whenever one of his shows opened. If the show was a hit, he would go to the party, drink a glass of wine, dance with his favorite chorus girl, and say, 'Well, it worked out this time.' If the show was a flop, he would have his glass of wine, dance with his favorite chorus girl, and say, 'Well, this time it didn't work out.' That was it. The ritual never changed. It's helped me a lot during

flops to know they are part of what we do. Don't get too deceived by success, but don't get too deceived by a flop either.⁵

Is that what is meant by the "Abbott Touch"? Stoic practicality? Always moving forward? Just do the work as best you can and harbor no regrets? After so many productions and years of collaborating with hundreds of people, Abbott's Touch is still elusive. The term was certainly not coined by Abbott himself. It was perhaps first used in one of the many theatre reviews over the decades. But whoever first referred to the director's productions as having the Abbott Touch, the phrase stuck and by the end of the 1930s it was used so often that Abbott himself found it vague and even annoying. Writing in 1963 in his autobiography, he addresses the well-worn moniker.

> 'Exactly what is the Abbott touch?' an interviewer asked me the other day. 'I make them say their final syllables,' I answered. A joke, but with much sense to it. One of the major faults of too many productions is that the actors have sloppy diction. It requires great persistence to get a play clearly spoken, and the actor who swallows his words is cheating.⁶

This observation was made before they started using body microphones on actors in musicals and even plays. Would Abbott think that today's over-amplified shows are any improvement? And there must be more to the Abbott Touch than diction. "If I were to give a serious answer to the question about my method," Abbott explained, "I would say that the quality which I impart to a show that may make it seem different is taste. By taste, I mean artistic judgement—the decision as to just how much to do or not do, at what point to leave one scene and get into another."⁷ In response to the observation that his plays are fast-paced, Abbott wrote, "The one thing a play should not have is just simple uncontrolled speed. The director who thinks that pace is just hurry makes a tragic mistake and produces a noisy, violent hodgepodge devoid of any illusion."⁸ Good pacing in a play or musical *is* an illusion, as we have seen with Abbott's staging of farce and his way of keeping multi-set musicals moving forward. But, once again, one asks if the Abbott Touch was more than tempo. Ethan Mordden, in his book about 1940s musicals *Beautiful Mornin'*, doesn't think there is much to Abbott beyond pace. "As producer and director, Abbott kept [his musicals] taut and bouncy. He didn't need strong story lines or character development to make a hit show. What Abbott knew was editing wordy scripts, pointing a scene, a joke, an exit, and getting false but pleasantly functional performances from his actors."⁹ Yet often the story lines *were* strong and the performances *were* often much more refined than "false" or "functional." Certainly this was true in many of the plays and even in a number of musicals. Abbott was interested in truth in the characters and the logic in the plotting. He just didn't like to talk about it. Samuel L. Leiter, in his book on "great" directors, explains how this was done. "Despite his distaste for psychological exploration of characters and situations, Abbott's directions were always rooted in motivation. Everything had a reason, nothing was done purely for effect. He listened carefully, constantly seeking justified, natural, and unforced readings."[10] Hal Prince, who worked with Abbott on more projects than perhaps anyone else, put it more bluntly in his memoir.

> George Abbott has never been a man to set someone dancing without motivation. In this respect, the 'Abbott Touch' has been consistently misunderstood. Dancing characters dance, doors are slammed *only* when characters out of emotion would slam them, and there is no such thing as a funny reading of a line.[11]

Misunderstood or oversimplified, the Abbott Touch was there. It's gone now because such an elusive thing is not very evident in his writing for the theatre. It was in Abbott's direction, in the way he approached a production, the way he worked with people, and even in the way he made an audience feel. I return to Prince to have the last word: "Abbott's work, even when it fails, *never* gives you a feeling of uneasiness. It has foundation. You never sit in a theatre and think, Oh God, what's going to happen? You know people are going to make entrances and exits like professionals. You are in good hands."[12]

APPENDICES

George Abbott's New York Theatre Productions

The Misleading Lady [25 Nov 1913] play by Charles W. Goddard, Paul Dickey [Fulton Thea; 183p] Cast included: Lewis Stone, Inez Buck, Frank Sylvester, Alice Wilson, Gladys Wilson, Albert Sackett, John Cumberland, Jane Quinn, William H. Sams, Robert Cain, Abbott. Produced by William H. Harris. Directed by Holbrook Blinn.

Lightnin' [26 Aug 1918] comedy by Winchell Smith and Frank Bacon [Gaiety Thea; 1,291p] Cast included: Frank Bacon, Ralph Morgan, Beatrice Nichols, Jesse Pringle, Paul Stantton, Harry Davenport, Jane Oaker, Sam Colt, Minnie Palmer, Sidney Coburn, Sue Wilson. Produced by John Golden. Play doctored by Abbott.

Daddies [5 Sept 1918] comedy by John L. Hobble [Belasco Thea; 340p] Cast included: Jeanne Eagels, Bruce McRae, John W. Cope, S. K. Walker, Abbott, Edwards Davis, Edith King, Lorna Volare, George Giddens, Winifred Fraser. Produced and directed by David Belasco.

The Broken Wing [29 Nov 1920] play by Paul Dickey, Charles W. Goddard [48th St Thea; 171p] Cast included: Charles Trowbridge, Inez Plummer, Henry Duggan, Alphonz Ethier, Louis Wolheim, Abbott. Directed by Paul Dickey.

Zander the Great [9 April 1923] comedy by Salisbury Field [Empire Thea; 80p] Cast included: Alice Brady, Edwin Mills, Joseph Allen, Abbott, Jerome Patrick. Produced by Charles Frohman, Inc. Directed by David Burton.

White Desert [18 Oct 1923] play by Maxwell Anderson [Princess Thea; 12p] Cast included: Frank Shannon, Berth Merrill, Abbott. Produced and directed by Brock Pemberton.

Hell-Bent fer Heaven [4 Jan 1924] play by Hatcher Hughes [Klaw Thea; 122p; Pulitzer Prize] Cast included: Augustin Duncan, Abbott, Glenn Anders, Margaret

Borough, John F. Hamilton, Clara Blandick. Produced by Marc Klaw. Directed by Augustin Duncan.

Lazybones [22 Sept 1924] play by Owen Davis [Vanderbilt Thea; 79p] Cast included: Abbott, Martha Bryan-Allen, Amelia Gardner, Beth Merrill, Elizabeth Patterson, Leona Hogarth, Willard Robertson. Produced by Sam H. Harris. Directed by Guthrie McClintic.

Processional [12 Jan 1925] play by John Howard Lawson [Garrick Thea; 96p] Cast included: Abbott, Blanche Friderici, June Walker, Philip Loeb, Ben Gauer, William T. Hays. Produced by the Theatre Guild. Directed by Philip Moeller.

The Fall Guy [10 March 1925] comedy by James Gleason, Abbott [Eltinge Thea; 176p]. Cast included: Ernest Truex, Hartley Power, Henry Mortimer, Beatrice Noyes, Ralph Sipperly, Dorothy Peterson. Produced by the Shuberts. Co-directed by Abbott and Gleason.

A Holy Terror [28 Sept 1925] play by Winchell Smith, Abbott [George M. Cohan Thea; 32p] Cast included: Abbott, Leona Hogarth, Leila Bennett, John F. Morisey, Frank Monroe, Bennet Musson, Elizabeth Allen. Produced by John Golden. Co-directed by Abbott and Smith.

Love 'Em and Leave 'Em [3 Feb 1926] comedy by Abbott, John V. A. Weaver [Sam H. Harris Thea; 152p] Cast included: Florence Johns, Katherine Wilson, Donald Meek, Camilla Crume, Donald MacDonald, Eda Heineman, Thomas Chalmers, Joseph Bell. Produced by Jed Harris. Directed by Abbott.

Broadway [16 Sept 1926] play by Philip Dunning, Abbott [Broadhurst Thea; 603p] Cast included: Lee Tracy, Sylvia Field, Robert Glecker, John Wray, Paul Porcasi, Millard Mitchell, Clare Woodbury, Edith Van Cleve, William Foran, Thomas Jackson. Produced by Jed Harris. Directed by Abbott.

Chicago [30 Dec 1926] comedy by Maurine Watkins [Music Box Thea; 172p] Cast included: Francine Larrimore, Charles Bickford, Edward Ellis, Charles Halton, Eda Heineman, Juliette Crosby, Isabelle Winlocke, Dorothy Stickney, Robert Barrat, Ferike Boros. Produced by Sam H. Harris. Directed by Abbott.

Spread Eagle [4 April 1927] play by George S. Brooks, Walter B. Lister [Martin Beck Thea; 80p] Cast included: Fritz Williams, Felix Kremb, Allen Vincent, Osgood Perkins, Donald Meek, Aline MacMahon, Malcolm Duncan, Fred House, Charles D. Brown. Produced by Jed Harris. Directed by Abbott.

Four Walls [19 Sept 1927] play by Dana Burnet, Abbott [John Golden Thea; 144p] Cast included: Muni Wisenfrend/Paul Muni, Averell Harris, Edward Keane, William Pawley, Clara Langner, Lee Strasberg, Jeanne Greene. Produced by John Golden. Directed by Abbott.

Coquette [8 Nov 1927] play by Abbott, Ann Preston Bridges [Maxine Elliott Thea; 366p] Cast included: Helen Hayes, Charles Waldron, Elliot Cabot, Andrew Lawlor, Jr., Una Merkle, Frederick Burton. Produced by Jed Harris. Directed by Abbott.

Bless You, Sister [26 Dec 1927] play by John Meehan, Robert Riskin [Forrest Thea; 24p] Cast included: Alice Brady, Charles Bickford, Robert Ames, George Alison, Mildred MacLeod, George Lessey, Dorothy Estabrook. Produced by A. E. Riskin and R. R. Riskin. Script doctored and directed by Abbott.

Gentlemen of the Press [27 Aug 1928] play by Ward Morehouse [Henry Miller Thea; 128p] Cast included: John Cromwell, Hugh O'Connell, Granville Bates, Duncan Penwarden, William Pawley, Millard Mitchell, Russel Crouse, Betty Lancaster. Produced by Thomas E. Jackson and H. S. Kraft. Directed by Abbott.

Ringside [29 Aug 1928] play by Edward E. Paramore, Jr., Hyatt Daab, Abbott [Broadhurst Thea; 37p] Cast included: Robert Gleckner, Richard Taber, Suzanne Caubaye, Craig Williams, Joseph Crehan, John Meehan, Donald Heywood, Yvonne Grey, Brian Donlevy, William Franklin. Produced by Gene Buck. Directed by Abbott.

Jarnegan [24 Sept 1928] play by Charles Beahan, Garrett Fort [Longacre Thea; 136p] Cast included Richard Bennett, Joan Bennett, Robert Cain, Margaret Mower, James H. Bell, Wynne Gibson, Henry O'Neill, Mabel Allyn, Ruthelma Stevens. Produced by Charles K. Gordon and Paul Streger. Script doctored and directed by Abbott.

Poppa [24 Dec 1928] comedy by Bella and Samuel Spewack [Biltmore Thea; 96p] Cast included: Jachial Goldsmith, William E. Morris, Harold Waldridge, Anna Apple, Mary Ricard, Wilton C. Herman, Paula Walter, Edward Shaw. Produced by H. S. Kraft. Script doctored and directed by Abbott.

Those We Love [19 Feb 1930] play by Abbott, S. K. Lauren [John Golden Thea; 77p] Cast included: Abbott, Armina Marshall, Edwin Phillips, Helen Flint, Franklyn Fox, Percy Kilbride, Josephine Hull, Charles Waldron. Produced by Philip Dunning. Directed by Abbott.

Louder, Please [12 Nov 1931] comedy by Norman Krasna [Masque Thea; 68p] Cast included: Lee Tracy, Louise Brooks, Robert Gleckner, Millard Mitchell, Percy Kilbride, J. H. Stoddard. Produced by A. L. Jones. Directed by Abbott.

Lilly Turner [19 Sept 1932] play by Philip Dunning, Abbott [Morosco Thea; 24p] Cast included: Dorothy Hall, James Bell, Robert Barrat, John Litel, Percy Kilbride, Joseph Creahan, Granville Bates, Clare Woodbury. Produced and directed by Abbott and Dunning.

The Great Magoo [2 Dec 1932] play by Ben Hecht, Gene Fowler [Selwyn Thea; 11p] Cast included: Paul Kelly, Claire Carlton, Victor Kilian, Dennie Moore,

Charlotte Granville, Millard Mitchell, Jack Hazzard. Produced by Billy Rose. Directed by Abbott.

Twentieth Century [29 Dec 1932] farce by Ben Hecht, Charles MacArthur [Broadhurst Thea; 152p] Cast included: Moffat Johnston, Eugenie Leontovich, Etienne Girardot, Matt Briggs, William Frawley, Roy Roberts, Henry Sherwood. Co-produced by Philip Dunning and Abbott. Directed by Abbott.

Heat Lightning [15 Sept 1933] play by Leon Abrams, Abbott [Booth Thea; 44p] Cast included: Jean Dixon, Emily Lowry, Robert Glecker, Robert Sloane. Co-produced by Philip Dunning and Abbott. Directed by Abbott.

The Drums Begin [24 Nov 1933] play by Howard Irving Young [Shubert Thea; 11p] Cast included: Walter Abel, Judith Anderson, Moffat Johnston, José Ruben, Kent Smith, Lionel Stander, William Foran, Robert Gleckler. Co-produced by Abbott and Philip Dunning. Directed by Abbott.

John Brown [22 Jan 1934] play by Ronald Gow [Ethel Barrymore Thea; 2p] Cast included: Abbott, William Corbett, Alma Kruger, John Emery, Oliver Barbour, Whitney Bourne, Edna Hagan, Iris Whitney, Herbert Yost. Produced and directed by Abbott.

Kill That Story [29 Aug 1934] comedy by Harry Madden, Philip Dunning [Booth Thea; 117p] Cast included: Matt Briggs, James Bell, Emily Lowry, Royal Dana Tracy, William Lynn, Wyrley Birch, William Foran, Gloria Grafton. Co-produced by Abbott and Philip Dunning. Directed by Abbott.

Small Miracle [26 Sept 1934] melodrama by Norman Krasna [John Golden Thea; 117p] Cast included: Ilka Chase, Joseph Spurin-Celleia, Myron McCormick, Owen Martin, Joseph King, Edward Crandall, Fraye Gilbert. Produced by Courtney Burr. Directed by Abbott.

Ladies 'Money [1 Nov 1934] play by Abbott [Ethel Barrymore Thea; 36p] Cast included: Hal K. Dawson, Eric Linden, Robert R. Sloan, Jerome Cowan, Joyce Arling, Lora Rogers, Margaret Mullen, James P. Hoffman, Margaret Callahan. Produced by Courtney Burr. Directed by Abbott.

Page Miss Glory [27 Nov 1934] comedy by Joseph Schrank, Philip Dunning [Mansfield Thea; 63p] Cast included: Charles D. Brown, James Stewart, Dorothy Hall, Bruce MacFarlane, Jane Seymour, Harry Bellaver, Peggy Shannon, Royal Beal. Produced by Laurence Schwab and Philip Dunning. Directed by Abbott.

Three Men on a Horse [30 Jan 1935] farce by John Cecil Holm, Abbott [Playhouse Thea; 835p] Cast included: William Lynn, Sam Levene, Teddy Hart, Millard Mitchell, Shirley Booth, Joyce Arling, Frank Camp, Richard Huey, Edith Van Cleve. Produced by Alex Yokel. Directed by Abbott.

Jumbo [16 Nov 1935] musical comedy by Ben Hecht, Charles MacArthur (bk), Richard Rodgers (mu), Lorenz Hart (lyr) [Hippodrome Thea; 233p] Cast included: Jimmy Durante, Donald Novis, Gloria Grafton, W. J. McCarthy, Arthur Sinclair, Bob Lawrence, George Watts, A. P. Kaye, Poodles Hanneford, Paul Whiteman and his Orchestra. Songs: The Most Beautiful Girl in the World; My Romance; Little Girl Blue; The Circus Is on Parade; Over and Over Again. Produced by Billy Rose. Choreographed by Marjery Fielding. Directed by John Murray Anderson and Abbott.

Boy Meets Girl [27 Nov 1935] farce by Bella and Sam Spewack [Cort Thea; 669p] Cast included: Allyn Joslyn, Jerome Cowan, Charles McClelland, Joyce Arling, James MacColl, Everett H. Sloane, Garson Kanin, Royal Beal, John Clarke. Produced and directed by Abbott.

On Your Toes [11 April 1936] musical comedy by Abbott (bk), Richard Rodgers (bk, mu), Lorenz Hart (bk, lyr) [Imperial Thea; 315p] Cast included: Ray Bolger, Doris Carson, Tamara Geva, Demetrios Vilan, David Morris, Monty Woolley, Luella Gear. Songs: There's a Small Hotel; Glad to Be Unhappy; It's Got to Be Love; On Your Toes; Quiet Night; The Heart Is Quicker Than the Eye; The Three B's; Too Good for the Average Man. Produced by Dwight Deere Wiman. Choreographed by George Balanchine. Directed by Worthington Miner, Abbott.

Sweet River [28 Oct 1936] play by Abbott [51st St Thea; 5p] Cast included: Walter Price, Margaret Mullen, Juan Hernandez, Betty Philson, Inge Hardison, Matt Briggs. Produced and directed by Abbott.

Brother Rat [16 Dec 1936] farce by John Monks, Jr., Fred F. Finklehoffe [Biltmore Thea; 577p] Cast included: Eddie Albert, José Ferrer, Jack Albertson, Kathleen Fitz, Ezra Stone, Carroll Ashburn, Robert Foulk, Mary Mason. Produced and directed by Abbott.

Room Service [19 May 1937] farce by John Murray, Allen Boretz [Cort Thea; 500p] Cast included: Sam Levene, Eddie Albert, Cliff Dunstan, Donald McBride, Betty Field, Philip Loeb, Teddy Hart, Margaret Mullen, Philip Wood. Produced and directed by Abbott.

Angel Island [20 Oct 1937] comedy by Mrs. Bernie Angus [National Thea; 21p] Cast included: Carroll Ashburn, Lea Penman, Eric Wollencott, Arlene Francis, Clyde Fillmore, Doro Merande, Edith Van Cleve, David Hoffman. Produced and directed by Abbott.

Brown Sugar [2 Dec 1937] melodrama by Mrs. Bernie Angus [Biltmore Thea; 4p] Cast included: Juan Hernandez, Christola Williams, Beulah E. Edmonds, Canada Lee, George W. Smith, Richard Huey, Richard McMyers, Ruby Elzy, Butterfly McQueen, Georgette Harvey, T. Burton Smith. Produced and directed by Abbott.

All That Glitters [19 Jan 1938] farce by John Baragwanath, Kenneth Simpson [Biltmore Thea; 69p] Cast included: Arlene Francis, Allyn Joslyn, Helen Gardner, Judson Laire, Royal Beal, Jean Casto, Everett Sloane, Edith Van Cleve, Barry Sullivan. Produced and directed by Abbott.

What a Life [13 April 1938] comedy by Clifford Goldsmith [Biltmore Thea; 538p] Cast included: Ezra Stone, Vaughan Glaser, Lea Penman, James Cormer, Betty Field, Arthur Pierson, Ruth Mattson, Eddie Bracken, William Mendreck, Joyce Arling. Produced and directed by Abbott.

You Never Know [21 Sept 1938] musical comedy by Rowland Leigh (bk), Cole Porter (mu, lyr) [Winter Garden Thea; 78p] Cast included: Clifton Webb, Rex O'Malley, Libby Holman, Lupe Velez, Charles Kemper, Toby Wing, Paul and Grace Hartman, June Preisser. Songs: At Long Last Love; From Alpha to Omega; By Candlelight; What Shall I Do?; You Never Know; What Is That Tune. Produced by the Shubert Brothers. Choreographed by Robert Alton. Directed by Rowland Leigh. Book and direction doctored by Abbott.

The Boys From Syracuse [23 Nov 1938] musical comedy by Abbott (bk), Richard Rodgers (mu), Lorenz Hart (lyr) [Alvin Thea; 235p] Cast included: Eddie Albert, Jimmy Savo, Ronald Graham, Teddy Hart, Muriel Angelus, Wynn Murray, Marcy Westcott, John O'Shaughnessy, Carroll Ashburn, Betty Bruce. Songs: Falling in Love With Love; This Can't Be Love; Dear Old Syracuse; Sing for Your Supper; The Shortest Day of the Year; He and She; What Can You Do With a Man?; You Have Cast Your Shadow on the Sea; Oh, Diogenes. Choreography by George Balanchine. Produced and directed by Abbott.

The Primrose Path [4 Jan 1939] comedy by Robert Buckner, Walter Hart [Biltmore Thea; 166p] Cast included: Florida Friebus, Helen Westley, Betty Garde, Betty Field, Philip Wood, Marilyn Erskine, Philip, Leslie Barrett, Russell Hardie, Clyde Fillmore. Produced and directed by Abbott.

See My Lawyer [27 Sept 1939] farce by Richard Mailbaum, Harry Clork [Biltmore Thea; 224p] Cast included: Milton Berle, Gary Merrill, Millard Mitchell, Eddie Nugent, Teddy Hart, Mary Rolfe, Robin Raymond, Fleming Ward, David Hoffman. Produced by Abbott. Directed by Ezra Hunt.

Too Many Girls [18 Oct 1939] musical comedy by George Marion, Jr. (bk), Richard Rodgers (mu), Lorenz Hart (lyr) [Imperial Thea; 249p] Cast included: Richard Kollmar, Eddie Bracken, Hal LeRoy, Desi Arnaz, Marcy Westcott, Clyde Fillmore, Mary Jane Walsh, Dioso Costello, Leila Ernst. Songs: I Didn't Know What Time It Was; Give It Back to the Indians; She Could Shake Her Maracas; Love Never Went to College; I Like to Recognize the Tune; All Dressed Up (Spic and Spanish). Choreography by Robert Alton. Produced and directed by Abbott.

Ring Two [22 Nov 1939] comedy by Gladys Hurlbut [Henry Miller Thea; 5p] Cast included: June Walker, Paul McGrath, Tom Powers, Betty Field, Edith Van Cleve, Gene Tierney. Produced and directed by Abbott.

The Unconquered [13 Feb 1940] play by Ayn Rand [Biltmore Thea; 6p] Cast included: John Emery, Helen Craig, Dean Jagger, Horace Cooper, Marshall Bradford, Lea Penman. Produced and directed by Abbott.

Goodbye in the Night [18 March 1940] melodrama by Jerome Mayer [Biltmore Tea; 8p] Cast included: James Bell, Owen Martin, Mary Mason, Paul Ballantyne, Jean Adair, Millard Mitchell, Edith Van Cleve, Natalie Schafer, William Swetland. Produced and directed by George Abbott.

Pal Joey [25 Dec 1940] musical play by John O'Hara (bk), Richard Rodgers (mu), Lorenz Hart (lyr) [Ethel Barrymore Thea; 374p] Cast included: Gene Kelly, Vivienne Segal, Leila Ernst, Jean Casto, June Havoc, Jack Durant. Songs: Bewitched; I Could Write a Book; Zip; You Mustn't Kick It Around; Den of Iniquity; Take Him; That Terrific Rainbow; The Flower Garden of My Heart. Choreographed by Robert Alton. Produced and directed by Abbott.

Best Foot Forward [1 Oct 1941] musical comedy by John Cecil Holm (bk), Hugh Martin, Ralph Blane (mu, lyr) [Ethel Barrymore Thea; 326p] Cast included: Gil Stratton, Jr., Rosemary Lane, Maureen Cannon, Nancy Walker, Marty May, Victoria Schools, June Allyson, Tommy Dix, Kenneth Bowers, Jack Jordan, Jr. Songs: Buckle Down, Winsocki; Just a Little Joint with a Juke Box; The Three B's; I Know You By Heart. Choreographed by Gene Kelly. Produced and directed by Abbott.

Jason [21 Jan 1942] play by Samson Raphaelson [Hudson Thea; 125p] Cast included: Alexander Knox, Nicholas Conte, Helen Walker, William Niles, E. G. Marshall, Raymond Greenleaf. Produced by Abbott. Directed by Samson Raphaelson.

Beat the Band [14 Oct 1942] musical comedy by George Marion, Jr. (bk, lyr), Abbott (bk), Johnny Green (mu) [46th St Thea; 68p] Cast included: Jack Whiting, Susan Miller, Jerry Lester, Juanita Juarez, Joan Caulfield, Romo Vincent. Songs: I'm Physical, You're Cultured; Keep it Casual; America Loves a Band; Let's Comb Beaches. Choreographed by David Lichine. Produced and directed by Abbott.

Sweet Charity [28 Dec 1942] comedy by Irving Brecher, Manuel Seff [Mansfield Thea; 8p] Cast included: Enid Markey, Philip Loeb, Viola Roache, Mildred Todd, Jane Seymour, Mary Sargent, Dort Clark. Produced by Alfred Bloomingdale. Directed by Abbott.

Kiss and Tell [17 March 1943] comedy by F. Hugh Herbert [Biltmore Thea; 956p] Cast included: Judith Parrish, Richard Widmark, Joan Caulfield, Robert White,

Jessie Royce Landis, Robert Keith, Lulu Mae Hubbard, Robert Lynn, Francis Bavier. Produced and directed by Abbott.

Get Away Old Man [24 Nov 1943] comedy by William Saroyan [Cort Thea; 13p] Cast included: Ed Begley, Richard Widmark, Glenn Anders, Beatrice Pearson, Joyce Mathews, Hilda Vaughn. Produced and directed by Abbott.

A Highland Fling [28 April 1944] comedy by Margaret Curtis [Plymouth Thea; 28p] Cast included: Ralph Forbes, Margaret Curtis, Karl Swenson, Frances Reid, Patti Brady, John Ireland, Marguerite Clifton. Produced and directed by Abbott.

Snafu [25 Oct 1944] comedy by Louis Solomon, Harold Buchman [Hudson Thea; 158p] Cast included: Billy Redfield, Russell Hardie, Elspeth Eric, Bethel Leslie, Patricia Kirkland, Enid Markey, Dort Clark, Ann Dere. Produced and directed by Abbott.

On the Town [28 Dec 1944] musical comedy by Adolph Green, Betty Comden (bk, lyr), Leonard Bernstein (mu) [Adelphi Thea; 463p] Cast included: Cris Alexander, Adolph Green, John Battles, Nancy Walker, Sono Osato, Betty Comden, Alice Pearce, Susan Steell, Robert Chisholm. Songs: New York, New York; Some Other Time; I Get Carried Away; Lonely Town; Lucky to Be Me; Come Up to My Place; You Got Me; I Can Cook Too. Produced by Oliver Smith and Paul Feigay. Choreography by Jerome Robbins. Directed by Abbott.

Billion Dollar Baby [21 Dec 1945] musical comedy by Betty Comden, Adolph Green (bk, lyr), Morton Gould (mu) [Alvin Thea; 220p] Cast included: Joan McCracken, Danny Daniels, Don DeLeo, David Burns, Robert Chisholm, Mitzi Green, William Tabbert, James Mitchell, Shirley Van, Emily Ross. Songs: Dreams Come True; Broadway Blossom; One Track Mind; There I'd Be. Produced by Paul Feigay and Oliver Smith. Choreography by Jerome Robbins. Directed by Abbott.

The Dancer [5 June 1946] melodrama by Milton Lewis, Julian Funt [Biltmore Thea; 5p] Cast included: Anton Dolin, Colin Keith-Johnston, Helen Flint, Bethel Leslie. Produced by Abbott. Directed by Everett Sloane.

Beggar's Holiday [26 Dec 1946] musical play by John Latouche (bk, lyr), Duke Ellington (mu) [Broadway Thea; 108p] Cast included: Alfred Drake, Jet MacDonald, Zero Mostel, Rollin Smith, Avon Long, Mildred Smith, Dorothy Johnson, Bernice Parks, Marie Bryant. Songs: When I Walk With You; Take Love Easy; I Wanna Be Bad; The Wrong Side of the Railroad Tracks; Maybe I Should Change My Ways. Produced by Perry Watkins and John R. Sheppard, Jr. Choreographed by Valerie Bettis. Directed by Nicholas Ray. Book and direction doctored by Abbott.

It Takes Two [3 Feb 1947] comedy by Virginia Faulkner, Dana Suesse [Biltmore Thea; 8p] Cast included: Martha Scott, Hugh Marlowe, Anthony Ross, Vivian Vance, John Forsythe. Produced by Abbott and Richard Aldrich. Directed by Abbott.

Barefoot Boy with Cheek [3 April 1947] musical comedy by Max Shulman (bk) Sidney Lippman (mu), Sylvia Dee (lyr) [Martin Beck Thea; 108p] Cast included: Nancy Walker, Billy Redfield, Ellen Hanley, Red Buttons, Jack Williams, Nathaniel Frey, Philip Coolidge, Jerry Austen, Shirley Van. Songs: Everything Leads Right Back to Love; I Knew I'd Know; Little Yetta's Gonna Get a Man. Choreographed by Richard Barstow. Produced and directed by Abbott.

High Button Shoes [9 Oct 1947] musical comedy by Stephen Longstreet, Abbott (bk), Jule Styne (mu), Sammy Cahn (lyr) [Century Thea; 727p] Cast included: Phil Silvers, Joey Faye, Jack McCauley, Nanette Fabray, Mark Dawson, Nathaniel Frey, Helen Gallagher, Johnny Stewart, Lois Lee. Songs: Papa, Won't You Dance With Me?; I Still Get Jealous; There's Nothing Like a Model T; On a Sunday By the Sea; Nobody Ever Died for Dear Old Rutgers. Produced by Monte Proser and Joseph Kipness. Choreography by Jerome Robbins. Directed by Abbott.

Look, Ma, I'm Dancin'! [29 Jan 1948] musical comedy by Jerome Lawrence, Robert E. Lee (bk), Hugh Martin (mu, lyr) [Adelphi Thea; 188p] Cast included: Nancy Walker, Alexander March, Harold Lang, Janet Reed, Alice Pearce, Tommy Rall, Katharine Sergava, Don Liberto, Virginia Gorski. Songs: Shauny O'Shay; I'm the First Girl; Gotta Dance; The Two of Us; If You'll Be Mine; I'm Tired of Texas. Choreographed by Jerome Robbins. Produced and directed by Abbott.

Where's Charley? [11 Oct 1948] musical comedy by Abbott (bk), Frank Loesser (mu, lyr) [St. James Thea; 792p] Cast included: Ray Bolger, Allyn Ann McLerie, Doretta Morrow, Byron Palmer, Horace Cooper, Jane Lawrence, Paul England, John Lynda. Songs: Once in Love With Amy; Make a Miracle; The New Ashmolean Marching Society and Students' Conservatory Band; My Darling, My Darling; At the Red Rose Cotillion; Serenade With Asides. Produced by Cy Feuer and Ernest H. Martin. Choreography by George Balanchine. Directed by Abbott.

Mrs. Gibbons' Boys [4 May 1949] comedy by Will Glickman, Joseph Stein [Music Box Thea; 5p] Cast included: Lois Bolton, Ray Walston, Richard Carlyle, Tom Lewis, Royal Dano, Francis Compton, Glenda Ferrell. Produced and directed by Abbott.

Touch and Go [13 Oct 1949] musical revue by Jean and Walter Kerr (skts, lyr), Jay Gorney (mu) [Broadhurst Thea; 176p] Cast included: Peggy Cass, George Hall, Nancy Andrews, Helen Gallagher, Louie Nye, Dick Sykes. Songs I'll Be All Right in a Hundred Years; Funny Little Old World; This Had Better Be Love; Broadway Love Song; Wish Me Luck. Produced by Abbott and George Hall. Choreographed by Helen Tamiris. Directed by Walter Kerr.

Tickets, Please! [27 April 1950] musical revue by Harry Herrmann, Edmund Rice, Jack Roche, Ted Luce (skts), Lyn Duddy, Joan Edwards, Mel Tolkin, Lucille Kallen and Clay Warnick (mu, lyr) [Coronet Thea; 245p] Cast included: Paul and Grace

Hartman, Jack Albertson, Roger Price, Mildred Hughes, Dorothy Jarnac, and Larry Kert. Produced by Arthur Klein. Choreographed by Joan Mann. Directed by Mervyn Nelson. Book and direction doctored by Abbott.

Call Me Madam [12 Oct 1950] musical comedy by Howard Lindsay, Russel Crouse (bk), Irving Berlin (mu, lyr) [Imperial Thea; 644p] Cast included: Ethel Merman, Paul Lukas, Russell Nype, Galina Talva. Songs: You're Just in Love; The Hostess With The Mostes 'on the Ball; Marrying for Love; It's a Lovely Day Today; The Best Thing for You; They Like Ike. Produced by Leland Hayward. Choreographed by Jerome Robbins. Directed by Abbott.

Out of This World [21 Dec 1950] musical comedy by Dwight Taylor, Reginald Lawrence (bk), Cole Porter (mu, lyr) [New Century Thea; 157p] Cast included: Charlotte Greenwood, George Jongeyans, Priscilla Gillette, William Redfield, William Eythe, David Burns. Songs: Use Your Imagination; Nobody's Chasing Me; I Am Loved; I Sleep Easier Now. Produced by Arnold Saint-Subber and Lemuel Ayers. Choreographed by Hanya Holm. Directed by Agnes de Mille and Abbott.

A Tree Grows in Brooklyn [19 April 1951] musical play by Betty Smith, Abbott (bk), Arthur Schwartz (mu), Dorothy Fields (lyr) [Alvin Thea; 270p] Cast included: Shirley Booth, Johnny Johnston, Marcia Van Dyke, Nomi Mitty, Nathaniel Frey, Albert Linville, Lou Willis, Jr. Songs: Make the Man Love Me; I'll Buy You a Star; He Had Refinement; Love Is the Reason; Look Who's Dancing. Choreographed by Herbert Ross. Produced and directed by Abbott.

The Number (30 Oct 1951) melodrama by Arthur Carter [Biltmore Thea; 87p] Cast included: Martha Scott, Mervyn Vye, Dane Clark, Jennie Goldstein, Anatol Winogradoff, Louise Larabee. Produced by Paul Vroom and Irving Cooper. Directed by Abbott.

In Any Language [7 Oct 1952] comedy by Edmund Beloin, Henry Garson [Cort Thea; 45p] Cast included: Uta Hagen, Walter Matthau, Eileen Heckart, Dino Terranova, Nita Naldi. Produced by Jule Styne and George Abbott. Directed by Abbott.

Wonderful Town [25 Feb 1953] musical comedy by Joseph Fields, Jerome Chodorov (bk), Leonard Bernstein (mu), Betty Comden, Adolph Green (lyr) [Winter Garden Thea; 559p; Tony Award] Cast included: Rosalind Russell, Edith Adams, George Gaynes, Cris Alexander, Dort Clark, Henry Lascoe. Songs: Ohio; It's Love; One Hundred Easy Ways; A Quiet Girl; Never Felt This Way Before (A Little Bit in Love); Conga! Produced by Robert Fryer. Choreographed by Donald Saddler. Directed by Abbott.

Me and Juliet [28 May 1953] musical play by Oscar Hammerstein (bk, lyr), Richard Rodgers (mu) [Majestic Thea; 358p] Cast included: Bill Hayes, Isabel Bigley, Mark

Dawson, Ray Walston, Joan McCracken, Arthur Maxwell, George S. Irving. Songs: No Other Love; It's Me; Marriage Type Love; I'm Your Girl; Intermission Talk; The Big Black Giant. Produced by Richard Rodgers and Oscar Hammerstein II. Choreographed by Robert Alton. Directed by Abbott.

The Pajama Game [13 May 1954] musical comedy by Abbott, Richard Bissell (bk), Richard Adler, Jerry Ross (mu, lyr) [St. James Thea; 1,063p; Tony Award] Cast included: John Raitt, Janis Paige, Carol Haney, Eddie Foy, Jr., Reta Shaw, Stanley Prager, Buzz Miller. Songs: Hey There; Hernando's Hideaway; Steam Heat; I'm Not at All in Love; I'll Never Be Jealous Again; Think of the Time I Save; There Once Was a Man. Produced by Frederick Brisson, Robert E. Griffith and Harold S. Prince. Choreography by Bob Fosse. Directed by Abbott and Jerome Robbins.

On Your Toes [11 Oct 1954] revival of the musical comedy by Abbott (bk), Richard Rodgers (bk, mu), Lorenz Hart (bk, lyr) [46th St. Thea; 64p] Cast included: Bobby Van, Vera Zorina, Kay Coulter, Elaine Stritch, Ben Astar. Produced by Richard Rodgers. Choreography by George Balanchine. Directed by Abbott.

Damn Yankees [5 May 1955] musical comedy by Abbott, Douglass Wallop (bk), Richard Adler, Jerry Ross (mu, lyr) [46th St. Thea; 1,019p; Tony Award] Cast included: Gwen Verdon, Ray Walston, Stephen Douglass, Bob Shafer, Shannon Bolin, Russ Brown, Nathaniel Frey, Eddie Phillips, Rae Allen, Jean Stapleton, Albert Linville, Jimmie Komack. Songs: Heart; Whatever Lola Wants; Two Lost Souls; Those Were the Good Old Days; A Little Brains—A Little Talent; Near to You; Who's Got the Pain?; A Man Doesn't Know. Produced by Frederick Brisson, Robert E. Griffith and Harold S. Prince. Choreography by Bob Fosse. Directed by Abbott.

The Skin of Our Teeth [17 Aug 1955] revival of a play by Thornton Wilder [ANTA Thea; 22p] Cast included: Abbott, Helen Hayes, Mary Martin, Florence Reed, Don Murray, Heller Halliday. Produced by Robert Whitehead. Directed by Alan Schneider.

New Girl in Town [14 May 1957] musical play by Abbott (bk), Bob Merrill (mu, lyr) [46th St. Thea; 431p]: Cast included: Gwen Verdon, George Wallace, Cameron Prud'hoome, Thelma Ritter, Lulu Bates, Mara Lynn, Jeff Killion. Songs: It's Good to Be Alive; Flings; Sunshine Girl; There Ain't No Flies on Me; On the Farm. Produced by Frederick Brisson, Robert E. Griffith and Harold S. Prince. Choreography by Bob Fosse. Directed by Abbott.

Drink to Me Only [8 Oct 1958] comedy by Abram S. Ginnes, Ira Wallach [54th St. Thea; 77p] Cast included: Tom Poston, Paul Hartman, Georgeann Johnson, John McGiver, Jack Gilford, Undine Forrest, Sherry Britton, Royal Beal. Produced by George Ross and John Robert Lloyd. Directed by Abbott.

Fiorello! [23 Nov 1959] musical play by Jerome Weidman, Abbott (bk), Jerry Bock (mu), Sheldon Harnick (lyr) [Broadhurst Thea; 795p; Pulitzer Prize, Tony Award]

Cast included: Tom Bosley, Howard Da Silva, Ellen Hanley, Patricia Wilson, Nathaniel Frey, Pat Stanley, Mark Dawson, Eileen Rodgers. Songs: Politics and Poker; When Did I Fall in Love?; Little Tin Box; The Very Next Man; I Love a Cop; Gentleman Jimmy; Til Tomorrow. Produced by Harold Prince and Robert E. Choreographed by Peter Gennaro. Directed by Abbott.

Once Upon a Mattress [25 Nov 1959] musical comedy by Jay Thompson, Dean Fuller (bk), Marshall Barer (bk, lyr), Mary Rodgers (mu) [Alvin Thea; 460p] Cast included: Carol Burnett, Joe Bova, Jane White, Jack Gilford, Harry Snow, Allen Case, Anne Jones, Matt Mattox. Songs: Happily Ever After; In a Little While; Shy; Yesterday I Loved You; Very Soft Shoes; Normandy; Sensitivity. Produced by T. Edward Hambleton, Norris Houghton and William and Jean Eckart. Choreographed by Joe Layton. Directed by Abbott.

Tenderloin [17 Oct 1960] musical play by Abbott, Jerome Weidman (bk), Jerry Bock (mu), Sheldon Harnick (lyr) [46th St. Thea; 216p] Cast included: Maurice Evans, Ron Husmann, Wynne Miller, Ralph Dunn, Eileen Rodgers, Lee Becker, Raymond Bramley, Irene Kane, Rex Everhart. Songs: Artificial Flowers; Little Old New York; Good Clean Fun; The Picture of Happiness; How the Money Changes Hands. Produced by Harold Prince and Robert E. Griffith. Choreographed by Joe Layton. Directed by Abbott.

A Call on Kuprin [25 May 1961] play by Jerome Lawrence, Robert E. Lee [Broadhurst Thea; 12p] Cast included: Jeffrey Lynn, George Voskovec, Eugenie Leontovich, William Swetland, Leon Janney, John Garson, Marie Baratoff, Dabney Coleman, Claude Horton. Produced by Robert E. Griffith and Harold S. Prince. Directed by Abbott.

Take Her, She's Mine [21 Dec 1961] comedy by Phoebe and Henry Ephron [Biltmore Thea; 404p] Cast included: Art Carney, Elizabeth Ashley, Phyllis Thaxter, June Harding. Produced by Harold Prince. Directed by Abbott.

A Funny Thing Happened on the Way to the Forum [8 May 1962] musical comedy by Burt Shevelove, Larry Gelbart (bk), Stephen Sondheim (mu, lyr) [Alvin Thea; 964p; Tony Award] Cast included: Zero Mostel, Brian Davies, Jack Gilford, David Burns, Ruth Kobart, Preshy Marker, Ronald Holgate, John Carradine. Songs: Comedy Tonight; Everybody Ought to Have a Maid; Lovely; Pretty Little Picture; I'm Calm; Impossible. Produced by Harold Prince. Choreographed by Jack Cole and (uncredited) Jerome Robbins. Directed by Abbott.

Never Too Late [27 Nov 1962] comedy by Sumner Arthur Long [Playhouse Thea; 1,007p] Cast included: Paul Ford, Maureen O'Sullivan, Fran Sharon, Orson Bean. Produced by Elliot Martin and Daniel Hollywood. Directed by Abbott.

Fade Out—Fade In [26 May 1964] musical comedy by Betty Comden, Adolph Green (bk, lyr), Jule Styne (mu) [Mark Hellinger Thea; 271p] Cast included: Carol

Burnett, Lou Jacobi, Dick Patterson, Jack Cassidy, Tiger Haynes, Tina Louise, Mitchell Jason. Songs: The Usher From the Mezzanine; You Mustn't Be Discouraged; My Fortune Is My Face; Close Harmony; Call Me Savage. Produced by Lester Osterman, Jr. and Jule Styne. Choreographed by Ernest Flatt. Directed by Abbott.

Flora, the Red Menace [11 May 1965] musical comedy by Abbott, Robert Russell (bk), John Kander (mu), Fred Ebb (lyr) [Alvin Thea; 87p] Cast included: Liza Minnelli, Bob Dishy, Mary Louise Wilson, Cathyrn Damon, James Cresson. Songs: A Quiet Thing; Dear Love; You Are You; Sing Happy; All I Need Is One Good Break. Produced by Harold Prince. Choreographed by Lee Theodore. Directed by Abbott.

Anya [29 Nov 1965] musical play by Abbott, Guy Bolton (bk), Sergei Rachmaninoff (mu), Robert Wright, George Forrest (mu, lyr) [Ziegfeld Thea; 16p] Cast included: Constance Towers, Michael Kermyan, Lillian Gish, Irra Petina, George S. Irving, John Michael King, Karen Shepard. Songs: If This Is Goodbye; Little Hands; A Song From Somewhere. Produced by Fred R. Fehlhaber. Choreographed by Hanya Holm. Directed by Abbott.

Help Stamp Out Marriage! [29 Sept 1966] comedy by Keith Waterhouse, Willis Hall [Booth Thea; 20p] Cast included: Valerie French, Roddy Maude-Roxby, Ann Bell, Francis Matthews. Produced by Theatre Guild Productions, Inc., Peter Bridge and Don Herbert. Directed by Abbott.

Agatha Sue, I Love You [14 Dec 1966] comedy by Abe Einhorn [Henry Miller Thea; 5p] Cast included: Ray Walston, Corbett Monica, Lee Lawson, Betty Garde, Renee Taylor. Produced by Judith Abbott and Edwin Wilson. Directed by Abbott.

How Now, Dow Jones [7 Dec 1967] musical comedy by Max Shulman (bk), Elmer Bernstein (mu), Carolyn Leigh (lyr) [Lunt-Fontanne Thea; 220p] Cast included: Anthony Roberts, Brenda Vaccaro, Hiram Sherman, Malyn Mason, Rex Everhart, Charlotte Jones, Sammy Smith, Barnard Hughes, Jennifer Darling. Songs: Step to the Rear; One of Those Moments; He's Here!; Walk Away. Produced by David Merrick. Choreographed by Gillian Lynne. Directed by Abbott.

*The Education of H*Y*M*A*N K*A*P*L*A*N* [4 April 1968] musical comedy by Benjamin Bernard Zavin (bk), Paul Nassau, Oscar Brand (mu, lyr) [Alvin Thea; 28p] Cast included: Tom Bosley, Nathaniel Frey, Hal Linden, Barbara Minkus, Dick Latessa, Gary Krawford, Donna McKechnie, Mimi Sloan. Songs: Anything Is Possible; Loving You; The Day I Met Your Father. Produced by André Goulston, Jack Farren and Stephen Mellow. Choreographed by Jaime Rogers. Directed by Abbott.

The Fig Leaves Are Falling [2 Jan 1969] musical comedy by Allan Sherman (bk, lyr), Albert Hague (mu) [Broadhurst Thea; 4p] Cast included: Barry Nelson,

Dorothy Loudon, Jenny O'Hare, Kenneth Kimmins, David Cassidy. Songs: For the Rest of My Life; Did I Ever Really Live?; Today I Saw a Rose. Produced by Joseph Harris, Lawrence Carr and John Bowab. Choreographed by Eddie Gasper. Directed by Abbott.

Three Men on a Horse [16 Oct 1969] revival of the farce by John Cecil Holm, Abbott [Lyceum Thea; 100p] Cast included: Sam Levene, Jack Gilford, Rosemary Prinz, Dorothy Loudon, Hal Linden, Paul Ford, Butterfly McQueen, Leon Janney, Gloria Bleezarde. Produced by Ken Gaston, Leonard J. Goldberg and Bud Fillippo. Directed by Abbott.

Norman, Is that You? [19 Feb 1970] comedy by Ron Clark, Sam Bobrick [Lyceum Thea; 12p] Cast included: Lou Jacobi, Maureen Stapleton, Martin Huston, Walter Willison, Dorothy Emmerson. Produced by Harold D. Cohen. Directed by Abbott.

Not Now, Darling [29 Oct 1970] comedy by Ray Cooney, John Chapman [Brooks Atkinson Thea; 21p] Cast included: Norman Wisdom, Rex Garner, Claude Horton, Jean Cameron, M'el Dowd, Curt Dawson, Ardyth Kaiser. Produced by James M. Nederlander and George M. Steinbrenner III. Directed by Abbott.

The Pajama Game [9 Dec 1973] revival of the musical comedy by Abbott, Richard Bissell (bk), Richard Adler, Jerry Ross (mu, lyr) [Lunt-Fontanne Thea; 65p] Cast included: Hal Linden, Barbara McNair, Cab Calloway, Sharon Miller, Tiger Haynes, Willard Waterman, Mary Jo Catlett. Produced by Richard Adler and Bert Wood. Choreography by Zoya Leporska. Directed by Abbott.

Music Is [20 Dec 1976] musical comedy by Abbott (bk), Richard Adler (mu), Will Holt (lyr) [St. James Thea; 8p] Cast included: Catherine Cox, Sherry Mathis, Christopher Hewett, David Holliday, David Sabin, Joel Higgins, Joe Ponazecki, Laura Waterbury. Songs: Please Be Human; Should I Speak of Loving You?; No Matter Where; I Am It. Produced by Richard Adler, Roger Berlind and Edward R. Downe, Jr. Choreographed by Patricia Birch. Directed by Abbott.

On Your Toes [6 March 1983] revival of the musical comedy by Abbott (bk), Richard Rodgers (bk, mu), Lorenz Hart (bk, lyr) [Virginia Thea; 505p; Tony Award]. Cast included: Lara Teeter, Natalia Makarova, Christine Andreas, Dina Merrill, George S. Irving. Produced by Alfred De Liagre, Jr., Roger L. Stevens, John Mauceri, Donald R. Seawell and André Pastoria. Choreographed by Donald Saddler. Directed by Abbott.

Tropicana [29 May 1986] a musical by Abbott (bk), Robert Nassif (mu & lyr), Peter Napolitano (lyr) [Musical Theatre Works; 16p] Cast included: Lara Teeter, Roxann Cabalero, Constance Carpenter, Edmund Lyndeck, T. J. Harris, Natalie Costa, Poli Rogers, Nicholas Augustus. Choreographed by Donald Saddler. Directed by Abbott.

Broadway [25 June 1987] revival of a play by Philip Dunning, Abbott [Royale Thea; 4p] Cast included: Richard Poe, Peggy Taphorn, Lonny Price, Bruce Adler, K. T. Sullivan, Hal Robinson, Dorothy Stanley, Jennifer M. Thorsby, David Rogers. Produced by Frank Goodman. Directed by Abbott.

Frankie [6 Oct 1989] a musical by Abbott (bk), Joseph Turrin (mu), Gloria Nisssenson (lyr) [York Thea; 20p] Cast included: Richard White, Elizabeth Walsh, Ellia English, Gil Rogers, Casper Roos, Mark Zimmerman, Kim Moore. Directed by Abbott and Donald Saddler.

Damn Yankees [3 March 1994] revival of the musical comedy by Abbott, Douglass Wallop, Jack O'Brien (bk), Richard Adler, Jerry Ross (mu, lyr) [Marquis Thea; 533p] Cast included: Victor Garber, Bebe Neuwirth, Jarrod Emmick, Dennis Kelly, Linda Stephens, Vicki Lewis, Dick Latessa, Scott Wise, Jeff Blumenkrantz, Gregory Jbara. Produced by Mitchell Maxwell, PolyGram Diversified Entertainment, etc. Choreographed by Rob Marshall. Directed by Jack O'Brien. Script changes supervised by Abbott.

Films of George Abbott

The Impostor [Empire All Star Corp. 1918] based on the play by Leonard Merrick, Michael Morton; screenplay by Anthony Paul Kelly. Cast includes: Anna Murdock, David Powell, Lionel Adams, Ritchie Ling, Charlotte Granville, Abbott. Directed by Abbott and Dell Henderson.

Love 'Em and Leave 'Em [Famous Players-Lasky Corp. 1926] based on the play by Abbott, John V. A. Weaver; screenplay by Townsend Martin. Cast includes: Louise Brooks, Evelyn Brent, Lawrence Gray, Osgood Perkins, Jack Egan, Marcia Harris. Produced by William LeBaron. Directed by Frank Tuttle.

Hills of Peril [Fox 1927] based on the play *A Holy Terror* by Winchell Smith, Abbott; screenplay by Jack Jungmeyer. Cast includes: Buck Jones, Georgia Hale, Louis Natheaux, Marjorie Beebe, Duke Green, Bob Kortman. Produced by William Fox. Directed by Lambert Hillyer.

Four Walls [MGM 1928] based on the play by Abbott, Dana Burnet; screenplay by Abbott. Cast includes: John Gilbert, Joan Crawford, Vera Gordon, Carmel Myers, Robert Emmett O'Connor. Produced by Mary Pickford and Sam Taylor. Directed by William Nigh.

Coquette [United Artists 1929] based on the play by Abbott, Ann Preston Bridgers; screenplay by John Gray, Allen McNeil. Cast includes: Mary Pickford, Johnny Mack Brown, Matt Moore, John St. Polis, William Janney, Henry Kolker, Louise Beavers. Directed by Sam Taylor.

The Carnival Man [Paramount 1929] Screenplay by Abbott. Cast includes: Walter Huston, Nan Sunderland. Directed by Abbott. (short)

Broadway [Universal 1929] based on the play by Abbott, Philip Dunning; screenplay by Abbott, etc. Cast includes: Glenn Tryon, Merna Kennedy, Robert Ellis, Paul Porcasi, Leslie Fenton, Evelyn Brent, Otis Harlan, Thomas Jackson, Marian Lord. Produced by Carl Laemmle, Jr.. Directed by Paul Fejos.

The Bishop's Candlesticks [Paramount 1929] based on the play by Norman McKinnell; screenplay by McKinnell. Cast includes: Walter Huston, Charles S. Abbe, Josephine Hull, Duncan Penwarden. Directed by Abbott. (short)

Why Bring that Up? [Paramount 1929] Screenplay by Abbott, etc. Cast includes: Charles Mack, George Moran, Evelyn Brent, Harry Green, Bert Swor, Freeman Wood, Helen Lynch. Directed by Abbott.

The Saturday Night Kid [Paramount 1929] based on the play *Love 'Em and Leave 'Em* by Abbott, John V. A. Weaver; screenplay by Ethel Doherty. Cast includes: Clara Bow, Jean Arthur, James Hall, Edna May Oliver, Charles Sellon, Ethel Wales. Directed by A. Edward Sunderland.

Night Parade [RKO 1929] based on the play *Ringside* by Edward E. Paramore, Jr., Hyatt Daab, Abbott; screenplay by George O'Hara, James Gruen. Cast includes: Aileen Pringle, Hugh Trevor, Dorothy Gulliver, Robert Ellis, Ann Pennington, Lloyd Ingraham. Produced by William LeBaron. Directed by Malcolm St. Clair.

Half Way to Heaven [Paramount 1929] Screenplay by Abbott. Cast includes: Charles "Buddy" Rogers, Jean Arthur, Paul Lukas, Helen Ware, Edna West, Irving Bacon, Michael Stuart. Produced by Jesse L. Lasky. Directed by Abbott.

El Dios del Mar [Paramount 1930] based on the film *The Sea God* by Abbott; Screenplay by Josep Carner Ribalta. Cast includes: Ramón Pereda, Rosita Moreno, Julio Villarreal, Francisco Moreno, Manuel Arbó. Directed by Francisco Moreno (as Paco Moreno) and Edward D. Venturini.

All Quiet on the Western Front [Universal 1930] based on the novel by Erich Maria Remarque; screenplay by Maxwell Anderson, Abbott, Del Andrews. Cast includes: Lew Ayres, Louis Wolheim, John Wray, Arnold Lucy, Ben Alexander, Scott Kolk, Owen Davis, Jr., Walter Rogers, William Bakewell. Produced by Carl Laemmle, Jr. Directed by Lewis Milestone.

The Fall Guy [RKO 1930] based on the play by Abbott, James Gleason; screenplay by Tim Whelan. Cast includes: Jack Mulhall, Mae Clarke, Ned Sparks, Wynn Gibson, Pat O'Malley, Thomas E. Jackson. Produced by William LeBaron and William Sistrom. Directed by Leslie Pearce.

Manslaughter [Paramount 1930] based on the novel by Alice Duer Miller; screenplay by Abbott. Cast includes: Claudette Colbert, Fredric March, Emma Dunn, Natalie Morehead, Richard Tucker, Hilda Vaughn. Produced by Adolph Zukor. Directed by Abbott.

The Sea God [Paramount 1930] based on the story "The Lost God" by John Russell; screenplay by Abbott. Cast includes: Richard Arlen, Fay Wray, Eugene Pallette, Robert Gleckler, Ivan F. Simpson, Maurice Black. Produced by Jesse L. Lasky. Directed by Abbott.

Stolen Heaven [Paramount 1931] Screenplay by Abbott, Dana Burnet. Cast includes: Nancy Carroll, Phillips Holmes, Louis Calhern, Edward Kean, Joan Carr, Dagmar Oakland. Directed by Abbott.

La Incorregible [Paramount 1931] based on the screenplay *Manslaughter* by Abbott. Cast includes: Enriqueta Serrano, Tony D'Algy, Gabriel Algara, Marita Ángeles, Ricardo Baroja, Carmen Muñoz. Directed by Leo Mittler.

Sombras del circo [Paramount 1931] based on the screenplay *Half Way to Heaven* by Abbott. Cast includes: Amelia Muñoz, Tony D'Algy, Félix de Pomés, Antonia Arévalo, Miguel Ligero, Alfredo Hurtado. Directed by Adelqui Migliar.

À *mi-chemin du ciel* [Paramount 1931] Screenplay by Abbott, Alberto Cavalcanti. Cast includes: Janine Merrey, Jeanne Marie-Laurent, Enrique Rivero, Thomy Bourdelle, Jean Mercanton, Ketty Loloff, Marguerite Moreno. Directed by Alberto Cavalcanti.

Secrets of a Secretary [Paramount 1931] Screenplay by Abbott. Cast includes: Claudette Colbert, Herbert Marshall, Georges Metaxa, Betty Lawford, Mary Boland, Berton Churchill, Averell Harris, Betty Garde. Directed by Abbott.

My Sin [Paramount 1931] Screenplay by Owen Davis, Adelaide Heilbron, Abbott. Cast includes: Tallulah Bankhead, Fredric March, Harry Davenport, Scott Kolk, Anne Sutherland, Margaret Adams, Jay Fassett, Lily Cahill. Produced and directed by Abbott.

The Cheat [Paramount 1931] Screenplay by Harry Hervey. Cast includes: Tallulah Bankhead, Harvey Stephens, Irving Pichel, Ann Andrews, Jay Fassett, William Ingersoll. Directed by Abbott and Berthold Viertel.

Halvvägs till himlen [Paramount 1932] based on the play by Henry Leyford Gates; screenplay by Abbott. Cast includes: Elisabeth Frisk, Haakon Hjelde, Edvin Adolphson, Karin Swanström, Torben Meyer. Directed by Rune Carlsten and Stellan Windrow.

Those We Love [K.B.S. Prod. 1932] based on the play by Abbott, S. K. Lauren; screenplay by F. Hugh Herbert. Cast includes: Mary Astor, Kenneth MacKenna,

Lilyan Tashman, Hale Hamilton, Tommy Conlon, Earle Foxe. Produced by Philip Dunning and John Golden. Directed by Robert Florey.

Lilly Turner [First National 1933] based on the play by Abbott, Philip Dunning; screenplay by Gene Markey, Kathryn Scola. Cast includes: Ruth Chatterton, George Brent, Frank McHugh, Guy Kibbee, Robert Barrat, Ruth Donnelly, Marjorie Gateson. Directed by William A. Wellman.

Heat Lightning [Warner Bros. 1934] based on the play by Abbott, Leon Abrams; screenplay by Brown Holmes, Warren Duff. Cast includes: Aline MacMahon, Ann Dvorak, Preston Foster, Lyle Talbot, Glenda Farrell, Frank McHugh, Ruth Donnelly, Theodore Newton, Willard Robertson. Produced by Samuel Bischoff. Directed by Mervyn LeRoy.

Straight Is the Way [MGM 1934] based on the play by Abbott, Dana Burnet; screenplay by Bernard Schubert. Cast includes: Franchot Tone, May Robson, Karen Morley, Gladys George, Nat Pendleton, Jack La Rue, C. Henry Gordon. Produced by Lucien Hubbard. Directed by Paul Sloane.

Three Men on a Horse [First National 1936] based on the play by Abbott, John Cecil Holm; screenplay by Laird Doyle. Cast includes: Sam Levene, Frank McHugh, Joan Blondell, Allen Jenkins, Teddy Hart, Guy Kibbee, Carol Hughes, Edgar Kennedy, Paul Harvey, Eddie "Rochester" Anderson. Produced and directed by Mervyn LeRoy.

On Your Toes [Warner Bros 1939] based on the musical comedy by Abbott (bk), Richard Rodgers (bk, mu), Lorenz Hart (bk, lyr); screenplay by Jerry Wald, Richard Macauley. Cast includes: Vera Zorina, Eddie Albert, Alan Hale, Frank McHugh, James Gleason, Leonid Kinskey, Gloria Dickson, Queen Smith, Donald O'Connor. Choreography by George Balanchine. Produced by Robert Lord. Directed by Ray Enright.

Too Many Girls [RKO 1940] based on the musical comedy by George Marion, Jr. (bk), Richard Rodgers (mu), Lorenz Hart (lyr); screenplay by John Twist. Cast includes: Lucille Ball, Richard Carlson, Ann Miller, Eddie Bracken, Frances Langford, Desi Arnaz, Hal Le Roy, Libby Bennett. Produced by Harry E. Edington. Choreography by LeRoy Prinz. Directed by Abbott.

The Boys from Syracuse [Universal 1940] based on the musical comedy by Abbott (bk), Richard Rodgers (mu), Lorenz Hart (lyr); screenplay by Charles Grayson, etc. Cast includes: Allan Jones, Irene Hervey, Martha Raye, Joe Penner, Alan Mowbray, Charles Butterworth, Rosemary Lane. Produced by Jules Levey. Choreography by Dave Gould. Directed by A. Edward Sutherland.

Highway West [Warner Bros 1941] based on the play *Heat Lightning* by Abbott, Leon Abrams; screenplay by Allen Rivkin, Charles Kenyon, Kenneth Gamet. Cast includes: Brenda Marshall, Arthur Kennedy, William Lundigan, Olympe Bradna, Slim Summerville, Willie Best. Produced by Edmund Grainger. Directed by William C. McGann.

Broadway [Universal 1942] based on the play by Abbott, Philip Dunning; screenplay by Felix Jackson, John Bright. Cast includes: George Raft, Pat O'Brien, Janet Blair, Broderick Crawford, Marjorie Rambou, S. Z. Sakall. Produced by Bruce Manning and Frank Shaw. Directed by William A. Seiter.

Beat the Band [RKO 1947] based on the play by Abbott, George Marion, Jr.; screenplay by Lawrence Kimble. Cast includes: Frances Langford, Ralph Edwards, Philip Terry, June Clayworth, Mabel Paige, Andrew Combes, Donald MacBride. Produced by Michael Kraike and Sid Rogell. Directed by John H. Auer.

The Pajama Game [Warner Bros 1957] based on the musical by Abbott, Richard Bissell (bk), Richard Adler, Jerry Ross (mu, lyr); screenplay by Abbott. Cast includes: Doris Day, John Raitt, Carol Haney, Eddie Foy, Jr., Reta Shaw, Barbara Nichols. Produced by Abbott, Stanley Donen, and Frederick Brisson. Choreography by Bob Fosse. Directed by Abbott and Stanley Donen.

Damn Yankees [Warner Bros 1958] based on the musical by Abbott, Douglass Wallop (bk), Richard Adler, Jerry Ross (mu, lyr); screenplay by Abbott. Cast includes: Gwen Verdon, Ray Walston, Russ Brown, Nathaniel Frey, Eddie Phillips, Rae Allen, Jean Stapleton, Albert Linville, Jimmie Komack. New song: There's Something About An Empty Chair. Produced by Abbott, Stanley Donen, and Frederick Brisson. Choreography by Bob Fosse. Directed by Abbott and Stanley Donen.

George Abbott's Awards and Honors

1930   Academy Award nomination for Best Achievement in Writing: *All Quiet on the Western Front* (co-author)

1955   Tony Award for Best Musical: *The Pajama Game* (co-author)

1956   Tony Award for Best Musical: *Damn Yankees* (co-author)

1956   Writers Guild of America Award nomination for Best Written American Musical: *The Pajama Game* (co-author)

1957   Writers Guild of America Award nomination for Best Written American Musical: *Damn Yankees*

1958   Tony Award nomination for Best Musical: *New Girl in Town* (author)

1959   Directors Guild of America Award nomination for Outstanding Directorial Achievement in Motion Pictures: *Damn Yankees* (co-director)

1960 Tony Award for Best Direction of a Musical: *Fiorello!*

1960 Tony Award for Best Musical: *Fiorello!* (co-author)

1960 Pulitzer Prize for Drama: *Fiorello!* (co-author)

1963 Tony Award nomination for Best Direction of a Play: *Never Too Late*

1963 Tony Award for Best Direction of a Musical: *A Funny Thing Happened on the Way to the Forum*

1965 The 54th Street Theatre was rechristened the George Abbott Theater in his honor; building demolished in 1970

1965 George Abbott Way, the section of West 45th Street northwest of Times Square, designated

1968 Tony Award nomination for Best Direction of a Musical: *How Now, Dow Jones*

1972 Inducted into the American Theatre Hall of Fame.

1976 Special Tony Award: The Lawrence Langer Award

1976 New York City's Handel Medallion

1982 Kennedy Center Lifetime Achievement Award

1983 Drama Desk Award for Outstanding Director of a Musical: *On Your Toes* (revival)

1987 Special Tony Award on the occasion of his 100th birthday

1990 National Medal of Arts by the National Endowment of the Arts

NOTES

Preface

1   Abbott, George, *Mister Abbott* (New York: Random House, 1963), 106.
2   Abbott, *Mister Abbott*, 252.

Prologue

1   Abbott, *Mister Abbott*, 1.

Chapter 1

1   Abbott, *Mister Abbott*, 99.
2   Abbott, *Mister Abbott*, 105.
3   Bordman, Gerald, *American Theatre: A Chronicle of Comedy and Drama, 1914–1930* (New York: Oxford University Press, 1995), 205
4   Abbott, *Mister Abbott*, 108.

Chapter 2

1   Mantle, Burns (ed), *The Best Plays of 1924–1925* (Boston: Small, Maynard & Co, 1925), 271.
2   Sheward, David. *It's a Hit: The Back Stage Book of Longest-Running Broadway Shows* (New York: Back Stage Books, 1994), 25.
3   Dunning, Philip, and George Abbott, *Broadway* (New York: Samuel French, Inc., 1925), 9–10.
4   Dunning, *Broadway,* 26.
5   Abbott, *Mister Abbott*, 118.

6 Dunning, *Broadway*, 3.
7 Mantle, Burns (ed), *The Best Plays of 1926–1927* (Boston: Small, Maynard & Co, 1927), 14.
8 Bordman, Gerald, *American Theatre: A Chronicle of Comedy and Drama, 1914–1930* (New York: Oxford University Press, 1995), 318.
9 Abbott, *Mister Abbott*, 128.
10 Mantle, Burns (ed), *The Best Plays of 1927–1928* (New York: Dodd, Mead & Co, 1928), 166.
11 Abbott, *Mister Abbott*, 129–30.

Chapter 3

1 Mantle, Burns (ed), *The Best Plays of 1933–1934* (New York: Dodd, Mead & Co, 1934), 8.
2 Abbott, *Mister Abbott*, 178.
3 Bordman, Gerald, *American Theatre: A Chronicle of Comedy and Drama, 1930–1969* (New York: Oxford University Press, 1996), 175.
4 Mayhew, Robert (ed). *Ayn Rand's The Unconquered* (New York: Palgrave MacMillan, 2014).
5 Abbott, *Mister Abbott*, 171–2.

Chapter 4

1 Abbott, *Mister Abbott*, 174.
2 Aronson, Lisa, and Frank Rich, *The Theatre Art of Boris Aronson* (New York: Alfred A. Knopf, 1987), 60.
3 Abbott, *Mister Abbott*, 176.
4 Mantle, Burns (ed), *The Best Plays of 1935–1936* (New York: Dodd, Mead & Co, 1936), 204.
5 Sheward, *It's a Hit*, 44.
6 Bordman, Gerald, *American Theatre: A Chronicle of Comedy and Drama, 1930-*, 154.
7 Mantle, Burns (ed), *The Best Plays of 1937–1938* (New York: Dodd, Mead & Co, 1938), 332.
8 Mantle, *The Best Plays of 1937–1938*, 334.

Chapter 5

1 Abbott, *Mister Abbott*, 86.
2 Abbott, *Mister Abbott*, 86.

3 Abbott, *Mister Abbott*, 130.
4 Abbott, *Mister Abbott*, 135.
5 Abbott, *Mister Abbott*, 134.
6 Abbott, *Mister Abbott*, 134.
7 Abbott, *Mister Abbott*, 135.
8 Abbott, *Mister Abbott*, 138.
9 Abbott, *Mister Abbott*, 144.

Chapter 6

1 Rodgers, Richard, *Musical Stages* (New York: Random House, 1975), 173.
2 Abbott, *Mister Abbott*, 177–8.
3 Rodgers, *Musical Stages*, 174.
4 Abbott, George, and Richard Rodgers, Lorenz Hart, *On Your Toes* (New York: Rodgers and Hammerstein Theatre Library, 1936/1985), 12–13.
5 Abbott, George, and Richard Rodgers, Lorenz Hart, *The Boys from Syracuse* (New York: Rodgers and Hammerstein Theatre Library, 1938), 37.
6 Abbott, etc., *The Boys from Syracuse*, 19.
7 Abbott, etc., *The Boys from Syracuse*, 22.
8 Henderson, Mary C., *Mielziner: Master of Modern Stage Design* (New York: Back Stage Books, 2001), 122.
9 Rodgers, *Musical Stages*, 191.
10 Abbott, *Mister Abbott*, 187.
11 Abbott, *Mister Abbott*, 187.
12 Mantle, Burns (ed), *The Best Plays of 1939–1940* (New York: Dodd, Mead & Co, 1940), 5.
13 Mordden, Ethan, *Beautiful Mornin': The Broadway Musical in the 1940s* (New York: Oxford University Press, 1999), 8.
14 Abbott, *Mister Abbott*, 198.
15 Nathan, George Jean, *The Theatre Book of The Year, 1942–1943* (Cranbury, NJ: Associated University Presses, Inc., 1943/1971), 102.
16 Abbott, *Mister Abbott*, 196.

Chapter 7

1 Nathan, *The Theatre Book of The Year, 1942–1943*, 197.
2 Abbott, *Mister Abbott*, 199.
3 Nathan, George Jean, *The Theatre Book of The Year, 1943–1944* (Cranbury, NJ: Associated University Presses, Inc., 1944/1972), 256.

4   Abbott, *Mister Abbott*, 199.
5   Abbott, *Mister Abbott*, 199.
6   Nathan, *The Theatre Book of The Year, 1943–1944*, 145.
7   Nathan, *The Theatre Book of The Year, 1943–1944*, 316.
8   Nathan, *The Theatre Book of The Year, 1943–1944*, 317.
9   Nathan, George Jean, *The Theatre Book of The Year, 1944–1945* (Cranbury, NJ: Associated University Presses, Inc., 1945/1972), 118.

Chapter 8

1   Mordden, *Beautiful Mornin'*, 122.
2   Abbott, *Mister Abbott*, 199–200.
3   Abbott, *Mister Abbott*, 200.
4   Abbott, *Mister Abbott*, 200.
5   Nathan, *The Theatre Book of The Year, 1944–1945*, 238.
6   Nathan, George Jean, *The Theatre Book of The Year, 1946–1947* (Cranbury, NJ: Associated University Presses, Inc., 1947/1975), 361.
7   Sheward, *It's a Hit*, 96.
8   Abbott, *Mister Abbott*, 219.
9   Mordden, *Beautiful Mornin'*, 205.
10 Abbott, *Mister Abbott*, 221.
11 Abbott, *Mister Abbott*, 221.
12 Mordden, *Beautiful Mornin'*, 192.
13 Nathan, George Jean, *The Theatre Book of The Year, 1947–1948* (Cranbury, NJ: Associated University Presses, Inc., 1948/1975), 247.
14 Abbott, *Mister Abbott*, 222.
15 Abbott, George, and Frank Loesser, *Where's Charley?* (New York: Edwin H. Morris & Co., 1948/1964), 5.
16 Abbott, *Mister Abbott*, 224.
17 Abbott, *Where's Charley?*, 60.
18 Abbott, *Mister Abbott*, 225.

Chapter 9

1   Nathan, *The Theatre Book of The Year, 1946–1947*, 35.
2   Nathan, *The Theatre Book of The Year, 1946–1947*, 61.
3   Kronenberger, Louis (ed), *The Best Plays of 1960–1961* (New York: Dodd, Mead & Co, 1961), 12.

4 Prince, Harold, *Sense of Occasion*, (Milwaukee, WI: Applause Theatre and Film Books, 2017), 67.
5 Abbott, *Mister Abbott*, 256.
6 Abbott, *Mister Abbott*, 256.
7 Abbott, *Mister Abbott*, 257.
8 Abbott, *Mister Abbott*, 258.

Chapter 10

1 O'Hara, John, *Pal Joey* (New York: Popular Library, 1939/1968), 66.
2 Abbott, *Mister Abbott*, 194.
3 O'Hara, John, Richard Rodgers, and Lorenz Hart, *Pal Joey* (New York: Popular Library, 1952/1968), 150-2.
4 Hart, Dorothy, and Robert Kimball, *The Complete Lyrics of Lorenz Hart* (New York: Alfred A. Knopf, 1986), 272.
5 O'Hara, *Pal Joey*, 223.
6 Abbott, *Mister Abbott*, 217.
7 Abbott, *Mister Abbott*, 217.
8 Nathan, George Jean, *The Theatre Book of The Year, 1945-1946*. (Cranbury, NJ: Associated University Presses, Inc., 1946/1974), 257.
9 Smith, Betty, and George Abbott, Dorothy Fields, Arthur Schwartz, *A Tree Grows in Brooklyn* (New York: Harper & Brothers, 1951), 158.
10 Smith, *A Tree Grows in Brooklyn*, 25-6.
11 Abbott, *Mister Abbott*, 254.
12 Abbott, *Mister Abbott*, 254.
13 Prince, *Sense of Occasion*, 31.
14 Prince, *Sense of Occasion*, 31.
15 Abbott, George, and Bob Merrill, *New Girl in Town* (New York: Random House, 1958), 27.
16 Abbott, *Mister Abbott*, 262-3.
17 Prince, *Sense of Occasion*, 52.
18 Weidman, Jerome, and George Abbott, Sheldon Harnick, Jerry Bock, *Fiorello!* (New York: Random House, 1960), 72.
19 Prince, *Sense of Occasion*, 63.
20 Prince, *Sense of Occasion*, 65.
21 Lambert, Philip, *To Broadway, To Life! The Musical Theatre of Bock and Harnick* (New York: Oxford University Press, 2011), 87.
22 Weidman, Jerome, and George Abbott, Sheldon Harnick, Jerry Bock, *Tenderloin* (New York: Random House, 1961), 3-4.
23 Altman, Richard, and Mervyn Kaufman, *The Making of a Musical: Fiddler on the Roof*, (New York: Crown Publishers, 1971), 26.

24 Altman, *The Making of a Musical*, 26.
25 Prince *Sense of Occasion*, 64.
26 Lambert, *To Broadway! To Life!*, 92.
27 Prince, *Sense of Occasion*, 2.
28 Prince, *Sense of Occasion*, 3.
29 Prince, *Sense of Occasion*, 3.

Chapter 11

1 Bergreen, Laurence, *As Thousands Cheer: The Life of Irving Berlin* (New York: Viking Press, 1990), 501–2.
2 Abbott, *Mister Abbott*, 227.
3 Abbott, *Mister Abbott*, 227.
4 Abbott, *Mister Abbott*, 233.
5 Abbott, *Mister Abbott*, 233–4.
6 Abbott, *Mister Abbott*, 234.
7 Rodgers, *Musical Stages*, 281.
8 Abbott, *Mister Abbott*, 243–4.
9 Mordden, Ethan, *Rodgers and Hammerstein* (New York: Harry N. Abrams, 1992), 150.
10 Rodgers, *Musical Stages*, 283.
11 Abbott, *Mister Abbott*, 243–4.
12 Prince, *Sense of Occasion*, 13.
13 Abbott, *Mister Abbott*, 248.
14 Adler, Richard, with Lee Davis, *You Gotta Have Heart* (New York: Donald I. Fine, Inc, 1990), 37.
15 Adler, *You Gotta Have Heart*, 37.
16 Abbott, George, and Richard Bissell, Richard Adler, Jerry Ross, *The Pajama Game* (New York: Random House, 1954), 5.
17 Abbott, etc, *The Pajama Game*, 6.
18 Abbott, etc, *The Pajama Game*, 31.
19 Prince, *Sense of Occasion*, 14.
20 Adler, *You Gotta Have Heart*, 42–3.
21 Adler, *You Gotta Have Heart*, 51.
22 Prince, *Sense of Occasion*, 30.
23 Prince, *Sense of Occasion*, 19.
24 Harris, Andrew B., *The Performing Set: The Broadway Designs of William and Jean Eckart* (Denton, TX: University of North Texas Press, 2006), 94.
25 Abbott, George, and Douglass Wallop, Richard Adler, Jerry Ross, *Damn Yankees* (New York: Random House, 1956), 62.

26 Abbott, etc., *Damn Yankees*, 52.
27 Adler, *You Gotta Have Heart*, 72.
28 Harris, *The Performing Set*, 46.
29 Harris, *The Performing Set*, 53.
30 Harris, *The Performing Set*, 53.
31 Harris, *The Performing Set*, 57.

Chapter 12

1 Abbott, *Mister Abbott*, 267.
2 Prince, *Sense of Occasion*, 83.
3 Abbott, *Mister Abbott*, 267–8.
4 Abbott, *Mister Abbott*, 268.
5 Hewes, Henry (ed), *The Best Plays of 1962–1963* (New York: Dodd, Mead & Co, 1963), 11.
6 Mordden, Ethan, *Coming Up Roses: The Broadway Musical in the 1950s* (New York: Oxford University Press, 1998), 226.
7 Harris, Andrew B., *The Performing Set: The Broadway Designs of William and Jean Eckart* (Denton, TX: University of North Texas Press, 2006), 107.
8 Abbott, *Mister Abbott*, 262.
9 Harris, *The Performing Set*, 110.
10 Harris, *The Performing Set*, 111.
11 Burnett, Carol, *One More Time: A Memoir* (New York: Random House, 1986) 291.
12 Harris, *The Performing Set*, 112.
13 Burnett, *One More Time*, 291.
14 Abbott, *Mister Abbott*, 268.
15 Prince, *Sense of Occasion*, 91.
16 Prince, *Sense of Occasion*, 91.
17 Prince, *Sense of Occasion*, 92.
18 Sondheim, Stephen, *Finishing the Hat: Collected Lyrics (1954–1981)*. (New York: Alfred A. Knopf, 2010), 87.
19 Sondheim, *Finishing the Hat*, 87.
20 Prince, *Sense of Occasion*, 94.

Chapter 13

1 Abbott, *Mister Abbott*, 268.
2 Abbott, *Mister Abbott*, 268.

3. Suskin, Steven, *Second Act Trouble: Behind the Scenes at Broadway's Big Musical Bombs* (New York: Applause Books, 2006), 88.
4. Suskin, *Second Act Trouble*, 94.
5. Prince, *Sense of Occasion*, 117.
6. Prince, *Sense of Occasion*, 117.
7. Kander, John, and Fred Ebb with Greg Lawrence, *Colored Lights: Forty Years of Words and Music, Show Biz, Collaboration, and All That Jazz* (New York: Faber & Faber, 2003), 39.
8. Kander, etc., *Colored Lights*, 43.
9. Harris, *The Performing Set*, 164.
10. Harris, *The Performing Set*, 164.
11. Harris, *The Performing Set*, 165.
12. Kander, etc., *Colored Lights*, 44.
13. Kander, etc., *Colored Lights*, 44.
14. Prince, *Sense of Occasion*, 117.
15. Abbott, George, and Robert Russell, John Kander, Fred Ebb, *Flora, the Red Menace* (New York: Samuel French, Inc., 1965), 24–5.
16. Kander, etc., *Colored Lights*, 49.
17. Kander, etc., *Colored Lights*, 49–50.
18. Mordden, Ethan, *Open a New Window: The Broadway Musical in the 1960s* (New York: Palgrave Macmillan, 2001), 86.
19. Mandelbaum, Ken, *Not Since Carrie: 40 Years of Broadway Musical Flops* (New York: St. Martin's Press, 1991), 237.
20. Goldman, William, *The Season: A Candid Look at Broadway* (New York: Harcourt, Brace and World, 1969), 360.
21. Harris, *The Performing Set*, 188.
22. Harris, *The Performing Set*, 190.
23. Goldman, *The Season*, 366.
24. Mandelbaum, *Not Since Carrie*, 289–90.
25. Harris, *The Performing Set*, 198.
26. Suskin, Steven, *More Opening Night on Broadway* (New York: Schirmer Books, 1997), 627.
27. Adler, *You Gotta Have Heart*, 270.
28. Author's interview with Lara Teeter, 16 June 2021.
29. Author's interview with Robert Lindsey-Nassif, 29 June 2021.
30. Author's interview with Joseph Turrin, 2 June 2021.
31. Turrin interview.
32. Turrin interview.
33. Turrin interview.
34. Turrin interview.
35. Turrin interview.

36 Guernsey, Otis L., Jr., and Jeffrey Sweet (eds), *The Best Plays of 1989–1990* (New York: Applause Theatre Books, 1990), 453.

37 Turrin interview.

Chapter 14

1 Suskin, *More Opening Night on Broadway*, 697.

2 Teeter interview.

3 Teeter interview.

4 Lindsey-Nassif interview.

5 Lindsey-Nassif interview.

6 Lindsey-Nassif interview.

7 O'Brien, Jack, *Jack Be Nimble: The Accidental Education of an Intentional Director* (New York: Farrar, Straus & Giroux, 2013), 286.

Epilogue

1 Turrin interview.

2 Turrin interview

3 Goldman, *The Season*, 359.

4 Adler, etc., *You Gotta Have Heart*, 273.

5 Kander, etc., *Colored Lights*, 51.

6 Abbott, *Mister Abbott*, 263–4.

7 Abbott, *Mister Abbott*, 264.

8 Abbott, *Mister Abbott*, 265.

9 Mordden, *Beautiful Mornin'*, 8.

10 Leiter, Samuel L., *The Great Directors* (New York: Facts on File, Inc., 1994), 3.

11 Prince, *Sense of Occasion*, 28.

12 Prince, *Sense of Occasion*, 30.

SELECTED BIBLIOGRAPHY

Abbott, George. *Mister Abbott*. New York: Random House, 1963.
Abbott, George, and Frank Loesser. *Where's Charley?* New York: Edwin H. Morris & Co., 1948/1964.
Abbott, George, and Bob Merrill. *New Girl in Town*. New York: Random House, 1958.
Abbott, George, and Richard Bissell, Richard Adler, Jerry Ross. *The Pajama Game*. New York: Random House, 1954.
Abbott, George, and Richard Rodgers, Lorenz Hart. *The Boys from Syracuse*. New York: Rodgers and Hammerstein Theatre Library, 1938.
Abbott, George, and Richard Rodgers, Lorenz Hart. *On Your Toes*. New York: Rodgers and Hammerstein Theatre Library, 1936/1985.
Abbott, George, and Robert Russell, John Kander, Fred Ebb. *Flora, the Red Menace*. New York: Samuel French, Inc., 1965.
Abbott, George, and Douglass Wallop, Richard Adler, Jerry Ross. *Damn Yankees*. New York: Random House, 1956.
Adler, Richard, and Lee Davis. *You Gotta Have Heart*. New York: Donald I. Fine, Inc., 1990.
Alpert, Hollis. *Broadway: 125 Years of Musical Theatre*. New York: Arcade, 1991.
Altman, Richard, and Mervyn Kaufman. *The Making of a Musical: Fiddler on the Roof*. New York: Crown, 1971.
Appelbaum, Stanley (ed). *The New York Stage Famous Productions in Photographs (1883–1939)*. New York: Dover Publications, 1976.
Aronson, Lisa, and Frank Rich. *The Theatre Art of Boris Aronson*. New York: Alfred A. Knopf, 1987.
Atkinson, Brooks. *Broadway* (revised edn). New York: Macmillan, 1974.
Atkinson, Brooks. *The Lively Years: 1920–1973* (2nd edn). Brownsboro, AL: Ardent Writer Press, 2019.
Banfield, Stephen. *Sondheim's Broadway Musicals*. Ann Arbor: University of Michigan Press, 1993.
Banham, Martin (ed). *The Cambridge Guide to Theatre*. New York: Cambridge University Press, 1992.
Bates, J. Douglas. *The Pulitzer Prize*. New York: Birch Lane, 1991.
Benchley, Robert. *Benchley at the Theatre: Dramatic Criticism, 1920–1940*. Ipswich, MA: Ipswich Press, 1995.
Bergreen, Laurence. *As Thousands Cheer: The Life of Irving Berlin*. New York: Viking Press, 1990.
Bernstein, Leonard. *Findings*. New York: Simon & Schuster, 1982.
The Best Plays. 90 editions. Editors: Garrison Sherwood and John Chapman (1894–1919); Burns Mantle (1919–1947); John Chapman (1947–1952); Louis Kronenberger (1952–1961); Henry Hewes (1961–1964); Otis L. Guernsey, Jr. (1964–2000); Jeffrey

Eric Jenkins (2000–2009). New York: Dodd, Mead & Co., 1894–1988; New York: Applause Theatre Book Publishers, 1988–1993; New York: Limelight Editions, 1994–2009.

Block, Geoffrey. *Enchanted Evenings: The Broadway Musical from Show Boat to Lloyd Webber* (2nd edn). New York: Oxford University Press, 2009.

Bloom, Ken. *Broadway: An Encyclopedic Guide to the History, People and Places of Times Square*. New York: Facts on File, 1991.

Bloom, Ken, and Frank Vlastnik. *Broadway Musicals: The 101 Greatest Shows of All Time*. New York: Black Dog & Leventhal Publishers, 2004.

Bordman, Gerald. *American Theatre: A Chronicle of Comedy & Drama, 1914–1930*. New York: Oxford University Press, 1995.

Bordman, Gerald. *American Theatre: A Chronicle of Comedy & Drama, 1930–1969*. New York: Oxford University Press, 1996.

Bordman, Gerald, and Thomas S. Hischak. *The Oxford Companion to American Theatre* (3rd edn). New York: Oxford University Press, 2004.

Bordman, Gerald, and Richard Norton. *American Musical Theatre: A Chronicle* (4th edn). New York: Oxford University Press, 2010.

Brantley, Ben (ed). *The New York Times Book of Broadway*. New York: St. Martin's Press, 2001.

Brown, Jared. *Zero Mostel: A Biography*. New York: Antheneum, 1989.

Brown, John Mason. *Dramatis Personae: A Retrospective Show*. New York: Viking Press, 1963.

Burnett, Carol. *One More Time: A Memoir*. New York: Random House, 1986.

Dunning, Philip, and George Abbott. *Broadway*. New York: Samuel French, Inc., 1925.

Everett, William A., and Paul R. Laird (eds). *The Cambridge Companion to the Musical*. (3rd edn.) Cambridge, UK: Cambridge University Press, 2017.

Ewen, D. A. *With a Song in His Heart: The Story of Richard Rodgers*. New York: Holt, Rinehart and Winston, 2000.

Fordin, Hugh. *Getting to Know Him: A Biography of Oscar Hammerstein II*. New York: Random House, 1977.

Ganzl, Kurt. *Ganzl's Encyclopedia of the Musical Theatre*. New York: Schirmer Books, 1993.

Gelbart, Larry. *Laughing Matters*. New York: Random House, 1998.

Goldman, William. *The Season: A Candid Look at Broadway*. New York: Harcourt, Brace and World, 1969.

Gottfried, Martin. *Opening Nights: Theatre Criticism of the Sixties*. New York: G. P. Putnam's Sons, 1972.

Gottfried, Martin. *Jed Harris, the Curse of Genius*. New York: Little, Brown & Co., 1984.

Grant, Mark N. *The Rise and Fall of the Broadway Musical*. Boston: Northeastern University Press, 2004.

Green, Stanley, and Cary Ginell. *Encyclopedia of the Musical Theatre*. New York: Dood, Meade & Co, 1976.

Green, Stanley, and Cary Ginell. *The World of Musical Comedy*. New York: A.S. Barnes & Co., 1980.

Green, Stanley, and Cary Ginell. *Broadway Musicals Show By Show* (6th edn). Guilford, CT: Applause Theatre & Cinema Books, 2019.

Grode, Eric. *The Book of Broadway: The 150 Definitive Plays and Musicals*. Minneapolis: Voyageur Press, 2015.

Harris, Andrew B. *The Performing Set: The Broadway Designs of William and Jean Eckart*. Denton, TX: University of North Texas Press, 2016.

Hart, Dorothy, and Robert Kimball. *The Complete Lyrics of Lorenz Hart*. New York: Alfred A. Knopf, 1986.
Hartnoll, Phyllis. *The Oxford Companion to the Theatre*. New York: Oxford University Press, 1983.
Henderson, Mary C. *Theatre in America*. New York: Harry N. Abrams, Inc., 1986.
Henderson, Mary C. *Mielziner: Master of Modern Stage Design*. New York: Back Stage Books, 2001.
Henderson, Mary C. *The City and the Theatre*. New York: Back Stage Books, 2004.
Hirsch, Foster. *Harold Prince and the American Musical* (rev. edn). New York: Applause, 2005.
Hischak, Thomas S. *American Theatre: A Chronicle of Comedy and Drama, 1969–2000*. New York: Oxford University Press, 2001.
Hischak, Thomas S. *Boy Loses Girl: Broadway's Librettists*. Lanham, MD: Scarecrow Press, 2002.
Hischak, Thomas S. *Through the Screen Door: What Happened to the Broadway Musical When It Went to Hollywood*. Lanham, MD: Scarecrow, 2004.
Hischak, Thomas S. *The Oxford Companion to the American Musical: Theatre, Film and Television*. New York: Oxford University Press, 2008.
Hischak, Thomas S. *Broadway Plays and Musicals: Descriptions and Essential Facts of More Than 14,000 Shows Through 2007*. Jefferson, NC: McFarland and Co., 2009.
Hischak, Thomas S. *The 100 Greatest American Plays*. Lanham, MD: Rowman & Littlefield, 2017.
Hughes, Glenn. *A History of the American Theatre, 1700–1950*. New York: Samuel French, Inc., 1951.
Ilson, Carol. *Harold Prince: From Pajama Game to Phantom of the Opera*. Ann Arbor: U.M.I. Research Press, 1989.
Jackson, Arthur. *The Best Musicals From Show Boat to A Chorus Line*. New York: Crown Publishers, 1977.
Jones, John Bush. *Our Musicals, Ourselves*. Lebanon, NH: University Press of New England, 2003.
Jowitt, Debrah. *Jerome Robbins: His Life, His Theatre, His Dance*. New York: Simon & Schuster, 2004.
Kander, John, and Fred Ebb with Greg Lawrence. *Colored Lights: Forty Years of Words and Music, Show Biz, Collaboration, and All That Jazz*. New York: Faber & Faber, 2003.
Kantor, Michael, and Laurence Maslon. *Broadway: The American Musical*. New York: Bullfinch Press, 2004.
Kennedy, Michael Patrick, and John Muir. *Musicals*. Glasgow, UK: Harper Collins Publishers, 1997.
Kerr, Walter. *Journey to the Center of the Theatre*. New York: Alfred A. Knopf, 1979.
Kissel, Howard. *David Merrick: The Abominable Showman*. New York: Applause Books, 2000.
Lamb, Andrew. *150 Years of Popular Musical Theatre*. New Haven, CT: Yale University Press, 2000.
Lambert, Philip. *To Broadway, to Life: The Musical Theatre of Bock and Harnick*. New York: Oxford University Press, 2011.
Laufe, Abe. *Anatomy of a Hit: Long-Run Plays on Broadway: 1900 to the Present Day*. New York: Hawthorn, 1966.
Lawrence, Greg. *Dance with Demons: The Life of Jerome Robbins*. New York: G. P. Putnam's Sons, 2001.

Leiter, Samuel L. *The Great Directors*. New York: Facts on File, Inc., 1994.
Leopold, David. *Irving Berlin's Show Business*. New York: Harry N. Abrams, 2005.
Leve, James. *Kander and Ebb*. New Haven, CT: Yale University Press, 2009
Lindberg, Julianne. *Pal Joey: The History of a Heel*. New York: Oxford University Press, 2020.
Loesser, Susan. *Frank Loesser: A Most Remarkable Fella*. New York: Donald I. Fine, Inc., 1993.
Lynch, Richard Chigley. *Broadway on Record: A Directory of New York Cast Recordings of Musical Shows, 1931–1986*. Westport, CT: Greenwood Press, 1987.
Lynch, Richard Chigley. *Broadway, Movie, TV, and Studio Cast Musicals on Record*. Westport, CT: Greenwood Press, 1996.
Mandelbaum, Ken. *Not Since Carrie: 40 Years of Broadway Musical Flops*. New York: St. Martin's Press, 1991.
Marx, Samuel, and Jan Clayton. *Rodgers and Hart: Bewitched, Bothered and Bewildered*. New York: Putnam, 1976.
Mayhew, Robert (ed). *Ayn Rand's The Unconquered*. New York: Palgrave MacMillan, 2014.
McBrien, William. *Cole Porter*. New York: Vintage Press, 2011.
McMillan, Scott. *The Musical as Drama: A Study of the Principals and Conventions Behind Musical Shows from Kern to Sondheim*. Princeton, NJ: Princeton University Press, 2006.
Merman, Ethel, with George Eells. *Merman: An Autobiography*. New York: Simon & Schuster, 1978.
Mielziner, Jo. *Designing for the Theatre*. New York: Bramhall House, 1965.
Miller, Scott. *Rebels With Applause: Broadway's Groundbreaking Musicals*. Portsmouth, NH: Heinemann Drama, 2001.
Mordden, Ethan. *Rodgers and Hammerstein*. New York: Harry N. Abrams, 1992.
Mordden, Ethan. *Open a New Window: The Broadway Musical in the 1960s*. New York: Oxford Press, 2001.
Mordden, Ethan. *Coming Up Roses: The Broadway Musical in the 1950s*. New York: Oxford Press, 1998.
Mordden, Ethan. *Beautiful Mornin': The Broadway Musical in the 1940s*. New York: Oxford Press, 1999.
Mordden, Ethan. *Make Believe: The Broadway Musical in the 1920s*. New York: Palgrave Macmillan, 2001.
Mordden, Ethan. *The Happiest Corpse I've Ever Seen: The Last 25 Years of the Broadway Musical*. New York: Palgrave Macmillan, 2004.
Mordden, Ethan. *Sing for Your Supper: The Broadway Musical in the 1930s*. New York: Palgrave Macmillan, 2005.
Mordden, Ethan. *All That Glittered: The Golden Age of Drama on Broadway, 1919–1959*. New York: St. Martin's Press, 2007.
Morehouse, Ward. *Matinee Tomorrow: Fifty Years of Our Theatre* (2nd edn). New York: McGraw-Hill, 1949/2001.
Nathan, George Jean. *The Theatre Book of The Year, 1942–1943*. Cranbury, NJ: Associated University Presses, Inc., 1943/1971.
Nathan, George Jean. *The Theatre Book of The Year, 1943–1944*. Cranbury, NJ: Associated University Presses, Inc., 1944/1972.
Nathan, George Jean. *The Theatre Book of The Year, 1944–1945*. Cranbury, NJ: Associated University Presses, Inc., 1945/1972.
Nathan, George Jean. *The Theatre Book of The Year, 1945–1946*. Cranbury, NJ: Associated University Presses, Inc., 1946/1974.

Nathan, George Jean. *The Theatre Book of The Year, 1946-1947.* Cranbury, NJ: Associated University Presses, Inc., 1947/1975.
Nathan, George Jean. *The Theatre Book of The Year, 1947-1948.* Cranbury, NJ: Associated University Presses, Inc., 1948/1975.
Nolan, Frederick. *The Sound of their Music: The Story of Rodgers and Hammerstein.* (rev. edn). New York: Walker & Company, 2002.
Norton, Richard C. *A Chronology of American Musical Theatre* (3 vols). New York: Oxford University Press, 2002.
O'Brien, Jack. *Jack Be Nimble: The Accidental Education of an Intentional Director.* New York: Farrar, Straus & Giroux, 2013.
O'Hara, John. *Pal Joey.* New York: Popular Library, 1939/1968.
O'Hara, John, Richard Rodgers, and Lorenz Hart. *Pal Joey.* New York: Popular Library, 1952/1968.
Parker, Dorothy, and Kevin C. Fitzpatrick (ed). *Dorothy Parker: Complete Broadway, 1918-1923.* Bloomington, IN: iUniverse LLC, 2014.
Patinkin, Sheldon. *No Legs, No Jokes, No Chance: A History of the American Musical Theatre.* Evanston, IL: Northwestern University Press, 2008.
Pender, Rick. *The Stephen Sondheim Encyclopedia.* Lanham, MD: Rowman & Littlefield, 2021.
Portantier, Michael (ed). *The TheatreMania Guide to Musical Theatre Recordings.* New York: Backstage Books, 2004.
Prince, Harold. *Sense of Occasion.* Milwaukee: Applause Theatre and Cinema Books, 2017.
Raymond, Jack. *Show Music on Record, From the 1890s to the 1980s.* New York: Frederick Ungar Publishing Co., 1982.
Rich, Frank, and Lisa Aronson. *The Theatre of Boris Aronson.* New York: Alfred A. Knopf, 1987.
Rodgers, Richard. *Musical Stages: An Autobiography.* New York: Random House, 1975.
Sabinson, Harvey. *Darling, You Were Wonderful.* Washington, DC: H. Regnery, 1977.
Sainer, Arthur. *Zero Dances: A Biography of Zero Mostel.* New York: Limelight, 1998.
Schneider, Robert W., and Shannon Agnew (eds). *Fifty Key Stage Musicals.* New York: Routledge, 2022.
Secrest, Meryle. *Stephen Sondheim.* New York: Knopf, 1998.
Secrest, Meryle. *Somewhere for Me: A Biography of Richard Rodgers.* New York: Knopf, 2001.
Sheward, David. *It's a Hit: The Back Stage Book of Longest-Running Broadway Shows, 1884 to the Present.* New York: Watson-Guptill Publications-BPI Communications, Inc., 1994.
Singer, Barry. *Ever After: The Last Years of Musical Theatre and Beyond.* New York: Applause Theatre and Cinema Books, 2004.
Smith, Betty, and George Abbott, Dorothy Fields, Arthur Schwartz. *A Tree Grows in Brooklyn.* New York: Harper & Brothers, 1951.
Smith, Cecil, and Glenn Litton. *Musical Comedy in America.* (2nd edn.) New York: Theatre Arts Books, 1981.
Sondheim, Stephen. *Finishing the Hat: Collected Lyrics (1954-1981).* New York: Alfred A. Knopf, 2010.
Stewart, John. *Broadway Musicals, 1946-2000.* Jefferson, NC: McFarland, 2006.
Suskin, Steven. *Opening Night on Broadway: A Critical Quotebook of the Golden Era of the Musical Theatre.* New York: Schirmer Books, 1990.
Suskin, Steven. *More Opening Night on Broadway.* New York: Schirmer Books, 1997.

Suskin, Steven. *Second Act Trouble: Behind the Scenes at Broadway's Big Musical Bombs*. New York: Applause Books, 2006.
Swain, Joseph P. *The Broadway Musical: A Critical and Musical Survey*. New York: Oxford University Press, 1990.
Taylor, Theodore. *Jule: The Story of Composer Jule Styne*. New York: Random House, 1979.
Theatre World. 64 editions. Editors: Daniel C. Blum (1946–1964), John Willis (1964–2007), John Willis and Ben Hodges (2005–2008); New York: Norman McDonald Associate, 1946–1949; New York: Greenberg, Publisher, 1949–1957; Philadelphia: Chilton, 1957–1964; New York: Crown Publishers: 1964–1991; New York: Applause Theatre Book Publishers, 1991–2008.
Thelanen, Lawrence. *The Show Makers: Great Directors of the American Musical Theatre*. New York: Routledge, 2000.
Toohey, John L. *A History of the Pulitzer Prize Plays*. New York: The Citadel Press, 1967.
Vaill, Amanda. *Somewhere: The Life of Jerome Robbins*. New York: Broadway Books, 2006.
Wasson, Sam. *Fosse: The Biography*. Boston: Houghton Mifflin Harcourt, 2013.
Weidman, Jerome, and George Abbott, Sheldon Harnick, Jerry Bock. *Fiorello!* New York: Random House, 1960.
Weidman, Jerome, and George Abbott, Sheldon Harnick, Jerry Bock. *Tenderloin*. New York: Random House, 1961.
Wilmeth, Don. B., and Tice Miller (eds). *Cambridge Guide to American Theatre*. New York: Cambridge University Press, 1993.
Winkler, Kevin. *Big Deal: Bob Fosse and Dance in the American Theatre*. New York: Oxford University Press, 2019.
Zadan, Craig. *Sondheim & Co*. (2nd edn). New York: Harper & Row, 1986.

INDEX

Pages in **bold** type indicate a photograph.

7 1/2 Cents 148

Abbott, Edna Lewis 5–6, 12, 15, 17, 62–3
Abbott, George
   awards given to 151, 197, 225–6
   birth of 4
   childhood of 4–5
   daughter of 15, 63, 180
   death of 200
   education of 5–6
   in rehearsal with 1–3
   marriages of 3, 12, 80, 197
   parents of 4–5
   street named after 179
   tally of hits and flops 202–3
   television 138
   theatre named after 179
Abbott, Joy Valderrama 197, 201
Abbott, Judith 15, 63, 180
Abel, Walter 36
Abie's Irish Rose 153
About Face 53
Abrams, Leon 36
Act One 3
Adams, Edith 143–4
Adams, Samuel Hopkins 136
Adler, Richard 103, 147–8, 150, 152, 153, 155, 157, 175, 187–9, 194, 200, 203
Agatha Sue, I Love You 180
Albert, Eddie 52–3, 71, 73
Albertson, Jack 52–3
Aldrich Family, The 57
Aldrich, Richard 116, 147–52
Alexander, Cris 104

Alice Adams 52
All Quiet on the Western Front 61–2, **88**
All that Glitters 54–5
Allegro 145
Allen, Arthur 9
Allyson, June, 78, **93**
Altman, Richard 137
Alton, Robert 77, 124, 141, 146–7
Americana 113
Ames, Robert 30
Anastasia 177
Anastasia Game, The 179
Anders, Glenn 16, 83
Anderson, John 58
Anderson, John Murray 68–9
Anderson, Judith 26–7
Anderson, Leroy 143
Anderson, Maxwell 16, 17, 23, 61
Andreas, Christine 196–7
Andrews, Nancy 114
Angel Island 38–9, 55
Angelus, Muriel 73
Angus, Mrs. Bernie 38–9
Anna Christie 43, 129–30
Annie Get Your Gun 139, 141
Anya 177–9
Arlen, Harold 32
Arlen, Richard 62
Arling, Joyce 33, 48, 50
Arnaz, Desi 76–7
Aronson, Boris 33, 41, 48–9
Arthur, Jean 60, 61
Ashburn, Carroll 38
Ashley, Elizabeth 159–60

Astaire, Fred 69
Astar, Ben 152
Aston, Frank 138
Atkinson, Brooks 27, 28, 30, 31, 32, 33, 36, 38, 39, 49, 51, 54, 58, 79, 117, 124–5, 146, 164
Atwill, Lester 174
Auntie Mame 118
Ayers, Lemuel 142
Ayres, Lew 61, **88**

Bacon, Frank 12
Bacon, Lloyd 51
Bailey, Pearl 186
Baker, George Pierce 6, 26, 80
Baker, Josephine 172
Balanchine, George 70–1, 75, 91, 112, 140, 147, 153, 195–6
Baldwin, Alec 47
Ball, Lucille 77, 78
Ballantyne, Paul 41
Ballard, Kaye 145
Banjo Eyes 50
Bankhead, Tallulah 64–5
Baragwanath, John 55
Barefoot Boy with Cheek 107–8
Barer, Marshall 161–3
Barnes, Clive 181, 185, 186, 187, 194
Barnes, Howard 109
Barrat, Robert 36
Barrere, Jean 152
Barrymore, Ethel 10
Barrymore, John 10, 47
Barrymore, Lionel 37
Battles, John 104
Beahan, Charles 31
Beal, Royal 50–1
Bean, Orson **100**, 161
Beat the Band 78–9
Beaton, Cecil 137
Beggar's Holiday 126–7
Beggar's Opera, The 126
Begley, Ed 83
Behrman, S. N. 41
Belasco, David 13–14, 22, 35, 45
Belita 156
Bell, Ann 180
Bell, James 36, 38, 41
Beloin, Edmund 117

Benchley, Robert 32, 39, 49, 55, 75
Bennett, Joan 31
Bennett, Linda 145
Bennett, Michael 181
Bennett, Richard 31
Bennett, Tony 150
Benny, Jack 44
Bergasse, Joshua 106
Bergreen, Laurence 140
Berkeley, Busby 172
Berle, Milton 57, 166, 200
Berlin, Irving 95, 103, 139–41, 143
Berlind, Roger 187
Bernstein, Elmer 181
Bernstein, Leonard 103–6, 142–4, 197
Best Foot Forward 77–8, **93**, 105, 107, 175
Besterman, Doug 199
Beyond the Horizon 43
Bickford, Charles 26, 30
Bigley, Isabel 145
Billion Dollar Baby 106–7
Billy Rose's Jumbo 47, 58, 67–9, **90**
Birch, Patricia 188
Bishops Candlesticks, The 60
Bissell, Richard 148–9, 152
Black Crook, The 154
Blane, Ralph 77–8
Bless You, Sister 29–30
Blitzstein, Marc 126
Blondell, Joan 50
Blumenkrantz, Jeff **102**
Blyden, Larry 168
Bobrick, Sam 186
Bock, Jerry 99, 132–4, 135–6
Body Beautiful, The 133
Bogart, Humphrey 24
Boland, Mary 10
Bolger, Ray 70–1, **91, 95**, 103, 111, 113, 176, 195
Bolin, Shannon 153
Bolton, Guy 177
Bolton, Lois 116
Booth, Shirley 48–9, **90, 96**, 127–9
Borman, Gerald 18
Boretz, Allen 53
Borodin, Alexandre 178
Borough, Margaret 16
Bosley, Tom **99**, 133–4, 182–3
Bova, Joe **99**, 162

Bow, Clara 60, 62
Bowab, John 185
Bowers, Kenneth **93**
Boy Meets Girl 50–1, 117
Boys From Syracuse, The 73–6, **92**, 111, 165–6, 187–8
Bracken, Eddie 53, 57, 76–7
Brackett, Charles 26, 29, 31, 64
Brady, Alice 10, 15–16, 29–30
Brand, Oscar 182
Braunagel, Don 200
Brecher, Irving 82
Brecht, Bertolt 126
Brent, Evelyn 60
Bridgers, Ann Preston 15, 28
Briggs, Matt 38, 46
Brisson, Frederick 130
Britton, Sherry 118
Broadway 24–6, 36, 43, 60, 197–9
Broken Wing, The 14, 15
Bron, Heywood 14
Brooks, George S. 27
Brooks, Louise 32, 60
Brother Rat 51–3
Brother Rat and a Baby 53
Brown, Charles D. 33
Brown, John Mason 56, 82
Brown Sugar 39, 55
Brown, Zach 195
Bruce, Carol 125
Bryan-Allen, Martha 18
Buchman, Harold 85
Buck, Gene 31
Buck, Inez 11
Buckner, Robert 39
Burnet, Dana 27, 63
Burnett, Carol **99**, 103, 161–5, 171–4, 203
Burns, David **100**, 106, 141, 165–7, 176
Burr, Courtney 33, 35
Butler, David 113
Buttons, Red 107, 183
Buzzell, Edward 78

Cabalero, Roxann 189
Cabaret 138, 176
Cabot, Elliot 28
Cagney, James 24, 51
Cahn, Sammy 108–9
Cain, Robert 31

Calhern, Louis 63
Call Me Madam **95**, 139–41, 176
Call on Kuprin, A 118
Calleia, Joseph Spurin 14
Calloway, Cab 152, 194
Cannon, Maureen 77
Carlson, Richard 77
Carlton, Claire 32
Carlyle, Richard 116
Carney, Art 159–60
Carnival Man, The 60
Carpenter, Constance 190
Carr, Lawrence 185
Carradine, John **100**, 165–6
Carroll, Nancy 63
Carson, Doris 70
Carter, Arthur 117
Caryll, Ivan 10
Case, Allen 162
Cass, Peggy 114
Cassidy, Jack 172–3
Casto, Jean 117
Cats 197
Caubaye, Suzanne 30
Caulfield, Joan 82, **93**
Cerf, Bennett 3
Chadman, Christopher 125
Champion, Gower 109, 136
Channing, Carol 142, 144, 172
Channing, Stockard 125
Chapman, John (critic) 105, 107, 128, 130, 142, 156, 173
Chapman, John (playwright) 187
Charades 138
Charley's Aunt 95, 111
Chase, Ilka 32
Cheat, The 64–5
Chicago 26–7
Chisholm, Robert 106
Chodorov, Jerome 143–4
Church, George **91**
Churchill, Burton 64
Cirker & Robbins 46
Clark, Bobby 156
Clark, Dane 117
Clark, Dort 85
Clark, Ron 186
Clark, Wallis 15
Clement, Josephine 7

Clork, Harry 57
Coe, George 181
Cohan, George M. 10, 23, 44, 58
Cohn, Harry 143–4
Colbert, Claudette 62, 63–4
Cole, Jack 167
Coleman, Robert 110, 141, 146, 151, 168
Colt, Alvin 94
Comden, Betty 103–7, 142–4, 171–2
Come Back, Little Sheba 128
Comedy of Errors, The 73–5, 111, 165–6, 188
Congdon, James 181
Compton, Francis 116
Connelly, Marc 14–15
Connick, Harry, Jr. 152
Conte, Nicholas 81
Cooney, Ray 187
Cooper, Horace 111, 113
Cooper, Jackie 57
Copeland, Joan 125
Coquette 15, 28–30, 43, 60
Corbett, William 37
Corbin, John 15, 16
Costa, Natalie 190
Costello, Diosa 76
Coulter, Kay 152
Cowan, Jerome 33, 50–1
Coward, Noel 3
Cox, Catherine 188
Craig, Helen 40–1
Craig, James 17
Crandall, Edward 32
Crane, William H. 10
Crawford, Joan 60
Crews, Laura Hope 10
Cromer, James 56
Cromwell, John 30
Crosby, Bing 140
Crosby, Gary 140
Crouse, Russel 139
Crume, Camilla 23
Curtis, Margaret 84

Da Silva, Howard 133–4
Daab, Hyatt 30
Daddies 13–14
Damn Yankees **98**, **102**, 130, 147, 153–7, 176, 187, 199–200

Damon, Cathryn 174
Dancer, The 115–16
Daniels, Danny 106
Dano, Royal 116
Darin, Bobby 137
Davies, Brian 166
Davis, Owen 17
Davis, Sammy, Jr. 184
Dawson, Hal K. 33
Dawson, Mark 108, 134
Day, Doris 69, 130, 152
de Mille, Agnes 197
De Santis, Joe 117
Dee, Sylvia 107
DeLeo, Don 106
DeMille, Cecil B. 62, 64
Desire Under the Elms 43
Dickey, Paul 11, 14
Dinner at Eight 49
Dishy, Bob **101**, 174
Dix, Tommy 78
Dixon, Jean 36
Dolin, Anton 115
Donen, Stanley 106, 152, 156
Douglas, Gilbert 15
Douglas, Larry 152
Douglass, Stephen **98**, 153
Dowling, Eddie 83
Downe, Edward R. 187
Drake, Alfred 126
Drew, John 10
Drink to Me Only 118, 179
Drums Begin, The 36–7
du Bois, Raoul Pene 97
Duggan, Henry 14
Dulcy 14–15, 28
Duncan, Augustin 16–17, 22
Dunning, Philip 24–5, 32, 33, 35–6, 37, 38, 45, 197
Dunstan, Cliff 53
Durante, Jimmy 68–9

Eagels, Jeanne 13–14, 26
Ebb, Fred 27, 101, 103, 174–7, 203
Eckart, William and Jean 99, 134, 152, 155, 160–1, 162–4, 172–3, 175, 183, 185–8
Edelman, Maurice 118
Edens, Roger 106

Edmonds, Beulah E. 39
Education of H*Y*M*A*N K*A*P*L*A*N, The 182–4
Einhorn, Abe 180
Ellington, Duke 126, 187
Ellis, Edward 26
Elzy, Ruby 39
Emery, John 40
Emick, Jarrod 200
Emmerson, Dorothy 186
Endgame 119
England, George 179
England, Paul 111
English, Illia 190
Entertainers, The 173
Ephron, Nora 160
Ephron, Phoebe and Henry 159
Eric, Elspeth 32, 85
Ernst, Leila 122
Erskine, Marilyn 39
Erwin, Trudi 77, 125
Ethier, Alphonz 14
Evans, Maurice 136
Eythe, William 141–2

Fabray, Nanette 108
Fade Out – Fade In 171–4
Fairbanks, Douglas, 10
Fall Guy, The 15, 21–3, 43, 87, 187
Fancy Free 103–4
Farren, Jack 183
Faulkner, Virginia 116
Faye, Joey 108
February Hill 39
Fehlhaber, Fred 177
Feigay, Paul 104
Ferguson, Elsie 10
Ferrer, José 47, 52–3
Feuer, Cy 111
Ffolks, David 95
Fiddler on the Roof 184
Field, Betty 39, 40, 56
Field, Salisbury 15
Field, Sylvia 24
Fields, Dorothy 129, 143
Fields, Herbert 143
Fields, Joseph 143–4
Fig Leaves Are Falling, The 184–6
Fillmore, Clyde 76

Finklehoffe, Fred F. 51–2
Fiorello! **99**, 132–6, 139, 176
Fitz, Kathleen 52
Flatt, Ernest 172
Flint, Helen 31, 116
Flora, the Red Menace **101**, 174–7, 203
Flournoy, Richard 33
Fontanne, Lynn 14–15
Forbes, Ralph 84
Forbes-Robertson, J. 10
Ford, Hugh 25
Ford, Paul **100**, 161, 194
Forrest, George 178–9
Forrerst, Undine 118
Forsythe, John 116
Fort, Garrett 31
Fosse, Bob 98, 103, 125, 130, 144, 150–2, 154–6, 194, 197, 200
Four Walls 27–8, 60
Fowler, Gene 32
Foxx, Redd 186
Foy, Eddie, Jr. 149
Francis, Arlene 55
Frankenstein 190, 192
Frankie **101**, 190–2
Frawley, William 46
Freed, Arthur 78, 104–6
French, Valerie 180
Friderici, Barbara 18
Friebus, Florida 39
Friml, Rudolf 10
Front Page, The 30, 45–6
Fryer, Robert 127, 142–3
Fuller, Dean 162
Funny Girl 172–3
Funny Thing Happened on the Way to the Forum, A **100**, 161, 165–8, 176, 187, 202
Funt, Julian 115

Gabriel, Gilbert 52
Gaige, Crosby 25
Gallagher, Helen 114, 176
Garber, Victor 200
Garde, Betty 39, 180
Gardner, Helen 55
Garland, Judy 175
Garland, Robert 109
Garner, Rex 187

Garrett, Betty 106, 144
Garrick Gaieties, The 144
Garry Moore Show, The 163
Garson, Henry 117
Gaver, Jack 171
Gay, John 126
Gaynor, Mitzi 154
Gear, Luella 70
Gelbart, Larry 165-7
Gennaro, Peter 134
Gentlemen of the Press 30
George, Grace 10
Gershwin, George 103
Gershwin, Ira 103
Gest, Morris 45
Get Away, Old Man 83-4
Geva, Tamara 70, **91**
Gibbs, Wolcott 36, 38, 71, 78, 83, 85, 116, 124
Gilbert, John 60
Gilford, Jack 49, **100**, 118, 162-3, 165-6, 168, 194
Gillette, Priscilla 141
Ginnes, Abram S. 118
Giradot, Etienne 46
Gish, Lillian 178-9
Gleason, James 15, 21-2, 87
Gleckler, Robert 24, 30, 32, 36, 62
Glickman, Will 116
Goddard, Charles W. 11, 14
Goff, Charles 190
Goldberg, Whoopie 168
Golden Apple, The 155
Golden, John 12, 23, 35
Goldman, William 184, 202
Goldsmith, Clifford 55, 57
Goldwyn, Samuel 201
Good, Jack 163
Goodbye in the Night 41
Gordon, Max 143
Gorki, Maxim 84
Gorme, Eydie 174-5
Gorney, Jay 113
Gottfried, Martin 184, 185, 195
Gould, Morton 106
Goulston, André 183
Gow, Ronald 37
Grafton, Gloria 68
Graham, Ronald 73

Grand Hotel 47
Great Magoo, The 32-3
Green, Adolph 103-7, 142-4, 171-2
Green, Johnny 79
Green, Mitzi 106
Greenberg, Richard 125
Greenwood, Charlotte 142
Greer, Jo Ann 125
Greig, Edvard 178
Grey, Joel 167
Griffith, Hugh 136
Griffith, Raymond **88**
Griffith, Robert E. 118, 130, 132-3, 135-6, 148, 150, 156, 159, 203
Grumpy 10
Guernsey, Otis L. 128
Gussow, Mel 192
Guys and Dolls 49
Gypsy 147, 166

Hagen, Uta 117-18
Hague, Albert 185
Hair 138
Halfway to Heaven 61
Hall, Dorothy 33, 35
Hall, Ellen 82
Hall, George 114
Hall, Willis 180
Halliday, David 188
Halliday, Heller 119
Halton, Charles 26
Hamilton, John F. 16-17
Hamlet 56, 114
Hammerstein, Oscar 141, 145-7
Hammond, Percy 15, 22, 26, 46
Haney, Carol 149, 176
Hanley, Ellen 107, 134
Harburg, E. Y. 32, 113
Harding, June 160
Harnick, Sheldon 99, 103, 132-4, 135-6
Happy New Year 195
Harris, Andrew B. 155, 163
Harris, Barbara 167
Harris, Henry B. 11
Harris, J. T. 190
Harris, Jed 24-5, 27, 28-9, 35, 45
Harris, Joe 163
Harris, Joseph 185
Harris, Sam H. 18, 26, 53

Harris, William, Jr. 11
Harris, William, Sr. 11
Hart, Bret 15
Hart, Lorenz 67–9, 73, 74–5, 76–8, 92, 122–5
Hart, Moss 3
Hart, Teddy 48–50, 53, 57, 73–4
Hart, Walter 39
Hartman, Paul 118, 152
Harvey, Georgette 39
Hatcher, Hughes 16–17
Hayes, Bill 145
Hayes, Helen 28–9, 119–20
Haynes, Tiger 172
Hayward, Leland 139, 143
Hayworth, Rita 125
Hazard, Lawrence 33
Head of the Family, The 6
Heat Lightning 36
Heche, Ann 47
Hecht, Ben 32, 45–6, 50, 68, 89
Heckart, Eileen 117
Heineman, Eda 26
Hell-bent fer Heaven 16–17
Hello, Dolly! 172–3
Help Stamp Out Marriage 180, 187
Henderson, Dale 60
Henderson, Florence 172
Henrietta 10
Herbert, F. Hugh 82
Herbert, Victor 10
Hernandez, Juan 39
Hewes, Henry 161
Hewett, Christopher 188
Higgins, Joel 188
High Button Shoes **94**, 108–9
High Jinks 10
Highland Fling, A 84–5
Hills of Peril 60
Hobble, John L. 13
Hogarth, Leona 23
Holgate, Ronald 166
Holliday, Judy 142
Hollywood, Daniel 161
Holm, Hanya 142
Holm, John Cecil 47–9, 77–8, 193
Holmes, Phillips 63
Holt, Will 187–8
Holy Terror, A 23, 60

Honor Bright 52
Hoover, J. Edgar 209
Horne, Lena 126
Horwitt, Arnold B. 143
Houseman, John 126
How Now, Dow Jones 176, 181–2
Huey, Richard 39
Hugh Martin Show, The 138
Hughes, Carol 50
Hughes, Elinor 176
Hugo, Victor 60
Hull, Josephine 31
Hunt, Ezra 57
Hunter, Tab 156
Hurlbut, Gladys 40
Husmann, Ron 137
Huston, Martin 186
Huston, Walter 37, 60

I Can Get It for You Wholesale 133
I Married an Angel 124
Ibsen, Henrik 29
Imposter, The 60
In Any Language 117
Inherit the Wind 118
Irving, George S. 178, 195
Is Zat So? 21
It Takes Two 116

Jacobi, Lou 172, 186
Jackson, Thomas 24
Jaffe, Sam 31
Jagger, Dean 40
Jarnegan 31
Jason 81–2
Jbara, Gregory **102**
Jeanmarie, Zizi 154
Jenkins, Allen 50
Jerome Robbins' Broadway 109
John Brown 37
Johns, Florence 23
Johnson, Albert 90
Johnston, Johnny **96**, 127
Johnston, Moffat 45
Jones, Anne 162
Jongeyans, George 141
Joslyn, Allyn 50–1, 55
Jumbo 47, 58, 67–9, **90**

Kahn, Madeline 181
Kander, John 27, 101, 103, 174–7, 203
Kanin, Garson 49, 53
Kaufman, George S. 14–15, 58
Kay, Hershy 188
Kaye, Judy 152
Kean, Jane 152
Keith, Robert 83
Keith-Johnston, Colin 115
Kelly, Dennis 200
Kelly, Gene 78, **92**, 103, 106, 122, 124–5
Kelly, George 17
Kelly, Paul 32
Kermoyan, Michael 178–9
Kern, Jerome 103
Kerr, Jean 113–14
Kerr, Walter 113–14, 135, 144, 151, 156, 160, 176, 179, 180, 182
Key, Leonard 125
Kidd, Michael 113
Kilbride, Percy 31, 36
Kill that Story 37–8
Kimmins, Kenneth 185
King and I, The 146
King, John Michael 178
King, Joseph 32
King, Martin Luther 184
Kipness, Joseph 108, 113
Kismet 178
Kiss and Tell 82–3, 85, **93**
Kiss Me, Kate 51, 141, 142
Kissel, Howard 188
Klaw, Alonso 16–17
Klugman, Jack 49, 185
Knox, Alexander 81
Kobart, Ruth 166
Kolk, Scott 64
Kollmar, Richard 76
Kramer, Mimi 198
Krawford, Gary 182
Krasna, Norman 32
Kremb, Felix 27
Kronenberger, Louis 105, 110, 119, 126, 153
Kwamina 194

Ladies Money 33
LaGuardia, Fiorello 132–5
LaGuardia, Marie 133

Laire, Judson 55
Lambert, Philip 136
Lane, Burton 143
Lane, Nathan 168
Lane, Rosemary 77, **93**
Lang, Harold 110, 124
Lang, Walter 141
Langford, Frances 77
Lansbury, Angela 172
Lardner, John 118
Larrimore, Francine 26
Latessa, Dick **102**
Latouche, John 104, 126
Lauren, S. K. 31
Lawford, Betty 64
Lawrence, Jane 111
Lawrence, Jerome 109, 118
Lawrence, Megan 152
Lawrence, Reginald 142
Lawson, John Howard 18
Lawson, Lee 180
Layton, Joe 99, 137, 164
Lazybones 17–18
Leave It to Me! 125
Lee, Canada 39
Lee, Lois 108
Lee, Robert E. 109, 118
Leigh, Carolyn 181
Leigh, Janet 144
Leiter, Samuel L. 204
Lemmon, Jack 144
Leontovich, Eugenie 41, 45, 47, **89**, 118
Leporska, Zoya 194
Lerner, Alan Jay 103
LeRoy, Hal 76–7
LeRoy, Mervyn 50
Les Misérables 60
Leslie, Bethel 85, 116
Lester, Jerry 79
Lester, Richard 168
Let It Ride! 50
Levene, Sam 48–50, 53, **90**, 193
Lewis, Jerry 200
Lewis, Milton 115
Lewis, Tom 116
Lewis, Vicki 200
Life with Father 58
Lightnin' 12–13, 18
Lillie, Beatrice 172

Lilly Turner 35–6
Lincoln, Victoria 39
Linden, Eric 33
Linden, Hal 49, 152, 183, 194
Lindfors, Viveca 125
Lindsay, Howard 139–40
Lindsay, John 183
Lindsey-Nassif, Robert 189–90, 197–9
Lippman, Sidney 107
Lister, Walter B. 27
Litel, John 36
Little Café, The 10
Little Night Music, A 194
Lloyd-Webber, Andrew 191
Loeb, Philip 18, 53
Loesser, Frank 103, 111, 113, 148
Loewe, Frederick 103
Logan, Ella 143
Lombard, Carole 47
Long, Arthur Sumner 160
Longstreet, Stephen 108
Look Ma, I'm Dancin' 109–10, 179
Louder, Please 32, 43
Loudon, Dorothy 49, 185, 194
Louise, Tina 172
Louisiana Purchase 132, 139
Love 'Em and Leave 'Em 23–4, 43, 60
Love Is Just Around the Corner 174
Lowry, Emily 36, 38
Luck of Roaring Camp, The 15
Lukas, Paul 61, 140
Lundborg, Arne 50
Lyndeck, Edmund 189
Lynn, Jeffrey 117, 118
Lynn, William 48, **90**, 193
Lynne, Gillian 181

MacArthur, Charles 45–6, 50, 68, 89
McBride, Donald 53
McCarton, John 138, 180
McCarthy, Joe 174, 200
McCarthy, W. J. 68
McCauley, Jack 108
McClelland, Charles 50
McClain, John 131, 142, 151, 168
McClelland, Kay 145
McClintic, Guthrie 18, 22
MacColl, James 50
McCormick, Myron 32

McCracken, Joan 106, 145
MacDonald, Donald 23
MacDonald, Jet 126
MacDonald, Kyle 114
McGiver, John 118
McGrath, Paul 40
McHugh, Frank 50
Mack & Mabel 109
Mack, Charles 60
Mack, Johnny 79
McKean, Michael 152
McKeever, Jaquelyn 145
McKenny, Ruth 142
MacLaine, Shirley **97**
McLerie, Allyn Ann 111, 113
MacMahon, Horace **90**
McMein, Neysa 80
McNair, Barbara 152, 194
MacPherson, Aimee Semple 29
McQueen, Butterfly 39
McRae, Bruce 13
MacRae, Gordon 53
Madden, Harry 38
Mailbaum, Richard 57
Mandelbaum, Ken 178, 184
Manslaughter 62
Mantello, Joe 125, 197
Mantle, Burns 17, 22, 37, 56, 77
March, Alexander 110
March, Fredric 62, 64
Marion, George, Jr. 76, 79
Makarova, Natalia 176, 195–7
Marker, Preshy 166
Marks, Joe E. 176
Marlowe, Hugh 77–8, 116
Marshall, Armina 31
Marshall, Herbert 64
Marshall, Kathleen 145, 152, 165
Marshall, Rob 200
Martin, Eliot 161
Martin, Ernest H. 111
Martin, Hugh 77–8, 109–10, 138
Martin, Mary 119–20, 172
Martin, Owen 32, 41
Martins, Peter 195
Marx Brothers 54, 201
Mason, Marlyn 181–2
Mason, Mary 41
Mathis, Sherry 188

Matthau, Walter 117
Matthews, Francis 180
Maude, Cyril 10
Maude-Roxby, Roddy 180
Maurette, Marcelle 177
May, Marty 77
Mayer, Jerome 40–1
Me and Juliet 145–7
Mears, Martha 78
Meehan, John 29–30
Meek, Donald 23–4
Meeker, Ralph 150
Meet Me in St. Louis 78
Meisner, Sanford 18
Mellow, Stephen 183
Merman, Ethel **95**, 140–1, 176
Merrick, David 136, 166, 180–2
Merrill, Beth 16
Merrill, Bob 130–1
Merrill, Dina 195
Mesta, Peal 139
Metaxa, Georges 63
Meyerberg, Michael 83
Middleman, Arnold 192
Mielziner, Jo 71–2, 74, 77, 92, 124, 128, 146–7
Milestone, Lewis 61
Miller, Alice Duer 62
Miller, Ann 77, 106
Miller, Benjamin 107
Miller, Sharron 152, 194
Miller, Susan 79
Miller, Wynne 137
Millholland, Charles Bruce 45
Mills, Edwin 15
Miner, Worthington 71
Minkus, Barbara 183
Minnelli, Liza 78, **101**, 103, 174–7, 203
Minnelli, Vincente 175
Minot, Anna 117
Miracle Worker, The 132
Misleading Lady, The 11–12, 14
Miss Liberty 140
Mitchell, Millard 48–9, 57
Mitty, Nomi 127
Moeller, Philip 18, 22
Monica, Corbett 180
Monks,. John, Jr., 51–2
Monterey, Carlotta 130

Moon Over Buffalo 174
Moore, Crista 145
Moran, George 60
Mordden, Ethan 104, 146, 161, 177, 204
Morehouse, Ward 30, 113
Morgan, Ralph 12
Morris, David 70
Morris, William E. 31
Morrow, Doretta 111
Mortimer, Henry 21
Mostel, Zero **100**, 126, 165–8, 176
Mr. Cooper's Left Hand 85
Mrs. Gibbon's Boys 116–17
Mullen, Margaret 38
Munez, Richard 152
Muni, Paul 28
Munshin, Jules 106, 185
Murdock, Anna 60
Murphy, Donna 145
Murphy, George 54
Murray, Arthur 200
Murray, Don 119
Murray, John 53
Murray, Wynn 73
Music Is 187–9, 203
Musser, Tharon 164
Musson, Bennet 23
My Fair Lady 184, 196
My Sin 64
My Sister Eileen 143
My Three Angels 51

Nadel, Norman 160, 173, 175, 179
Napolitano, Peter 189
Nassau, Paul 182
Nathan, George Jean 79–80, 82, 83, 84–5, 107, 116, 126
Nelson, Barry 185
Nemetz, Lenora 152
Nesor, Al 49, 194
Neuwirth, Bebe 200
Never Too Late **100**, 159, 160–1, 202
New Girl in Town 129–32, 139, 176
New Henrietta, The 10
Nichols, Beatrice 12
Nichols, Lewis 84, 116
Nichols, Mike 197
Night of January 16th 41
Nissenson, Gloria **101**, 191

Norman, Is that You? 186
Not Now, Darling 187
Novak, Kim 125
Novis, Donald 68
Nugent, Eddie 57
Number, The 117
Nye, Louis (Lewis) 114
Nype, Russell **95**, 140–1, 176

O'Brien, Jack 199–200
O'Brien, Pat 51
O'Connor, Donald 141
Oenslager, Donald 38
Of Thee I Sing 132, 135
O'Hara, Jenny 185
O'Hara, John 121–5
O'Hara, Kelli 152
Ohio Lady, The 12
Oklahoma! 80, 105, 107, 121, 141
Oliver, Edna May 60
O'Malley, Muriel 114
On the Town **94**, 103–6, 107, 109, 121, 132, 142, 164, 179
On the Twentieth Century 47
On Your Toes 2, 67, 68, 69–73, 75, **91**, 111, 121, 152–3, 176, 189, 195–7
Once Upon a Mattress **99**, 161–5, 172
One Shoe Off 85
O'Neill, Eugene 6, 43, 129–31
O'Shaughnessy, John 73
Osato, Sono 104–5
Osterman, Lester 171, 173
O'Sullivan, Maureen **100**, 161
Out of This World 141–2

Page Miss Glory 33
Paige, Janis **97**, 148
Pajama Game, The **97**, 118, 130, 147–52, 153, 176, 187, 194–5
Pal Joey 58, **92**, 121–6, 152, 162, 195
Pallette, Eugene 62
Palmer,. Byron 111
Papp, Joseph 189
Paramore, Edward E. Jr., 30
Parker, Dorothy 14, 15
Parker, Sarah Jessica 164
Parrish, Judith 82
Passing Show, The 10
Patrick, Jerome 15

Patterson, Dick 172
Pearson, Beatrice 83
Pemberton, Brock 16, 22
Penman, Lea 38, 56
Penn, Arthur 132–3, 181
Perkins, Osgood 27
Perry, Lawrence 79
Peters, Roger 197
Petina, Irra 178–9
Petrified Forest, The 36
Phantom of the Opera, The 191
Phillips, Edwin 31–2
Philson, Betty 38
Pichel, Irving 64
Pickford, Mary 60
Plautus 165
Play On 187
Plummer, Inez 15
Poppa 31, 43
Porter, Cole 73, 124, 141–2, 143
Poston, Tom 118
Potash and Perlmutter 10
Powell, David 60
Power, Hartley 21
Powers, Tom 40
Price, Lonny 198
Primrose Path, The 39–40
Prince, Harold 103, 118–19, 130–1, 132–3, 135–8, 148, 150–1, 159–60, 166–7, 174–7, 187, 189–90, 192, 197–9, 201, 203, 205
Princess and the Pea, The 161–2
Pringle, Jessie 12, 156
Prinz, LeRoy 77
Prinz, Rosemary 49, 194
Proser, Monte 108
Processional 18–19
Prud'homme, Cameron 131

Queen's Enemies, The 12
Quick, George 163

Rachmaninoff, Sergei 178
Rae, Charlotte 150
Rain 26
Raitt, John **97**, 148, 150
Rand, Ayn 40–1
Randall, Tony 49
Rando, John 106

Raphaelson, Samson 81
Rasco, Burton 105, 107
Ratoff, Gregory **89**
Ray, Nicholas 126
Raye, Martha 69, 163
Redfield, William (Billy) 85, 107, 141–2
Reed, Florence 119
Reid, Frances 84
Remarque, Erich Maria 61
*Return of H*Y*M*A*N K*A*P*L*A*N, The* 182
Rich, Frank 196
Richards, Lloyd 197
Ring Two 40
Ringside 30
Risch, Matthew 125
Riskin, Robert 29–30
Ritter, Thelma 131, 176
Rizzo, Frank 129
Robbins, Jerome 94, 103–4, 106–7, 109–10, 140, 142, 147, 150, 165–8, 201
Roberts, Anthony 181–2
Roberts, Roy 46, **89**
Robinson, Edward G. 24
Rodgers, Eileen 137
Rodgers, Mary 161–3
Rodgers, Richard 67–9, 71, 73–5, 76–7, 78, 92, 122, 124–5, 141, 145–7, 162
Rogers, Charles "Buddy" 61
Rogers, Gil 190
Rogers, Ginger 27
Rogers, Jamie, 183
Rogers, Will 44
Roman Holiday 175
Romeo and Juliet 68
Room Service 53–4, 117
Roos, Casper 190
Roosevelt, Eleanor 200
Rose, Billy 32, 67–9, 83
Ross, Anthony 116
Ross, Jerry 103, 147–52, 153, 155, 157
Rosten, Leo 182–4
Rothschilds, The 194
Rounseville, Robert 163
Roxie Hart 27
Russell, John 62
Russell, Robert 174
Russell, Rosalind **97**, 143–5, 176

Sabin, David 188
Sabinson, Harvey 173
Saddler, Donald 97, **101**, 143, 189–92, 195, 197
Saint Subber, Arnold 142
Saltzman, Avery 152
Sameth, Martin 107
Saroyan, William 82, 83–4, 124
Saturday Night Kid, The 60
Savo, Jimmy 73–4
Say, Darling 152
Schools, Victoria **93**
Schmidt, Douglas W. 199
Schneider, Alan 119
Schrank, Joseph 33
Schwartz, Arthur 129
Scott, Martha 116, 117
Scott, Sir Walter 4
Sea God, The 62
Seal, Elizabeth 156
Secrets of a Secretary 63–4
See My Lawyer 57–8
Seff, Manuel 82
Segal, Vivienne 122, 124–5
Seven Brides for Seven Brothers 195
Seven Keys to Baldpate 10
Shafer, Bob 153
Shannon, Frank 16
Sharaff, Irene 74, 92
Shea, Jere 200
Sheldon, Ned 6
Shelley, Mary 190–1
Shepard, Karen 178
Stephens, Linda 200
Sheppard, John R., Jr. 126
Sherman, Allan 184–5
Sherman, Hiram 176, 181
Sherwood, Henry 46
Sherwood, Robert 36
Shevelove, Burt 165–8
Sheward, David 24
Show-Off, The 17
Shubert Brothers 21, 70, 74
Shulman, Max 107, 181
Siegel, Sol C. 141
Silvers, Phil 108–9, 157, 166, 168
Simon, John 200
Simpson, Kenneth 55
Sinatra, Frank 54, 106, 125

Sinclair, Arthur 68
Sinclair, Mary 80
Singin' in the Rain 172
Sisters Like Them Handsome, The 108
Skin of Our Teeth, The 119–29
Sloan, Mimi 183
Sloan, Robert R. 33
Sloane, Robert 36
Small Miracle 32–3
Smith, Betty 127
Smith, Oliver 94, 104, 126
Smith, Rollin 126
Smith, Winchell 12, 23
Snafu 85
So Proudly We Hail 52
Solomon, Louis 85
Some Baby 12
Something for the Boys 80
Sondheim, Stephen 100, 103, 166–8, 192
Song of Norway 178
South Pacific 135
Spewack, Bella and Sam 31, 50–1
Spialek, Hans 195
Spread Eagle 27
Spurin-Celleia, Joseph 32
Stanislavski, Konstantin 47
Stanley, Pat 134, 152
Stanton, Paul 12
Stapleton, Maureen 186
State of the Union 139
Steam, Eloise 24
Stein, Joseph 116
Step Lively 54
Stephens, Harvey 64
Stephens, Linda 200
Stewart, James 33
Stimac, Anthony J. 190
Stolen Heaven 63
Stone, Ezra 55–7
Stone, Lewis 11
Stone, Sid 193
Stowe, Harriet Beecher 38
Strasberg, Lee 18
Stratton, Gil, Jr. 77
Streisand, Barbra 172, 174–5
Stritch, Elaine 145, 152
Stroman, Susan 197
Strong, Austin 12
Styne, Jule 103, 108–9, 117, 125, 171, 173

Sues, Leonard 79
Suesse, Dana 116
Sullivan, Jo 145
Swanson, Gloria 47
Sweet Charity 82
Sweet River 38, 52
Sweethearts 10
Swenson, Carl 84
Sykes, Dick 114
Sylvester, Frank 11

Tabbert, William 107
Taber, Richard 21, 30
Take Her, She's Mine 159–60
Tales from Shakespeare 4
Talva, Galina 140
Tamiris, Helen 113–14
Taubman, Howard 168, 175
Taylor, Dwight 141
Taylor, Renee 180
Taymor, Julie 197
Teeter, Lara 189–90, 195–7
Temple, Shirley 83, 172
Tenderloin 132, 135–8, 139
Thaxter, Phyllis 159
Theodore, Lee 176
Thirer, Irene 61
Thomas, Brandon 111
Thompson, David 176
Thompson, Jay 162
Those We Love 31–2
Three Men on a Horse 47–50, 53, **90**, 117, 193–4
Three Wise Fools 12
Threepenny Opera, The 126
Thurber, James 182
Tierney, Gene 40
Time of Your Life, The 83, 124
Tobacco Road 39
Todd, Mike 83–4
Too Many Girls 73, 76–7
Touch and Go 113–14
Towers, Constance 178–9
Toys in the Attic 132
Tracy, Lee 24, 32
Tree Grows in Brooklyn, A **96**, 127–9, 132
Tropicana 189–90, 197
Trowbridge, Charles 14
Truex, Ernest 21

Tully, Jim 31
Turrin, Joseph **101**, 190–1
Twelfth Night 187–8
Twentieth Century 44–7, **89**
Twilight Bar 85
Two for the Seesaw 132

Ullman, Tracy 165
Uncle Tom's Cabin 38, 52
Unconquered, The 40–1

Vaccaro, Brenda 181–2
Valleé, Rudy 57
Van, Bobby 152
Van Cleve, Edith 40
Van Dyke, Marcia **96**, 127
Vance, Vivian 116
Vera-Ellen, 106 141
Verdon, Gwen **98**, 129–32, 153–5, 176
Verna: USO Girl 190
Viertel, Berthold 64
Vilan, Demetrios 70
Vincent, Allen 27
Voskovec, George 118
Vye, Mervyn 117

Waiting for Godot 119
Waldridge, Harold 31
Waldron, Charles 28, 31
Walken, Christopher (Ronald) 78
Walker, Helen 81
Walker, Janet Hays 190
Walker, June 18–19, 40
Walker, Nancy 78, 103–5, 107, 109–10, 145, 162–3
Wallach, Eli 134
Wallach, Ira 118
Wallace, George 131
Wallop, Douglas 153–4
Walsh, Elizabeth 190
Walston, Ray 116, 145, 153, 176, 180
Walters, Charles 78
Walton, Tony 167
Warfield, David 10
Warner, Jack 156
Watch Your Step 139
Waterbury, Laura 188
Waterhouse, Keith 179
Watkins, Maurine 26

Watkins, Perry 126
Watt, Betty Lou 107
Watts, Richard, Jr. 54, 75, 107, 109, 113, 141, 156, 195
Wayne, Paula 78
We the Living 40–1
Weaver, V. A. 23
Webber, Andrew Lloyd 191
Weidman, Jerome 132–3, 135–6
Weill, Kurt 126
Welles, Orson 41, 55
Wesson, Dick 53
West, Mae 172
West Side Story 166, 201
Westcott, Marcy 76
Westley, Helen 39
Westley, John 15
What a Life! 55–7
What Price Glory? 23
Where's Charley? **95**, 111–13, 166, 176
White, Carmel 55
White Desert 16
White, Jane 162–3
White, Miles **94**
White, Richard 190
White, Robert 83
Whitehead, Robert 119
Whiteman, Paul 68
Whiting, Jack 79
Why Bring that Up? 60
Widmark, Richard 82, 83, **93**
Wilder, Thornton 119
Williams, Christola 39
Williams, Fritz 27
Williams, Tennessee 114
Willison, Walter 186
Wilson, Edwin 180
Wilson, Katherine 23
Wilson, Mary Louise 174
Wilson, Patricia 134
Wiman, Dwight Deere 70–1
Wisdom, Norman 187
Wise, Scott **102**
Wisenfrend, Muni (Paul Muni) 27–8
Wizard of Oz, The 71
Wolfe, George C. 197
Wonderful Town **97**, 142–5, 176
Wonderful World of Disney, The 165
Wood, Bert 194

Wood, Philip 39
Woolley, Monte 70
Wollcott, Alexander 14, 18, 26
Wray, Fay 62
Wray, John 24
Wright, Ethel 16
Wright, Robert 178–9

Year the Yankees Lost the Pennant, The 153
Yellow Jacket, The 11

Yokel, Alex 49
Young, Howard Irving 36
Young, Stark 18, 22
Your Own Thing 187–8

Zaks, Jerry 168
Zander the Great 15–16, 18
Zavin, Benjamin Bernard 182
Ziegfeld Follies 10, 106
Zorina, Vera 71, 152
Zukor, Adolph 62